ISOKON

and the Bauhaus in Britain

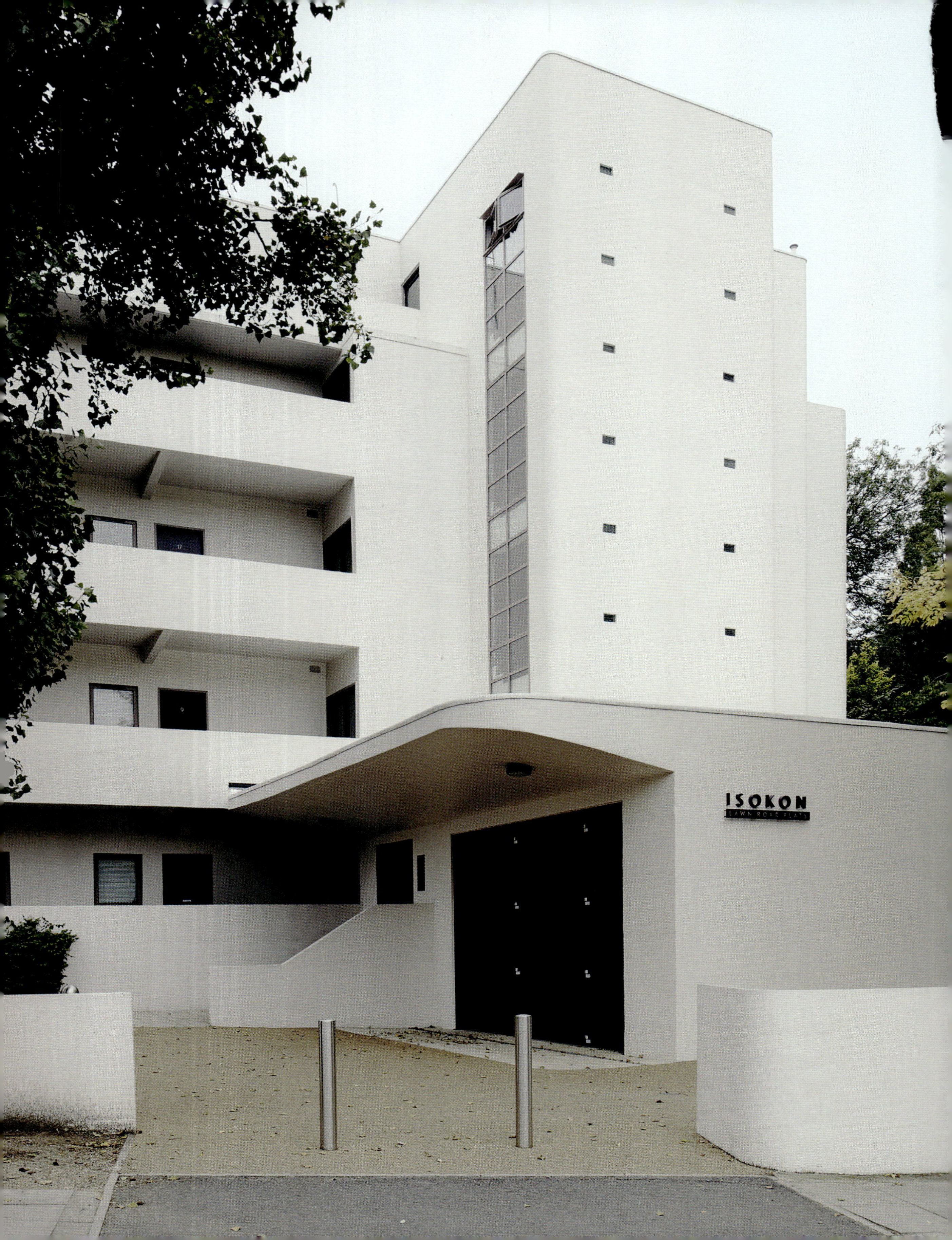
ISOKON
LAWN ROAD FLATS

ISOKON
and the Bauhaus in Britain

LEYLA DAYBELGE & MAGNUS ENGLUND

First published in the United Kingdom in 2019
by B.T. Batsford Ltd
43 Great Ormond Street
London WC1N 3HZ

An imprint of B.T. Batsford Holdings Ltd

ISBN: 9781849944915

A CIP catalogue record for this book is available
from the British Library.

10 9 8 7 6 5 4 3 2

Reproduction by ColourDepth Ltd, UK
Printed by Leo Paper Products, China

This book can be ordered direct from
the publisher www.batsfordbooks.com
or try your local bookshop.

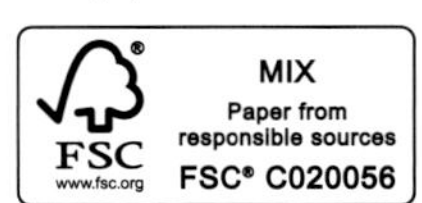

CONTENTS

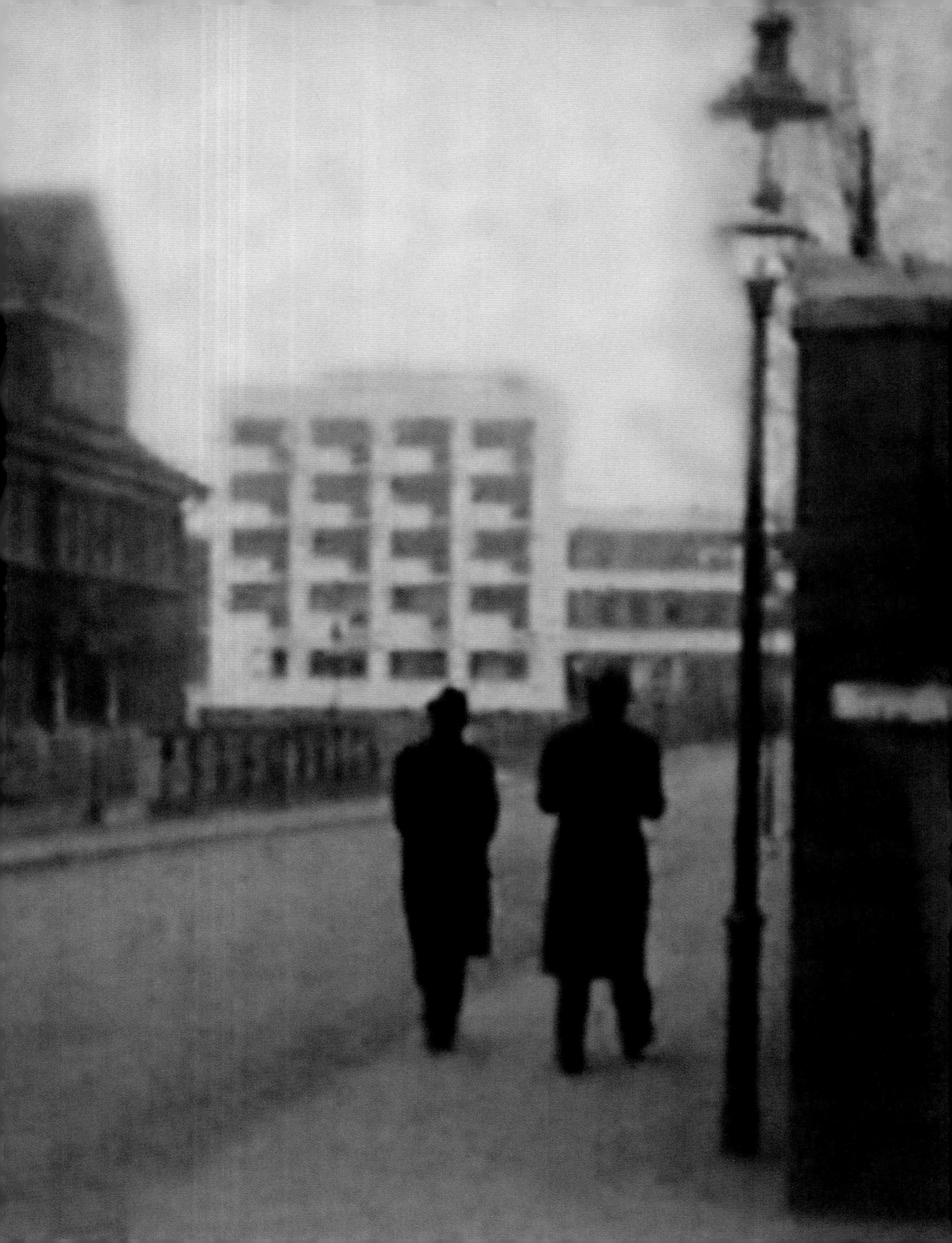

INTRODUCTION

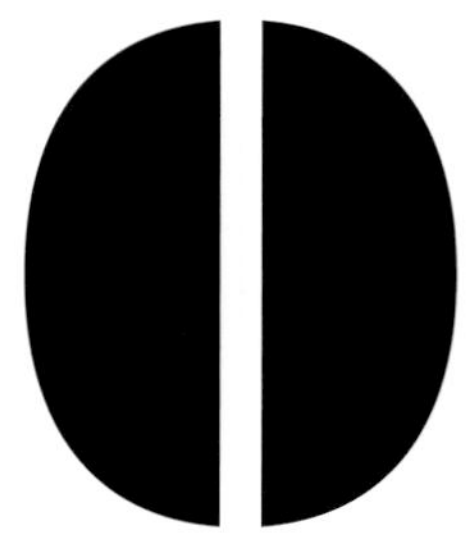 N A BITTERLY COLD DAY IN MARCH 1931, THREE travellers left the railway station in the provincial German town of Dessau, in the Free State of Anhalt. Dressed in long, dark overcoats and trilby hats, they made their way along a short street of 19th-century wooden-framed houses, bracing themselves against the biting wind. Turning a corner, they stopped in their tracks. Before them lay the Bauhaus, the revolutionary school of art, architecture and design founded by Walter Gropius. They gazed at the complex of stark, geometric buildings, linked by an aerial glass bridge. It was a powerful vision of the future.[1]

One of the three, the English entrepreneur Jack Pritchard, reached for his cine-camera. Sensing this was a moment for posterity, he filmed his friends, architects Wells Coates and Serge Chermayeff, as they strode ahead of him towards the Bauhaus. Then through the camera's lens, he avidly devoured the buildings' architectural details, sweeping back and forth across the vast glass curtain wall, cantilevered steel-framed balconies, flat roofs and grey and white concrete facades. The shots were unsteady, as his hands shook with excitement. The school building, which had opened just five years earlier in 1926, was now virtually deserted, under threat of imminent closure by the local Nazi party. In the Director's office they were told that 'Dr Gropius was no longer there, in fact no-one was there.'[2] Disappointed, but 'greatly impressed with the building as a building', the trio explored the site, peering into empty workshops, classrooms, theatre, offices, student apartments and refectory, absorbing everything, including the radical serif-free font of the typography proudly proclaiming the art school's name:

B
A
U
H
A
U
S

As snow began to fall, the men made the short journey to the nearby suburb of Törten. They wandered through the streets of small, low-cost, prefabricated houses that Walter Gropius had designed for industrial workers, leaving tracks of dark footprints in the gathering white.

Years later Pritchard recalled the significance of the visit: 'It had a very powerful impact on me. I did not know it then, but both the Bauhaus and Walter Gropius were to have an enormous influence on much of my future.'[3]

In fact, the Bauhaus, its ideas and protagonists would influence not just Pritchard's life, but also play a key role in the story of 20th-century design and architecture – in Britain and across the globe. Pritchard's cine footage, rediscovered in 2016, contains some of the earliest-known moving images of the art school, and was certainly the first to be brought back to Britain. It represents the beginning of an important dialogue between the ideas of the Bauhaus Masters and a group of pioneers of British Modernism, which will form the narrative of this book.

Founding members of the British Twentieth Century Group Pritchard, Canadian Coates and Russian-born Chermayeff were part of a small, but growing band of individuals in Britain embracing the new architecture at the start of the 1930s. The movement was already well established in continental Europe – particularly in France, the Netherlands and Germany, where the Weimar government had been swift to realize the economic imperative of marrying art and industry.

The three men had travelled from London to Stuttgart on the Orient Express, ostensibly on a business trip, but the journey became something of an architectural pilgrimage, taking in many of Germany's new modern developments – department stores, factories, private houses and residential estates.[4] In Stuttgart they toured the experimental 1927 Weissenhof Estate, the work of 17 architects and a showcase for the new techniques and materials of International Modernism. Erich Mendelsohn, one of the founders of the influential Der Ring group of architects, showed the trio over his Metalworkers' Union building in Berlin and entertained them at his spectacular new lakeside home, Am Rupenhorn.[5] While in the city, they also visited the vast Großsiedlung Siemensstadt Estate and Bruno Taut's monumental flat-roofed, horseshoe-shaped Hufeisensiedlung, built to house 3,000 members of the Gehag trade union.[6] They had seen, at first hand, Modernism not just as a style breaking with the past, but as the realization of a new Utopian vision, that architecture could improve the lives of ordinary men and women in the 20th century.[7]

Pritchard filmed most of the Modernist landmarks they visited and Chermayeff also kept a photographic diary of their trip to Germany, which he published in a jaunty article in *Architectural Review* (*AR*) in November that year.[8] The publication, and its stablemate *Architects' Journal* (*AJ*), both owned and edited by Hubert de Cronin Hastings, played a key role in disseminating Modernist ideas and imagery in late 1920s and 1930s Britain, but prior to the visit of Pritchard and his colleagues, relatively little was known about the Bauhaus. The earliest mention of Walter Gropius and the foundation of the Bauhaus (at its first location, in Weimar), appeared in the July 1924 edition of *AR* in a series about German architects.[9] At the time of the trio's visit the only image of the Dessau Bauhaus that had been published in Britain was a single photograph in Bruno Taut's 1929 book *Modern Architecture*, accompanied by the legend: 'House for Students at Dessau'.[10] The series of 14 *Bauhaus Bücher* (1925–30), edited by Walter Gropius and designed by Lászlo Móholy-Nagy had not yet been translated into English, so information about the school, its architecture and teaching methods was scarce and the proto-Modernists received only scant details from German magazines brought back to London, a few continental journals in the library of the Design and Industries Association, and the first-hand accounts of individuals such as Leonard and Dorothy Elmhirst, founders of Dartington Hall School in Devon, who had visited the Weimar Bauhaus in the early 1920s.[11]

On their return to London, Pritchard, Coates and Chermayeff no doubt discussed their experiences with their friend, the influential architecture critic and *bon viveur*, Philip Morton Shand. A fluent German speaker, he travelled extensively on the continent as a correspondent for both *AR* and *AJ* and first wrote about the Bauhaus in June 1931, *after* the trio's visit to Dessau. He was also instrumental in bringing Walter Gropius to Britain, first for an exhibition of his work at the Royal Institute of British Architects in May 1934 and, a few months later, to seek refuge from Nazi persecution. Morton Shand's role in the story is a key one, as a translator of Gropius's work and an early champion of plywood furniture.

Inspired by what they had seen in Germany, in autumn 1931 Jack Pritchard and Wells Coates set up Isokon, a company whose aim was to create mass-produced unit housing and furniture. Following discussions with Jack's wife Rosemary 'Molly' Pritchard, a Cambridge graduate and trainee psychiatrist, they abandoned their earlier plans to build a pair of houses in Hampstead. Instead, Molly drew up a new brief for Coates to build an apartment block of 'minimal' flats, aimed at young, middle-class professionals with an annual income of around £500 per year. Considering both domestic and spatial reform, she asked: 'How do we want to live? What sort of framework must we build around ourselves to make that living as pleasant as possible?'.[12]

Their conclusion was a community of small, serviced apartments with built-in furniture, into which tenants could move, bringing just 'a rug, a vase and a favourite painting'.[13] Completed in summer 1934, Wells Coates's Lawn Road Flats, or Isokon Building (as it later came to be known), is believed to be Britain's first reinforced-concrete apartment building and a Modernist manifesto in both a material and philosophical sense. Hampstead was the perfect locus for this experiment in social living, being home to key figures in the English avant-garde and a focal point for cultural refugees from Nazi Europe.

In a fitting coda to that snowy day in Dessau in March 1931, Pritchard went on to offer accommodation in the flats to three giants of the Modern movement, the Bauhaus professors Walter Gropius, László Moholy-Nagy and Marcel Breuer, who fled Germany as its political climate worsened. Pritchard employed them in his fledgling Isokon Furniture Company, to which they brought their considerable experience of industrial design. During their short stay in Britain between 1934 and 1937, they also worked on a wide range of other architectural and design projects, leaving their mark on British housing, education, retail, furniture, interior design and art. However, frustrated by the lack of opportunities in pre-war England they left London for the USA, where their work and teachings influenced a new generation of American architects and artists. After their departure, another Bauhäusler, the former metalwork professor Naum Slutzky, moved into the Lawn Road Flats and spent the rest of his life and career in Britain. Through his teaching work he championed the Bauhaus philosophy of marrying art with industry at the Royal College of Art and Birmingham College of Arts and Crafts.

The US work of Gropius, Breuer and Moholy-Nagy has been extensively documented, but the detailed story of the Bauhaus artists and their time in Britain has never been fully told. Similarly, although the Lawn Road Flats are frequently cited in histories of 20th-century British architecture, no comprehensive account of the Isokon Furniture Company has been published, other than Alastair Grieve's short 2004 account, an expanded essay originally written to accompany the 1974 exhibition 'Hampstead in the Thirties. A Committed Decade' at Camden Arts Centre.[14] David Burke's 2014 *The Lawn Road Flats: Spies, Writers and Artists* looks more specifically at the Flats' inhabitants, but with a strong emphasis on espionage.[15.]

This book attempts to tackle both stories, by providing a more in-depth examination of the Isokon flats – in their role as a crucible of Modernist ideas, and Jack and Molly Pritchard's relationship over many decades with the Bauhaus artists, both personally and in the context of the Isokon Furniture Company.

Jack Pritchard's greatest skill was as a catalyst. Between the 1930s and 1960s, he brought together some remarkably influential artists and thinkers of the time. The Flats and its social club, the Isobar, functioned rather like an old-fashioned telephone exchange, connecting era-defining people, conversations and ideas.

From the start, the Lawn Road Flats attracted a stellar cast of residents, who included artists, writers, scientists, architects, designers and, later, a network of notorious Soviet spies. The Bauhäuslers, Le Corbusier, Charlotte Perriand, Alvar Aalto, Bertrand Russell, Maxwell Fry, F.R.S. Yorke, Philip Morton Shand, Nikolaus Pevsner, Naum Gabo, Henry Moore, Edith Tudor-Hart, Frank Pick, Julian Huxley, Gerald Summers, Gordon Russell, Herbert Read, Agatha Christie, the Cambridge Five, even the first celebrity chef Philip Harben, all play key roles in the Isokon story. But it all begins with Jack and Molly Pritchard.

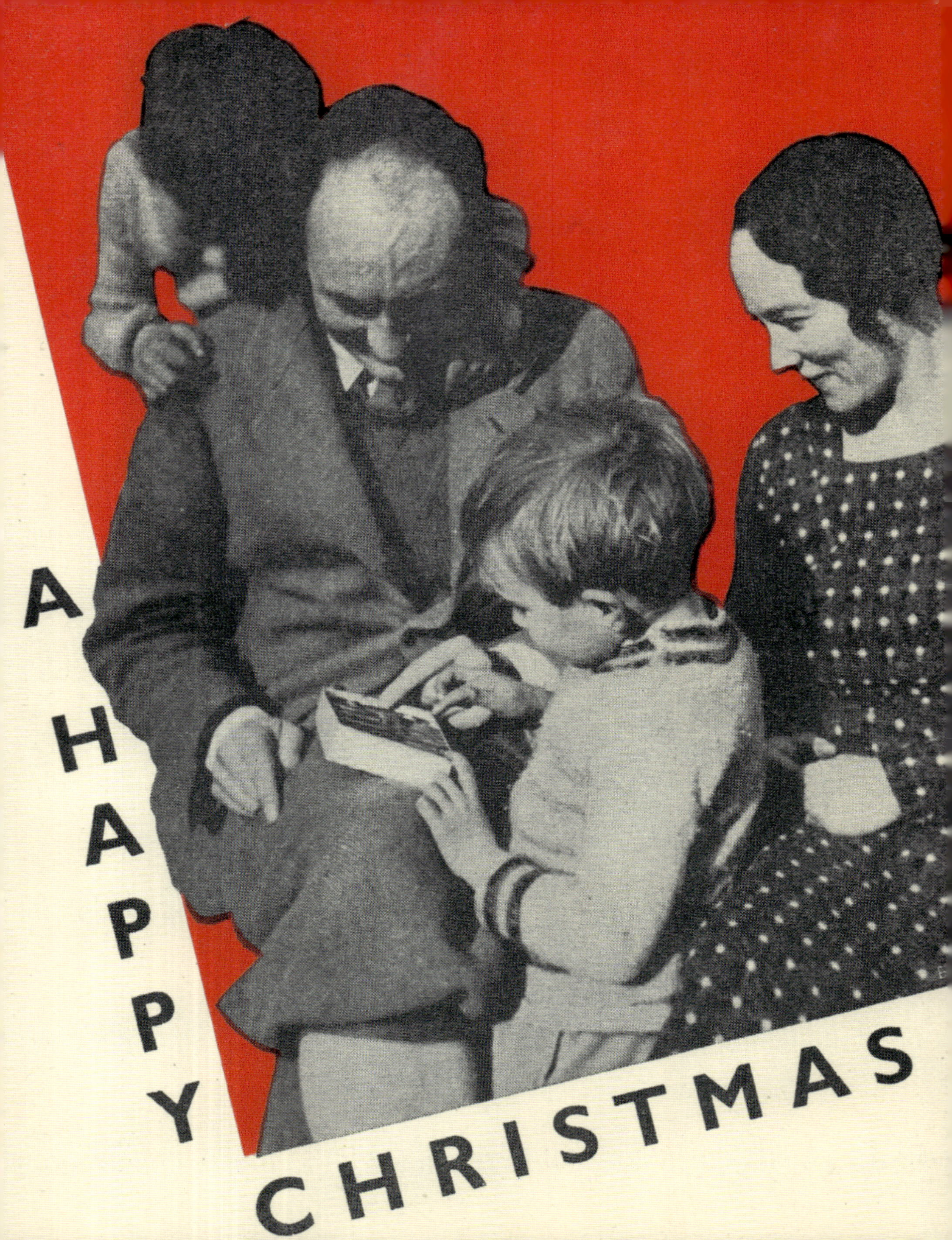

A HAPPY
CHRISTMAS

CHAPTER 1

JACK & MOLLY

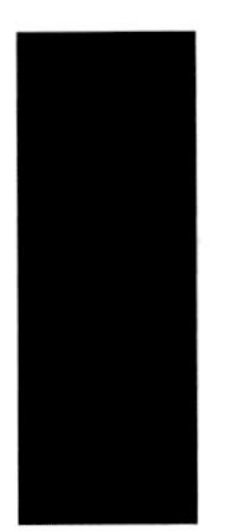**N THE SUMMER OF 1920, DURING HIS FIRST WEEK AT CAMBRIDGE,** Jack Craven Pritchard met his future wife. Joining a lively party of undergraduates punting on the River Cam, he was introduced to Rosemary 'Molly' Cooke and their mutual attraction was instantaneous: 'She and I seemed to know our feelings for each other from the start and, although there would be peccadilloes on the way, it was inevitable that Molly and I would ultimately come together.'[1]

On one level, their relationship was a classic case of opposites attracting. Pritchard was an extrovert and provocateur – his mantra was 'Live dangerously! Don't be comfortable. Take chances!' – while Molly was cool, reserved and highly intellectual. What they shared, however, was a need to challenge the status quo and a desire to order their world using scientific, rational facts.

They were both the children of successful London lawyers. Pritchard, born in 1899, was the son of barrister, Clive Fleetwood Pritchard, who from 1902–3 was the second Mayor of Hampstead. He and his wife Lilian were a cosmopolitan couple who travelled widely throughout Europe, including visiting Paris for the 1900 exhibition.[2] Jack and his three siblings were raised in a substantial red-brick villa in Hampstead's leafy Maresfield Gardens, which was, he remembered, a fine house for parties. Pritchard senior took a keen interest in interior design and was an indulgent father. His four children were given freedom to run a model train between their rooms on the upper floor of the house. It should have been an idyllic childhood, but dyslexia blighted Jack's early school days. He was unable to read until the age of 11 and felt his parents favoured his elder, more academic brother, Fleetwood, who was five years his senior. At 13, he followed Fleetwood to Oundle public school, and finally began to flourish under headmaster F.W. Sanderson (the first scientist to lead a public school), who encouraged Jack to question facts and think analytically. When it appeared Pritchard was not cut out for an academic career, he was channelled into the 'Army class', which prepared boys for practical careers in the services.

In 1914, Pritchard's father died and during the First World War his mother let out their Hampstead home to Belgian refugees. This gave the boy his first insight into the plight of those fleeing oppression and perhaps paved the way for his own generosity to political exiles some 20 years later. In 1917, he successfully applied for a place as a naval cadet at Keyham Naval College at Devonport. The closest Pritchard came to enemy action during his two years in the Navy, was when his ship, HMS *Lion* escorted German cruisers for internment in Scapa Flow. He disliked the snobbery of the services and the rote learning required to pass the exams. His brother, meanwhile, served in Italy and was awarded the Military Cross.

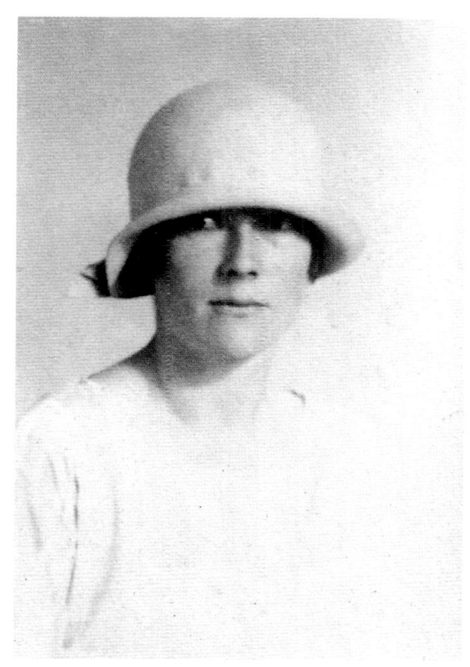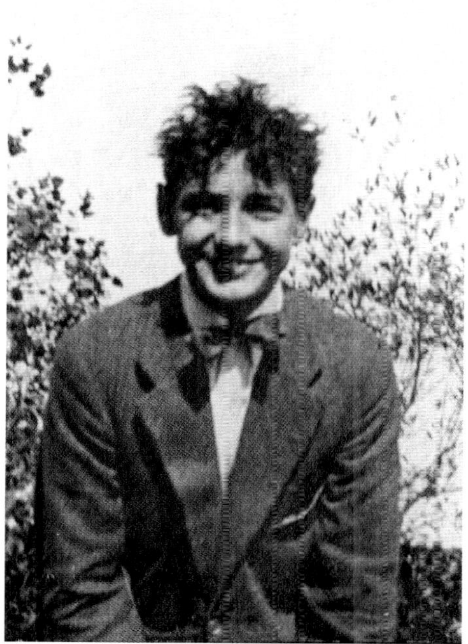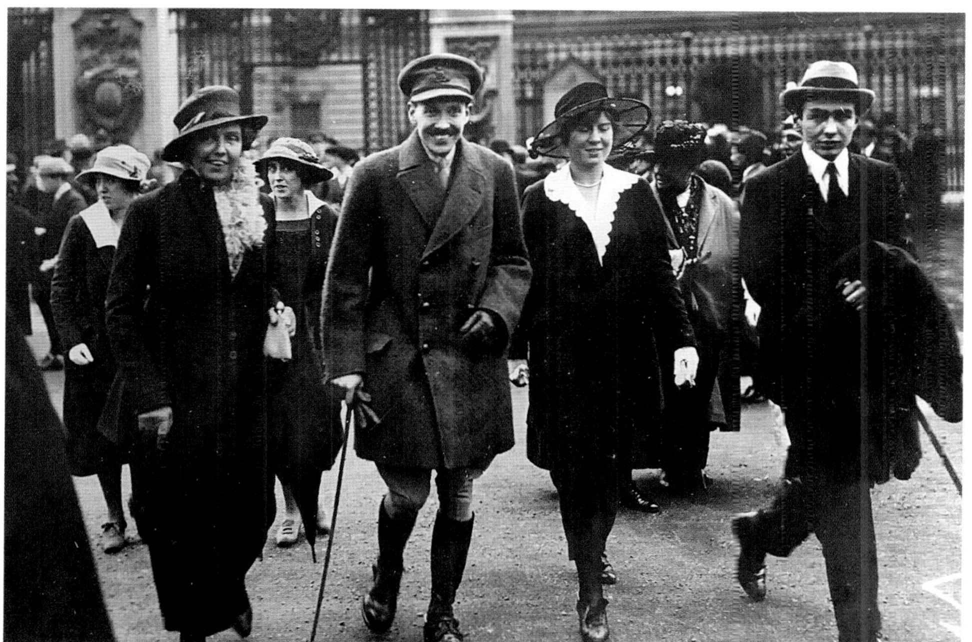

ABOVE LEFT: Rosemary 'Molly' Cooke, c.1920. ABOVE RIGHT: Jack Pritchard as a teenager. BELOW: The Pritchard family outside Buckingham Palace c.1919. Mrs Lilian Pritchard, Lieutenant Fleetwood Pritchard and his wife Miriam, and Jack. In the background: Jack's twin sisters Nancy and May.

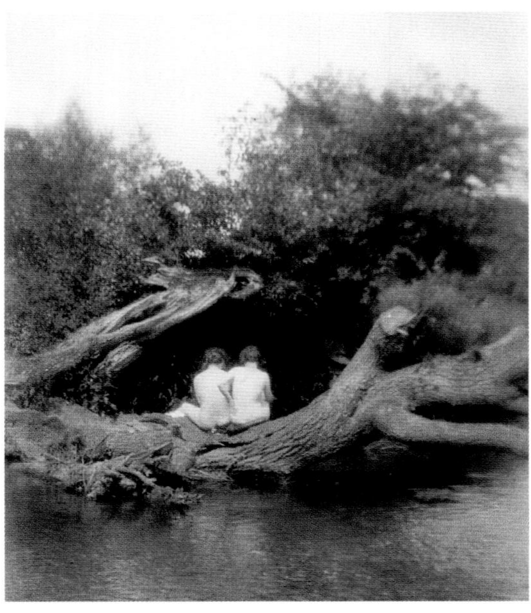

A photograph of the Pritchard family outside Buckingham Palace on the day of Fleetwood's investiture, hints at the rivalry already apparent between the brothers.

On leaving the Navy, Jack enrolled at the London Polytechnic in Regent Street and, proving that he was merely a later developer, won a place at Pembroke College, Cambridge to read Engineering and Economics.

Before going up to Cambridge, Pritchard went to the Pelman Laboratory of Applied Psychology in Bloomsbury Street, London to sit a detailed psychological aptitude test, a new development in career guidance. It showed that he was 'practical with facts, had strong visual and imaginative skills' and was 'original'.[3]

The Cambridge years were formative intellectually and politically for Pritchard and the alliances he and Molly forged during this period were to shape their lives and the entire Isokon project. He recalled: 'I could now do, think, reason why, and say what I liked and work out my own discipline. I worked hard, went to many lectures, some outside my subject and also had a good time. It was like bright sunlight and an ever-expanding view.'[4]

Rosemary 'Molly' Cooke was the precociously bright child of solicitor Henry Cooke and his wife Rose, who, prior to her marriage, had worked in an infant-welfare clinic in Marylebone. The middle child of three, Molly spent her early years in Streatham, before the family moved to Argyll Road in Kensington. Although well-to-do, the Cooke parents instilled in their children a contempt for wasting money. Molly and her siblings did not spend their weekly allowance on sweets 'like other children', but would save up for something 'really good' – a box of tin soldiers or a bow and arrow.[5]

Molly was a physical child, who enjoyed activities in which she could pit herself against nature – climbing trees, ice skating and above all horse riding. The Cooke household was an artistic and musical one, but Molly described herself as the 'black sheep', and a 'naughty and disagreeable child'. She claimed her mother sent her away to boarding school at the age of 9, for being 'too upsetting an influence on the family'. At Lingholt prep school in Surrey, she felt the first stirrings of a vocation:

> *My favourite teacher of all was Miss Fuller, the science teacher… most of all I remember her placing a prism on a ray of sunlight and showing us how the rainbow colours appeared on a sheet of white paper. After that day I was going to be a scientist; and to my mind, then, the peak of science was medicine.*[6]

Winning a scholarship to Cambridge from Godolphin and Latymer girl's school in 1920, Molly was one of a mere handful of women reading medicine. She attended lectures in chemistry, anatomy and physiology, in addition to long sessions in the lab. However, there was more to Molly than blue-stockinged medic. She and Jack were part of the hedonistic generation of Bright Young Things. Molly and her peers were discarding their corsets, smoking and driving cars. She revelled in the social side of Cambridge life, particularly the boat races and May Balls.[7] A photograph from her undergraduate days shows her with a friend, both sporting fashionable short bobs, sunbathing nude by the River Cam.

Pritchard's young American economics professor, Philip Sargant Florence, was to play an important role in Jack and Molly's life. In 1914, he travelled to Germany, visiting the Deutsche Werkbund exhibition in Cologne, and was one of the few in Britain to have seen the work of Walter Gropius. He and his wife Lella, a writer and feminist, held strong left-wing views and also introduced the Pritchards to the prominent Marxist historian Maurice Dobb, a central figure in the burgeoning Communist scene at Cambridge.

Through Florence, Jack and Molly also met the charismatic Henry Morris, Chief Education Officer for Cambridgeshire, whom Pritchard credited with 'changing his life'.[8] He became a frequent, rather shy visitor to Morris's elegant rooms in Trinity Street in Cambridge and joined a small group for long walks on Sundays, listening to his flamboyant friend declaim on mediocrity, insincerity in design and the narrowness of the education system.[9] Morris, who coined the phrase

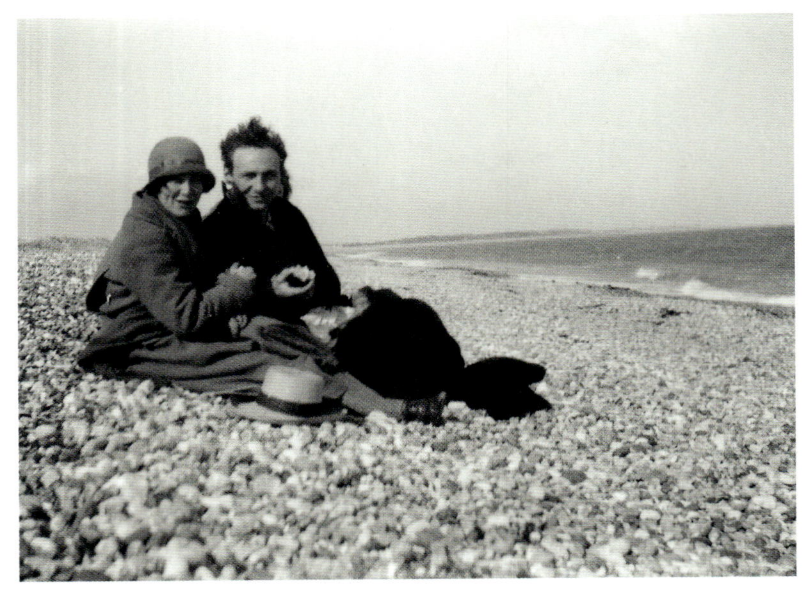

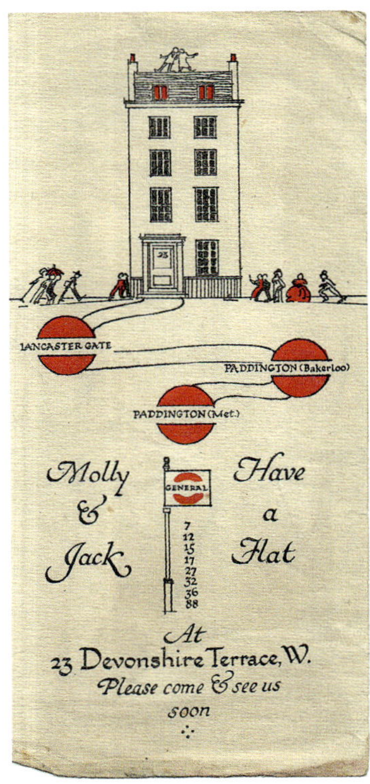

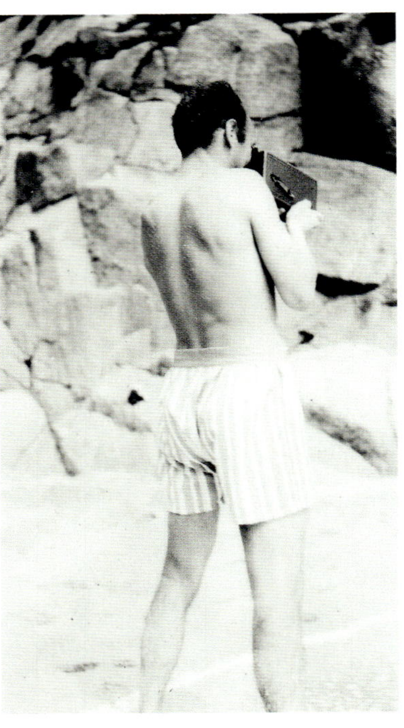

ABOVE, TOP: Jack and Molly Pritchard, 1924, Aldeburgh Beach, Suffolk. ABOVE LEFT: The Pritchards' at home card, 1924. ABOVE ,RIGHT: Jack with cine camera, Cornwall, late 1920s.

'education from cradle to grave', would later commission Gropius to design the influential Impington Village College, near Cambridge.

One Easter vacation, possibly inspired by Jerome K. Jerome's *Three Men in a Boat*, Pritchard and three friends travelled to London and back by canoe. Their round-trip, from the River Granta to Cadogan Pier in Chelsea, took nine days and was followed by the national press. On the day of his final university exam, Pritchard faced a dilemma. He had been invited to the wedding of a naval friend, which was taking place at 2.30pm in Surrey. His exam paper was due to finish at midday. How could he possibly attend? Revealing the entrepreneurial skills that would later stand him in good stead, he hired a three-passenger aeroplane and sold seats to his brother, two friends and his mother, who obligingly booked return tickets and made it to the wedding. Fittingly, his paper was on the economics of transport. Despite his many extensive extra-curricular activities, Pritchard left Cambridge with a first in Economics and a second in Engineering. Molly was awarded a first in Natural Sciences and completed her medical training at London's Charing Cross Hospital between 1921 and 1924.

The couple married at Kensington Registry Office in August 1924 and spent their honeymoon in Leven in Yorkshire, where Molly carried out a fortnight's locum. Returning to London, they set up home in Devonshire Terrace in Paddington. After the wedding, Molly continued postgraduate work in bacteriology and pathology at Charing Cross, reaching the post of assistant pathologist. She then moved to the drug manufacturer Glaxo to work on the newly discovered health benefits of cod-liver oil. Alfred Bacharach, a director of Glaxo, introduced Molly to the left-wing 1917 Club in Gerrard Street, Soho, where she began to lunch each day. Before long the Pritchards were socializing in the Bloomsbury Group circle.

In 1926 they moved to 79 Platt's Lane, a four-storey Edwardian house in Hampstead. Their first son Jonathan was born later that year, followed in 1928 by Jeremy. Influenced by the teachings of Dr Eric Pritchard, who had run Molly's mother's infant clinic in Marylebone, Molly and Jack followed a strict childcare regime with their boys, feeding them by the clock and rarely picking them up. Keen to test conventional wisdom on child development, Jack devised and patented a frame on wheels to assist his infant sons to walk from an early age.[10] Unusually for a woman of her class, Molly continued to study full-time after they were born, taking courses in psychopathology and psychology at University College London. Her interest in psychotherapy, that most 'modern' branch of medicine, was influenced by two Cambridge friends, Portia Holman and Doris Howard, who had already entered the profession. It was through Holman that Molly met Beatrix Tudor-Hart.

The daughter of Canadian artist Percyval Tudor-Hart, Beatrix spent her early childhood in Paris, spoke six languages and, defying her father, gained a scholarship to read Classics at Newnham College, Cambridge. She studied child psychology in Vienna and taught for a year at Beacon Hill, the progressive school in Sussex established by philosopher Bertrand Russell and his wife Dorothy. She also caught Jack's eye. 'She was a fine, tall girl, handsome and intelligent and was passionately concerned with education. She desperately wanted a child of her own. I was much impressed with her,' Jack recalled.[11] Beatrix and Jack embarked on an affair. While Molly was pregnant with her first child, Tudor-Hart invited the couple to stay at her father's villa in France. It was here that Jennifer, Beatrix's daughter with Jack, was conceived.[12] The Pritchards, in keeping with their progressive political and social views, adopted a relaxed attitude to marital fidelity and Molly, who went on to enjoy her own affair with architect Wells Coates, took a philosophical approach to the matter. However, according to family legend, Molly's mother was appalled that Beatrix was seen pushing a pram around Hampstead with Jack Pritchard's baby in it.[13]

In 1928, Beatrix and Molly set up The Children's Group, a nursery school on the top floor of the Pritchards' home, in Platt's Lane which their children attended. Molly's growing understanding of child psychology had caused her to regret the experimental, hands-off manner in which she and Jack had raised their infant sons. Influenced by Bertrand Russell's treatise *On Education* (and, no doubt, Beatrix Tudor-Hart) they sent Jonathan and Jeremy to Beacon Hill, where pupils were allowed to set their own boundaries. The Pritchards' interest in education was to last a lifetime.

Jack's first position on leaving Cambridge was as a graduate trainee with the Michelin Tyre Company. A stint followed selling advertising space for *The Field* and *World Today* magazines. His brother, Fleetwood, had established an influential advertising and public relations agency, Wood, Pritchard and Partners, with architectural historian and critic, John Gloag, who became a great friend and mentor to Jack. Gloag introduced him to the Design and Industries Association (DIA), an organization that aimed to forge ties between British manufacturers and designers. Its mantra was 'fitness for purpose' and between 1927 and 1932 the DIA published a series of important quarterly journals covering the latest developments in European architecture. Pritchard joined the editorial board of the DIA publication, *Design in Industry*, which enabled him: 'to meet a variety of people with somewhat similar interests and [it] provided confidence to experiment with new ideas.'

It was during these years that the Pritchard brothers began producing their own short films. They made several amusing Chaplin-esque shorts starring friends

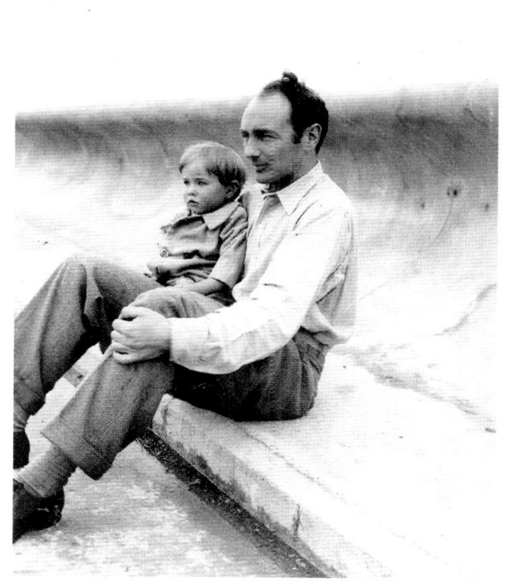

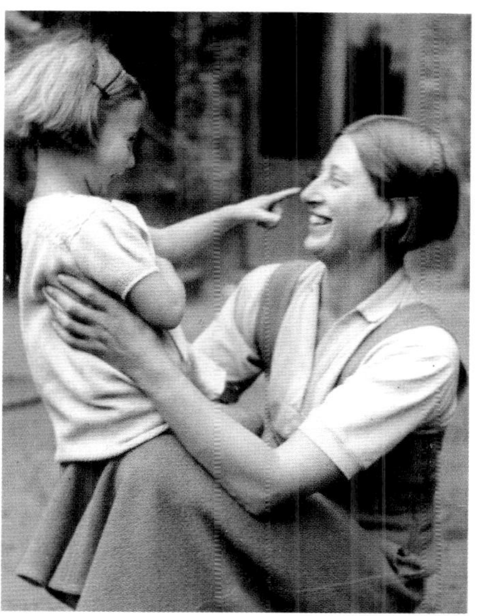

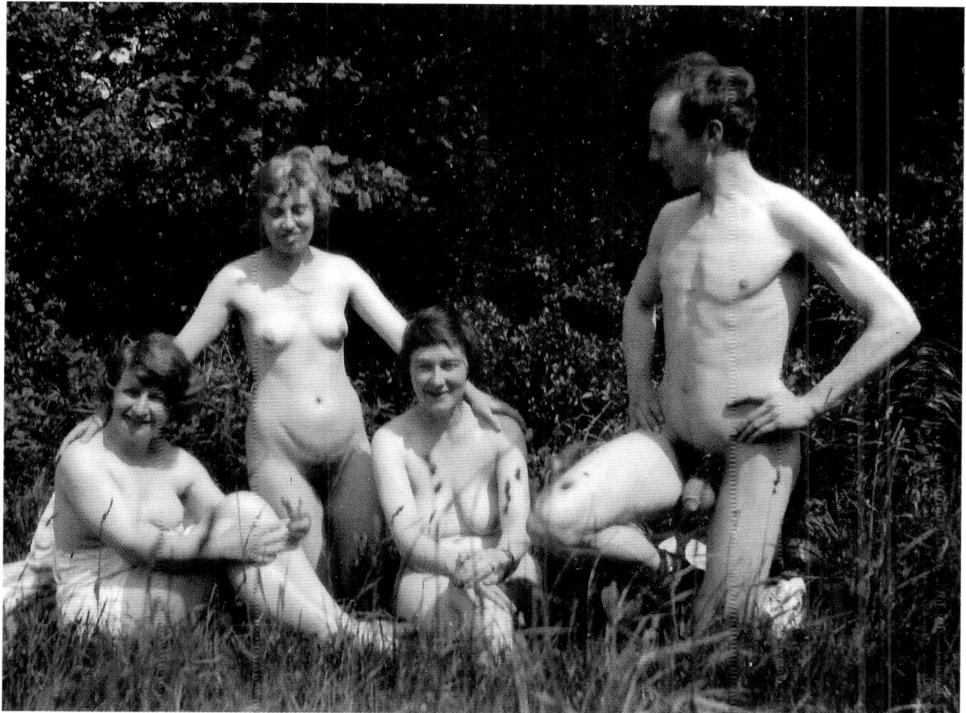

ABOVE, TOP-LEFT: Jack and Jeremy Pritchard, 1930. ABOVE TOP-RIGHT: Molly's friend and business partner, the brilliant Beatrix Tudor-Hart. She was also Jack's lover, and together they had a daughter, Jennifer. ABOVE: Nude sunbathing, as part of the Modernists' break with Victorian moral values: Jack, Molly and two friends.

and family. They also recorded idyllic holidays at Craven Cottage, the family's
seaside home at Southwold in Suffolk, where they sailed and built railway tracks
in the garden. A prophetic time-lapse sequence shows the adults building 'The
Little White House', a self-assembly, one-roomed garden house for the young
Pritchard cousins. It was minimal living in its simplest form. Jack and Fleetwood
also recorded their extensive foreign travels, including a visit to Morocco, where
the white, flat-roofed, geometric architecture is strikingly similar to what was then
being created by the European Modernists. Nude swimming, skiing, sailing – the
world captured on the Pritchards' cine reels shows a privileged and cosmopolitan
family, who played as hard as they worked. In 1927, the brothers established
The Projectors' Club, which screened commercial movies, documentaries and
members' productions.[14] It is entirely possible that Jack Pritchard showed the
footage of his 1931 architectural travels in Germany to members of the club.

In September 1925 Jack joined Venesta, a British company formed in 1897 to
import plywood from the Estonian manufacturer A.M. Luther. The firm initially
produced tea chests for the Indian and Ceylon tea trade and later diversified into
hatboxes and suitcases. By the 1920s, plywood was being adopted by the furniture
industry and by architects for interior construction. Pritchard could see the
enormous potential of the material, but it had something of an image problem,
which he was determined to tackle.

> *Plywood was then regarded as a cheap substitute for solid wood,*
> *even by some of those in the firm, and while I was principally*
> *employed to advertise and promote existing Venesta products,*
> *I believed it was important to find uses where its intrinsic*
> *qualities could be used.[15]*

He was tasked with finding a market for Plymax, a new Venesta product in
which thin metal sheets, such as copper and steel, were bonded to plywood,
creating a material of great strength. At John Gloag's suggestion, Jack placed an
advertisement in *The Times* describing the qualities of Plymax and asking for
suggestions for its use. Deciding to experiment himself, Pritchard designed a small
sideboard, with a Monel metal Plymax top and copper Plymax sides and doors,
which was manufactured by Crossley and Brown. The result – strictly geometric,
with exposed hinges and raised on cylindrical legs – which he nicknamed 'The
Oven' for its industrial appearance, is now in the collection of the Victoria and
Albert museum.

EARLY ENCOUNTERS WITH MODERNISM

Modernism in 1920s England was still very much in its infancy, but those seeking a visual language that broke with the past began to meet at Finella, the Cambridge home of the influential English don Mansfield Forbes. In 1927 Forbes commissioned the young Australian architect Raymond McGrath to transform the interiors of his Italianate Victorian villa. He believed 'that the furniture, buildings, habits and opinions of a past century [were] not suitable for modern people' and decreed that McGrath should employ only the very latest materials for the project.[16] McGrath chose Venesta Plymax for one of Finella's most outstanding features, a dramatic pair of pinky, copper-faced folding doors, which divided Forbes's drawing rooms. It was here, in the salons known as 'The Pinks', enjoying Forbes's legendary hospitality, that a small group of proto-Modernists met to hammer out the manifesto for MARS, the Modern Architectural Research Group, outlined further in the next chapter.

Pritchard's first encounter with a Modern interior had taken place in 1925, when he had visited the Exposition des Arts Décoratifs et Industriels Modernes in Paris and seen Le Corbusier's Pavillon de l'Espirit Nouveau. Tucked away amidst the Art Deco excess, this concrete, steel and glass 'minimum dwelling' was an essay in standardization and mass production. At the end of 1929, Pritchard returned to Paris. He visited the Salon d'Automne and was struck by Corbusier, Jeanneret and Perriand's one-roomed 'apartment for two' in which every item of furniture was multifunctional and ingeniously movable. Encouraged by John Gloag, he took the audacious step of asking Corbusier's architectural practice if it would design an exhibition stand for Venesta for the 1930 Building Trades Exhibition in London.

The brief was handed to Charlotte Perriand, with whom Jack struck up a lively friendship. He recalled she was:

A strikingly handsome girl, hair cropped and round her neck a string of white beads almost an inch in diameter… She showed me her flat, highly efficient and a sliding table that seemed to vanish into nowhere.[17]

Le Corbusier's 1925 Pavillon had been built around a living tree and Perriand borrowed a similar motif for the Venesta stand, incorporating a whole birch tree (which had to be specially imported) as a witty reference to the origins of

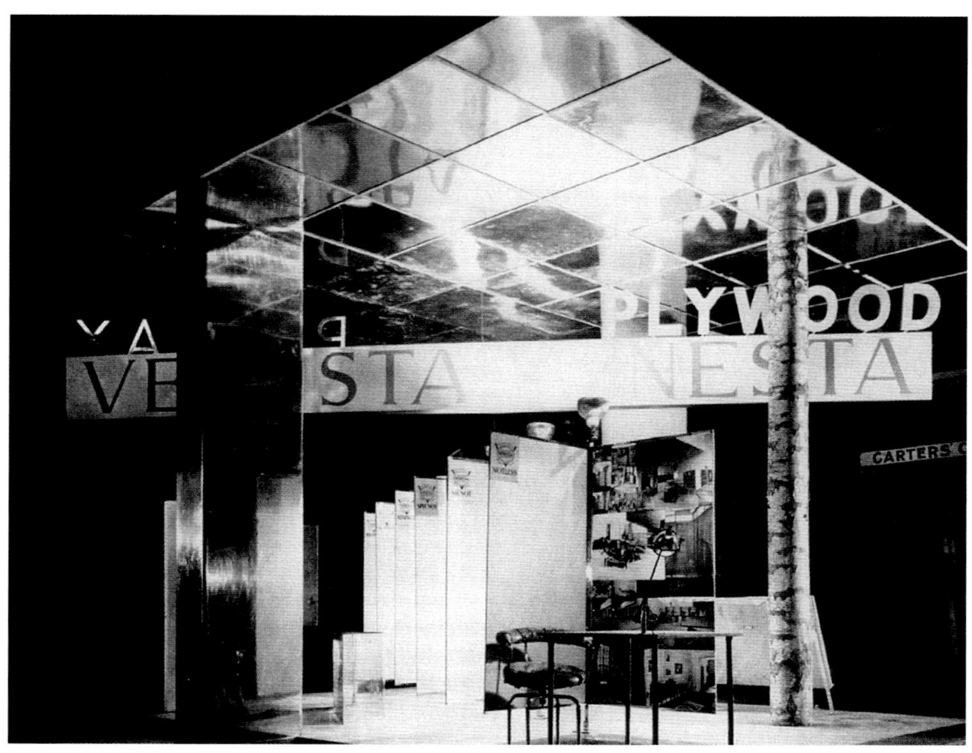

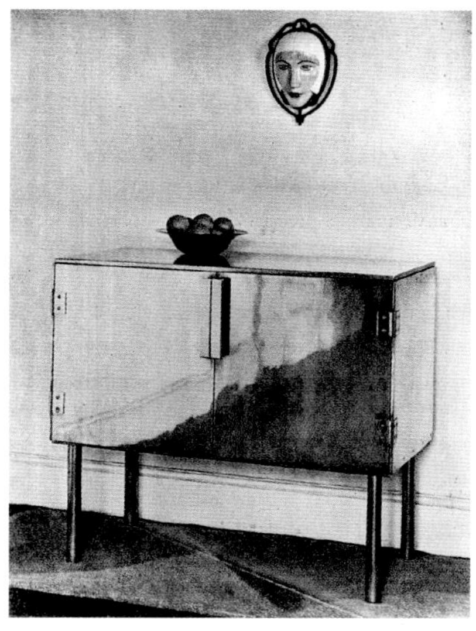

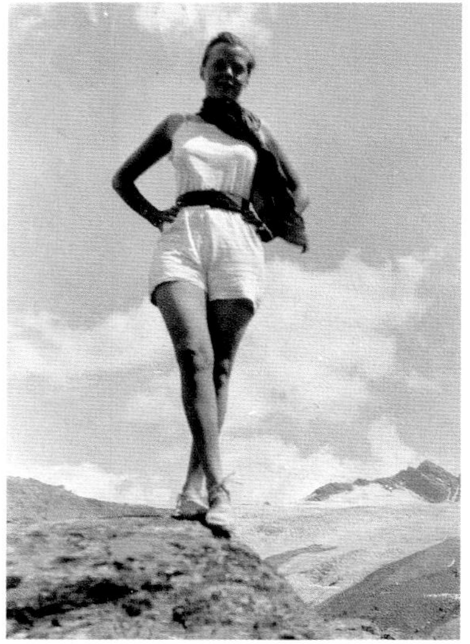

ABOVE, TOP: Charlotte Perriand's Venesta stand, 1930 Building Trades Exhibition, Olympia, London.
ABOVE LEFT: 'The Oven', Jack Pritchard's Plymax sideboard, 1929, now in the collection of the V&A.
ABOVE RIGHT: Designer Charlotte Perriand, who won many admirers on her visit to London in 1930.

plywood.[18] The stand, which consisted of a Plymax ceiling and pillar, showcased different grades and finishes of Venesta plywood (a sales approach Jack had pioneered), and demonstrated the various uses to which they might be put. Perriand travelled to London to supervise the installation and Jack made every effort to introduce the brilliant and beautiful young designer to his wide circle of architectural friends. He took a box at the Cambridge Theatre, where Serge Chermayeff had recently designed the interiors, and they had supper at the architect's home. He brought Perriand to Finella to meet Mansfield Forbes and Raymond McGrath, and he and Molly took her sailing on the River Blyth in Suffolk.[19] The Architectural Association (AA) held a dinner in her honour and Venesta's stand was favourably received in the September issues of *The Builder* and *The Architects' Journal*.

PRITCHARD POLITICS

Jack and Molly's commitment to Socialism had crystallized at Cambridge and they were now part of a firmly left-wing intellectual and social set, which believed the nation was losing its way after the Great War. The General Strike of 1926, which their Marxist friend Maurice Dobbs predicted would herald 'the great revolution', was a seminal moment for the couple. As the government imposed reduced wages and longer hours on the nation's miners, 1.7 million workers, including staff at Venesta's warehouse in Millwall and factory in Silvertown, downed tools in solidarity. Amidst a crackdown on the media, Jack and Molly volunteered to help the TUC distribute *The British Worker* newspaper. They borrowed a van and delivered the paper around London and as far afield as Leicester.

Pritchard increasingly believed that social and economic problems could be improved by better planning of available resources. It was a view shared by Gerald Barry, editor of *The Weekly Review* (later part of the *New Statesman*). Barry commissioned a young journalist, Max Nicholson, to draw up a Soviet-style National Plan, calling on a high-powered group of advisers from industry, commerce and the Bank of England to contribute ideas. Nicholson's influential article led to the creation of the think tank, 'Political and Economic Planning', of which Pritchard became a founding member (he claimed credit for inventing its acronym, 'PEP'). Other founding members, some of whom would resurface at the Lawn Road Flats and its club, the Isobar, included the founder of Dartington Hall school Leonard Elmhirst; zoologist Julian Huxley; research chemist Sir Henry Bunbury, journalist John Pinder; and industrialists Josiah Stamp and Israel Sieff. Over the course of three years, PEP produced a host of far-sighted policy studies on subjects including provision of a state health service, the education system, and, as war approached, air-raid precautions.

A VERY HAMPSTEAD COUPLE

In 1929, Molly and Jack bought a plot of land for £1,500 in Lawn Road, south-east Hampstead. The sloping plot faced a row of Edwardian houses and backed onto a wooded hillside with tennis courts beyond. It was conveniently located just a short walk from Belsize Park Underground in one direction and Hampstead Heath Overground in the other. In 1930, they asked Molly's sister Jill and her husband Harry Harrison, both AA-trained architects to design two houses for the site – one for themselves, and the other for Beatrix Tudor-Hart.[20]

> *We had not yet learnt the importance of the 'brief'. Harry made a first sketch. It was of a charming little neo-Georgian house that gave a nod to the modern. It was white amongst the trees, with corner windows. The drawing was shown at the Royal Academy.[21]*

Precisely when Jack and Molly rejected Cooke and Harrison's plan is not on record, nor is whether it caused a family rift, but the couple's interest in Modernism and their understanding of its capacity to effect positive social change were developing rapidly. Hampstead in the 1930s had a unique cultural and political micro-climate which made it the perfect birthplace for the Pritchards' forthcoming architectural experiment. Perched high above London, its hilly streets were a mixture of grand Victorian mansions, aspirational Edwardian terraces, seedy cobbled lanes and rundown mews. Between the wars, its open spaces and cheap studio space meant the village and area surrounding Lawn Road were home to a large number of British painters and sculptors. In the late 1920s, Tasker Road became the centre for a group of key figures in the English avant-garde. Barbara Hepworth, Henry Moore and Ben Nicholson lived and worked in the purpose-built Mall Studios. In 1932, they formed Unit One – a collective of 11 artists and architects to formally establish a Modern style in England. It was the first attempt to unite the aims of architecture and art, and its members included Nash, Nicholson, Hepworth, Moore and Wells Coates who were all united in their commitment to express 'a strictly contemporary spirit'. Their neighbour, the art historian Herbert Read, was instrumental in championing their work and he edited the manifesto which accompanied their group exhibition at the Mayor Gallery in Cork Street.[22] As the 1930s progressed and the political landscape darkened, a wave of important émigré artists and thinkers from Europe converged on this corner of North London. The streets of NW3 contained a truly remarkable concentration of intellectual talent. Most, along with Jack and Molly Pritchard, shared a belief that Socialism would deliver a better future.

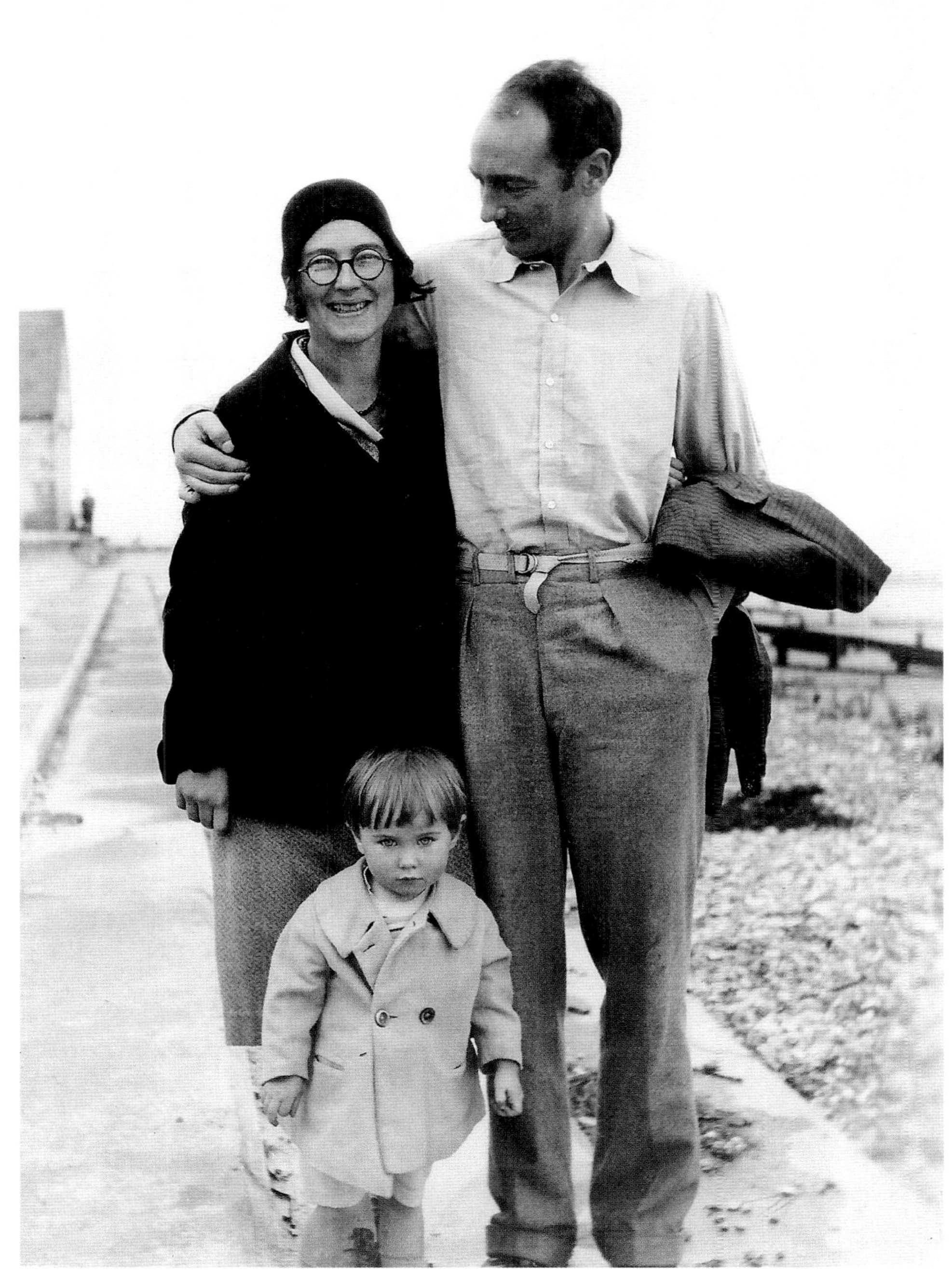

ABOVE: Jack and Molly Pritchard, 1928, Aldeburgh, Suffolk.

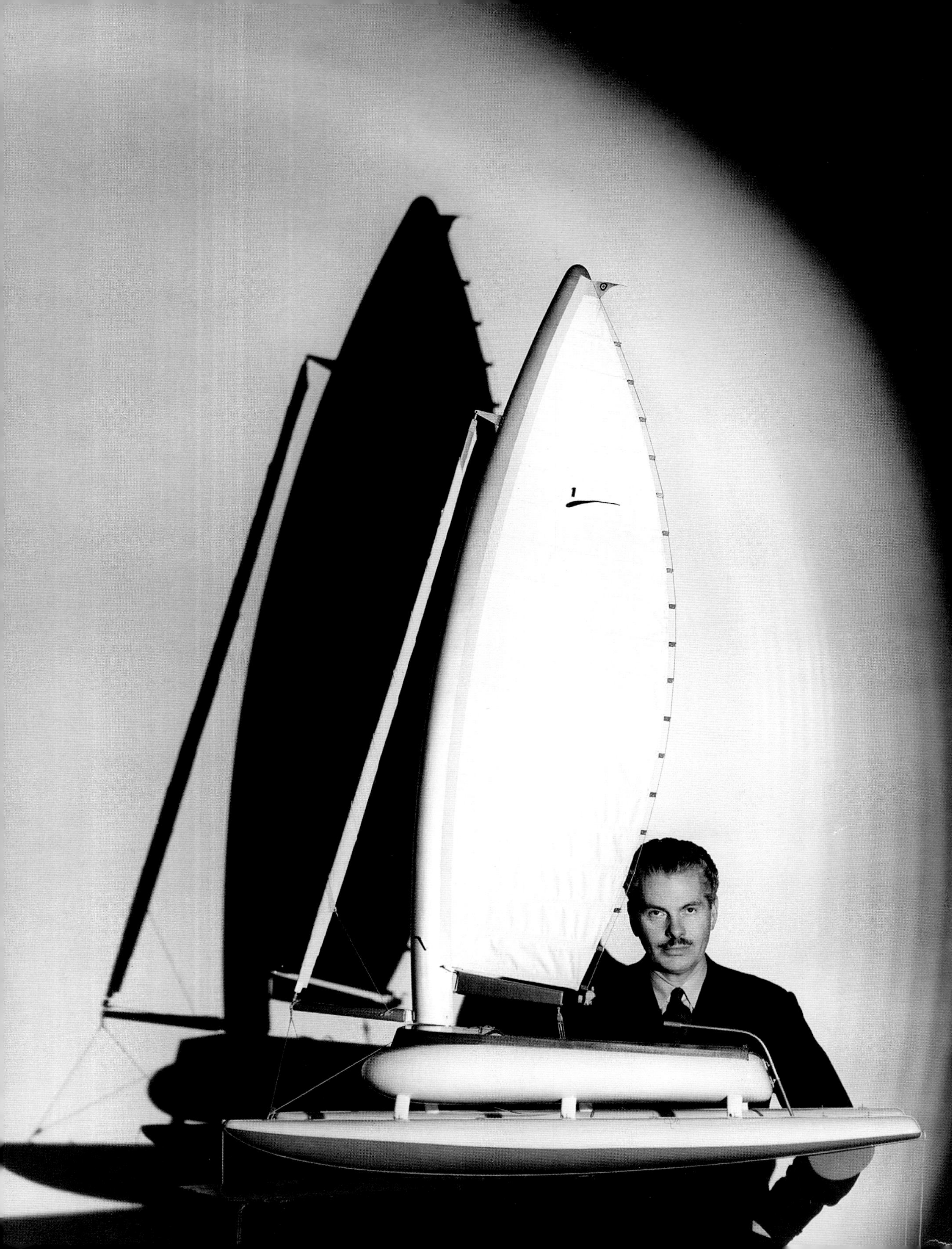

WELLS COATES

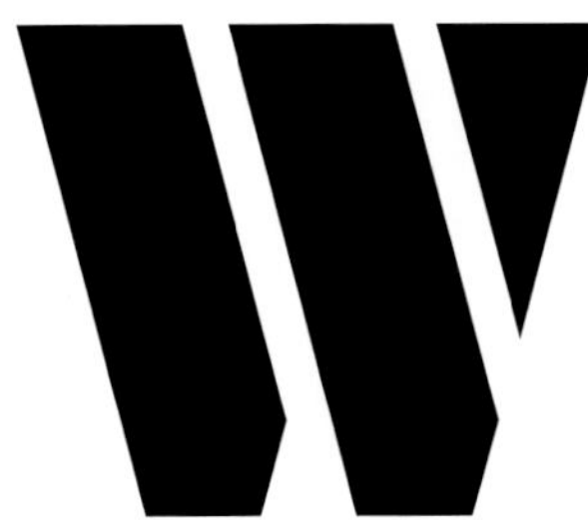

ELLS WINTEMUTE COATES'S UNORTHODOX education goes some way to explaining the singular and somewhat compartmentalized personality, described in his 1958 obituary by J.M. Richards, editor of *Architectural Review.* Wells was born in Japan in 1895, the eldest of six children to parents who were Canadian Methodist missionaries. Reverend Harper Havelock Coates was Professor of Philosophy and Religion at Aoyama theological college in Tokyo and prior to her marriage his formidable mother, Agnes Wintemute, had studied architecture under father of American Modern architecture Louis Sullivan in Chicago. The couple had arrived in Japan at the tail end of the Meiji era, a time of intense modernization, during which the country underwent far-reaching transformations. While the Japanese were reinventing themselves in a Western manner, Coates's parents made a concerted effort to incorporate many elements of traditional Japanese culture into their son's education. They employed an English tutor, George Edward Luckman Gauntlett, who, in addition to teaching Coates the usual Western academic curriculum, devised an unconventional and highly practical programme for their son. It included paper making and printing; silkworm-rearing, spinning and weaving; boat building; cooking and the traditional Japanese rituals of serving food. Coates also studied shorthand and typing and how to manage his finances, budgeting with the pocket money he was made to earn from his parents.[2] Coates was a driven and competitive child, highly attuned to the beauty of his surroundings and, from an early age, he was intrigued to discover the way in which things worked. In a diary entry from 1909, he described a family outing to the grand Mitsukoshi department store in Tokyo:

In 1913, when he was 17, his parents decided to return to Canada and he, his
father and Gauntlett turned the journey into a spectacular four-and-a-half month
Grand Tour, which Coates recorded in an illustrated diary. They made stops in
China, Java, Burma and India, the pyramids in Egypt and then sailed on to Europe,
where they visited Italy, Greece and England, before crossing the Atlantic to New
York. It was a rich and intense experience afforded to few young men of his
era and gave Coates a wealth of cultural references, with which he peppered his
conversation for the rest of his life.

In Vancouver, he enrolled at McGill University College, to begin a six-year
combined BA/BSc in Engineering. He chose the subject on his mother's advice,
as she believed it was the most practical training for an architect. However, after
the bespoke, one-to-one nature of his education in Japan, Coates found university
life hard to adjust to.

In November 1916, Coates took a break from university to enlist in the army.
He arrived in the trenches of France in 1917 with the Second Division of the
Canadian Gunners, but was disappointed to find himself charged with looking
after the battalion's horses, rather than fighting at the Front. Frustrated, he signed
up to the Royal Naval Air Service (which later merged into the Royal Air Force).
It was just over a decade since the Wright Brothers had taken to the skies in
the first powered flight and Coates now found himself at the very vanguard of
technology, in a new and rapidly developing field of warfare. The pared-back
functionality of the aircraft, the utility of the materials and the camaraderie of
working in a small team left their mark on him. Just as he completed his training,
the Armistice was announced and he returned to Canada disappointed at not
having seen any action. He completed his studies, receiving a First in Engineering
and won a scholarship to travel to London University, where he began work on his
PhD, a thesis on 'The Gases of the Diesel Engine'.

Since childhood, Coates had written and illustrated his own journals, and enjoyed the process of recording and ordering his impressions. These skills, combined with typing and shorthand now helped him gain a part-time job with the *Daily Express* newspaper and he quickly progressed from transcribing telephone messages to reporting. In 1925 he was posted to Paris for five months and in between assignments, he immersed himself in the city's modern art scene. Like Pritchard, he visited the seminal Exposition des Arts Décoratifs et Industriels Modernes, where he first saw the work of Le Corbusier.

Back in London, he began to mix with the artistic and literary circles of bohemian Bloomsbury. He was a regular at 'The Cave of Harmony' nightclub, owned by the flamboyant actress Elsa Lanchester, who would later become an important client. Other members included painters Paul Nash and John Banting, the writer Evelyn Waugh, and dancers Frederick Ashton and Rupert Doone. It was here that Coates met his future wife, Marion Grove, a beautiful, left-wing student at the London School of Economics. His own political views were evolving and, like Molly Pritchard, he joined Leonard Woolf's socialist 1917 Club, where he rubbed shoulders with writers H.G. Wells and Aldous Huxley, and the actor Charles Laughton.

The seminal figure from this period was Coates's 'first real male friend', Alfred Borgeaud, a fellow student at the University of London, with whom he embarked on an intellectual odyssey.[5] The pair voraciously devoured key texts in art, science and philosophy. They read the latest works of Modernist literature, including T.S. Eliot's recently published *The Waste Land*, which during their early courtship, Coates recited aloud to Marion Grove in his shabby Charlotte Street digs. By 1926, he had been promoted to Scientific Correspondent at the *Daily Express*, but he was becoming dissatisfied with his journalistic career and following a series of furious rows with Marion, he handed in his notice at the newspaper and on 24 April 1926, he and Borgeaud disappeared.

> *Our plans were made known to no-one … we decided to go to Canada for the summer, bought tickets at 5.30 pm and sailed the next day… Not a soul in the world knew where we had gone… We each carried a rucksack and a kit-bag. One suit of clothes, a rainproof, a small sleeping tent for two, some books … notebooks, this Corona typewriter, Fifty Pounds Sterling in a bank credit to be used only in an emergency and Five Pounds in Cash.*[6]

The pair embarked on a liberating trip through British Columbia, living on their wits, picking up casual work and jumping trains. On 29 September it ended in tragedy. Borgeaud fell from a freight train and was killed. Coates discovered his

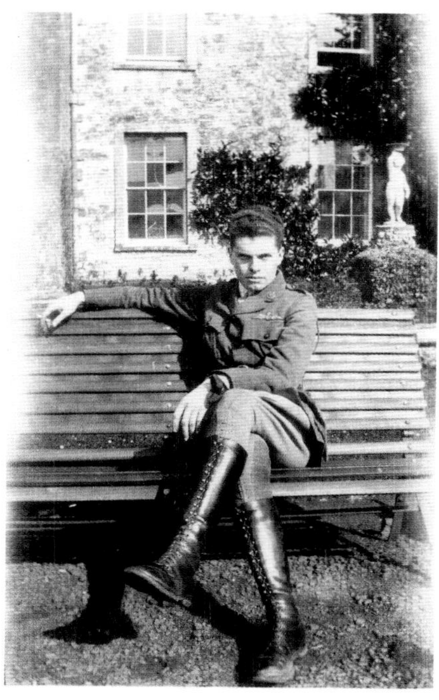

mangled body on the tracks and buried his friend.[7] Traumatized, he returned to London and in an act of catharsis, poured out his detailed memories of the trip in a 100-page letter to Marion. They were reconciled and married in August 1927.

Their two-roomed flat in Doughty Street provided Coates with his first design project. With a gift of £100 from Marion's grandmother, he bought some plain furniture from Heal's, laid down a utilitarian hair-cord carpet, covered the fireplace with aluminium sheeting and asked their friend, the artist John Banting, to decorate the walls and curtains with his linear surrealist drawings. His efforts at interior design were widely admired and their friends told Coates he 'should go in for this sort of thing'.[8]

In 1928, he met textile designer Alec Walker, who ran Cryséde, a company producing and retailing silk fabrics. Walker and his manager, Tom Heron, invited Coates to design fittings for their stores, the first of which opened in Cambridge in early 1929.

Coates designed a curved aluminium fascia on which the shop's name was spelt out in a thin Art Deco font. The plate-glass window revealed an elegant display of aluminium and plywood panels from which were draped columns of colourful silks. Inside, the walls were lined with sheets of veneered plywood and the fabrics were displayed in glass-fronted cabinets. The effect was light and simple, but *moderne* rather than truly Modern.

When Tom Heron left to form his own silk company, Cresta, he asked Wells to design the interiors of his factory in Welwyn Garden City and the first Cresta shop, in Brompton Road, Knightsbridge. Wells designed everything from the light fittings and stools to the company logo. Heron's son, the artist Patrick Heron, recalled the impact of the London store:

> *[it] made the most amazing use of the six letters CRESTA in square format and in very deep relief – I'd say they were two feet from back to front. While on the left-hand all of the recess from pavement to plate-window the letters SILKS projected so that they were legible only as you came along the pavement from the east: from straight in front, their form was totally abstract: very beautiful, very brilliant.[9]*

Coates had successfully created a distinctive visual brand identity for Cresta. Heron was delighted and he rolled out more branches in London, Bournemouth, Brighton and Bromley. For the exteriors, Coates used the same vocabulary of plate glass, Plymax and stainless steel. The store interiors were lined with oak and birch veneers and the fabrics were presented with a Japanese sense of space and restraint. The Cresta stores were featured in *Architectural Review* and also featured in *Building, Architecture Illustrated* and in *Architectural Record* in the US.[10]

Word reached Jack Pritchard at Venesta that a young architect was using plywood in an innovative manner and he got in touch with Cresta to request images of the stores to use in his company's marketing campaigns. Wells came to meet him at Venesta's office and the two men hit it off at once, agreeing to promote each other's work in a spirit of mutual 'back scratching'.[11]

Wells later told Pritchard: 'From the moment that I met you I knew instinctively that we were destined to do a job of work in this world, together someday.'[12]

For his part, Pritchard could see beyond Coates's charming veneer and realized that they shared a sense of mission about modern design and materials. He took him to Finella, and introduced him to its cabal of like-minded proto-Modernists. Keen to formalize their ideas with a manifesto of intent, they formed the Twentieth Century Group, whose first executive council included Raymond McGrath, Serge Chermayeff, Frederick Etchells (who had translated Le Corbusier's *Vers Une Architecture*) and Howard Robertson. Their aim was to 'define the principles to which contemporary design should conform' and they planned to promote British Modernism through an exhibition, like those in Sweden, Germany and France.[13] But splits emerged in the group and it soon broke up.

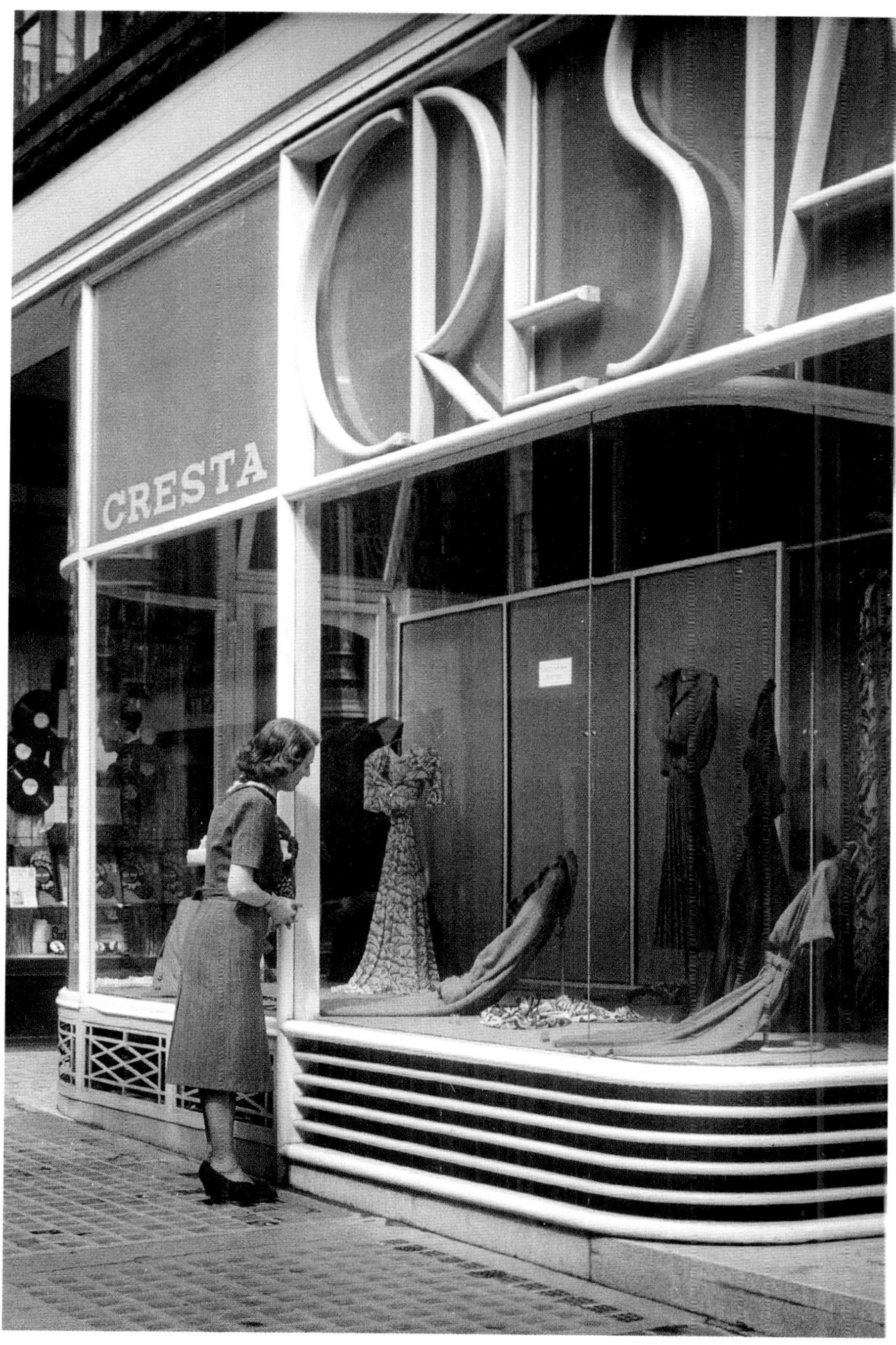

ABOVE: Cresta store facade and interiors, designed by Wells Coates, c.1930. It was Coates's innovative use of plywood in the Cresta chain which caught Jack Pritchard's eye. Coates designed everything from the company's logo to its stools.

What the group urgently needed was a more receptive cultural climate and more enlightened patrons to promote their work. Fortuitously for Coates, one soon arrived in the form of wealthy Labour MP George Russell Strauss, an acquaintance from the 1917 Club. Strauss commissioned Coates to transform his imposing Victorian mansion, One Kensington Palace Gardens, into a modern family home-cum-political salon. Coates stripped its interior of all its 19th-century features and used modern materials at every opportunity – Induroleum flooring, tubular-steel-framed furniture, plywood panelled walls. He installed Japanese-style sliding screens between the rooms, built-in electrical light fittings and used *shoji* screens instead of curtains. He also designed ingenious technological appliances, such as a service lift, which rose up through a concealed panel in the dining room floor to deliver food and drinks to guests.

To publicize the commission, he negotiated a large spread of before and after pictures in *Architectural Review* for a nine-page article he authored, entitled 'Furniture Today – Furniture Tomorrow'.[14]

His next commission was for actors Elsa Lanchester and Charles Laughton, who, since 1929, had been living in a 'lavender' marriage. They asked Coates to remodel their cluttered three-storey apartment at 34 Gordon Square and once again he stripped out the period detailing and rationalized the interior. He replaced interior doors with sliding screens decorated by artist John Armstrong, which could be pushed back to create a large, open-plan area for entertaining. The couple's separate bedrooms were lined with plywood panelling and he built-in plywood wardrobes faced with silken veneers. Wells chose unexpectedly utilitarian materials for the soft furnishings, such as roller-towel fabric for Laughton's curtains and shirting material for Lanchester's bedspread. The flat even contained a small gym to help Laughton keep in shape for his film roles.

A meeting at Finella with BBC producer Lance Sieveking (later a resident of the Lawn Road Flats) and the corporation's Assistant Comptroller, Valentine Goldsmith resulted in 'the greatest opportunity of modern decorative design the country had ever seen'[15]. In 1928 the BBC had commissioned architect Val Myer to build the new Broadcasting House in Portland Place and, in 1930, Coates, Raymond McGrath and Serge Chermayeff were asked to design the interiors. It was a high-profile and enormously challenging commission of national importance. Radio was still in its infancy and the building would house the very latest communications technology. Every single item had to be specially designed and, thanks to a government edict on imported goods, entirely made in Britain to boost the struggling economy. It was a huge coup for the new style of architecture and exactly the kind of project the Design and Industries Association had envisaged.

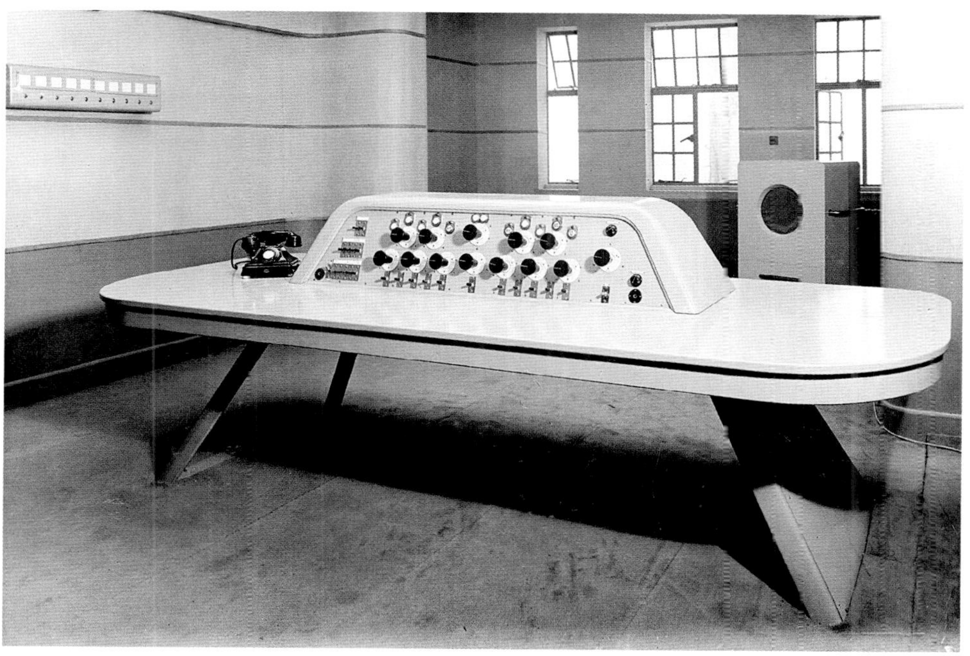

Coates and McGrath moved into Chermayeff's office in The Pantheon on Oxford Street and were soon dubbed 'the Three Musketeers' by the architectural press. Coates, with his PhD in Engineering, was given the most technical brief — the news and special-effects studios and control galleries. His experience as a pilot helped him conceive the cockpit-like broadcasting suites, where everything was within arm's reach. For the news studios, he designed a curved desk at which the announcer could move seamlessly on a swivel chair, from broadcasting a bulletin to operating a gramophone turntable. One of his most ingenious inventions was a ceiling-mounted, doubly counterbalanced floating microphone, which could be swung to any point in a studio and is still in use today. In the main sound studio Wells installed a rotating 'operating table' with seven different surfaces to create a huge range of sound effects. His dramatic control panel allowed producers to mix sounds from ten studios into a final broadcast. The work was enthusiastically received, with Coates singled out for special praise.

> *Mr Coates' rooms and their fittings are the finest achievements in the building and they show what the phrase, 'design in industry' cou'd mean if an introduction were effected between Mr Coates and a few industrialists.*[16]

By now Coates and Pritchard had become firm friends, with Coates initially seeing Jack as a replacement for the much-missed Borgeaud. Their friendship, based on so many shared interests, was consolidated on several trips to Europe, including their landmark visit to Germany with Serge Chermayeff in 1931. The cine footage of the visit, rediscovered in 2016, gives a remarkable insight into their road trip, including their in-jokes. Coates was renowned for his love of stylish clothing and immaculate appearance, and there are numerous shots of Coates's highly polished shoes.

In Berlin, Chermayeff arranged for them to visit Erich Mendelsohn, already something of an elder statesman of the new architecture. He must have enjoyed the company of the youthful trio, for in addition to entertaining them at his home, he invited them to come to his office to view his latest work. In an unpublished chapter from his memoirs, Jack Pritchard recalled the eventful evening that preceded their historic visit to the Dessau Bauhaus:

> We were to meet … at about 8:00 pm. We did not know if that meant that we were invited to supper, so we went to the Eden Hotel and drank some green cocktails. After we had seen the great man's drawings, he suggested that he and his charming wife would go and have a drink at a special place. We hoped for food but instead we had Cherry Cobblers [a cocktail of dry London gin and cherry brandy], very good but not on an empty stomach.
>
> Serge suggested we should go to a Russian restaurant he knew of. It was expensive and rather good. As we went in we had a vodka. Serge then ordered a blini for all of us. That was pancake covered with caviar, covered with pancake, covered with caviar, covered with pancake… etc. With vodka. We were getting in very good condition. Mendelsohn said we should now go to a dance hall where each table had a telephone so that you could exchange comments with anyone else you could see that you liked the look of. We got back to our hotel fairly successfully. Fortunately the hotel was by the station as we were to take an early train to Dessau to see the Bauhaus.
>
> Serge and I had some difficulty in getting Wells along in the morning. We were just in time to reach the back end of the train as it was about to start. We placed Wells on the step… The train started. Serge and I now decided how much to give the porter. We got on board and pushed Wells into the carriage. Unfortunately it was the dining car and Wells was more green than he should be. However we recovered by the time we arrived in Dessau.[17]

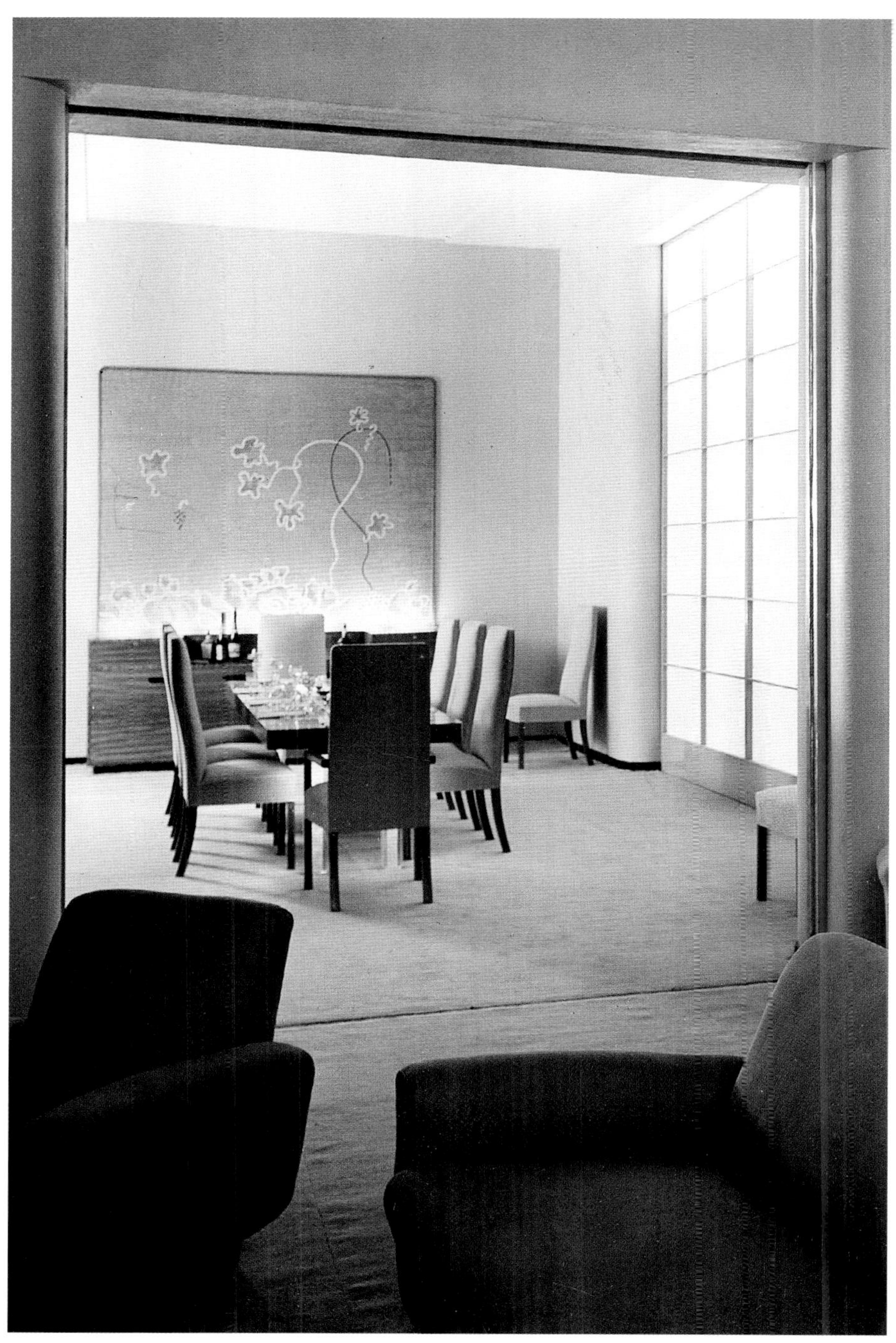

ABOVE: Coates's Japanese inspiration is evident in the dining room, One Kensington Palace Gardens, 1929.

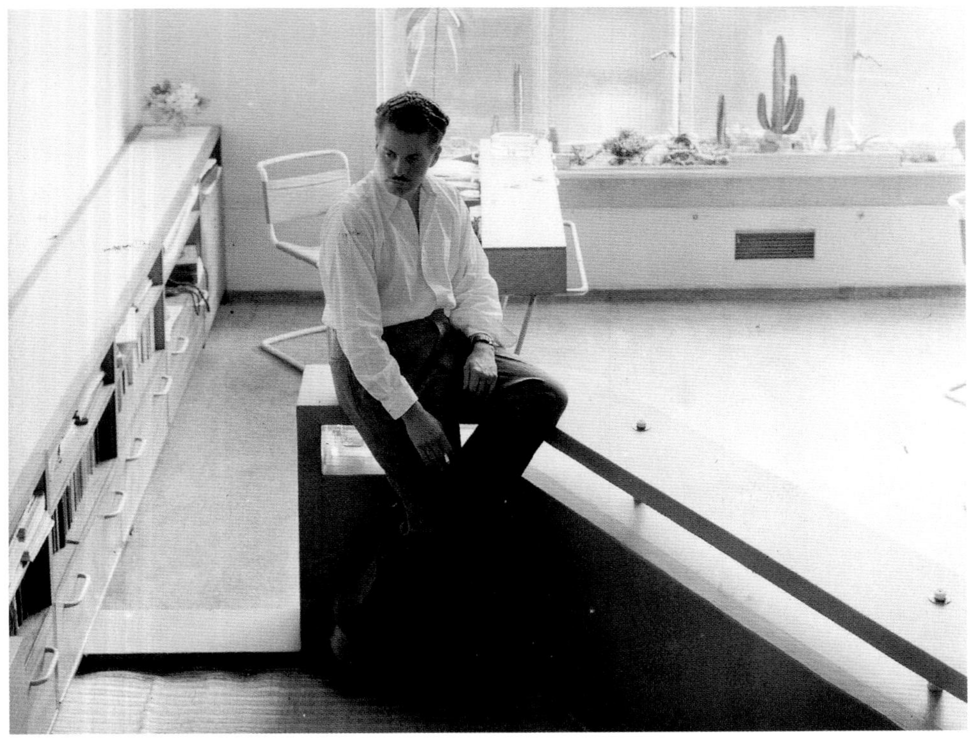

Hangovers behind them, the visit to the Bauhaus and Törten housing estate had a profound effect on both Coates and Pritchard and provided them with a business model and new ideas about materials which they believed would revolutionize British housing and furniture design. (Discussed further in chapter 4.)

In the space of three years Coates had moved from amateur decorator to one of the most technically accomplished designers working in England. He forged a network of like-minded allies in the fields of art, architecture and journalism and was instrumental in the first attempts at formalizing the aims of Modernism in Britain.

In 1932, the influential Les Congrès Internationaux d'Architecture Moderne (CIAM), whose members included Le Corbusier, Walter Gropius, Alvar Aalto and Sigfried Giedion, invited Philip Morton Shand to form a group representing England at CIAM congresses. He and Coates set up MARS, the Modern Architectural Research Group. The other founding members were architects Maxwell Fry and David Pleydell-Bouverie, critic John Gloag and publisher Hubert de Cronin Hastings. They stipulated that membership of the group should be kept

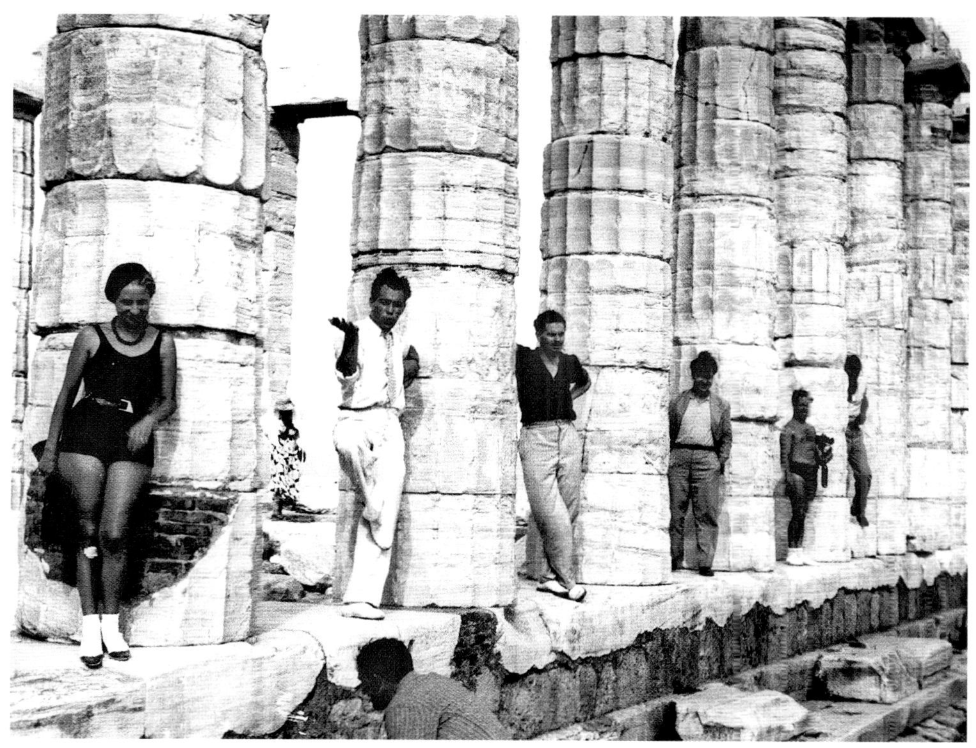

ABOVE: Coates (centre) with members of the CIAM Congress 1933, The Acropolis, Athens

select and small and would exclude certain people who were 'popular', but not 'modern' in the sense they understood. Those who fulfilled the criteria included: F.R.S. Yorke, Berthold Lubetkin, Amyas Connell, Basil Ward, Colin Lucas and Ernő Goldfinger. At the seminal CIAM conference of 1933, which took place on board the SS *Patris* sailing from Marseilles to Athens, Wells Coates, in his capacity as MARS's chairman, presented a report on future planning in London. It was here, by dint of his powerful intellect and force of personality that he met and took his place, quite naturally, among the leading figures of International Modernism.

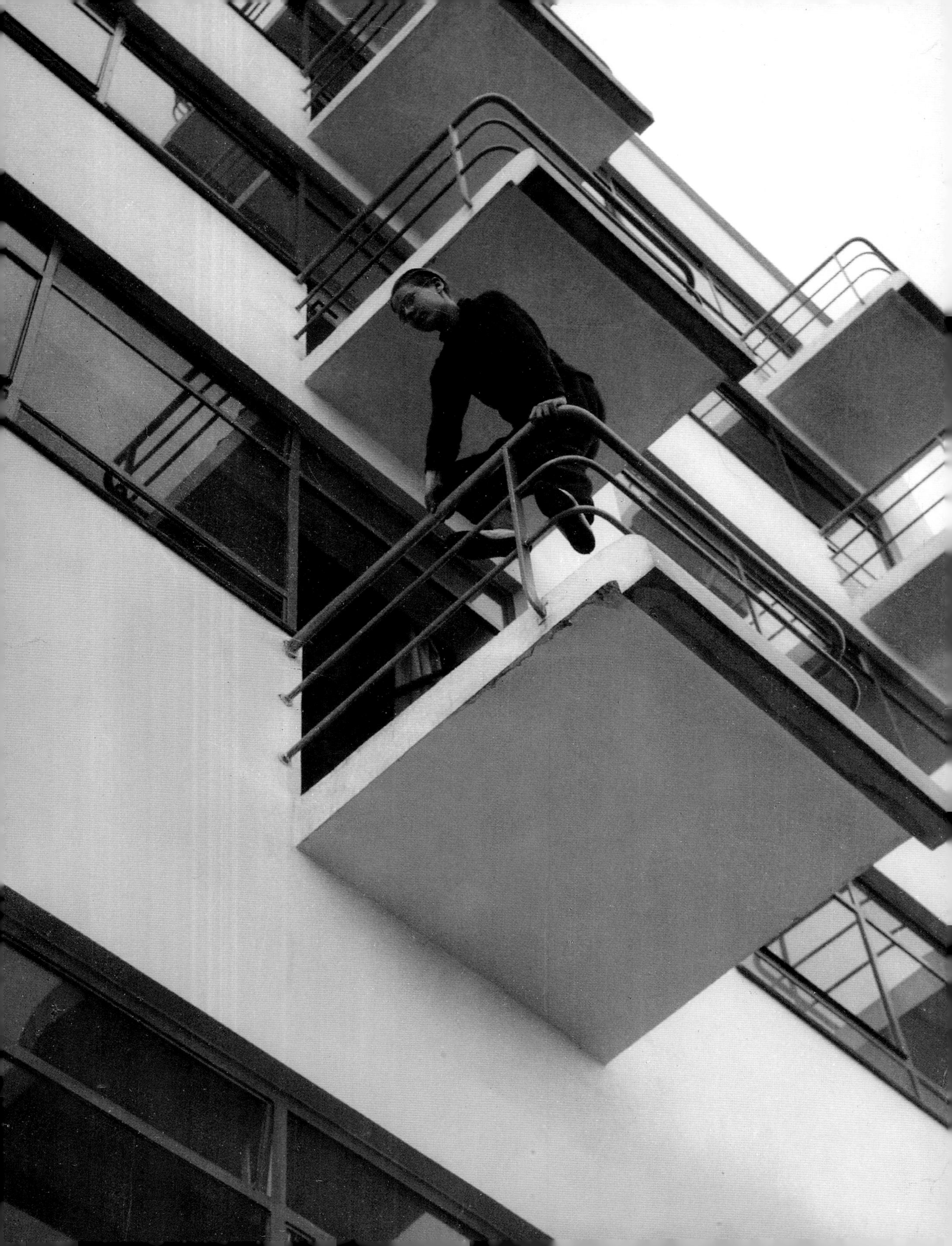

CHAPTER 3

THE BAUHAUS

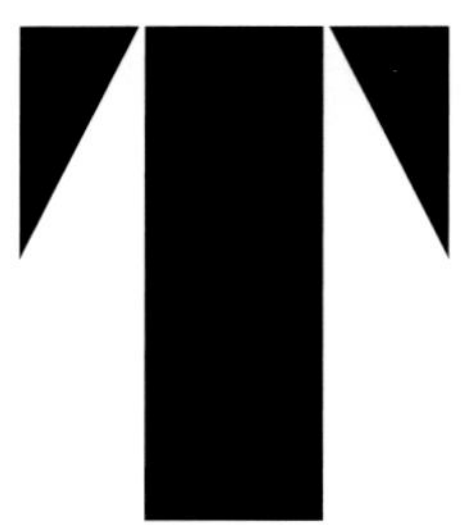HE DESERTED BUILDING THAT PRITCHARD, COATES
and Chermayeff visited in March 1931 was the second
incarnation of the Bauhaus. Throughout its short existence,
the art school was subject to the vicissitudes of German
politics, and by the time the Nazis finally shut it down in
Berlin in April 1933, it had been in three different locations,
some 280km apart.

Born in Berlin in 1883, its founder, Walter Gropius, began his architectural
training in the studio of Peter Behrens, a member of the Deutscher Werkbund.
The organization had been established in 1907 to bring together German artists
and industrialists, with the aim of making German companies and products
more competitive in the global markets. Behrens can be considered the first
'industrial designer' in history. Employed by the electricity giant AEG, he created
a total corporate identity for the company and remodelled its range of electrical
appliances, including fans, kettles and street lamps. In 1909, he designed a
monumental turbine hall for the firm. It was remarkable for its huge, full-height
steel-framed windows, which flooded the factory interior with light and became a
model for a new kind of industrial architecture.

In 1910 Gropius left Behrens's office and set up in practice with his colleague
Adolf Meyer. Their first major commission came from Carl Benscheidt, the owner
of a footwear company in Saxony, who wanted a radical new building to express
his company's break with the past. He had heard Gropius give a talk on the
importance of the working environment.[1]

> *Work must be established in places that give the workman,*
> *now a slave to industrial labour, not only light, air and hygiene,*
> *but also an indication of the great common idea that drives everything…*
> *The sophisticated industrialist will take all profitable steps to relieve*
> *the deadening monotony of factory work and alleviate its constraints.[2]*

The Faguswerk shoe-last factory, built between 1911 and 1913, was a workplace
both functional and humane. Gropius created a vast glass curtain wall, using steel-
framed windows, which wrapped around the building's corners. Supporting piers
were recessed and the building seemed to float on its black brick base, an effect
he called 'etherealization'. In 1914, he and Meyer built a landmark model factory
building for the inaugural Werkbund exhibition in Cologne. Its monumental
rectangular form was bookended by a pair of staircases enclosed in circular glass
towers, which framed the façade and exposed the building's inner structure.

The same year the Belgian architect and Werkbund member, Henry Van de

Velde resigned as Director of the Weimar School of Arts and Crafts and proposed Gropius as his successor. Before he could take up the position, World War I broke out and Gropius was called up for military service. He went on to serve his country with distinction as a cavalry officer and was twice awarded the Iron Cross. He also married Alma Mahler, widow of composer Gustav Mahler, and during their short and stormy marriage they produced a daughter, Manon. Returning to Berlin after the war, Gropius joined the Arbeitsrat fur Künst, a movement of artists and architects who believed modern architecture could deliver real social change.

> *It was then that the immensity of the mission of the architects of my own generation first dawned on me. I saw that an architect cannot hope to realize his ideas unless he can influence the industry of his country sufficiently for a new school of design to arise as a result; and unless that school succeeds in acquiring authoritative significance. I saw too, that to make this possible would require a whole staff of collaborators and assistants.[3]*

Having gained the approval of the Weimar authorities to amalgamate the School of Arts and Crafts with the Weimar Academy of Fine Art, he named the combined institution 'the state Bauhaus'. The title was symbolic. '*Bau*' meant 'building' and the title carried with it associations of medieval guild workers. His first 'collaborator' was the artist Lyonel Feininger who designed the cover of Gropius's Bauhaus manifesto of April 1919. Depicting the Expressionistic, medieval-style woodcut of a cathedral, it was circulated in German newspapers and art schools inviting students of all ages, nationalities and genders to apply. It declared:

> *Let us build a new guild of craftsmen, without the class distinctions which raise an arrogant barrier between craftsman and artist. Together let us conceive and create the new building of the future, which will embrace architecture and sculpture and painting in one unity and which will rise one day toward heaven from the hands of a million workers like the crystal symbol of a new faith.[4]*

Gropius drew up a syllabus for the school in which all students commenced with a preliminary six-month *Vorkurs*. He appointed artist and teacher Johannes Itten to run the *Vorkurs*, which was designed to challenge students' preconceptions and give them an understanding of materials, colour and form. In Itten's view it was the antithesis of the conventional 'beaux arts' training and would liberate the student's creative power.[5] Students who successfully completed this stage would be invited to enter a workshop as an apprentice, where they would receive specialized training in a specific craft such as metalwork, pottery, stained glass, bookbinding, printing, weaving or cabinet making. They would receive a combination of practical and formal instruction from two 'Masters' – an artist, known as a 'Master of Form' and a technician, known as a 'Workshop Master'. After three years they would take a journeyman's examination, after which they could proceed to the study of building, the very core of the Bauhaus curriculum. Gropius intended the Bauhaus to be self-funding, through sales of the students' products, which they would produce in collaboration with industry.

In reality, with inflation rampant and limited funds, he had enormous difficulty recruiting suitable craftsmen to act as Workshop Masters and the workshops were poorly equipped. The pottery students had to relocate to Dornburg, some 25km outside Weimar, to a pottery owned by Master of the Workshop, Max Crehan.

Gropius himself ran the woodwork department and, in 1920, his architectural practice (which he continued to run with Meyer), received a commission that gave him the opportunity to employ large numbers of Bauhaus students in a real commercial enterprise. It was a villa near Berlin, for the timber-merchant Adolf Sommerfeld. The house was made entirely from wood, much of it salvaged ships' timbers. The exterior resembled an Alpine chalet and with its extruding horizontal beams, owed much to Frank Lloyd Wright. Inside, Hungarian student Marcel Breuer created geometric wooden furniture as part of his journeyman's portfolio. The stained glass, lighting and door fittings were all created in the school's workshops. Dictated perhaps by the client, the building was Romantic, Expressionistic even, and seemingly the antithesis of Gropius's austere pre-war creations of steel and glass. It did, however, fulfil his dream of a cathedral of the crafts, uniting workers from different disciplines.

Between 1920 and 1922 Gropius managed to attract a number of high-profile artists to the school. Painters Paul Klee, Wassily Kandinsky and Georg Muche, and the artist and choreographer Oskar Schlemmer were made Masters of Form. However, Johannes Itten's influence over students was becoming a cause for concern. A mystic and follower of a religion known as Mazdaznan, he cut an eccentric figure around the school, wearing long, flowing robes of his own design, and adhered to an ascetic regime of fasting and vegetarianism. A growing number of students adopted Mazdaznan and his beliefs began to overshadow his talents as a teacher. Gropius felt his position as Director was becoming undermined. He eased Itten out of the school and moved the Bauhaus in a new direction.

Germany's post-war disenchantment with technology had abated and Gropius returned to his Machine Age ideals. The second phase of the Bauhaus began and a new appointment reflected this new direction. In 1923, Gropius appointed

Hungarian Constructivist artist László Moholy-Nagy as Master of the *Vorkurs*. He arrived at the Bauhaus like 'a pike in a pond full of goldfish'.[6] Where Itten had worn the garb of a monk, Moholy-Nagy donned that of a mechanic, dressing for the workshop in a blue boiler suit. Where Itten had been spiritual, Moholy-Nagy was supremely practical. He was a highly versatile artist who moved with ease between the media of paint, photography, sculpture and film.

> *The reality of our century is technology: the invention, construction and maintenance of machines. To be a user of machines is to be of the spirit of this century… Everyone is equal before the machine. I can use it, so can you. It can crush me: the same can happen to you. There is no tradition in technology, no class-consciousness. Everyone can be the machine's master or its slave.[7]*

Moholy-Nagy dispensed with Itten's quasi-spiritual exercises and replaced them with the study of basic techniques and materials and their practical application. He was assisted in running the *Vorkurs* by 'Young Master' Josef Albers, a gifted former student who ran the first semester and challenged students to test complex engineering theories using everyday materials such as paper and razor blades. Under Moholy-Nagy and Albers, experimentation was valued more highly than the finished result, with 'education by process' the new motto of the course.[8]

Moholy-Nagy was also made Master of the Metal Workshop and, together with fellow master Christian Dell, oversaw a period of intense productivity in which students were encouraged to create objects for mass production using industrial materials such as glass and steel. In the carpentry workshop, the new approach was also evident as leading talent Marcel Breuer produced a range of simple, geometric wooden furniture heavily influenced by the Dutch artistic movement *De Stijl*.

By the middle of 1923, the German economy was buckling under hyperinflation and Gropius was under intense pressure from the local government to show what the Bauhaus was achieving. The school was viewed with suspicion by local townspeople and the Nationalists accused the staff of having Communist sympathies. Gropius decided to hold an exhibition showcasing the new, more commercial direction in which he was taking the school, under the slogan: 'Art and Technology – A new Unity!' It was during a lecture tour he undertook to fund the project that he met his future wife Ilse (later 'Ise') Frank, who was seated in the front row of his audience in Hannover.

The centrepiece of the exhibition was the *Haus am Horn*. This was a prototype of a small, low-cost home, which Gropius hoped could be rolled out for staff and students in a settlement on the edge of Weimar. Designed by Georg Muche and Adolf Meyer and financed by Adolf Sommerfeld, it was built from mass-produced industrial materials and entirely furnished by the Bauhaus workshops. Moholy-Nagy designed the lights, which were made in the metal workshop and Marcel Breuer designed the furniture and the compact, functional kitchen.

Although favourably reviewed in international publications and visited by 15,000 people – many from abroad – the success of the Bauhaus exhibition only antagonized its enemies. A widely circulated publication known as 'The Yellow Brochure' accused Gropius and the Bauhaus School of subversion and Bolshevik sympathies.[9] The Nationalist party won a majority in the elections of February 1924 and by the end of the year announced they were halving the school's funding and would only offer six-month contracts to its masters. Gropius knew he was fighting a losing battle and took the decision to close the Weimar Bauhaus at the end of March 1925.

Several cities expressed an interest in rehousing the Bauhaus, but Gropius was won over by an invitation from Dr Fritz Hesse, the Mayor of Dessau. It was a prosperous city of 70,000 inhabitants, with thriving local industries and the only province in Germany still under Socialist rule. Gropius set to work designing the new school and the second Bauhaus, which opened in December 1926, was the successful realization of all his technical, social and architectural aspirations.

It consisted of three wings to house workshops and studios; a technical school of arts and crafts and the students' accommodation. Transparency was the keynote: at every opportunity, Gropius designed glass vistas to create a dialogue with the community beyond. The school of arts and crafts was a three-storey reinforced concrete block, housing classrooms, offices and Gropius's studio. It was linked by a raised glass bridge to the workshops. This wing, known locally as 'the Aquarium', was the signature building; its skin, a vast, glittering curtain wall, revealing the hive of creative activity within. Set on a base of recessed supports, it appeared to defy gravity. There was a canteen, lecture theatre and stage, which could be reconfigured to hold concerts and ballets. The lighting fixtures were created by the metal workshop and the tubular-steel furniture throughout the school was designed by Marcel Breuer.

Accommodation was provided for students in apartments, each with its own balcony, in a wing known as the Prellerhaus. 'All you had to do to call a friend was to step out on to your balcony and whistle,' remembered student Xanti Schawinsky, who credited Gropius's architecture with creating a 'wonderful community spirit'. It was a unique opportunity to combine living, learning and practice. Gropius designed four 'Masters' Houses' for senior teaching staff and their families, a short walk away, in an attractive copse of pine trees. Most of the Weimar teaching staff had moved with him to Dessau and several former pupils had now joined their ranks. The dual system of Masters of Form and Workshop Masters

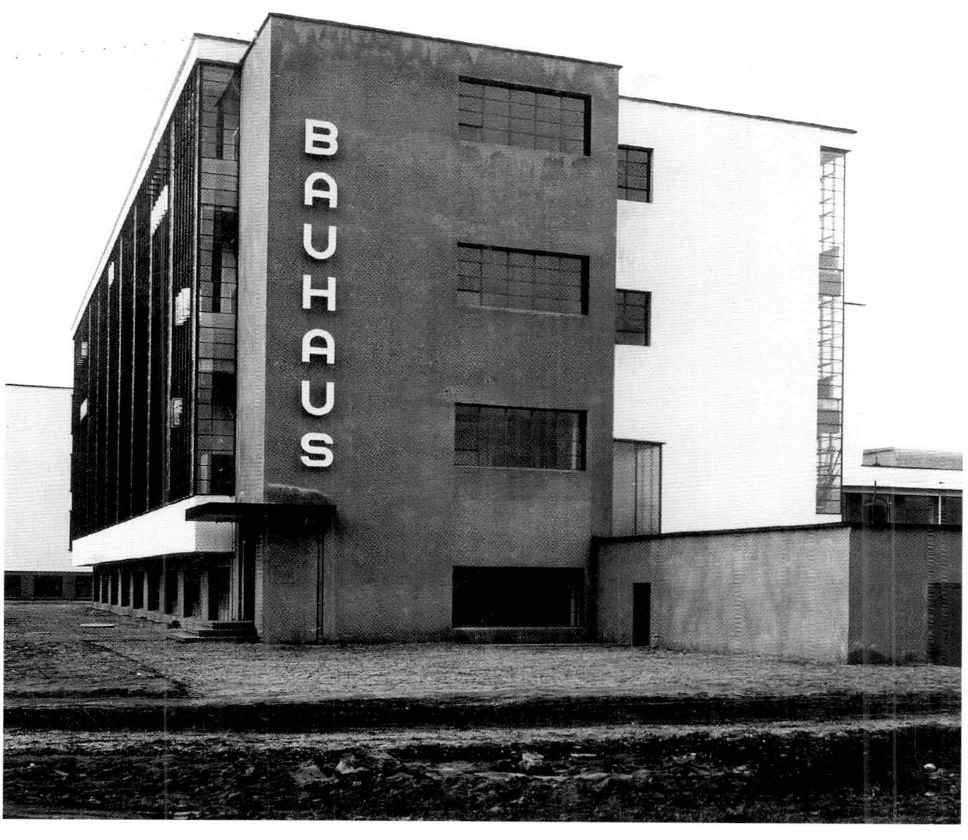

ABOVE: The Bauhaus building in Dessau, seen from the south-west. The famous lettering by Herbert Bayer was removed after the National Socialists took control of Dessau City Council in 1932.

was abandoned and, instead, specialized craftsmen were employed to assist in the workshops. Moholy-Nagy and Albers continued to teach the *Vorkurs* and Wassily Kandinsky and Paul Klee ran a compulsory course in Form.

The Dessau years of 1926–32 saw the school come of age and many of Gropius's aims brought to fruition. The Dessau workshops were now better equipped and had links with industry. The cabinet-making and metal workshops were amalgamated under Marcel Breuer and worked on standardized designs for household equipment and furniture. Inspired by the frame of the Adler bicycle he rode around campus, Breuer pioneered the development of tubular-steel furniture, including his landmark Wassily chair of 1925 and cantilevered S-shaped Cesca chair of 1928.

Young Master Herbert Bayer ran the printing department, which specialized in typography, layout and advertising. He was responsible for a new clarity in the school's graphic design, which gave it a distinctive visual identity, and he argued that upper-case letters and serifs were redundant. He also embarked on an affair with Ise Gropius. During this period, the school also published 14 influential Bauhaus books, in which leading architects and artists, including Gropius, Klee, van Doesburg and Mondrian, illustrated and elucidated their theories. These were edited by Gropius and Moholy-Nagy, who also designed their layout and covers.

Oskar Schlemmer ran the stage workshop. In addition to his ballets and experimental theatre productions, he was responsible for masterminding the school's spectacular themed entertainments, which became artworks in themselves. The most celebrated of these was the Metal Party of 1929. Guests dressed in costumes made from tin foil, cutlery and cooking pots and made their entrance sliding down a chute into a room filled with silver balls.

The first female Master, former student, Gunta Stölzl, ran the weaving workshop, one of the school's most commercially successful and productive departments from 1926–31. Inspired by Klee and Kandinsky's teachings on colour and form, these workshops successfully designed textiles for mass production and created innovative fabrics with acoustic and light-reflective properties.

In 1927, Gropius finally set up a department of architecture, open to students who had completed the preliminary course. He installed the Swiss architect Hannes Meyer as professor. It was to be a controversial choice, although Gropius was unaware of Meyer's extreme left-wing leanings at the time.

Gropius had set up his own private practice within the school and brought the department on board with several projects, including a commission from Dessau City Council to design an estate of low-cost housing for industrial workers in the nearby suburb of Törten. He drew up two basic housing models, using standardized components such as concrete walls, which could be manufactured on site. Each house took just three days to erect and provided invaluable practical experience for Bauhaus students, who were also involved in designing the furniture and fittings. The estate included a small block of flats with a cooperative shop beneath it, known as the Konsum Building.

However, the political climate was changing and Mayor Hesse, once a staunch ally, turned against the Bauhaus, threatening to slash its funding. Attacks against Gropius were growing from many quarters and the school was frequently satirized in the press. The final straw came when the publisher of the local newspaper refused to retract an article challenging the size of Gropius's fee for the Törten estate. On 4 February 1928, a battle-weary Gropius resigned. He appointed Hannes Meyer as his successor and left for private practice in Berlin. Breuer and Moholy-

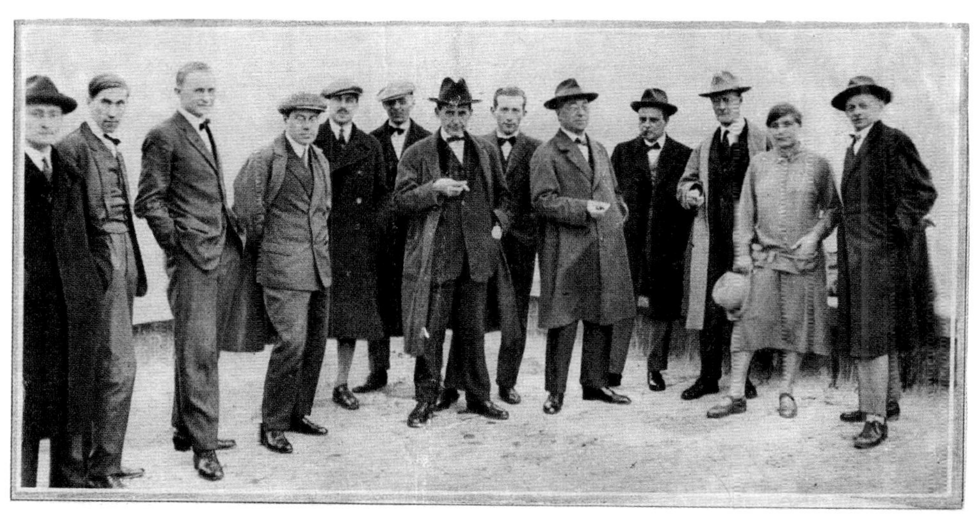

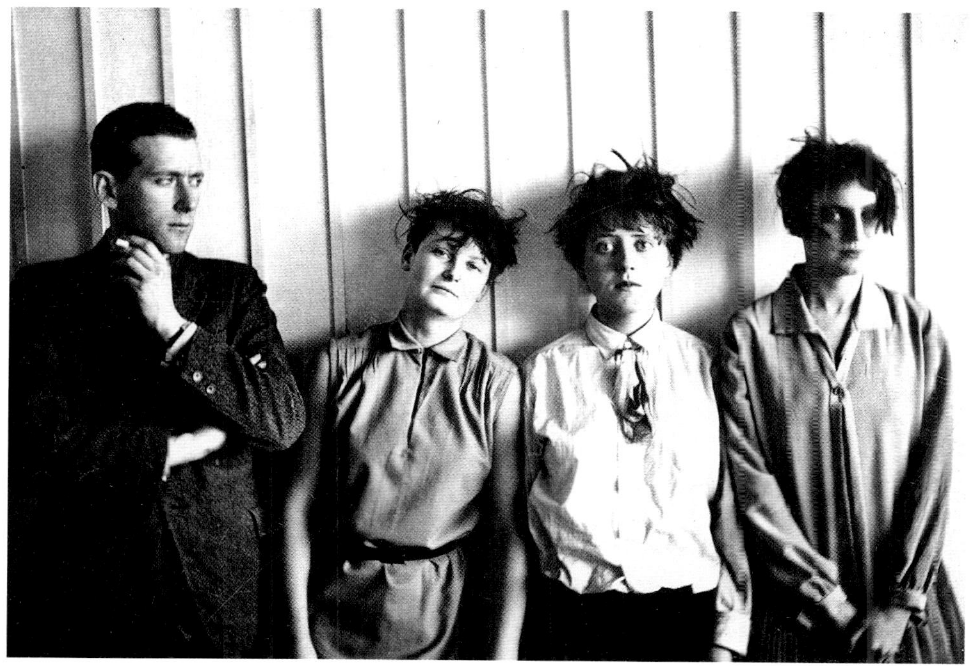

ABOVE, TOP: The Bauhaus masters on the roof of the Bauhaus building in Dessau in 1926. L–R: Josef Albers, Hinnerk Scheper, Georg Muche, László Moholy-Nagy, Herbert Bayer, Joost Schmidt, Walter Gropius, Marcel Breuer, Wassily Kandinsky, Paul Klee, Lyonel Feininger, Gunta Stölzl and Oskar Schlemmer. ABOVE: Marcel Breuer, then a junior master at the Bauhaus, and his 'harem' in 1927. From left to right: his first wife, Marta Erps-Breuer, Katt Both and Ruth Hollos-Consemüller.

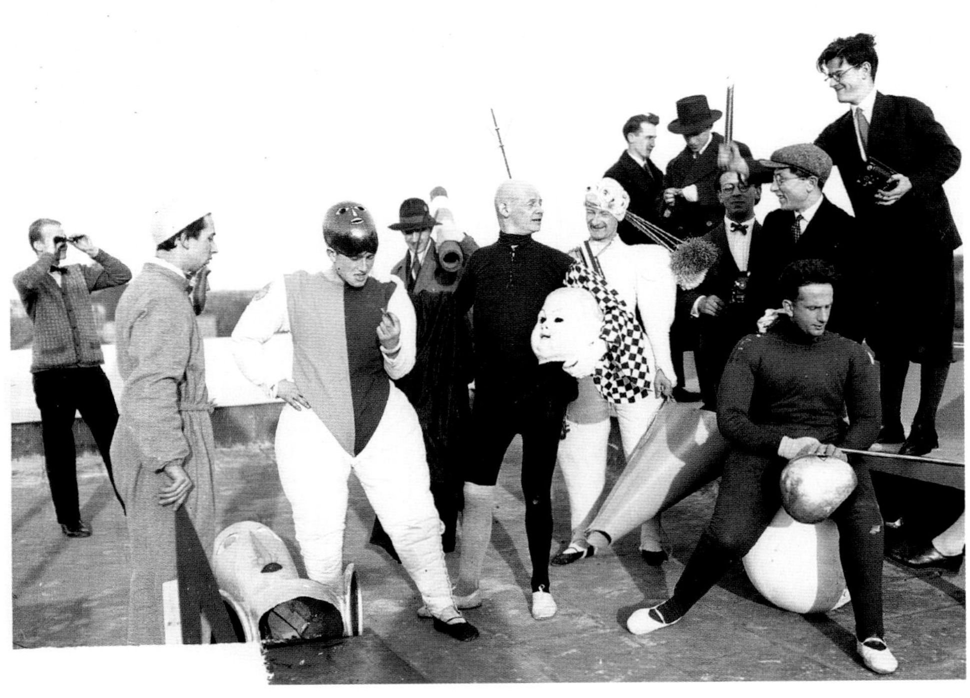

Nagy resigned in sympathy and followed him to Berlin. Gropius rewarded their loyalty by employing them on a commission for Dammerstock Siedlung housing estate at Karlsruhe, and on a number of apartment schemes in Berlin and Frankfurt.

Meyer headed the Bauhaus for the next two years, improving the school's links with industry and almost doubling its income. But his Marxist views did not go down well with Mayor Hesse. In August 1930, he was forced to resign amidst accusations of misusing Dessau city funds and the Communist students at the Bauhaus, who were growing in number, were ordered to leave. The administration tried to persuade Gropius to return, but he refused and instead recommended architect Mies van der Rohe (with whom he had worked as a young man in Behren's office) as Meyer's successor. Mies's first priority was to clamp down on discipline at the school and ban any political activity. The architectural department assumed even greater pre-eminence, with a new (some claimed 'bourgeois') emphasis on aesthetics and elegance. The metal, furniture and mural working workshops were amalgamated into an 'interior design' department.

Meanwhile, the Weimar Republic was badly hit by the Wall Street Crash and the Far Right was taking advantage of the economic chaos. In 1931, the Nazi party

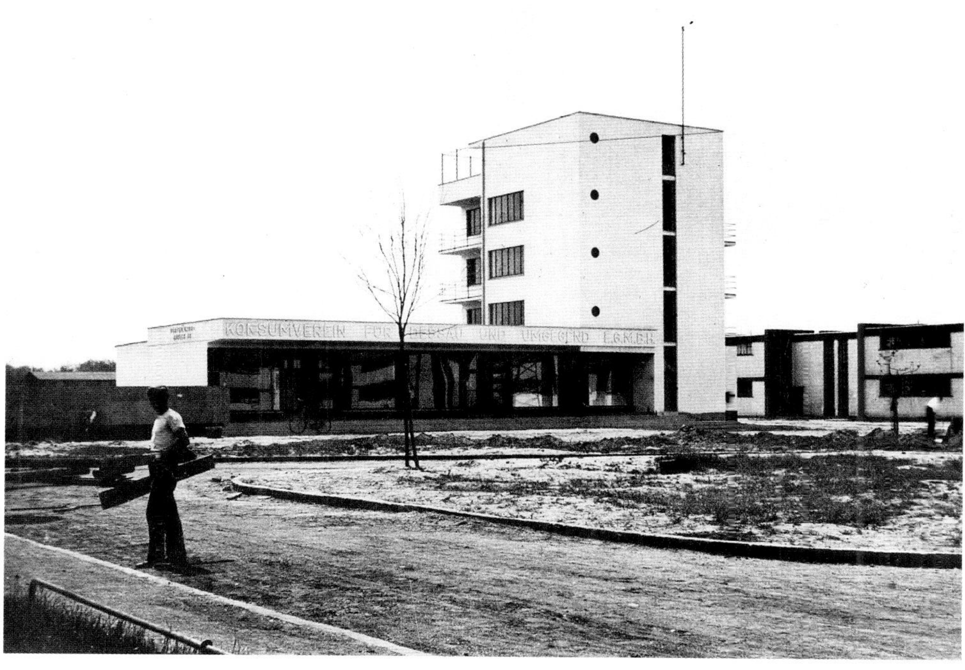

ABOVE: The Konsum Building was designed by Walter Gropius and built in 1928. It functioned as the centre point of the Törter Estate, towering over the surrounding buildings.

gained control of the Dessau city parliament. The school was accused once again of being Communist and its emphasis on International Modernism was declared 'anti-German' and decadent. The Nazis claimed most of the staff and students were Jews and that the architecture of the building itself was 'Jewish' – after all, flat roofs were not native to Germany. The Dessau authorities switched off all funding and shut the Bauhaus on 30 September 1932. Nazi officials smashed the school's windows and overturned its offices and workshops.

With no external funding, Mies moved the school to a former telephone factory in Berlin and reopened the Bauhaus as a private institution. But within months the Nazis had swept to power and Adolf Hitler was Chancellor. On 11 April 1933 the school was occupied by the Gestapo and searched for evidence of Communist activities. Staff and students without proper identification were loaded on trucks and taken away. On 10 August, Mies sent a letter to all Bauhaus students informing them that the Bauhaus was 'dissolved'.

The exodus to London began.

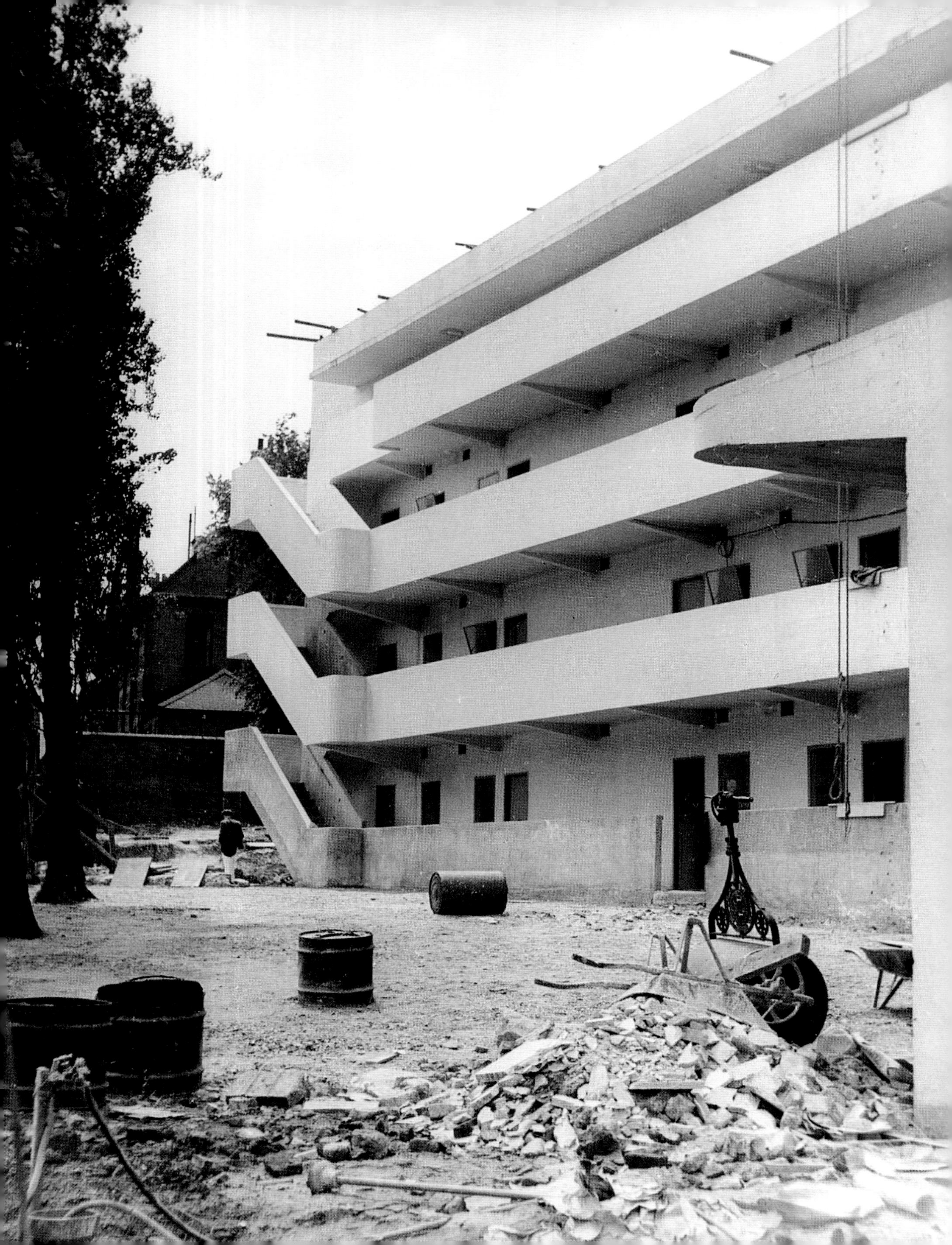

CHAPTER 4

BUILDING THE FLATS

During our discussions with Wells, Molly said that she supposed that really land in London should be used for more than one family. Wells, in one of his superior moods, said, 'Of course, I always knew that the right thing to do was to build flats rather than a house'.[1]

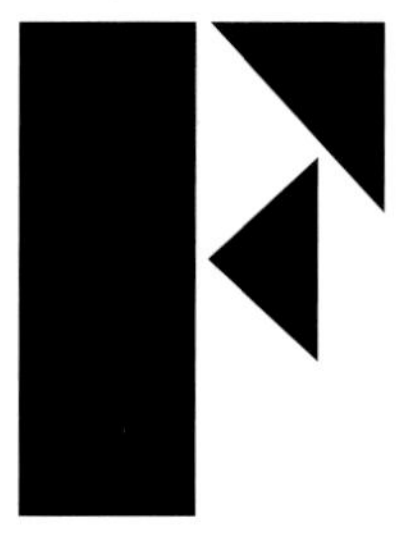OR YEARS, THE QUESTION OF WHO HAD FIRST suggested building a block of flats in Lawn Road was a bitter bone of contention between the Pritchards and Wells Coates. In early 1930, Jack and Molly took the considerable leap of faith of appointing the inexperienced Coates, who had never designed a building, as their architect. In the year since Jack had noticed his work for Cresta in the design press, both he and Molly had forged close relationships with the Canadian. Even so, constructing the flats was a turbulent process and one that put huge strain on their friendships.

'Molly's strong liking for him proved fortunate', Jack recalled '…since she was able to deal with his sometimes strange behaviour: he was very difficult at times.'[2]

It was Pritchard, entangled in his own affair with Beatrix Tudor-Hart, who had suggested Molly should gain some extra-marital 'experience' of her own. While her husband was working in Paris for Venesta in spring 1930, Molly invited Coates to dinner, although she confessed in a letter to Jack, 'I don't think I shall dare to flirt with him. Suppose he didn't want to flirt with me. I should feel snubbed and awkward and that would spoil such relations as had so far established.'[3] Her worries proved unfounded and they commenced an affair. She wrote to thank Jack for 'contriving to make it so plain to Wells what your views on sexual freedom were. I think you did it for me and it was lovely of you.[4]

The Pritchards, who had both turned 30, were keen to be actively involved in the design process and, together with Coates, spent much of the next year immersing themselves in architectural periodicals and refining their ideas. Coates succinctly described what they wished to achieve: 'The kind of place a man and a woman and family should live in, [in] this problem of the theatre of ordinary life, the theatre of modern living.'[5]

In March, in a reflection of their rapidly developing ties, they discussed building two linked houses, one for the Pritchards and their two boys, and a second, smaller house-cum-office for Coates, his wife Marion and daughter Laura. A single-storey building to house a nursery school run by Beatrix Tudor-Hart had also briefly been considered for the site and then shelved. Her relationship with Pritchard had ended bitterly, when he refused to accede to her demands to spend one night a week with her and their daughter, Jennifer.[6]

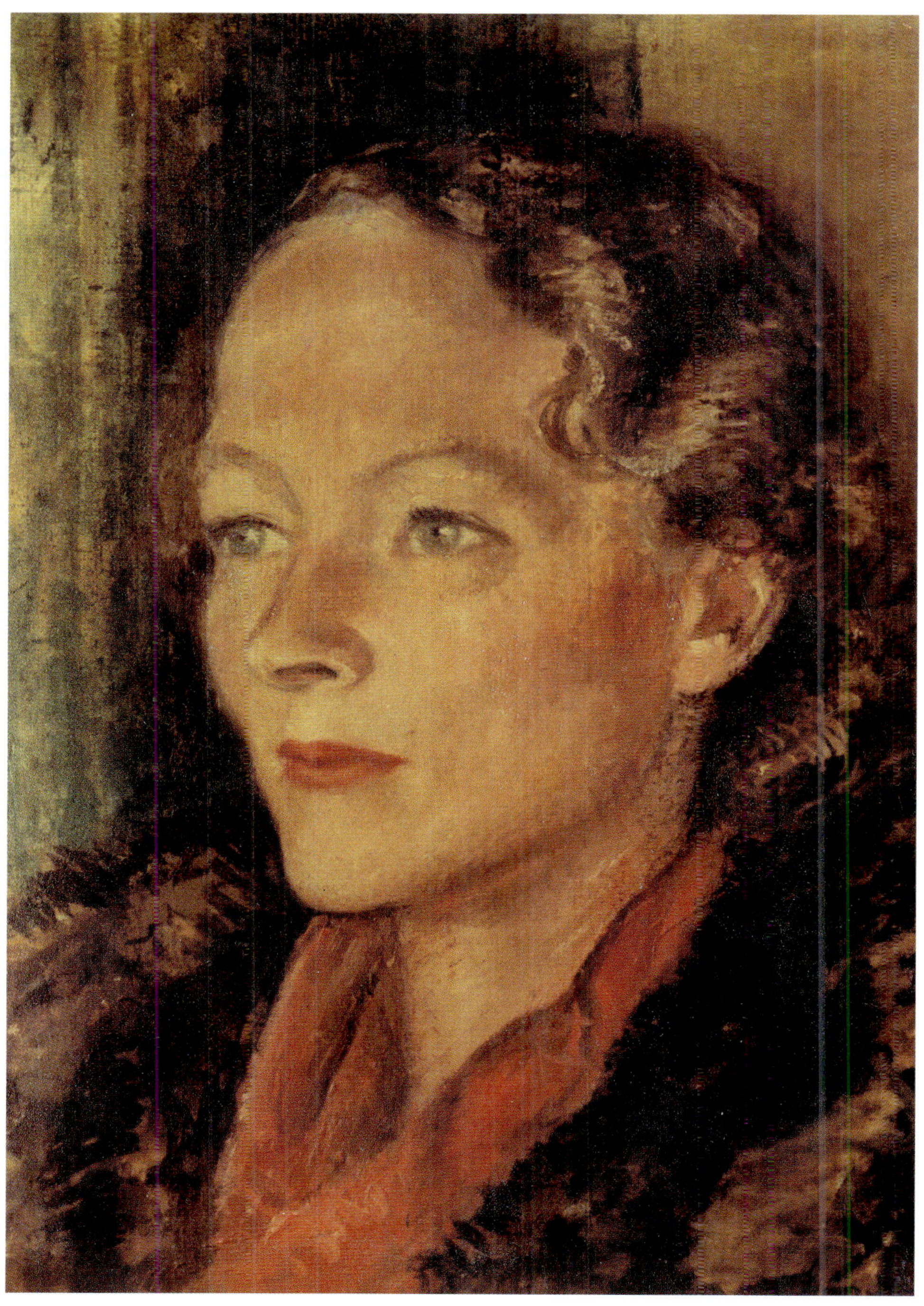

ABOVE: This portrait of Molly Fritchard, by an unknown artist, captures her fine-boned beauty.

In April, Coates and Molly planned to travel to Europe together to join Pritchard for a tour of Germany. [7] In the event Molly was too ill to travel so the two men made the nine-day trip without her, taking in Strasbourg, Karlsruhe, Heidelberg, Düsseldorf, Brussels and Paris. A highlight was the Weissenhof Estate in Stuttgart, where 17 Modernist architects each created a prototype of simple, low-cost workers' housing.

In July, Wells showed them some new designs he had drawn for a pair of L-shaped interlinked houses, constructed from reinforced concrete and raised on piloti, in the style of Le Corbusier. The Pritchards were 'bowled over' by them, but Jack enraged Coates by asking about practicalities and suggesting that he arranged the site, so that in future, they could easily be divided. Coates retorted in a fit of pique:

> *That idea of property – so much of this little garden is for you m'dear and this tweeny little wishy bit is for me, so there! – is dead, dead, dead… My scheme provides a place which every actor in a drama can call his own place, and further than that my idea of property does not go. This is the room where I sleep, this where I work, and this where I eat. That is the roof garden where everybody can turn out… This is the garden where everybody goes. It's like a park.* [8]

Molly's calming influence must have prevailed, for by September 1930, Pritchard and Coates had officially set up in business together as Wells Coates and Partners, 'to act as architects, engineers, designers, entrepreneurs and constructors of dwellings for modern people'. On the board of directors were Coates's father-in-law Frank Grove, lawyer Graham Maw, Henry John Sinclair, Lord Pentland and Edward Versluys. [9] Pritchard and Coates planned to use their two homes in Lawn Road as prototypes of the most 'up-to-date houses in the country and to incorporate every suitable modern method'. [10] Wells estimated each house would cost £2,000 to build, but they were unable to raise the necessary funds. The two men exchanged frustrated and recrimination-filled correspondence. Their building plans were put on ice.

In February 1931, in an attempt to put things back on a better business footing, Pritchard wrote to Coates outlining in more detail how they might market 'unit dwellings', selling them '&/or their contents either singly or as housing schemes'. He also suggested some new names for their company. 'I like the Russian type of name,' he wrote. [11] Coates, who was fond of using isometric drawings, responded enthusiastically: 'Why not Isometric Unit Construction (units of same measure),

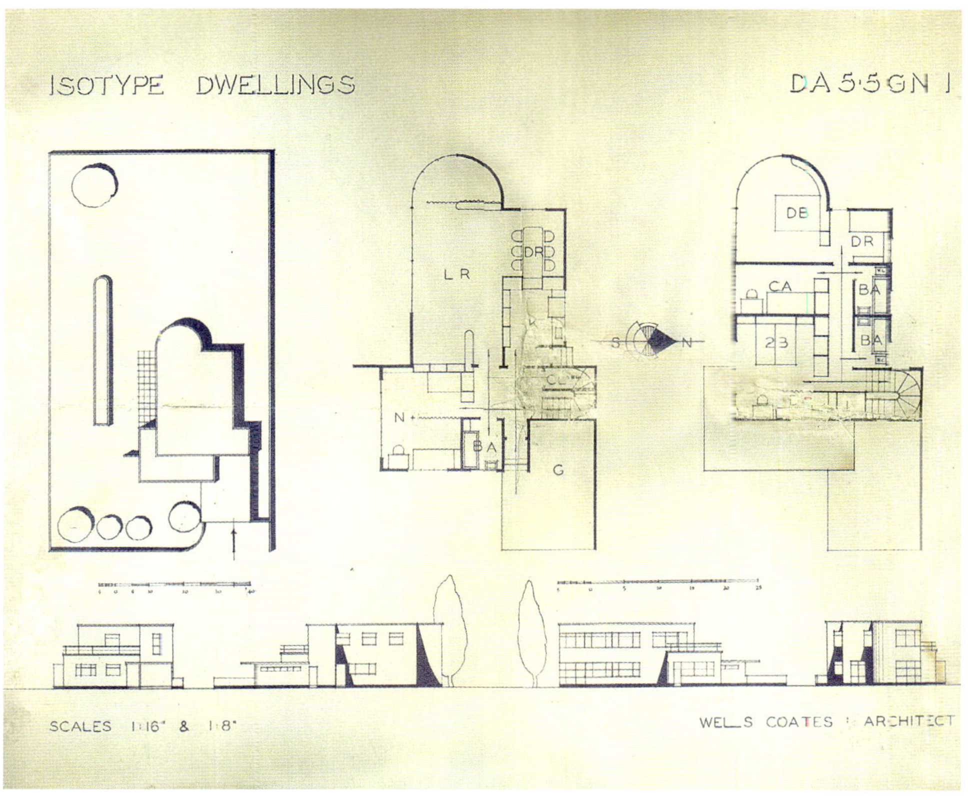

ABOVE: Designs for Isotype dwellings by Wells Coates, 1931.

ISOCON?' The finalized name, and its spelling as Isokon, was agreed over dinner at Rules restaurant in Covent Garden with Molly and Graham Maw.[12]

Coates was designated Isokon's Consultant Architect and Pritchard was given control of planning, marketing and publicity. Coates's first task was to design a number of prefabricated building components, which could be combined to create four different housing models, they dubbed Isotypes. He then designed a range of standardized built-in unit furniture, which would fit any shell the company might produce.

In March, Pritchard and Coates left for Germany with Serge Chermayeff, ostensibly to research the use of built-up plywood doors for Venesta. They returned to London inspired by their visit to Berlin and the Bauhaus. All their reading, foreign fact-finding and long conversations had given them fresh insight. One of the issues then preoccupying architects was how much space individuals needed to live in comfortably, and Molly queried whether it was really right that land in

London (which was in the throes of a housing crisis) should be used for a single family. Coates concurred, adding he had 'always thought they should build flats' on the site. Whoever truly came up with the idea, all three now leaped upon it as the only logical solution for the site. On 12 August 1931, Coates wrote to Jack: 'I note you agree to "minimum flats" and will proceed on these lines'.[13] The choice of the word 'minimum' was significant. In 1929, the second CIAM congress had chosen as its theme '*Die Wohnung fur das Existenzminimum*' (The Apartment for Minimal Living) and Walter Gropius had written an article exploring the issue.

Molly took the lead in drawing up the concept and technical brief for the flats. She sketched out their target audience as young professional men and (significantly) women, with incomes of around £500 a year, who had few possessions and would otherwise be condemned to living in digs.[14] They would offer a range of domestic services, including bed-making, clothes-washing, shoe-polishing, window-cleaning and dusting, and meals would be provided by a central kitchen. She asked Coates to design a block of approximately 20 one-room service flats with flexible space for sleeping, dressing and dining.[15] If convenient, the block should also comprise 'a few two-room flats with extra balcony space, which could be let for higher rents'. The maximum outlay for all this was (rather optimistically) not to exceed £5,000. The model she stated should 'in principle be suitable for duplication in other areas'.

Coates replied that he simply could not build 20 flats for £5,000, unless they were impossibly small and they cut all the central services. He suggested that they should build additional floors, to accommodate more apartments and thus spread their costs. His estimate was £8,000–9,000. He submitted an initial, rather basic scheme showing a typical floor plan of four minimum flats and two larger ones, symmetrically organized around a central staircase.

Coates had just set up in partnership with David Pleydell-Bouverie and was preoccupied with other commissions. As the months passed, tensions with Jack Pritchard arose again. Pritchard wanted to market their Isotype houses at the exhibition of British Industrial Art in Relation to the Home at Dorland Hall in Regent Street. He pressed Coates to finalize his designs and cut the costs. Coates suggested that it would be more sensible to use the space Isokon had reserved at Dorland Hall to show a full-scale model of a Minimum Flat. Pritchard finally agreed, but he demanded that Coates should also produce two models of Isotype houses, which they could include in the exhibition. Not surprisingly, given his workload, Coates was unable to fulfil both demands.

On 11 April 1933 Coates signed a new contract, agreeing he would be paid a fee of £580 for the design of the Lawn Road Flats. He was given an advance of £50 and in less than ten days, drew up a detailed 1/8-scale sketch for a typical

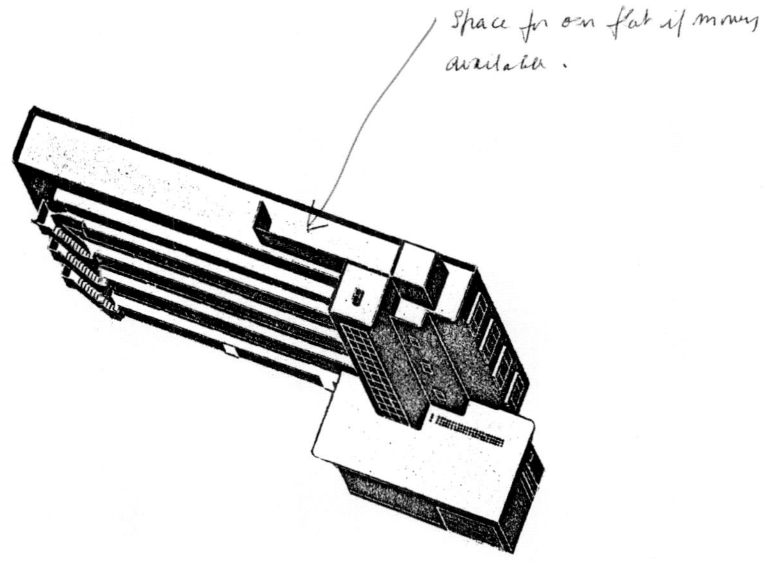

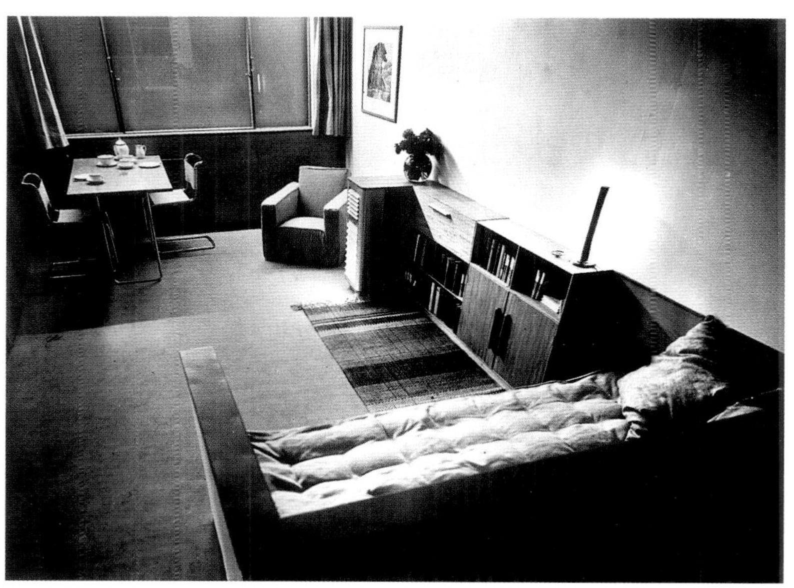

ABOVE, TOP: Isometric drawing of the Lawn Road Flats, 1933, by Wells Coates. The penthouse was added later. ABOVE: Minimum Flat, *British Industrial Art in Relation to the Home* exhibition, Dorland Hall, London, June 1933.

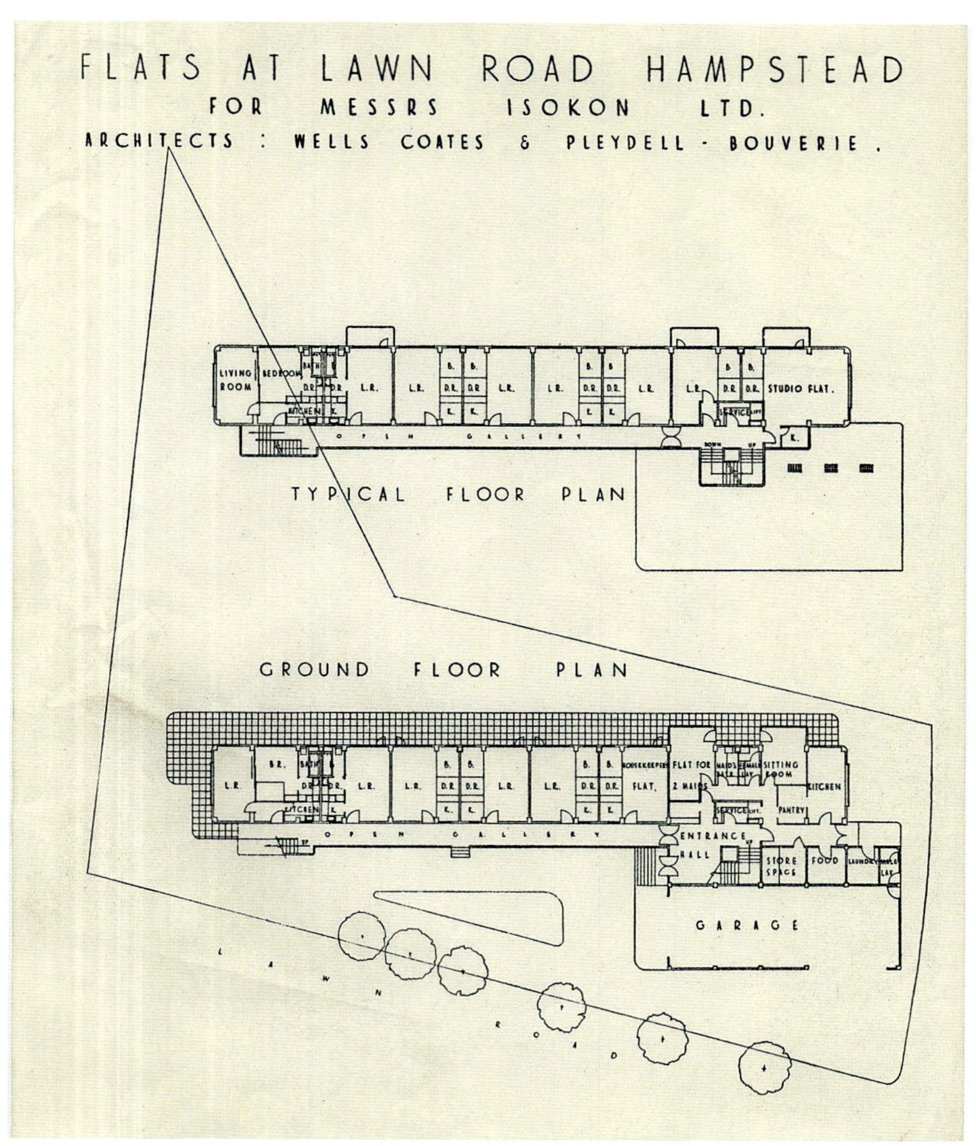

ABOVE: Floor plans for Flats at Lawn Road, Wells Coates, 1933.

floorplan. His prototype Minimum Flat was ready for exhibition at Dorland Hall in June 1933.

The fully furnished studio room measured 5.4 × 3.15m. It had a convertible bed-settee, a small sliding mahogany and tubular-steel dining table and cantilevered stacking chairs. Coates created a 'hearth scene' with an upholstered armchair and a built-in Isokon plywood unit comprising bookcase, radio, speakers and copper-fronted radiator. Sliding doors led to a bathroom and dressing room.[16] Fleetwood Pritchard created the accompanying advertising leaflet, which explained:

> *Isokon flats are designed to solve the problem of living comfortably and compactly. Everything that is unnecessary, inconvenient or 'labour-making' has been left out, but everything essential has been left in, and (more important) is in exactly the right position.*

Architectural Review, which devoted its entire July issue to the exhibition, declared Coates's design 'a brilliant feat of intelligent compression', adding that it was 'a welcome harbinger of a new way of life', for 'forward-regarding persons of culture with orderly minds and modest purses'. On the strength of the Dorland Hall exhibit, Pritchard managed to secure deposits for 12 flats.

Coates did not complete the Isotype house design for another year, when he sold the concept to building firm E & L Berg and they showed his two-storey Sunspan House at the *Daily Mail* Ideal Home Exhibition at Olympia.

Coates now produced his final detailed plans for the Lawn Road Flats. The proposal was a four-storey block, with access to the flats on each floor via external cantilevered galleries. There were to be three flat types within the building: 22 minimum flats; four larger double flats and three double studio flats, accessed via an internal staircase (a lift was too expensive). The flats had small kitchen windows at the front of the building ensuring privacy and large windows facing south-west at the rear, to catch the sun.

The Pritchards would have a large one-bedroom penthouse with a terrace (to be completed when they could afford it) and the unusual arrangement of a small separate apartment next door for their two young boys. A kitchen, staff quarters, laundry and garage for eight cars would be located on the ground floor. Coates placed the building at an acute angle to Lawn Road to accommodate two railway tunnels, which ran at right angles beneath the site.

It was the distillation of much that he had seen on his travels. The dominant visual motif – the horizontality of the cantilevered galleries – was offset by the emphatic vertical of the northern staircase tower (with its subtle evocation of

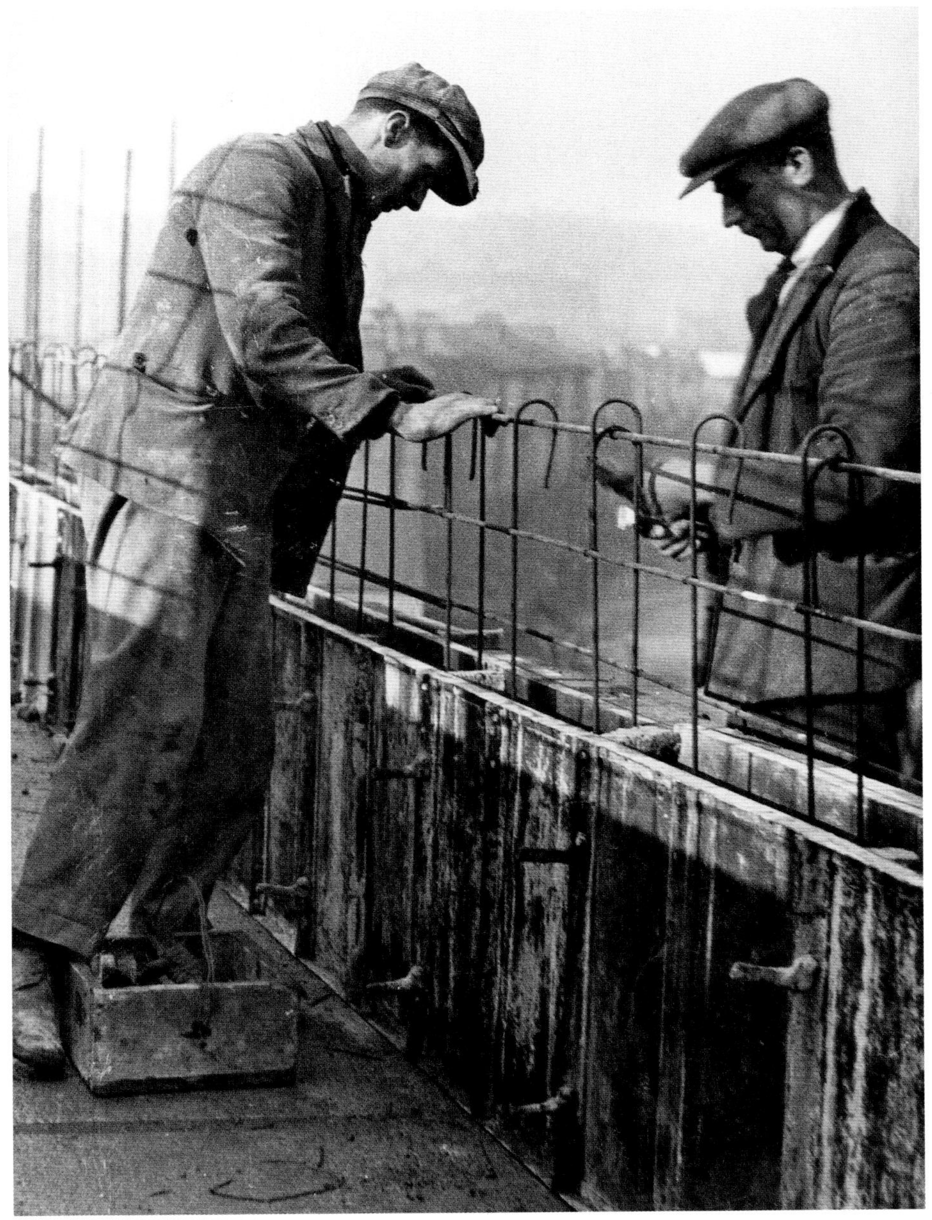

ABOVE: Construction workers position the steel rods used to reinforce the flats' exterior walls. The building firm of Barkers was entrusted with the experimental process, which was still in its infancy. The Lawn Road Flats was the earliest reinforced concrete apartment building in Britain.

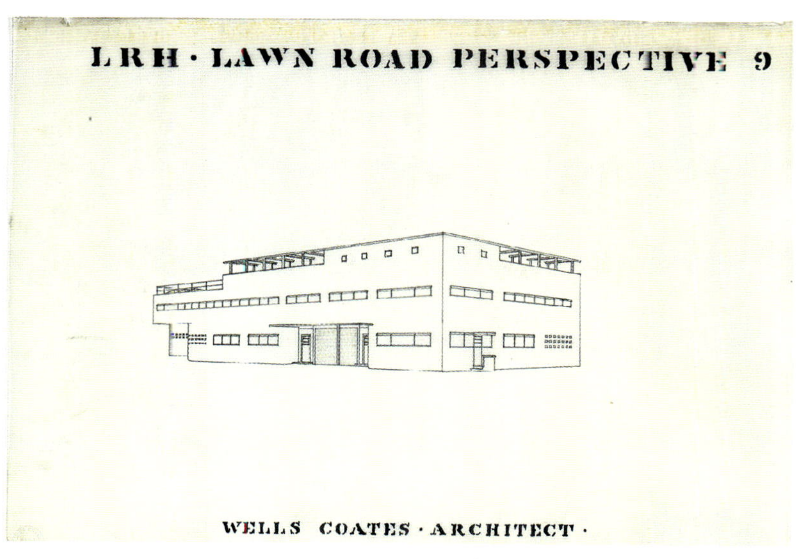

ABOVE: Early perspective sketch of the flats by Wells Coates. It replaced a plan for two houses for the Coates and Pritchard families and a nursery school for Beatrix Tudor-Hart.

Gropius's Konsum Building at Törten). The rear west facade was punctuated by cantilevered balconies with echoes of the students' wing at the Dessau Bauhaus. Inside the building, there were further nods to the housing experiments of Stuttgart and Frankfurt, in the severe ergonomic economy of the minimum flats' (1.4 × 1.52m) kitchens.[17]

To keep it as cheap and capable of reproduction as possible, the block was to be built from reinforced concrete. This was a bold decision. It was the first time the material had been used on this scale for a domestic building in Britain. In July 1933, Coates sent out his drawings for tender. The lowest offer of £13,587 came in from the East London building firm of Messrs George Barker whom he managed to beat down to £12,500. Building work would begin on 25 September 1933 and was due to be completed on 12th March 1934. It was arranged that Barkers would be paid £1,000 every fortnight.

Inexperienced in financial matters, the Pritchards found raising the funds far from straightforward. Between them they could put up just £5,000, so they took out a loan from a financier at a rate of 7.5% to cover the rest. Quickly it became apparent it was impossible for them to repay at such a high level of interest. Frank Pick, General Manager of London Transport and a member of the Design and Industries Association, told Pritchard: '… in the kindest way possible .. I was a silly young fool and that I must get rid of the lenders as soon as I could'.[18]

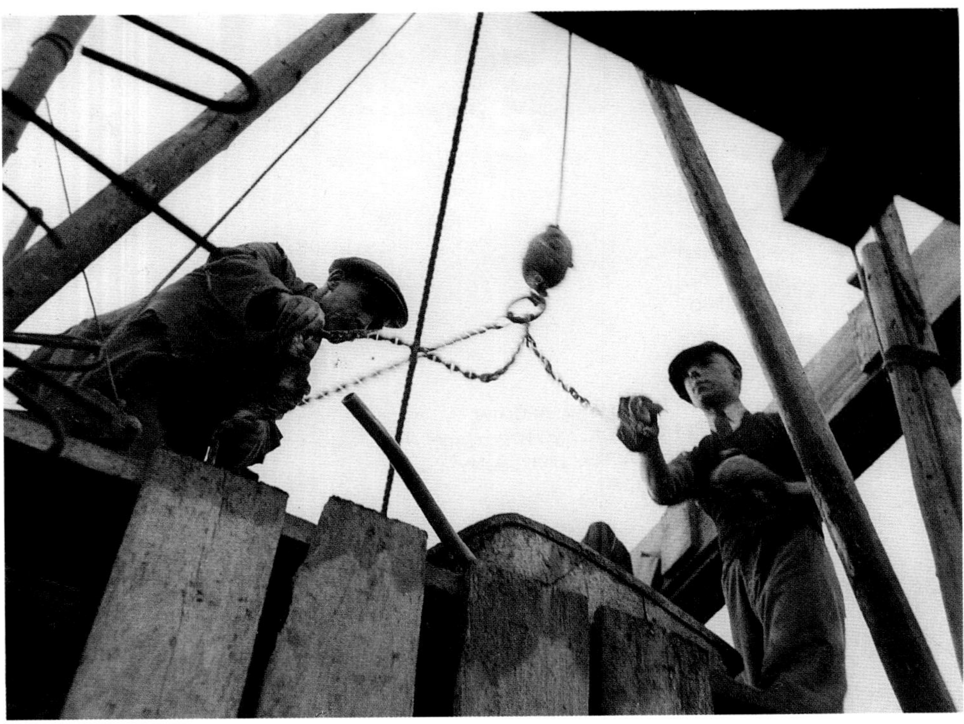

ABOVE: Workers on the flats' construction site, spring 1934.

By chance Pritchard met the manager of the District Bank in Waterloo Place, who, upon visiting the site and hearing about the Dorland Hall down-payments, agreed to loan them the money they needed at an ordinary, lower, bank lending rate. Work could proceed at last, but Pritchard's inexperience was to have further cost implications. His misunderstanding of London City Council's building regulations (he thought they had to give a formal seal of approval to the plans), meant that the start of work was delayed. Next, severe weather conditions hampered progress. The district surveyor did not allow concrete to be poured when the air temperature was below 39°F (3.8°C) and the unusually cold autumn and winter stole 37 days from their schedule. Construction finally began in 1934.

The pioneering nature of the concrete construction, which would give the building its smooth, sculptural appearance, meant Barker's workers needed to be closely supervised. The concrete walls, reinforced with steel rods, were 10cm (4in) thick and internally insulated with a 2.5cm (1in) layer of compressed cork, which had to be plastered over. The windows were steel-framed; internal walls between the flats were made from pumice blocks and the roof was covered with Indasco

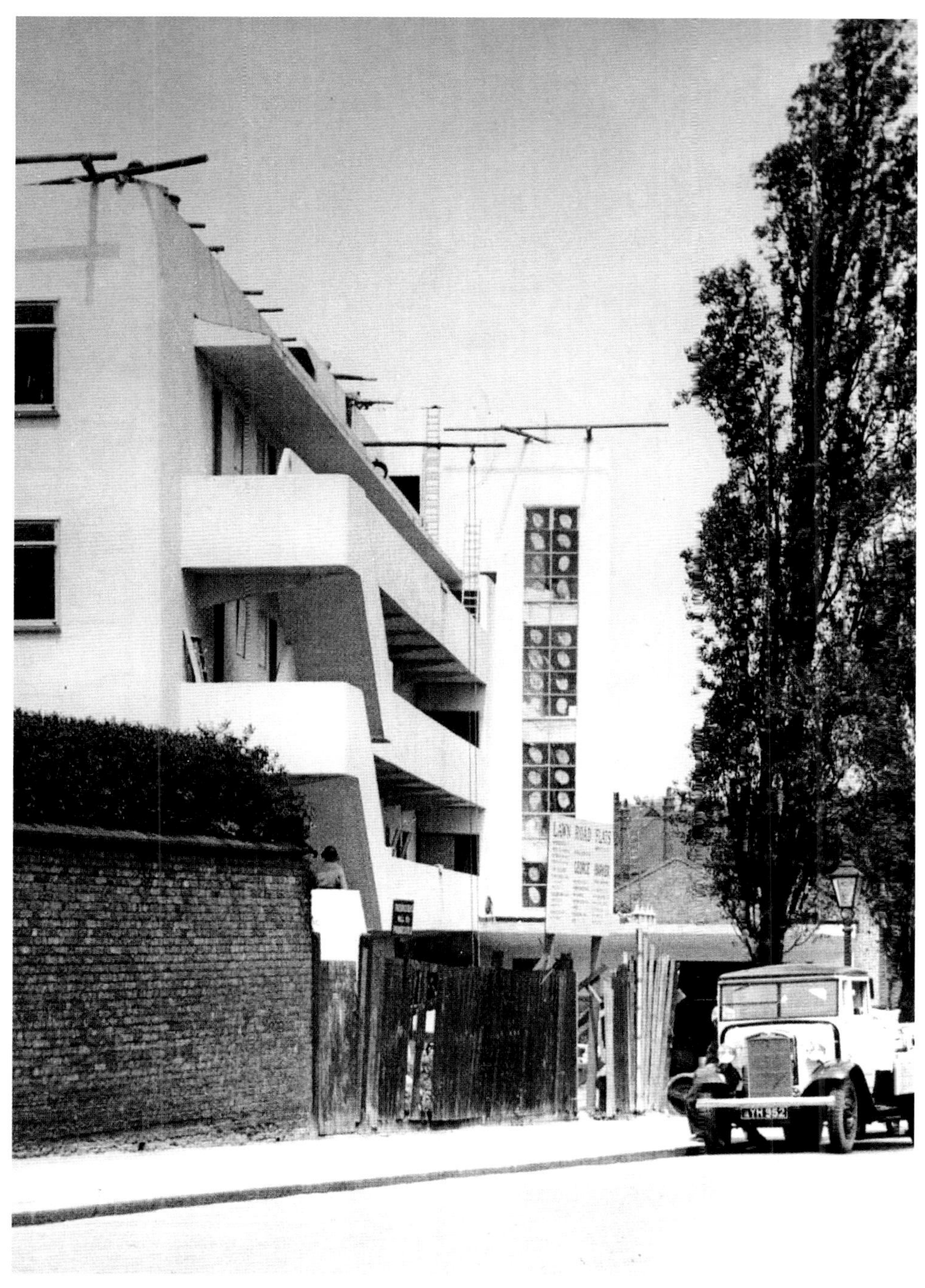

ABOVE: Construction nears completion with three cantilevered galleries completed, summer 1934.

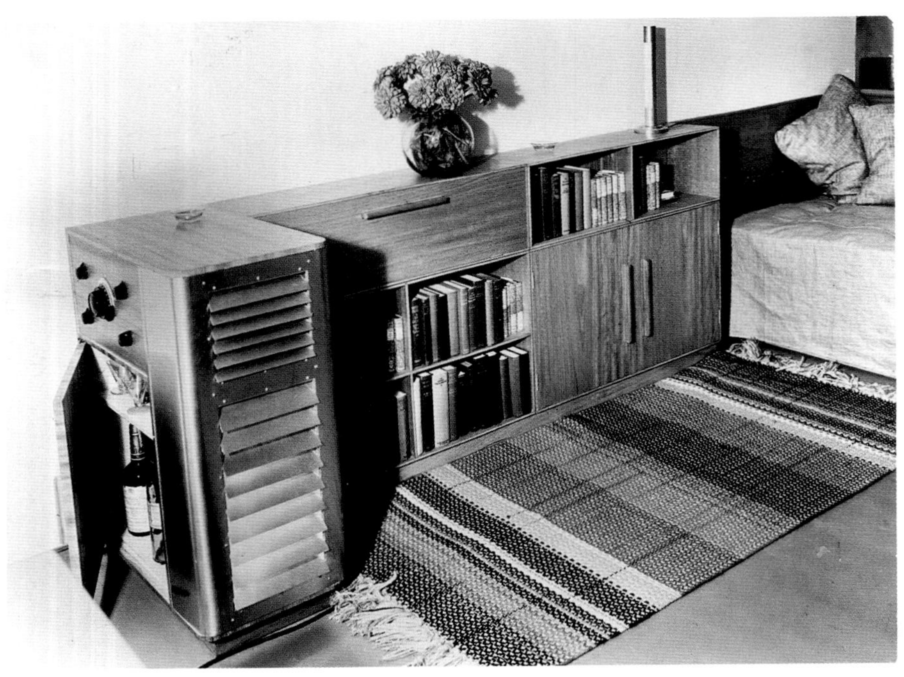

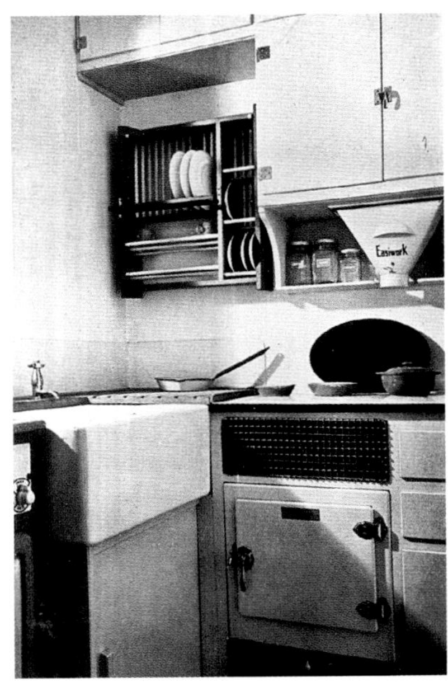

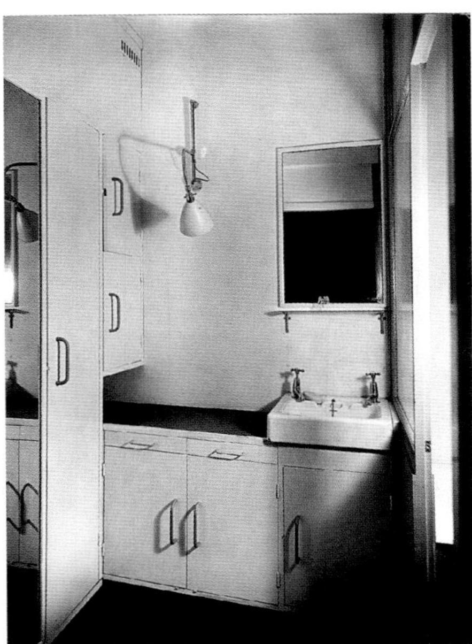

ABOVE, TOP: Wells Coates' Isokon hearth scene incorporating bookcases, radio and radiator, 1933.
ABOVE, LEFT: Each Minimum Flat had a compact kitchen with Belling oven and Electrolux refrigerator.
ABOVE, RIGHT: The lavatory and dressing room were accessed through sliding doors.

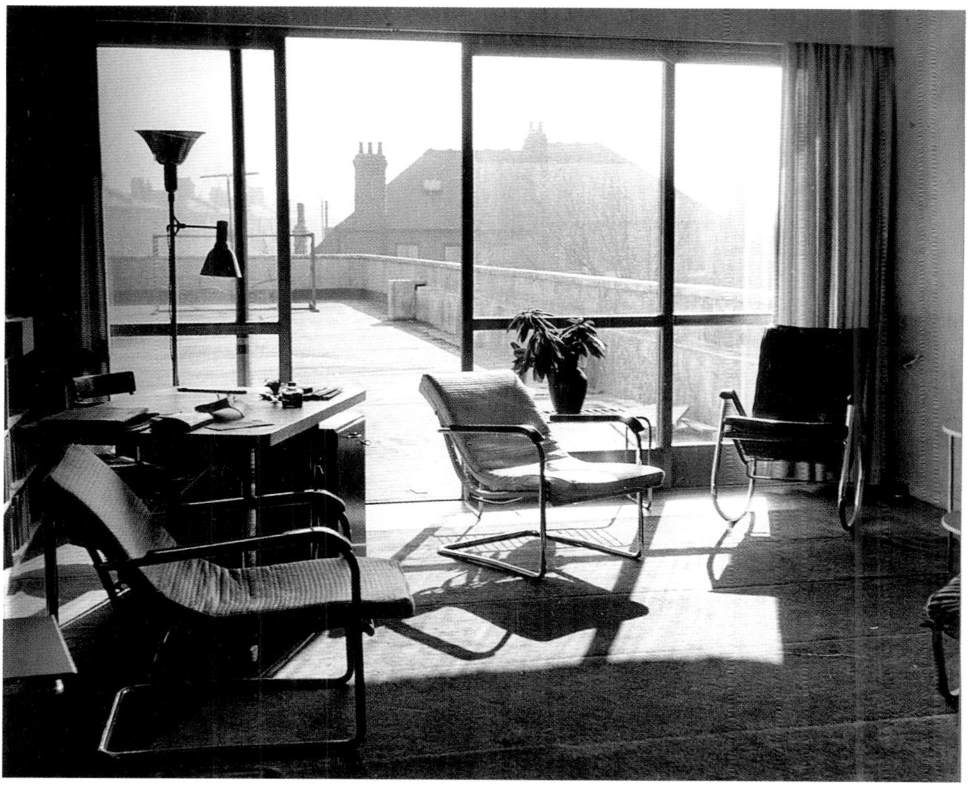

ABOVE: The Pritchards furnished the penthouse with tubular steel furniture purchased from the 'Wohnbedarf shop in Zurich. Sliding doors opened to a large roof terrace.

cold-process bitumen, the cheapest option Coates could find. Still working for Venesta (which had observed the Dorland Hall exhibition without comment), Pritchard sourced all the internal doors and materials for the built-in furniture from his employer.

The projected 'modern' lifestyle Molly had envisaged, dictated the flats' interior spec. Although just 5.4 x 4.67m, the minimum flats had an unusually high ceiling to create an illusion of spaciousness. A sliding table and single divan with mattress were included in the rent. Further living-room furniture, including the plywood unit bookcases, cupboards and electric fire unit with combined wireless and cocktail cabinet, could be bought from Isokon on a hire-purchase agreement. The bathroom, lavatory and dressing room were accessed through space-saving sliding doors. Each dressing room was fitted with a wall-mounted Bestlite, designed by Robert Dudley Best and produced by Birmingham manufacturer Best & Lloyd. The design was directly inspired by the German Rondella lamp from 1928 by

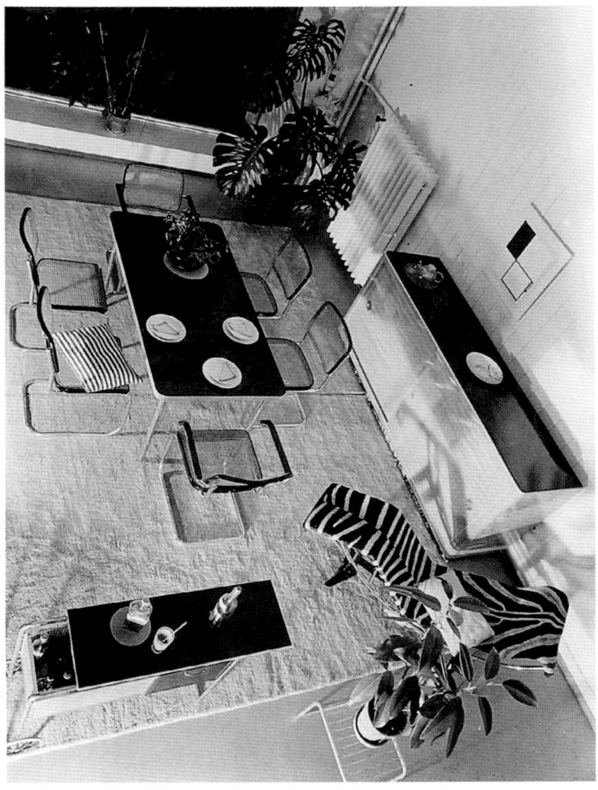

Christian Dell, foreman of the Bauhaus metal workshop at Weimar under László Moholy-Nagy. The double flats at the south end of the block, which came with a large bed and round table, offered more flexibility. A separate bedroom could be created by means of a sliding partition.

The tiny kitchens contained an electric Belling cooker, Electrolux refrigerator and built-in cupboards, with simple D-shaped handles designed by Coates. Residents were expected to do little cooking, but instead call down to the central kitchen and place their orders, which would be brought up via the service lift from a functional service kitchen and pantry on the ground floor. The rents would range from £96 to £170 per annum.[19]

Building was already underway when the couple finalized details of their own penthouse flat. Pritchard specified he would like a 2m (7ft) extension to their living room and plywood walls and floors throughout the apartment. As a result, Coates had to move the central service lift, so it could emerge inside the Pritchards' kitchen. The budget for the work was an additional £800, for which

Pritchard paid Coates a design fee of £5. He and Molly furnished the penthouse with the latest metal furniture by Marcel Breuer and Alvar Aalto, which they bought on a trip to Zurich from Sigfried Giedion's Wohnbedarf store.

Their growing haggling over costs, fees and schedule made it hard to imagine that the Coates and Pritchard families had once envisaged living in adjoining homes. In the four years since they had first employed him as their unknown and untested architect, Coates had transformed himself into one of the highest-profile proponents of Modernism in Britain. In early June 1934, with building work three months behind schedule, he wrote to Pritchard, enclosing an account with the following chilly ultimatum:

> *Would you please be good enough to settle the old items which go back nearly a year, otherwise they will have to be written off as debts … and our accountants will have to carry out the usual procedure for debt collection.*

A clamour was also rising from disappointed residents whose apartments were still not ready. Completion of the flats was therefore hastily rushed through, and the builders signed the job off on 26 June 1934. The work had come in over-budget, at £14,850 – nearly three times Molly's original estimate. On the same day, Jack and Molly took out a mortgage for £10,000 from the Manchester & County Bank. With so much invested in the venture, architect and clients were now desperate to generate as much publicity as they could, but as relations between them deteriorated (Coates' and Molly's affair was long over) they worked separately, rather than pooling their efforts. The Pritchards employed their own dedicated press agent Andrew Reid, and Philip Morton Shand and his wife, Sibyl, the Isokon secretary, helped with pitching stories. They agreed to give *Architectural Review* exclusive rights in the design press, with an article written by Molly outlining the concept behind the flats. Coates meanwhile was working simultaneously with many of the same publications. He wrote to Hubert de Cronin Hastings offering himself for interview, which, to the Pritchards' chagrin, led to Molly's article being dropped.

The Pritchards next planned a grand opening party to launch the flats. They drew up a guest list of influential press and asked local MP Thelma Cazalet to formally open the building. Monday 9 July 1934 was a brilliant summer's day and the flats, newly painted an almost imperceptible palest pink (a bespoke hue of white mixed with one part buff, as specified by Coates), must have been a dazzling sight as guests arrived in Lawn Road. They made their way up four floors to the roof terrace, for cocktails and canapés. There, outside the shell of the Pritchards'

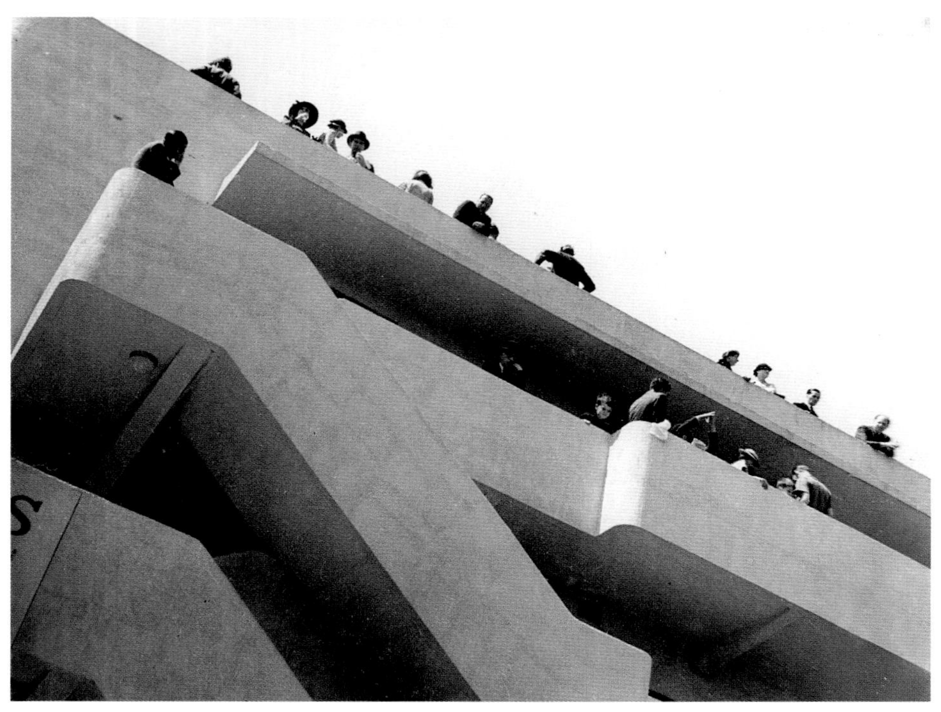

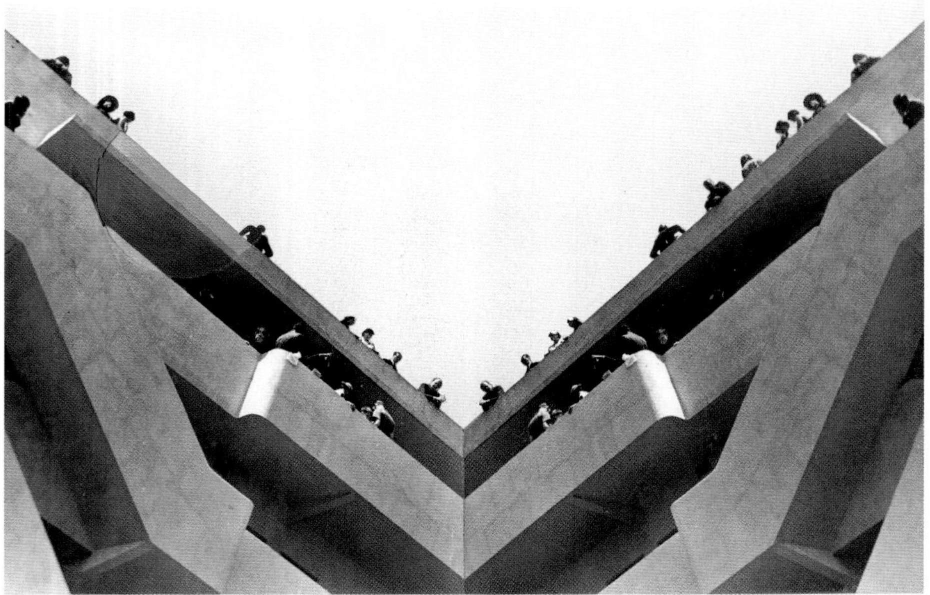

ABOVE: Edith Tudor-Hart photographed visitors on the roof terrace and galleries at the Grand Opening of the Lawn Road Flats, 9 July 1934.

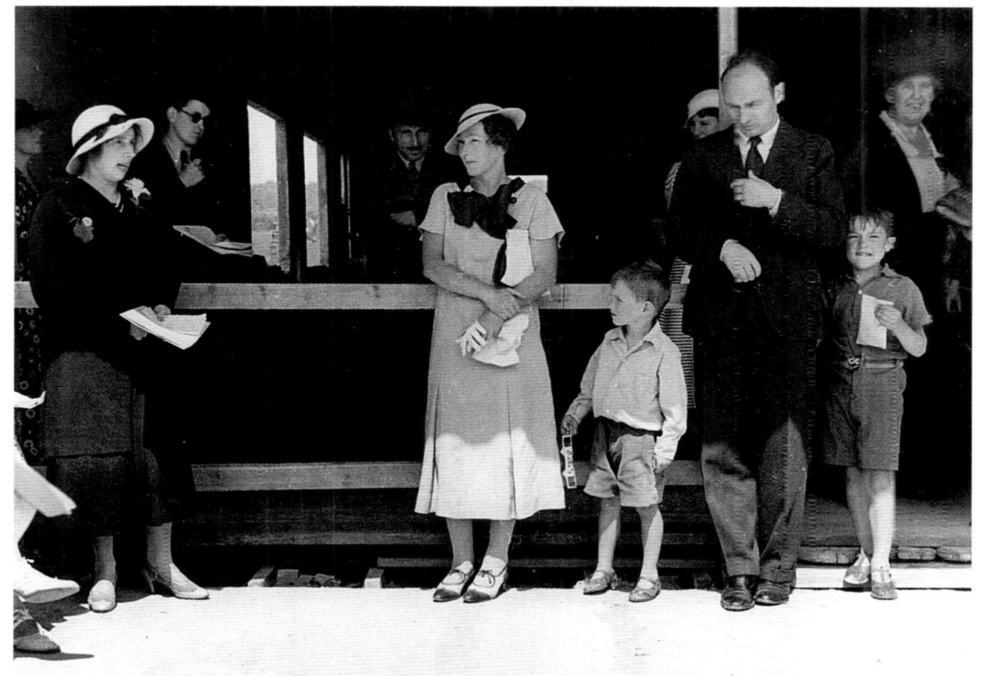

ABOVE: Opening day speeches: Thelma Cazalet MP, Molly and Jack Pritchard, Jeremy, Jonathan, and Mrs Lilian Pritchard, outside the still unfinished penthouse.

still unfinished penthouse, Molly took centre stage. Dressed in a pale skirt and blouse, a flamboyant bow at her neck and with a neatly trimmed white hat, she cut a cool, elegant figure. With Jack and her two young sons at her side, and their parents behind her, she delivered a speech to assembled friends, family and press. Watching from the crowd and no doubt seething with fury that she took credit for the concept and conspicuously failed to mention him by name was Wells Coates. Molly began:

> This building [...] is perhaps the most modern building in England. It
> is not only modern as an architectural piece – it expresses a revolutionary
> idea for living... Some of us felt that living in general, and living in cities
> in particular was far too complicated, expensive and dirty. To remedy this
> meant a revolution in approach to the problem. Not 'Here is a house or a
> flat, how shall we arrange ourselves and our possessions in it? How shall

*[...] We said to our Architect: 'Here is a site. We have so much money to
spend. We reckon it should provide so many flats. Each of these should be
designed for one or two persons and the following accommodation should be
provided:- bath space, dressing space, sleeping space, cooking space, dining
space and living space. Also there should be centrally provided: hot water,
heating, service and garage.' Whether the architect has solved this problem
to the best advantage I leave you to judge. Personally I can only say that the
planning of the flats seems to me perfectly adequate and perfectly simple, in
other words, perfect.*[20]

She announced that if the flats were a financial success, Isokon would open
similar blocks across the country, including more ambitious schemes for families,
which would include nursery schools.

Thelma Cazalet MP then added insult to the architect's injury by thanking
'Russell Coates' for creating a 'beautiful building'. She broke a bottle of beer over
the parapet and officially launched the flats.

The press coverage was extensive, positive and syndicated nationwide. Gerald
Barry (later director of the Festival of Britain) reported on the launch for *The
News Chronicle* and the significance of Coates's radical new building was not lost
on him:

*The experiment is the signpost to a new order – it represents in steel and
concrete the new attitude towards this business of living which is beginning
to emerge from our present-day chaos.*[21]

The *Observer* saw the Minimum Flat as heralding 'an interesting psychological
change. The modern mind does not seem to want the association of any personal
possessions; it wants to treat the place it lives in as something purely incidental to
its life, not dominating it.' The *Midland Daily Telegraph* compared life in the Flats to
that on board a luxury liner, but noted wryly that there was a lack of 'quarrelling
space, lounging space and muddle space'. Other publications hailed the building as

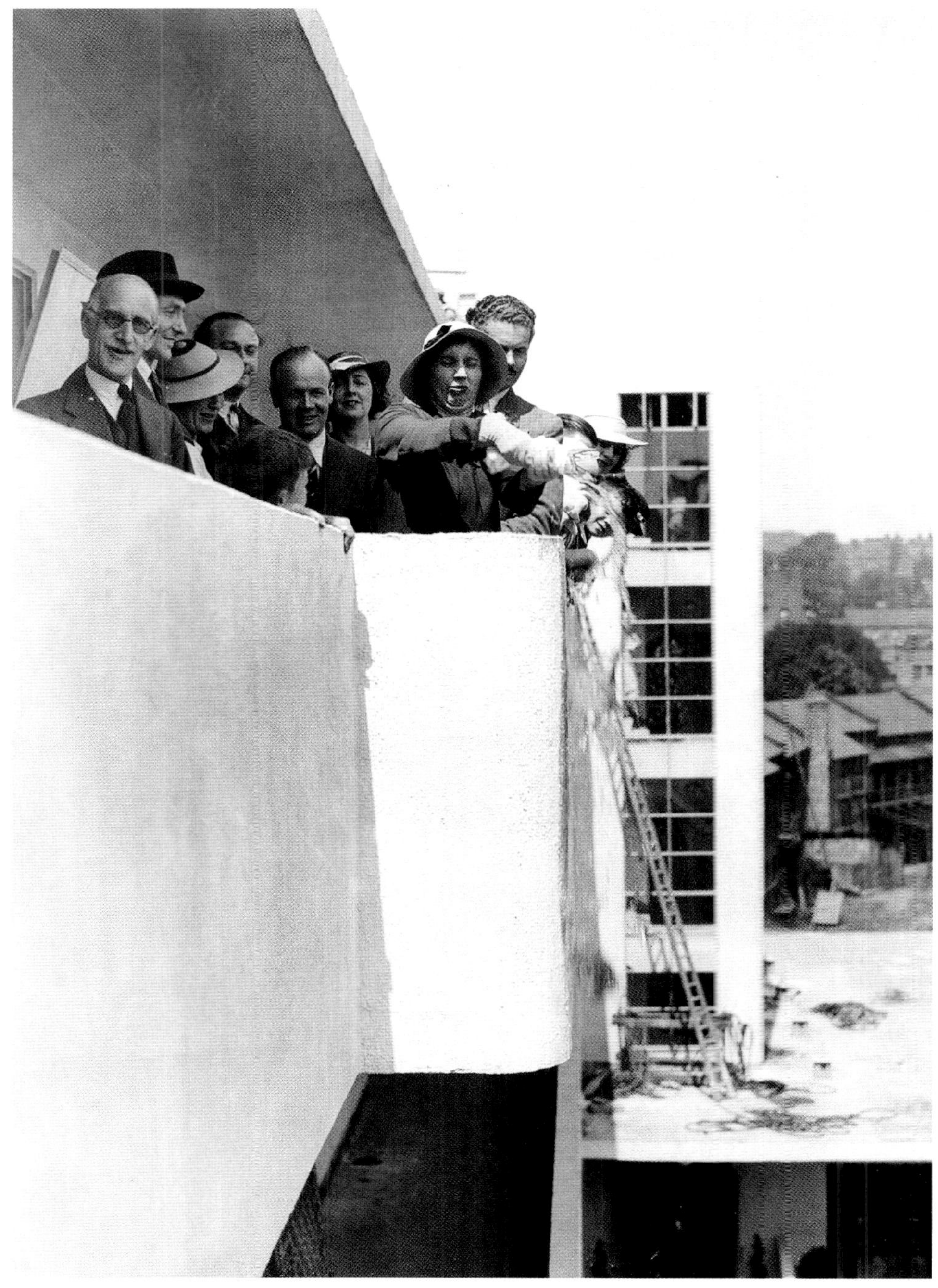

ABOVE: Thelma Cazalet MP breaks a bottle of beer to launch the flats. Wells Coates, whom she misnamed 'Russell' Coates in her speech. stands behind, surrounded by the Pritchard family.

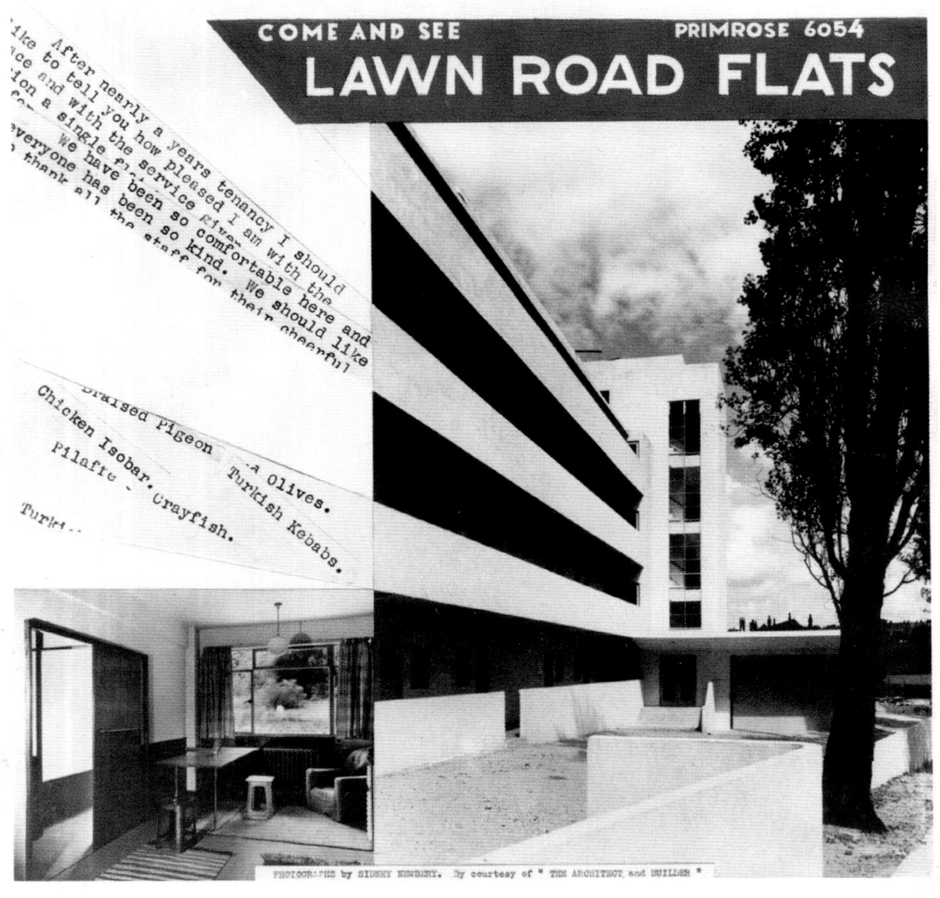

ABOVE: Advertisement from *Architect and Building News* with photography by Sydney Newbury c. 1937. The ad promotes Philip Harben's exotic cooking for the Isobar, including Turkish kebabs and olives, rarely seen in the British 1930s kitchen. Letting the flats was initially difficult, as tenants were required to sign up for long periods. The highest quoted rent of £170 a year represents the 2019 equivalent of £220 per week, calculated to be affordable for a single professional.

a feminist breakthrough, providing 'luxury flats for the bachelor girl' who would be freed from housework *(The Northern Despatch);* 'More Comfort – Less Work' *(Evening Standard)*; while the *Daily Mirror* headlined its story: 'Woman's Idea'.

With the building opened at last, the Pritchards headed straight to Cornwall for a short break. But after reading a copy of the *New Statesman*, which had also covered the launch, Pritchard could not resist firing off an indignant letter to its editor.

> *Dear Sir,*
>
> *In calling your attention to an error in your notice on the Lawn Road Flats last week, may I say how much those who are interested in the venture appreciate your remarks. The writer was in no way connected with the designing of the building which is the work of Mr Coates. The scheme, however, was inspired and instigated by my wife, Dr Rosemary Pritchard.*[22]

Maddox Properties, a firm of developers, approached Coates and offered him the prestigious commission of Embassy Court, a large seafront apartment block in Brighton. It was a chance to apply many of the lessons he had learned at Lawn Road. But the slight to his ego still rankled and he could not let it lie. In January 1935 he wrote to Jack and Molly:

> *It is certainly my view and the long one – that in the end you may realise what I have done for you both. In spite of your statement to the press and to private individuals, you know perfectly well that you have not 'inspired' the Lawn Road Flats, but that the whole idea of the small flats on that site was mine. I don't give a damn, and in the long run it is no harm at all, but that is my view.*[23]

Molly, who wisely did not show his letter to Jack, had the last word. She replied firmly, but with characteristic emollience:

> *You accuse me of putting over the flat idea as mine – well so it was – I felt you have been unkind when I have heard you put it over as yours – therefore the truth must be that, as a result of a germ dropped from you and another from me, the idea came to us both independently.*[24]

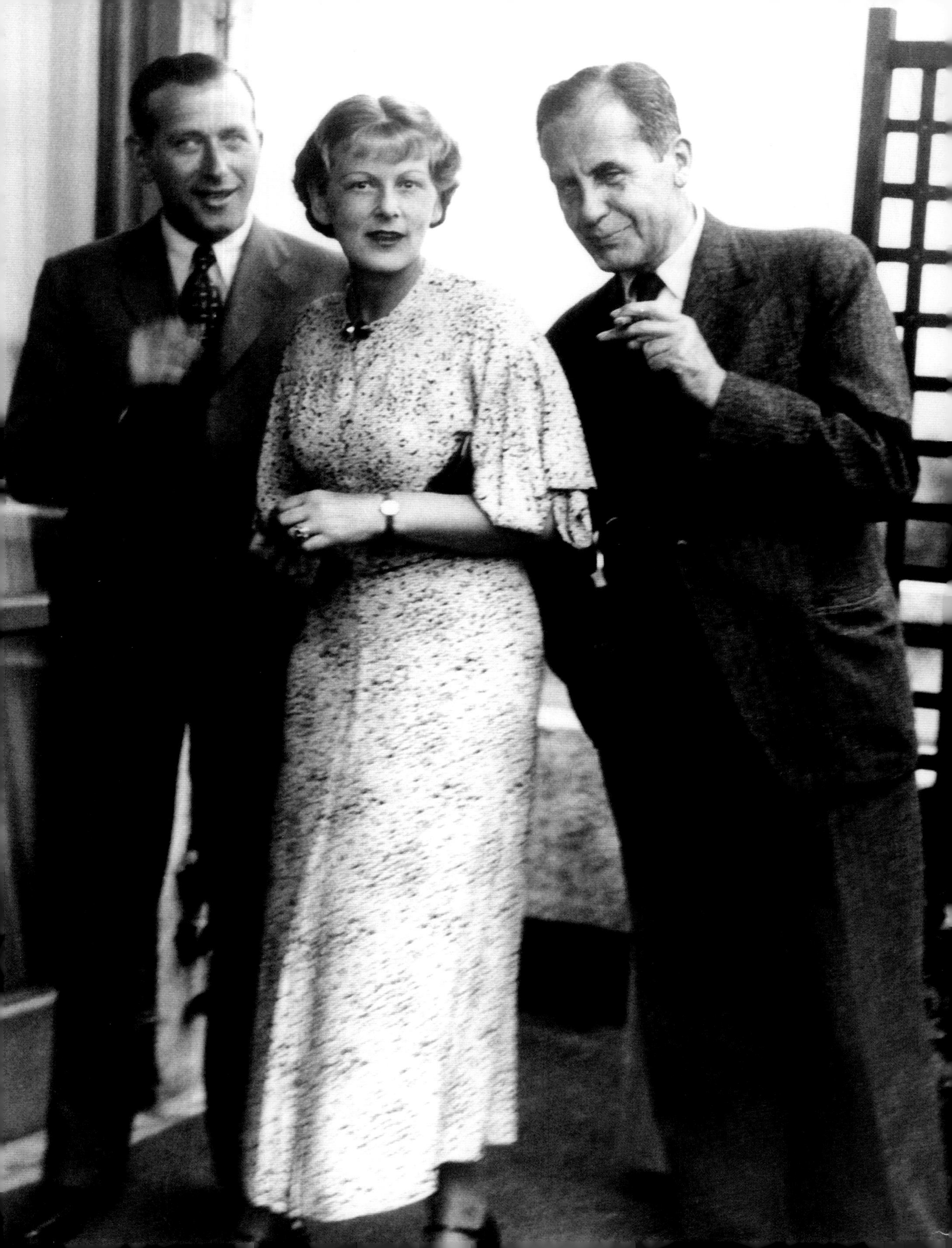

CHAPTER 5

THE ARRIVAL OF THE BAUHAUSLERS

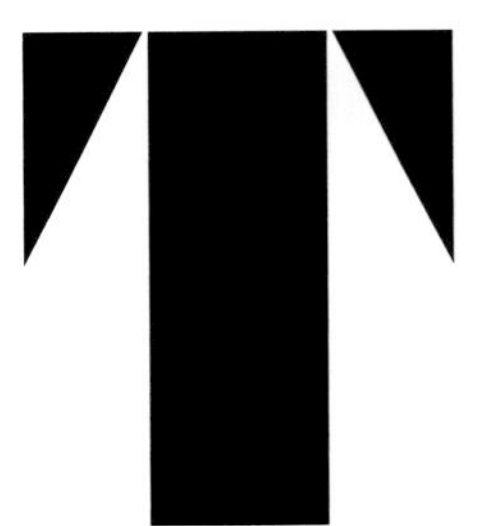 HE UTOPIAN VISION OF A NEW 'MODERN' WAY OF living offered by Lawn Road Flats appealed to a wide cross-section of what we would now refer to as the 'chattering classes'. The Pritchards' extensive social and professional circle encompassed the worlds of science, art, economics, politics, advertising and journalism and these were the spheres from which the flats' first residents were drawn. Many of the couple's oldest friends had been supporters of the Lawn Road project, and the first to spend a night in the flats were Jack's Economics professor from Cambridge, Philip Sargant Florence, and his American journalist wife, Lella, who slept in Flat 6, one of the double apartments at the south end of the building.

In the weeks following the opening and no doubt helped by the extensive press coverage, more flats were let. Art critic and painter Adrian Stokes (Flat 23), novelist Nicholas Monsarrat (Flat 29), Austrian ethnomusicologist Professor Erich von Hornbostel (Flat 6), German illustrator R.A. Brandt, brother of photographer Bill Brandt (Flat 26) and, briefly, the German Modernist architect Arthur Korn (Flat 24) became the first pioneers in Isokon's experiment in social living. But the haste with which the builders, Barkers, had been urged to complete the construction was soon evident. The tenant of Flat 21, Hon. Ralph Edward Gathorne-Hardy, on whom Evelyn Waugh is said to have based his character Miles Malpractice in *Vile Bodies*, wrote a waspish letter of complaint to Pritchard, comparing the living conditions unfavourably to a 'Mornington Crescent lodging house'.

> *Dear Sir,*
>
> *I wish to protest most strongly about some of the deficiencies in my flat…*
> *Twice a week since I have been in my flat the bath water has not been hot…*
> *The lock on my door is in such condition that it is now almost impossible*
> *to get in or out of my flat without using a great deal of physical force, the*
> *carpenters [sic] work is very bad indeed … the paintwork is of the shoddiest*
> *character imaginable… I should like you to look at the crevasses in my*
> *walls. The real trouble is, that although the design of the flat is admirable,*
> *I cannot help feeling that there has been a good deal of cheese-pairing [sic]*
> *in the joinery and decoration and arrangements.[1]*

Over the next few months there were further problems with the flat roof, water penetration and drainage. The boiler room flooded, flooring came up and distemper finishes inside the flats began to disintegrate. Wells Coates, Barkers and

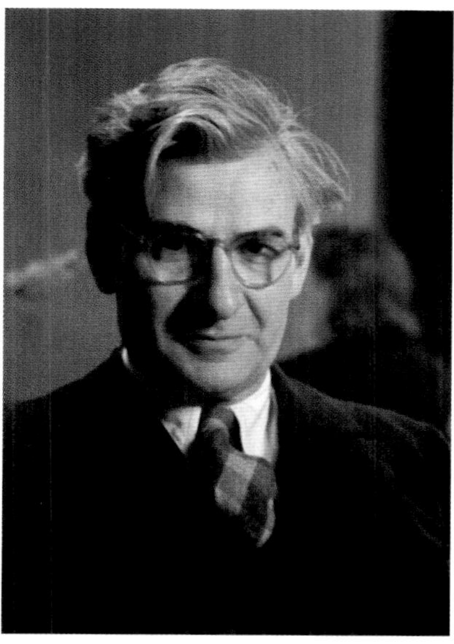

the surveyor were summoned to Lawn Road to carry out a full inspection, to resolve any issues within the building's warranty period.

While the Pritchards were endeavouring to fill the remaining flats, in Germany Walter Gropius was keeping an anxious eye on their progress. It would not be an exaggeration to state that his future and possibly even his life depended on the ability of the young English couple to make a success of the Lawn Road project. Over the last year, his situation in Berlin had become increasingly precarious. In 1933 he, Erich Mendelsohn and Mies van der Rohe had been invited to represent Germany in the Fifth Triennale Exhibition of Modern Decorative and Industrial Arts in Milan. Shortly before its opening, the Triennale's board was asked to eliminate two of the three German architects, on the grounds that their exhibits were 'undesirable from a German point of view'. Although the Italians refused to cooperate with this, the Militant Organization for German Culture proceeded to remove Gropius's lantern slides from the Deutscher Werkbund collection. When he questioned why they had done this, he was informed his work was 'too international'.[2]

In December 1933, he was summoned by Dessau police to answer charges of disloyalty and embezzlement. He was accused of having Communist sympathies and exploiting Bauhaus products for personal gain. Next, he discovered he had been listed under 'Culture Bolshevism' in an encyclopaedic, anti-Semitic publication entitled '*Sigilla Veri*'. This suggested he might be of Jewish origin and falsely attributed a large number of quotations to him, all of which he vehemently denied. In February 1934 he wrote to Carl Christoph Lörcher, leader of the Werkbund, passionately insisting he was of 'pure Aryan, German origin'.[3] He also argued that the new architecture should be valued as 'German intellectual property' and that because its originators were being ostracized, his country was now witnessing the humiliating spectacle of other nations such as Italy and France claiming the Modern movement as their own. In March 1934, he wrote to Professor Eugen Hönig, President of the Reich Chamber for the Creative Arts, who had called for 'packing case architecture' to be rejected by the New Reich. Gropius pleaded:

> *I am convinced in my innermost being that the victory of this new art of architecture, which was merely distorted by means of a travesty, will progress irresistibly throughout the world, because today there exists no other architectural movement of equal power, intellectual penetration and truthfulness.*[4]

In England, Philip Morton Shand was also promoting the new German architecture. He wrote to Gropius, inviting him to stage an exhibition of his work at the Royal Institute of British Architects (RIBA) in London. Morton Shand claimed the event, which was supported by RIBA secretary Ian MacAlister, would provide 'a kind of revolution for the architecture in England'.[5] He also arranged for Gropius to deliver a speech to the Design and Industries Association (DIA) on 'The Formal and Technical Problems of Modern Architecture and Planning', which he translated into English for him. These two events in May 1934 drew large numbers, including Jack Pritchard, Wells Coates and Serge Chermayeff. During his visit to London, Gropius stayed with architect Maxwell Fry, who recalled the impact his landmark speech made on the British Modernists:

> *Listening to this man speaking awkwardly in a language he had yet to adopt we realised that the task he set us would last our life-time, that we were concerned now not with architecture alone, but with society, and that he had filled us with a fervour as moral as it was aesthetic. When the applause ended the meeting broke up in a state of wild excitement and Gropius was shaking with emotion as he turned to thank me.*[6]

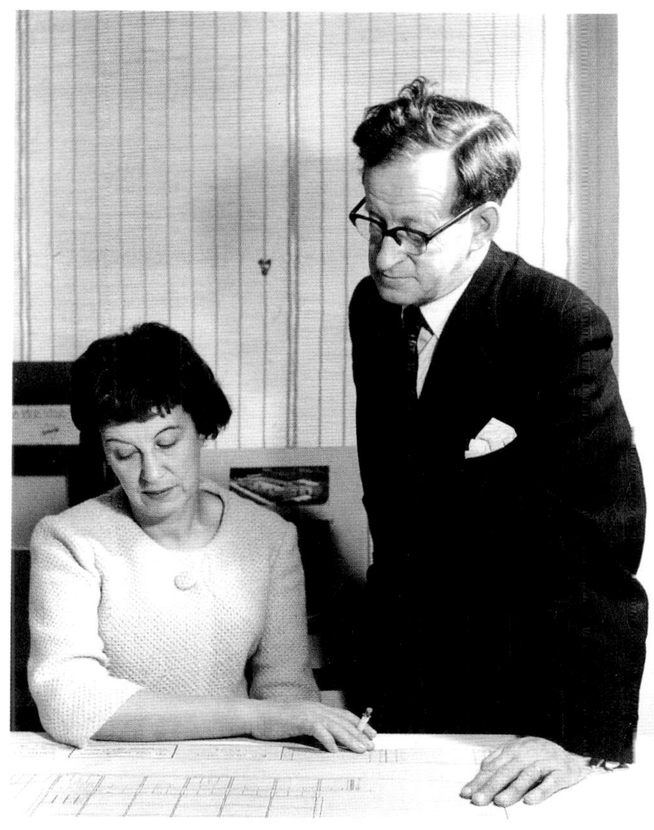

ABOVE: Architect Maxwell Fry with his wife, and later architectural partner, Jane Drew.

On his return to Berlin, Gropius continued to correspond with Morton Shand. He confided that he was in serious financial straits and was desperate for work. The strength of support he had received from the English architectural community on his trip had caused him to consider a move to London. He also revealed that his daughter Manon, who lived with her mother in Vienna, was seriously ill.

Morton Shand informed Pritchard and Fry that Gropius urgently needed to find employment in England. It was just weeks away from the opening of the Lawn Road Flats and Jack and Molly were already exploring the possibility of building a second Isokon block in Manchester. They had been offered a 3-acre site overlooking a river in the suburb of Didsbury by A.P. Simon, a member of the DIA, in return for shares in any development. Raising the capital, however, depended entirely on the Pritchards' ability to fill Lawn Road with tenants. Following the breakdown in their relationship with Coates, they were casting around for another architect and Pritchard agreed the job could be offered as a joint project to Walter Gropius and Maxwell Fry. Gropius would join the partnership of Adams, Thompson and Fry, solving the problem for Isokon of employing a foreign architect and giving Gropius a legitimate reason to leave Germany swiftly.

Pritchard wrote to Gropius explaining it was a small project, with a total budget of £14,000–15,000 and offered him a free apartment in the Lawn Road Flats during his stay in England.[7] Fry sent him further details of the site and explained their joint fee would be £450.

> *The site is at the end of a cul-de-sac development built around 1800. 3 acres. At the bottom of the garden is the river Mersey. House stands on land rising. The site has fine trees and lovely flowers and an extensive view to the south. JCP thinks we should build bigger flats than at LRF with a preponderance of 2 and 3 room flats and some even larger with a few 1-room bachelor flats on top. A.P. Simon is the chairman of the DIA in Manchester, a charming man doing much work for town planning design and common sense.[8]*

Momentum gathered to facilitate Gropius's move. Pritchard and Fry wrote to the Ministry of Labour explaining that Gropius possessed unique technical knowledge and had a world-class reputation.[9] Morton Shand advised Gropius that it would be advantageous to have his work published in Britain. He found him a journalistic commission and banked the small payment in London, so he would have some funds when he arrived. Art critic Herbert Read suggested publishing a book about his work through Faber & Faber, which would include the text of his influential talk at RIBA.

While his English supporters were endeavouring to bring him to Britain, A. Lawrence Kocher, the editor of the American journal *Architectural Record,* was simultaneously trying to lure him to the US. Kocher was keen to establish a Bauhaus-style art school with links to industry outside New York. He urged Gropius to bring an exhibition to America and also raised the possibility of a post for him at Columbia University. Gropius replied that he would consider his suggestion, but for the time being was set on England.

He had been invited to participate in an annual theatre conference taking place in Rome between 8–14 October. Mindful of possible reprisals and the risk of his possessions being seized were he to leave Germany without permission, he wrote to Professor Hönig asking for authorization to attend and travel on to London afterwards to work temporarily on 'a small housing construction'. He emphasized

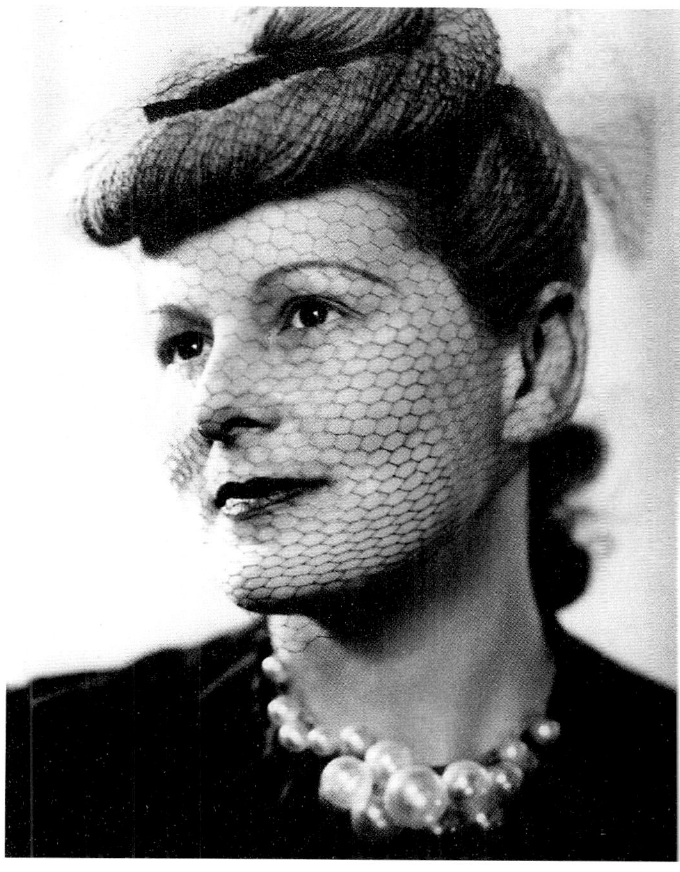

ABOVE: Ise Gropius, whom Jack Pritchard described as 'exceptionally beautiful and equally intelligent – a marvellous combination'.

it would be a short stay and that he was maintaining his permanent office in Berlin. Permission was granted and he and Ise left for Rome on 3 October.

In Lawn Road preparations for his arrival were under way. Jack, unaware that the great German architect was remarried and bringing his wife, had assigned him a single Minimum Flat. Isokon secretary Sibyl Morton Shand ordered curtains from Heal's, towels and bedlinen from Selfridges, and arranged for a private telephone to be installed in his flat.

On 18 October, Pritchard and Fry were waiting on the platform at Victoria station when Walter and Ise Gropius stepped off the train. Although taken aback by her presence, Pritchard was delighted to discover that Ise spoke fluent English. After exchanging pleasantries about the journey, he dashed off to ring Molly to swap the single flat they'd so carefully prepared, for a double, Flat 15. Conscious of the prestige of hosting an architect of Gropius's stature in their new block, the Pritchards did all they could to make Walter and Ise feel at home. During their first weekend in England, the Pritchards drove them to Stonehenge. Jack recalled:

> *As we drove west we passed large hoardings on the roadside. One read,*
> *'You are now entering the strong country.' I noticed that Ise whispered*
> *to Walter. A little further on there was another, which read simply,*
> *'Take Courage'. Walter asked me what was wrong with England that*
> *it needed all this propaganda. I stopped at a small pub and ordered*
> *Courage's bitter beer. They were much relieved.*

Within weeks Gropius had enrolled in English lessons and Pritchard introduced him to his great friend Henry Morris, Chief Education Officer of Cambridgeshire. He was delighted that, despite Gropius's very basic command of the language, 'it was remarkable how quickly they understood each other'.[10] A return visit was organized to Morris's rooms in Cambridge, which were filled with 18th-century furniture and hung with Impressionist pictures. Gropius wrote to his daughter:

> *I have found this visit really interesting; there is no doubt that this is a*
> *centre of culture with very old humus which could not easily be replaced.*
> *Now I understand the conservative attitude of the Englishman, which*
> *makes it difficult to recognize anything new.*[11]

The meeting with Morris would eventually lead to Gropius's most important architectural commission in Britain, Impington Village College (see Chapter 7). His primary aim in coming to England had been to establish a successful architectural practice but he quickly found himself in demand as an authority on educational matters. The Council for Art and Industry asked for his views on art teaching in English schools and he was invited to Edinburgh College of Art to speak on 'The Growth of the Modern Architectural Movement'. In December 1934, he was invited to Dartington Hall, near Totnes in Devon, by Leonard and Dorothy Elmhirst, who had visited and been inspired by the Weimar Bauhaus. On their large rural estate, the couple had built a progressive primary and secondary school and ran educational programmes for adults, teaching a range of subjects including arts, music, dance and drama. A showroom in London's Regent Street sold the school's products. Gropius described the set-up in a letter to German architect, Martin Wagner as 'a kind of English Bauhaus'.[12]

The Elmhirsts asked Gropius to advise on two ongoing architectural projects at Dartington: the conversion of a 14th-century barn into a 200-seater theatre and the construction of two cottages on the estate. Other proposed collaborations, including a paid role for Gropius advising on developing Dartington's products and links with industry, never came to fruition. Realizing the impecunious state in which Walter and Ise Gropius found themselves, the Elmhirsts sent them some money in the guise of a Christmas gift. Gropius thanked them effusively:

> *Your Christmas letter was like a fairy tale and gave us great surprise and delight. I wish I could find the right words in English … but apart from the material point of view it means so much to me to find in this country people who are really interested in the work I am doing.[13]*

Despite the warmth of his welcome in Britain, Gropius was depressed by the change in his circumstances and the cold and foggy weather. He asked for an electric heater to be installed in Flat 15 and wrote to Martin Wagner of his astonishment at the English love of open fires, which pumped smoke into the atmosphere:

> *Why are the English not doing anything against this continuing misery? I think the reason is puritan self-punishment. By the way, it is similar with the food … which is prepared in such a way one never gets pleasure out of it.*

The Nazis had strengthened their grip on Germany and it was becoming clear that the couple would have to stay in London longer than the six months they originally intended. Although desperately short of money they ordered some items for their flat – a bespoke plywood desk, a bedcover, and as they prepared for their first Christmas in the Lawn Road Flats, a dozen of the graphic, red Isokon Christmas cards, which Pritchard had commissioned from Bauhaus-trained photographer, Edith Tudor-Hart, who was married to Beatrix's brother Alex.

Gropius now made efforts to bring two of his closest Bauhaus allies to London. Marcel Breuer and László Moholy-Nagy had both resigned from the Bauhaus within days of Gropius's departure in January 1928. They had experienced difficulties relaunching private practices in a Germany increasingly under the thumb of the National Socialist party. Moholy-Nagy had first moved to Berlin and set up a studio where he explored the idea of building with light, through the

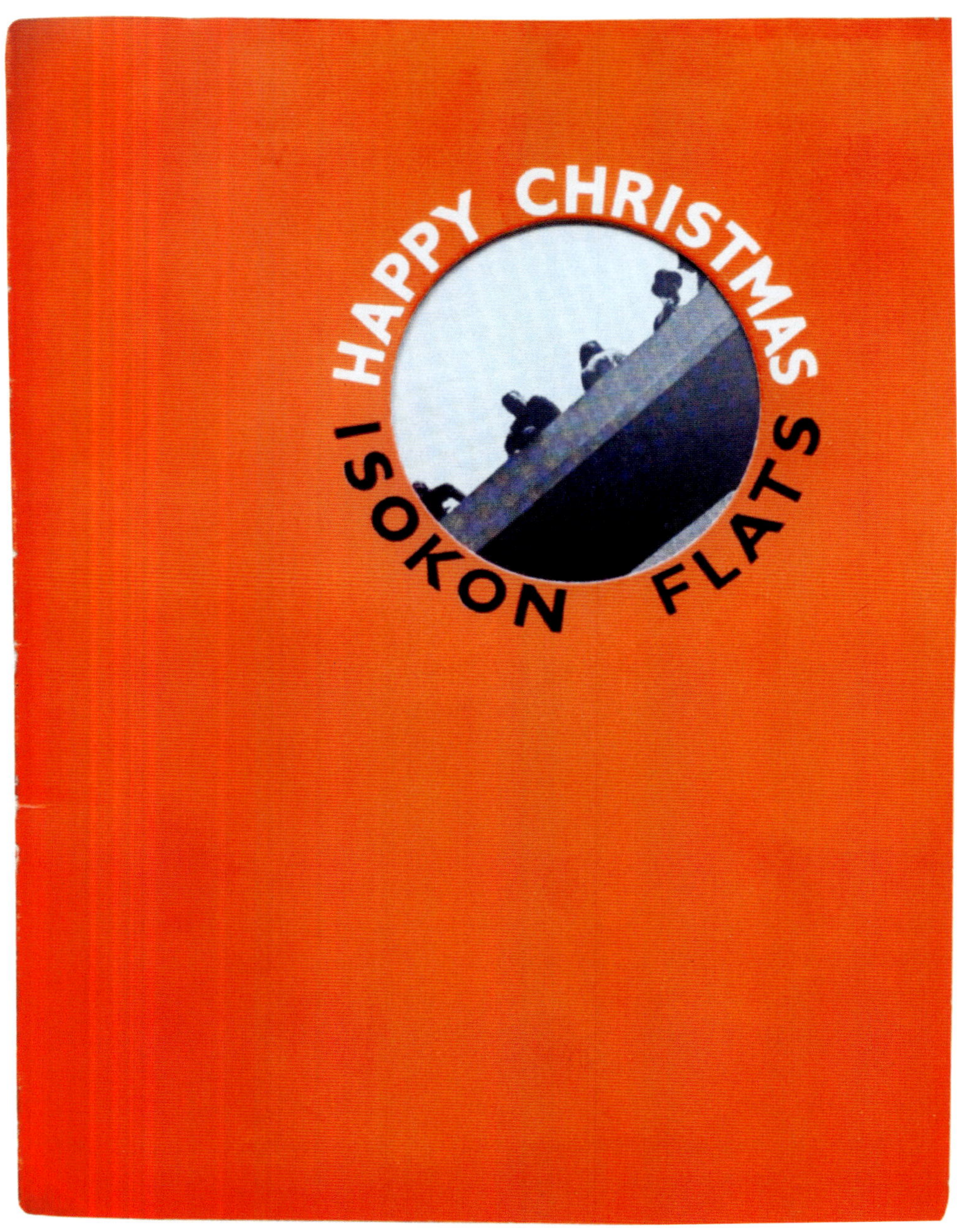

ABOVE: Edith Tudor-Hart designed the Lawn Road Flats distinctive Christmas card, 1934.

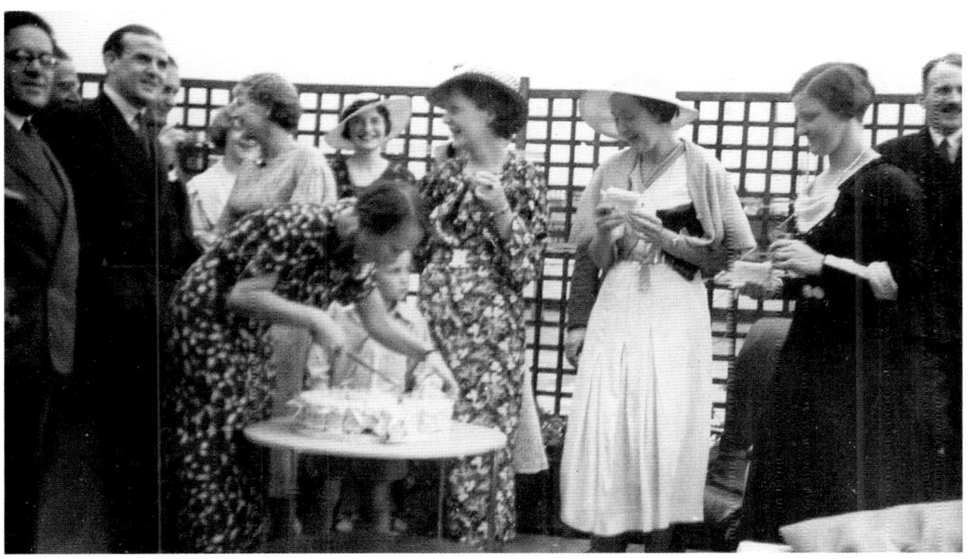

ABOVE: The Lawn Road Flats' first birthday party, July 1935. Sibyl Moholy-Nagy stands to the right of Molly Pritchard, who cuts the cake. Walter and Ise Gropius are to her left.

media of painting, photography and film. He worked as a designer for the Kroll Opera House, but his uncompromisingly modern staging of *Madame Butterfly*, led to accusations of cultural Bolshevism and he was shadowed by the SS. He met actress and scriptwriter Sybille Pietsche, they married in 1932 and their daughter Hattula was born the following year.

In 1933 Moholy-Nagy travelled with Sigfried Giedion to the first CIAM, where he met Philip Morton Shand, who urged him to visit London. He moved to Amsterdam, where he took up the post of creative director of the publication *International Textiles,* which gave him the chance to experiment with colour film and photography. In August 1934 he travelled to London and visited his first wife, former Bauhaus student and photographic artist Lucia Moholy (from whom he had divorced in 1929), and together they studied the colour-copy process at Kodak. Attracted by the British tradition of free thought and tolerance and encouraged by Gropius and an old friend, J.G. Crowther, science correspondent of *The Manchester Guardian,* he finally decided to move. He, Sibyl (her name now anglicized) and baby Hattula arrived in London on 20 May 1935, where Flat 16 was awaiting them in Lawn Road. His 'magnificent, infectious grin' endeared him to Jack Pritchard from their first meeting.[14]

It took longer for Gropius to persuade Marcel Breuer to join him. Despite the commercial success of the tubular-steel furniture he designed at the Bauhaus, Breuer's ambitions lay with architecture. Moving to Berlin in 1928, he set up his

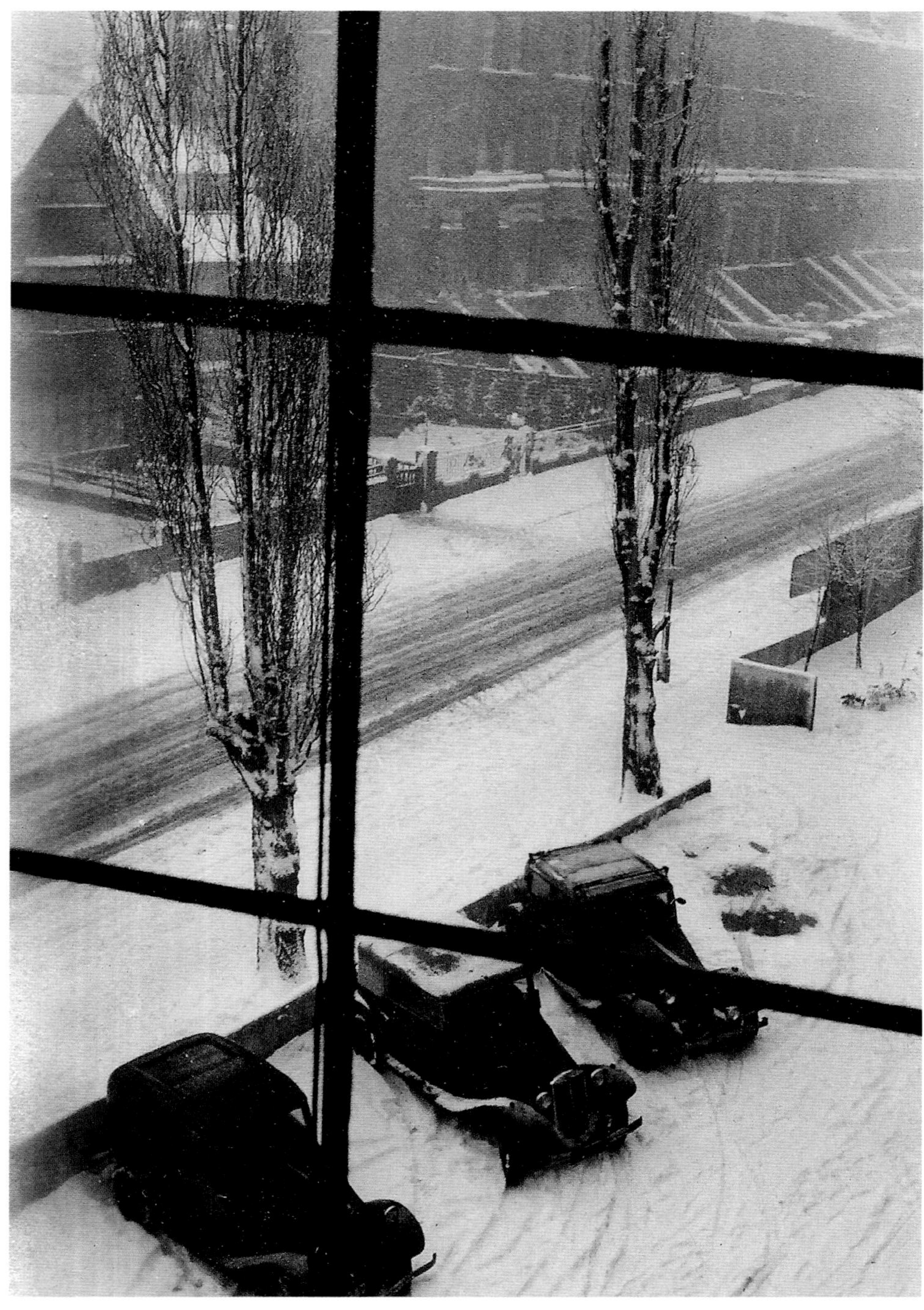

ABOVE: The winter of 1934 was a bitter one. The view from the staircase outside the penthouse over a snowy Lawn Road.

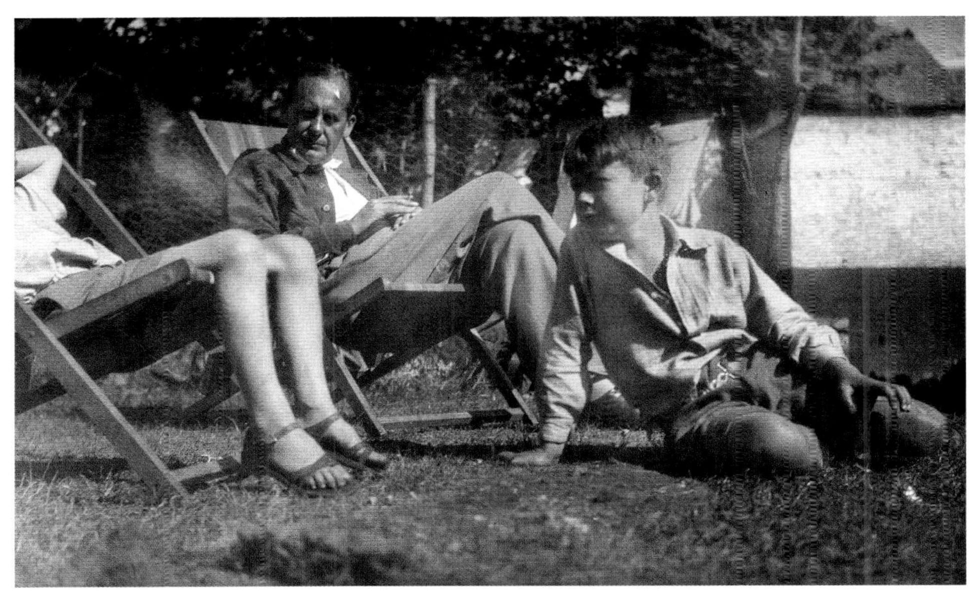

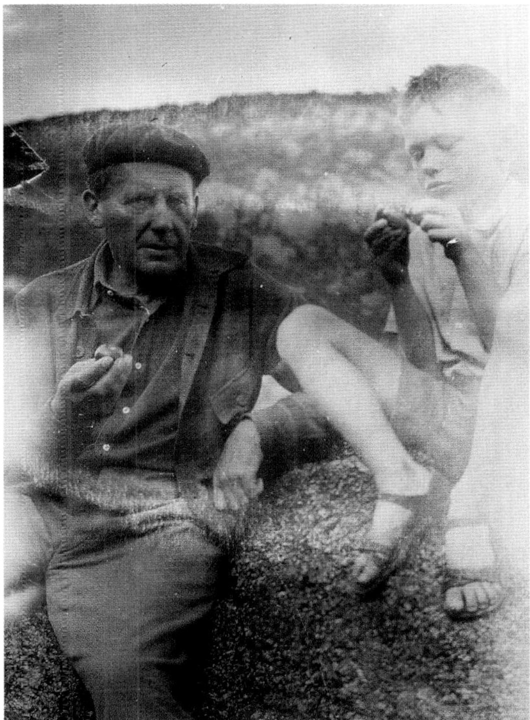

ABOVE, TOP: Walter Gropius with the Pritchard boys, Cornwall, summer 1935.
ABOVE: Gropius and Jeremy Pritchard eating plums in Cornwall, summer 1935.

own practice, but had to wait until 1931 for the Bund Deutscher Architekten to grant him entry. In 1932, thanks to help from Gropius, he won his first independent architectural commission, the Harnischmacher House in Wiesbaden. Although in 1926, he had formally renounced his Jewish faith before the Chief Rabbi of Frankfurt in order to marry his Bauhaus sweetheart, Marta Erps, his religious status was perceived as ambiguous, and in the anti-Semitic climate, work remained scarce. With no further commissions, he moved to Zürich, where he designed the new Wohnbedarf furniture store and two apartment buildings for Sigfried Giedion, before returning to his native Hungary. There, he met further frustration, as the Hungarian architects' organization refused him entry because of his Bauhaus background.

From December 1934 Gropius wrote urging him to move to England, but it took another six months before he visited London for the first time. He arrived in early summer 1935, and stayed in Flat 16, next door to Walter and Ise, just in time for the Lawn Road Flats' first birthday party, which Jack and Molly hosted on the penthouse terrace. Gropius introduced him to the architectural community, including MARS, whose Secretary was architect Francis Reginald Stevens (F.R.S.) Yorke, author of the influential book, *The Modern House*. Maxwell Fry described its impact.

> *It was hard to overestimate the value of that book, especially*
> *for someone ... that had not the money to travel: it was a real*
> *eye-opener and appearing as early as 1934, gave us a conspectus*
> *of the movement at the time we most needed it.*[15]

Breuer returned to London at the end of October 1935 and stayed in Flat 1. This time his visit coincided with another lively Lawn Road gathering, the Pritchards' General Election all-night party. He and F.R.S. Yorke now agreed to form an architectural partnership, as Gropius had done with Maxwell Fry. The modern art collector and diplomat's wife Lady 'Peter' Norton, whom Breuer had met whilst skiing, petitioned the Home Office on his behalf and on 20 November he obtained a long-term resident's permit to live and work in Britain. Breuer returned to Zürich and Budapest to put his affairs in order before his final move to London. In an effort to circumvent German Customs, he posted ahead a large sum of cash, the banknotes ingeniously hidden between the leaves of Hitler's *Mein Kampf*, which he addressed to Sibyl Moholy-Nagy at Lawn Road. When he arrived at the flats in December 1935 pandemonium ensued. She told him she had tossed the book out with the rubbish, thinking it was a joke in poor taste. Luckily, both book and cash were recovered and all was forgiven.

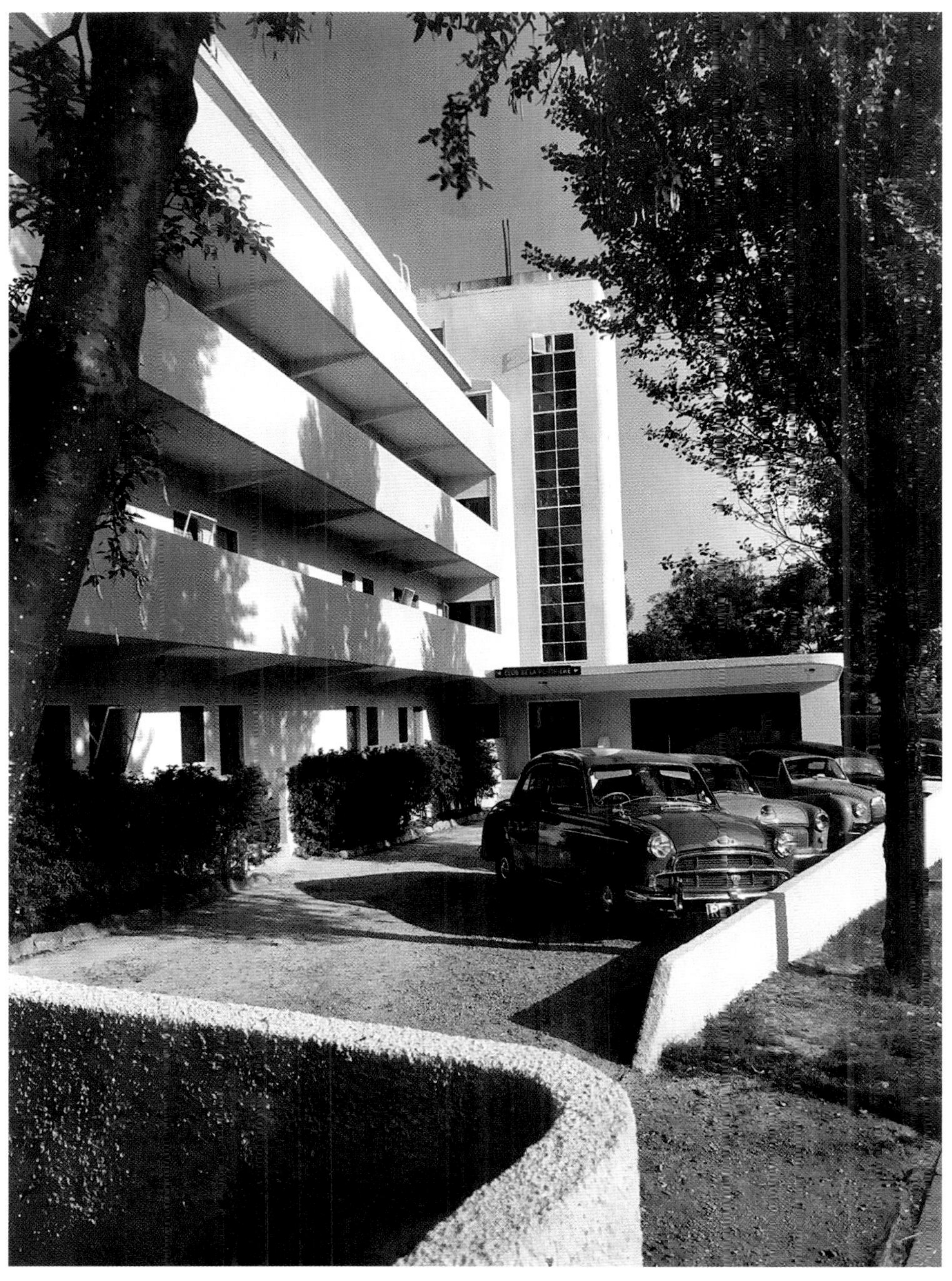

ABOVE: The Lawn Road flats with residents' cars parked outside, 1955.

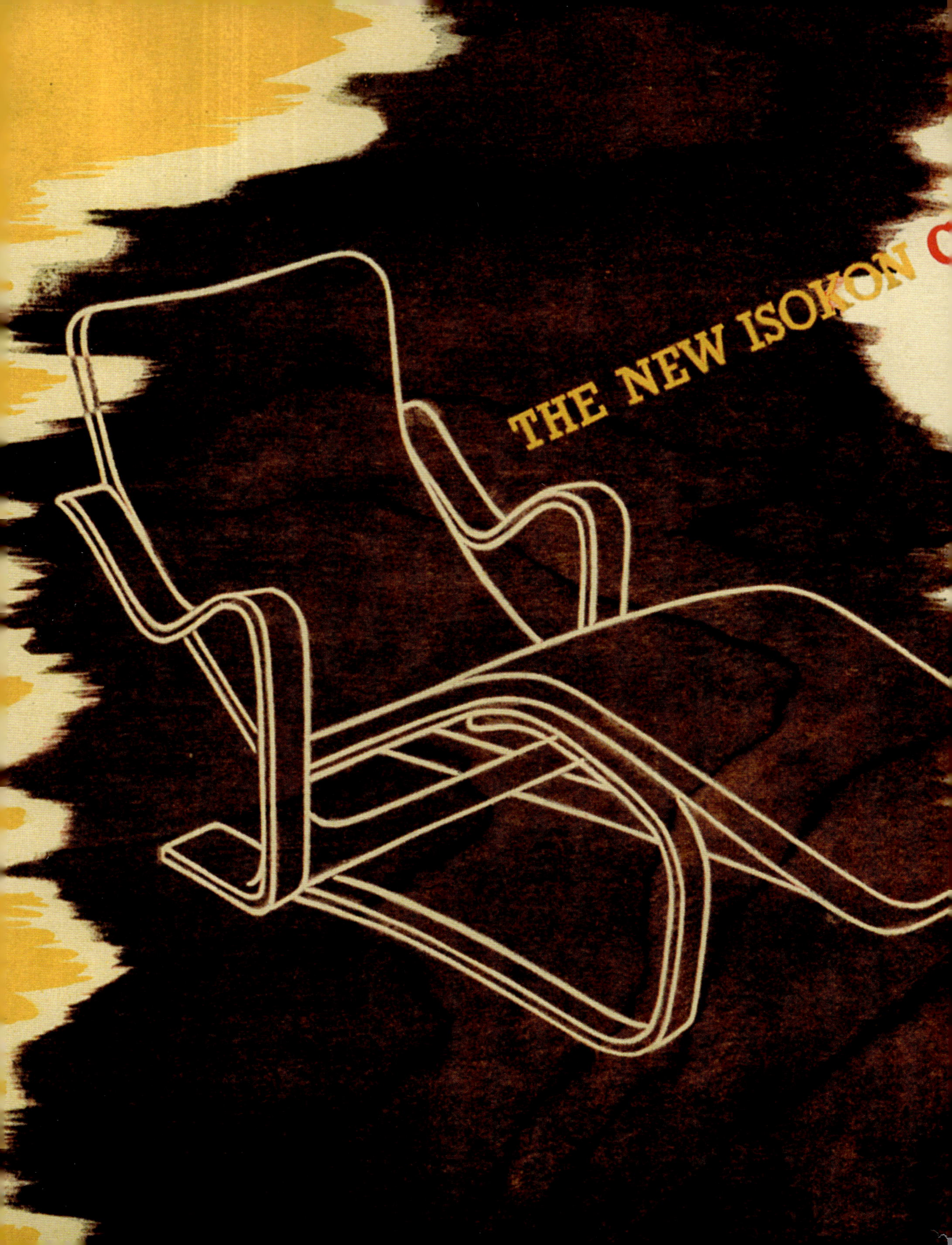
THE NEW ISOKON

ISOKON FURNITURE

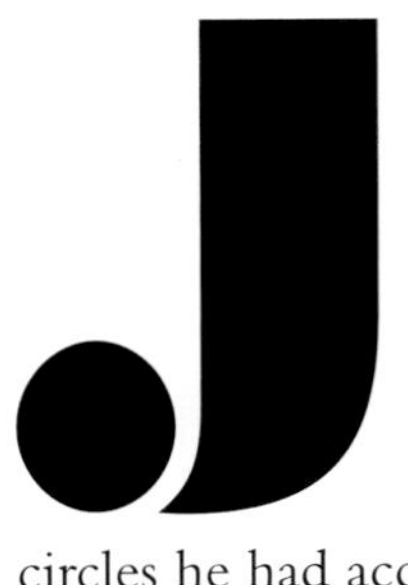

JACK PRITCHARD'S WORK WITH VENESTA HAD SHOWN him the enormous potential of plywood as a material of the future. Since joining the company in September 1925, he had travelled across Europe meeting manufacturers, suppliers and designers; visiting trade exhibitions and reporting on new markets and applications for the material. Such was his association with the product that in London's architectural circles he had acquired the moniker 'Plywood Pritchard'.

With his engineering background, Jack was keen to experiment with the material himself. In 1930, in collaboration with E. Arthur Brown, of north London furniture makers Crossley and Brown, he designed a walnut-veneered plywood desk, which was illustrated in the 1930 *Year Book* of *The Studio*.[1]

The same year, Coates designed a basic range of book units, which he expanded to become Isokon's first commercial product. They consisted of a series of modular cupboards and bookshelves, which could be stacked and arranged in multifunctional combinations. Priced at £4 17s they consisted of a single or double shelf, a single or double cupboard and a plinth. A desk could be created by using a plywood table top (44s) to bridge the units. By 1933, Isokon had sold 70 book units and two desk units. It has been claimed that Pritchard and Coates got the idea from an Austrian refugee they knew named Fried, who stored his possessions in stacked orange boxes. Coates redesigned these units to furnish the Minimum Flat at Dorland Hall in summer that year. Constructed with simple machine-made 'comb' joints to enable mass-production, they were priced from 9s 10d and available in a range of 12-mm (½in) Venesta plywood veneers.

Combined with the cocktail cabinet and radio, they sold well after the exhibition, but despite extensive press coverage and advertising in key publications over the next year, further orders were disappointing. Multifunctional unit furniture was also being developed and retailed during this period by Gordon Russell, Serge Chermayeff's Plan and Gerald Summers's Makers of Simple Furniture, but the pre-war British market for such items was limited.

It was the Finnish architect Alvar Aalto who first developed a highly influential vocabulary of curved, organic plywood forms with the furniture for his 1932 Paimio Tuberculosis Sanatorium. Aalto's furniture was first shown in Britain in November 1933 at the 'Wood Only' exhibition at Fortnum & Mason, organized by Philip Morton Shand and *Architectural Review*. This landmark exhibition demonstrated to British designers and consumers the aesthetic potential of plywood. In 1934, Morton Shand with his fellow architectural writer Geoffrey Boumphrey, founded Finmar, a company importing Aalto's furniture into Britain. Some time between 1930 and 1933, Pritchard designed the cantilevered Isokon

I S O K O N

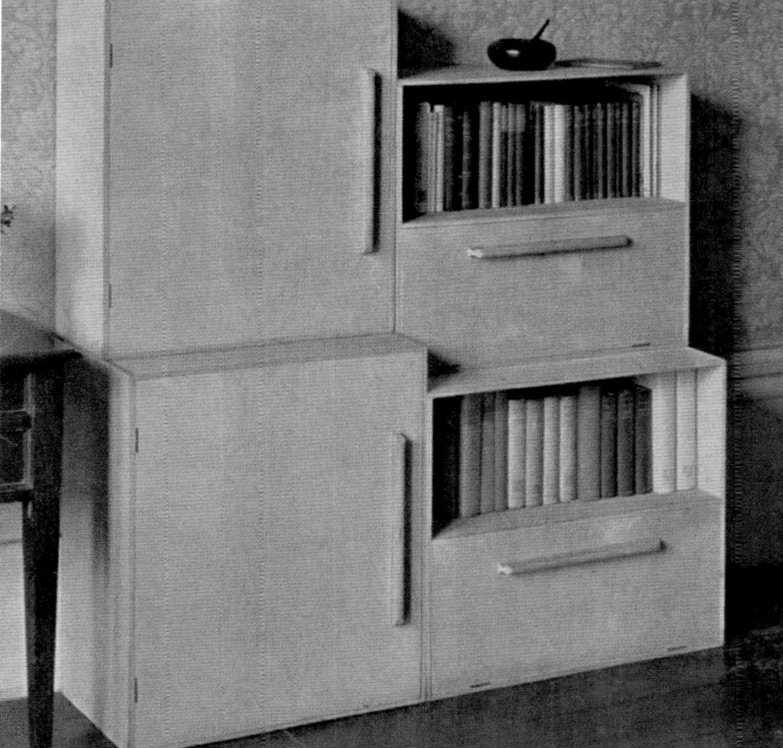

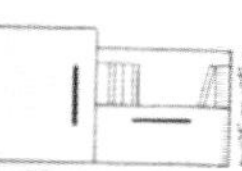

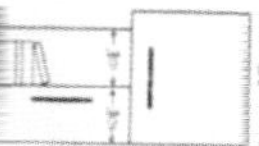

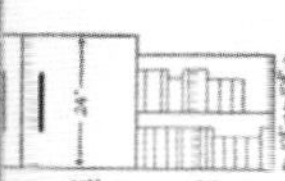

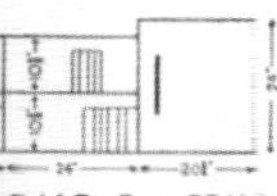

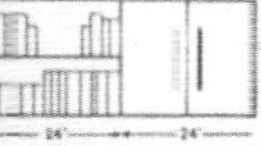

BOOK
UNITS

THE ABOVE IS GROUP ONE

ABOVE: Wells Coates's multifunctional book units, Isokon's first commercial product, 1930.

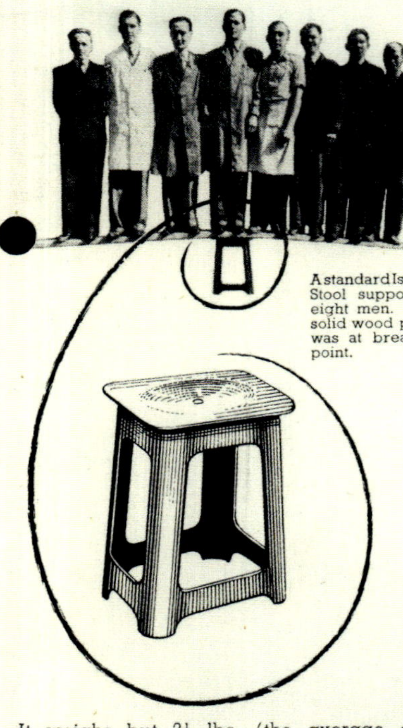

An AMAZING STOOL

There seems to be general agreement that an optician's stool should be

(a) comfortable,

(b) light, for easily moving about,

(c) strong,

(d) inexpensive

We have discovered such a stool. It is made by the Isokon Company, by whom we have been granted the distributing rights for the optical profession.

The Isokon stool is made throughout from scientifically bent, thin plywood. It weighs but 2½ lbs. (the average optician's stool weighs 13 lbs.), and can be lifted by the little finger. Yet, it is of such immense strength that it will support eight men—a weight of well over 1,000 lbs. The shaped seat provides a degree of comfort that is absent from many an upholstered stool.

D2654	Isokon Stool, finished in black cellulose - - **7/6** ea.

In natural oak or natural birch finish - - - 10/6 each

Note. The Isokon Stool cannot be supplied in finishes or colours other than the above.

CARRIAGE : An additional advantage arising out of the extraordinary lightness of the stool is the low carriage charge.

PACKING : By simplifying the packing of the stool we have been able also to make the packing charges correspondingly low, as follows :

Single stool	-	-	-	6d.
Two stools	-	-	-	9d.
Three stools	-	-	-	1/-

A SUGGESTION

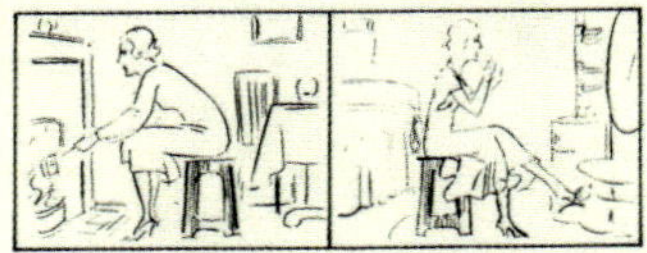

An optician writes : "Send me two more : They are just what I want for use in my own flat."

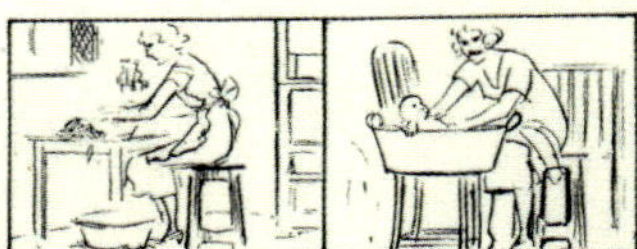

ABOVE: The light, yet strong Isokon Venesta stool (designer unknown), could be 'lifted by the little finger'.

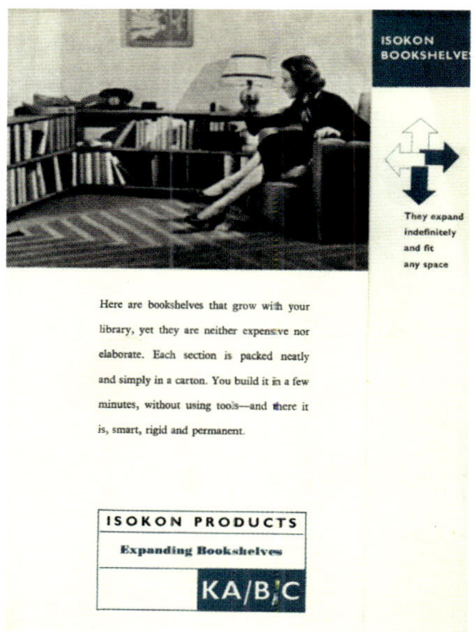

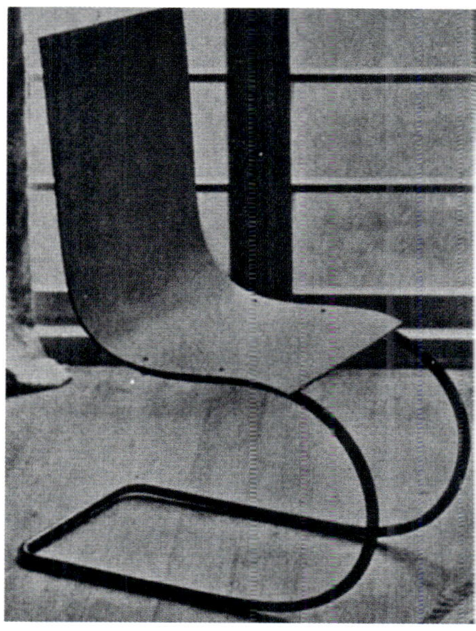

ABOVE, LEFT: Fleetwood Pritchard designed the Isokon Furniture Company's first product leaflets. ABOVE, LEFT: Jack Pritchard's Experimental Chair No.2, bent plywood seat by Venesta, tubular steel frame, 1933.

Experimental Chair No. 2, using one of Venesta's plywood tramcar seats mounted on a tubular steel frame. The chair, featured in *Design for Today* magazine in September 1933, was priced at 37s 6d, and is reminiscent of Aalto's stackable Chair 23, launched at the 'Rationalization of Small Apartments' exhibition in Helsinki in 1930 and sold in the early 1930s by Sigfried Giedion's Wohnbedarf store in Zurich. Whether Jack borrowed from Aalto consciously or otherwise, the Finnish designer would later launch a legal battle with Isokon over the design of one of its best-known products.

Apart from the few experimental examples cited above, Jack did not involve himself further in design and concentrated instead on the marketing side of the business while he and Coates were in partnership. They had envisaged Isokon as a vertically integrated business model whereby the Lawn Road tenants would rent an apartment and purchase Isokon's specially designed furniture. To this end, Coates had designed a plywood sliding table for the Minimum Flats, which could be moved around on tubular-steel runners, its top made, conveniently, from Venesta's flush plywood door. For the Double Flats, Coates chose a circular plywood table he had already used in the Cresta stores. It had a practical, 105cm (41in) diameter linoleum-covered top and three pink-painted metal legs.

From 1933 Isokon also offered for sale a small plywood stool, which it imported from Venesta. Created by an unknown designer and made in A.M. Luther's factory

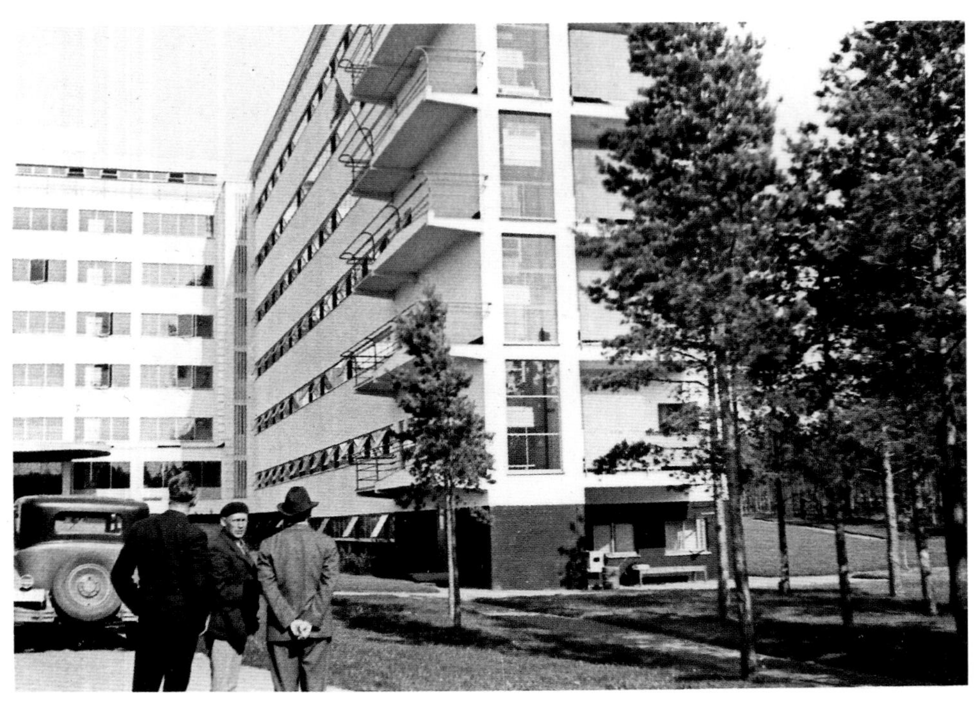

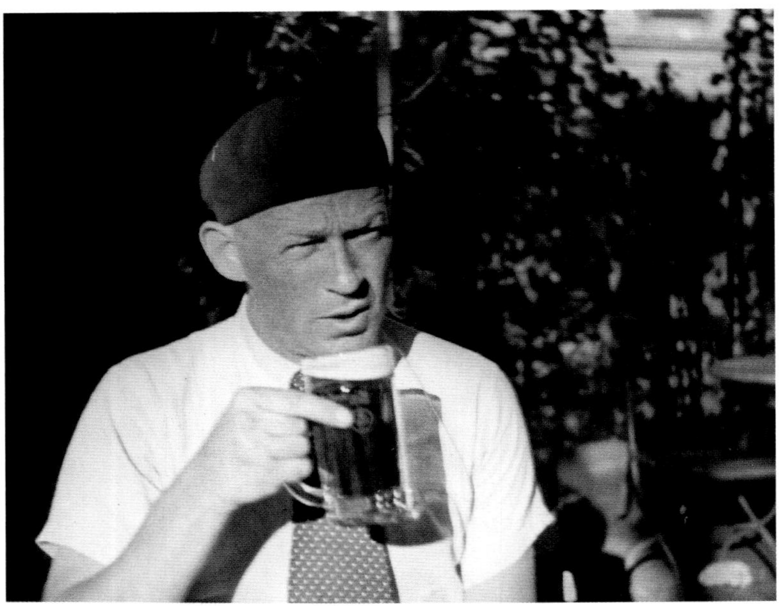

ABOVE, TOP: Philip Morton Shand, Alvar Aalto and Jack Pritchard at the Paimio sanatorium, Finland, August 1935. ABOVE: Alvar Aalto, August 1935, at the Venesta factory in Kirkkonummi, Finland.

in Estonia, the 2111 stool later came to be one of Pritchard's most versatile
products – used in the flats, the Isobar restaurant and reinvented later as a side
table by adding tray tops. Weighing just over 1kg, and measuring 45 × 33 × 33cm
(17¾ × 13 × 13in), its four-sided frame was made from a single bent sheet of
ply with large cut-outs in each side. The stool was so light it could be picked up
with a single finger and its square seat was detachable, making it easy to stack. It
was strong enough, so Isokon's advertisement claimed, to bear the weight of eight
men. It cost 7s 6d, in a black cellulose finish, or 10s 6d, in oak or birch veneer. The
design was hard to improve upon, although in 1936, Gropius proposed a slightly
altered version, with more extreme cut-outs, which never went into production.
Pritchard, realizing the stool could be transformed into a small side table, designed
two trays, one round, with a recessed underside and the other square, with wooden
blocks beneath it (model TR1), which could be slotted securely onto the stool.

The bitterness of Pritchard's rift with Wells Coates during the building of
the flats had made his position as chief designer at Isokon, as well as any future
working relationship, untenable. It was clear Pritchard would have to forge other
alliances if the business was to continue. In 1933, he had met Gerald Summers, a
young designer who was experimenting with plywood in his small workshop in
Charlotte Street. They had both been inspired by Aalto's exhibition in London that
year and were excited by the new organic forms the Finn had achieved. Pritchard
encouraged Summers to use the extremely thin and flexible 'aeroplane ply', created
for the aircraft industry, which helped him to develop his distinctive curvilinear
style, which reached its highpoint in Summers's iconic 1934 armchair, whose back,
legs and seat were cut from a single sheet of bent plywood.[2] Shortly after the Lawn
Road Flats opened, in October 1934, Pritchard reached an agreement to retail
Summers's plywood trolley through Isokon. Ideal as a means of transporting food
or even serving drinks in the flats, the trolley's three tiers are enfolded by a single,
supporting S-shaped sheet of plywood.

In August 1935, Venesta sent Pritchard to visit A.M. Luther's three factories in
the Baltics, a trip he made with Philip Morton Shand and Venesta director Graham
Reid. They travelled on to Finland to meet Morton Shand's new business partner,
Alvar Aalto. The architect took them to Turku, to tour the Korhonen factory
where his furniture was made and he showed them over the Paimio Sanatorium,
where they saw his pioneering plywood designs in their intended context.[3] The
experience made a great impression on Pritchard and within two months of his
return to London, he launched the Isokon Furniture Company (a subdivision of
the parent Isokon Control Company), to make and sell plywood furniture.

Pritchard had researched Finmar's turnover, which was then running at just over
£350 per week. He estimated that with his own experience and working with

progressive furniture stores across the country, he could more than double that in the space of two years.[4] He estimated he needed £3,000 to set up the business, £1,000 of which he would put up himself. He pitched the idea to Graham Reid, claiming it would create a new market for Venesta plywood and that they could learn much from Finmar's 'mistakes':

> *A good deal of this furniture is questionable as to comfort, but we can profit from their experience… We should begin aiming for the 'better class market'… During this time the product would be sold at relatively high prices and as the demand and production increased the price could be progressively lowered. The Finmar experience is worth recording here. They started off at a price which resulted in demand being greater than available supplies, so that they failed to equate the two and to reap a satisfactory profit, moreover they created bad will through late delivery.[5]*

Henry Rutherford, Chairman of Venesta, initially considered investing £1,000 in the new venture, but the idea was vetoed by his board, as was permission to use the company's Silvertown factory to make up Pritchard's models. Instead they agreed to provide advice, continue to supply Pritchard's new venture with plywood at a 25% discount and to act as agents importing Isokon furniture from A.M. Luther's factories in Tallinn.

In 1934 Jack and Molly had bought a set of three flat-pack bookshelves from Wohnbedarf in Zurich for their apartment. They were designed by Wilhelm Kienzle and made by the Swiss aluminium manufacturer Embru-Werke AG. Pritchard struck a licensing deal with the firm and the shelves became the first design marketed by the new Isokon Furniture Company.[6] Taylor-Law in Birmingham produced the metal 'grips' supporting the shelves, which were made from oak (24s) or deal (21s) and could hold up to a hundred books. Pritchard turned to Fleetwood to devise a marketing campaign and his agency made their self-assembly and packaging a selling point. Aimed at the 'shelf conscious', the 'Bookcase in a Carton' could be put together in three minutes without tools and 'Because you construct the bookcase yourself, you save money'. Pritchard appointed a number of nationwide agents for the Isokon shelves including: Heal's in London; Brown Muffs of Bradford; Mark Rowe & Sons in Exeter; and P.E. Gane in Bristol.

He also toyed with the idea of producing items in aluminium and asked Walter Gropius to create some designs including a range of aluminium teapots. In April 1935, Gropius designed a cylindrical waste-paper basket (36 × 27cm/14

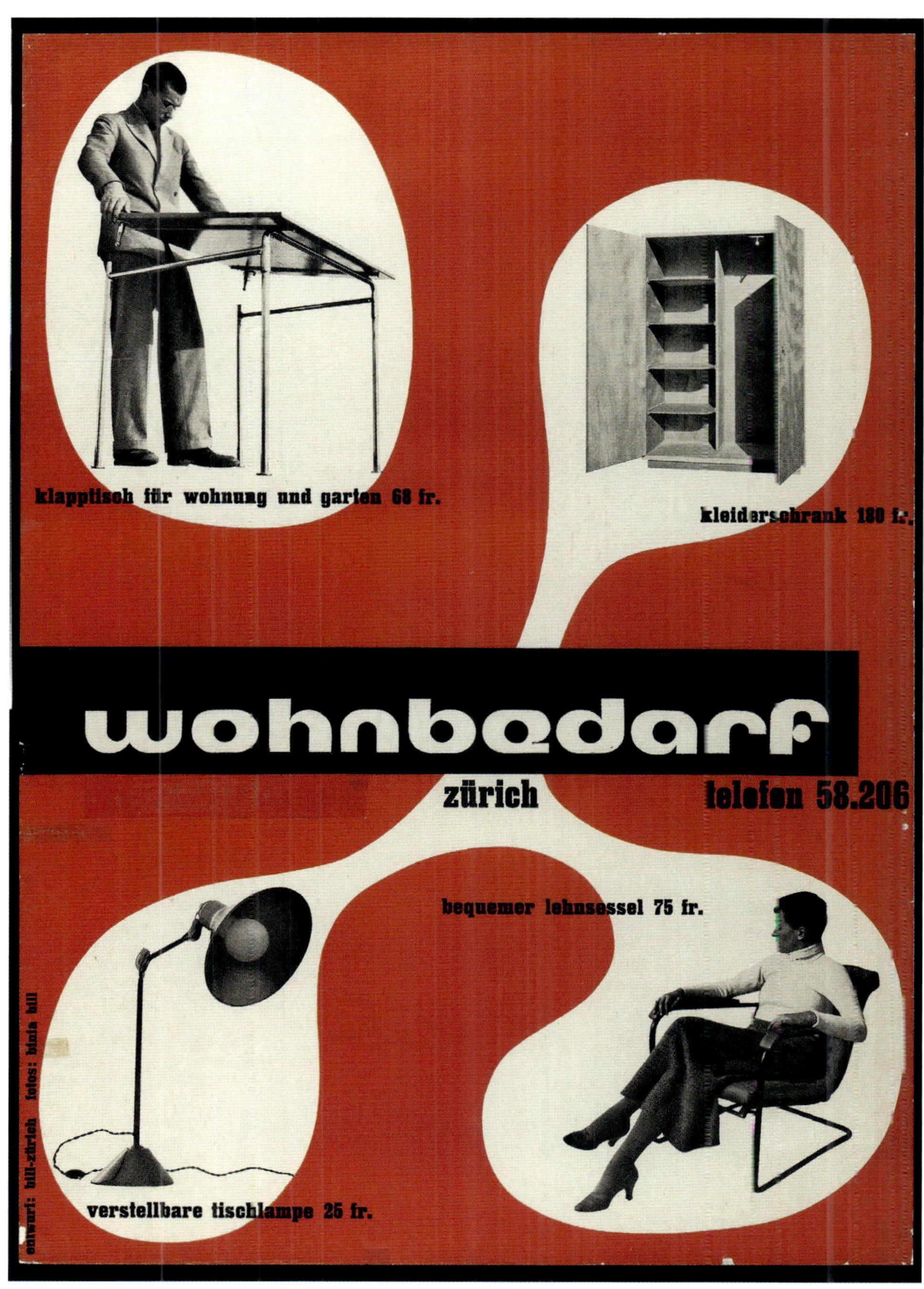

ABOVE: Advertising poster dated 1932 for Sigfried Giedion's shop Wohnbedarf in Zurich. The poster was both designed by and featured Binia and Max Bill. Marcel Breuer designed the interiors for the Wohnbedarf shops in both Basel and Zurich, together with Robert Winkler and Eduard Schöni.

× 10½cm), which was formed from a sheet of geometrically pierced aluminium. Pritchard sent this design to Taylor-Law, but the company balked at the cost of new equipment needed to produce the item.[7] Eventually he had a small number produced by the London Aluminium Company and the item was sold at Gordon Russell, which by this stage was employing architectural historian Nikolaus Pevsner, another German refugee, as the buyer for its Wigmore Street store.

Jack's first impression of Gropius had been as a 'formidable and silent' father figure, but as the months passed and communication between the two improved, the older man's warmth and humour became apparent. In October 1935 Pritchard appointed Gropius as the Isokon Furniture Company's Controller of Design. His salary was £165 per annum, the equivalent of the rent on his flat, and he was given a share in the company's profits.[8] Aware of the prestige the Bauhaus founder would confer on his fledgling company, Pritchard asked his press agent Andrew Reid to draw up an announcement, which appeared in a number of publications that spring:

> *The ideas developed by Professor Walter Gropius at the Bauhaus at Dessau are the inspiration behind the new organisation for the design and manufacture of furniture in Great Britain… Professor Gropius will both design himself and select suitable designers to undertake specific work under his guidance… It is particularly emphasised that the furniture will be thoroughly practical, with its aesthetic qualities dependent on form rather than superimposed adornment… Owing to its strength, lightness and flexibility, plywood will be the principal product used in constructing the first models.*

Naturally Gropius suggested Pritchard should employ his two former Bauhaus colleagues Marcel Breuer and László Moholy-Nagy in the business. Within a matter of months, Pritchard had three of the most celebrated names in 20th-century design working for his company.

On his arrival in London in winter 1935, Breuer was appointed Isokon's Chief Designer. Despite Pritchard's clubbable personality, the chemistry between the two was not instantaneous. The language barrier was a problem, particularly when it came to discussing fees and Breuer wrote to Gropius in December 1935 mentioning his difficulties reaching terms with Pritchard.[9] However, by January 1936, they signed an agreement giving Breuer a retainer of £200–300 a year and a royalty of 5% of the retail price of any of his furniture sold.[10] The initial

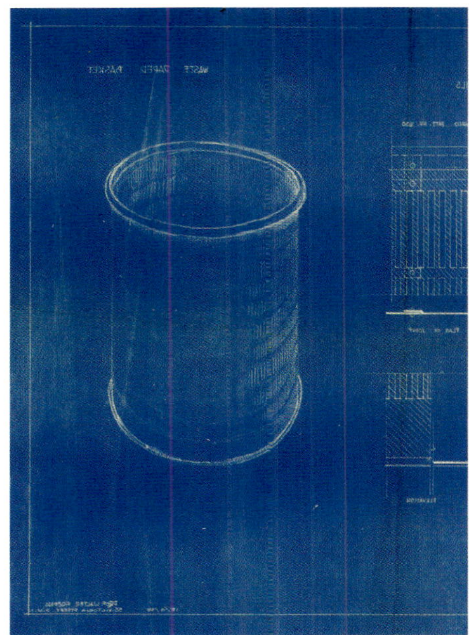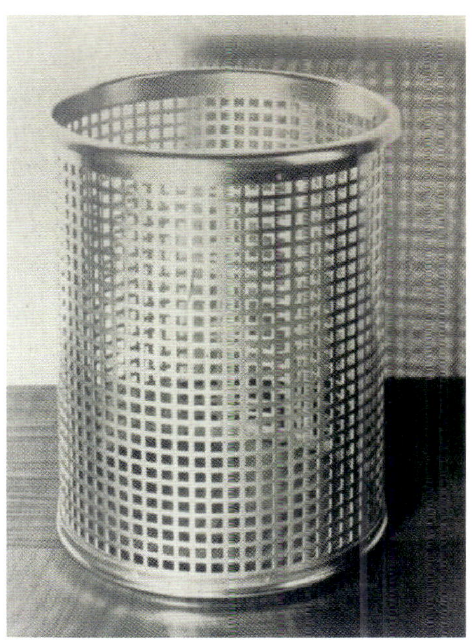

ABOVE, LEFT AND RIGHT: Blueprint and finished design, Walter Gropius's aluminium wastepaper basket for the Isokon Furniture Company, 1935.

awkwardness between the two, and Breuer's sometimes prickly personality, may be reasons why he did not continue living at Lawn Road, but in the New Year moved to 4 Tregunter Road in Chelsea, where his new partner F.R.S. Yorke lived and ran his studio. Even so, Breuer frequently returned to Lawn Road to play an active part in the social life of the flats.

By early 1936, László and Sibyl Moholy-Nagy were expecting their second daughter, Claudia. After four months in London they had moved to a small house at 7 Farm Walk in Hampstead Garden Suburb more suited to a family and with space for a studio.[11] As his work was already well known in artistic and architectural circles, Pritchard lost little time in asking Moholy-Nagy to design a full-page advertisement for Venesta plywood, which he placed in *Architectural Review* in February 1936. It featured a stylized composition of a tree wrapped in a scroll of birch plywood.[12]

The brief was simple, it avoided any need to emphasise technical quality or special aspect of the company's policy, just to indicate that Venesta plywood was both rigid and flexible. I relied on the impact I thought he would make… He worked fast; at first it seemed that he was too facile,

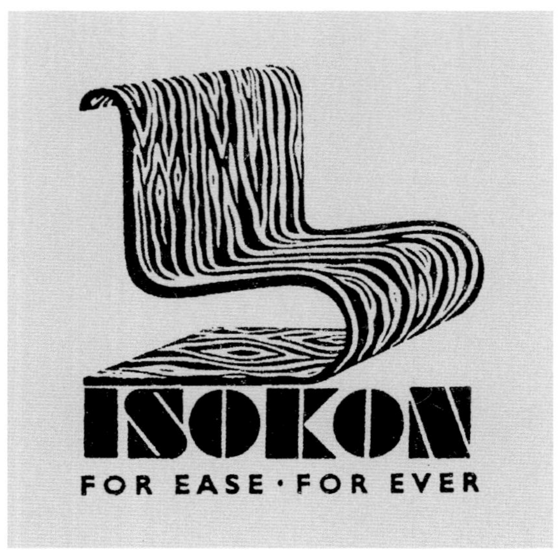

ABOVE: Isokon logotype designed by László Moholy-Nagy, 1936.

*but I soon realised it was the speed of his understanding and execution
at the same time, analysis and synthesis almost in one operation.[13]*

Moholy-Nagy next designed a 'trademark' for the Isokon Furniture Company.
He took the existing logo of an S-shaped plywood chair (devised by Fleetwood
Pritchard's firm) and infilled it with a graphic woodgrain pattern. He also designed
an elegant embossed letterhead for the company, adding the slogan, 'Designers of
New Furniture' and was paid 10 guineas for the work.[14]

At this point Pritchard resigned from Venesta, although Henry Rutherford, who
had valued his drive and imagination, kept him on a retainer as a consultant to the
firm for several more years. When Breuer had arrived in London, Jack and Molly
Pritchard were displaying one of his aluminium reclining chairs in the penthouse.
Breuer had begun experimenting with aluminium furniture in 1932, and was one
of the first designers to use it in a domestic context. He had designed the chair
in 1933 for an international aluminium furniture competition held in Paris and
it had been awarded two jury prizes. Manufactured by Embru-Werke AG, the
chair's seatback was formed from aluminium slats and Breuer had used one single
band of aluminium for the supporting frame, which he split in two and then bent
in separate directions. Gropius suggested that Breuer should create a plywood
version of the model, which became the Isokon Long Chair. Breuer produced his
first designs during the winter and New Year of 1935–6 and spent several further

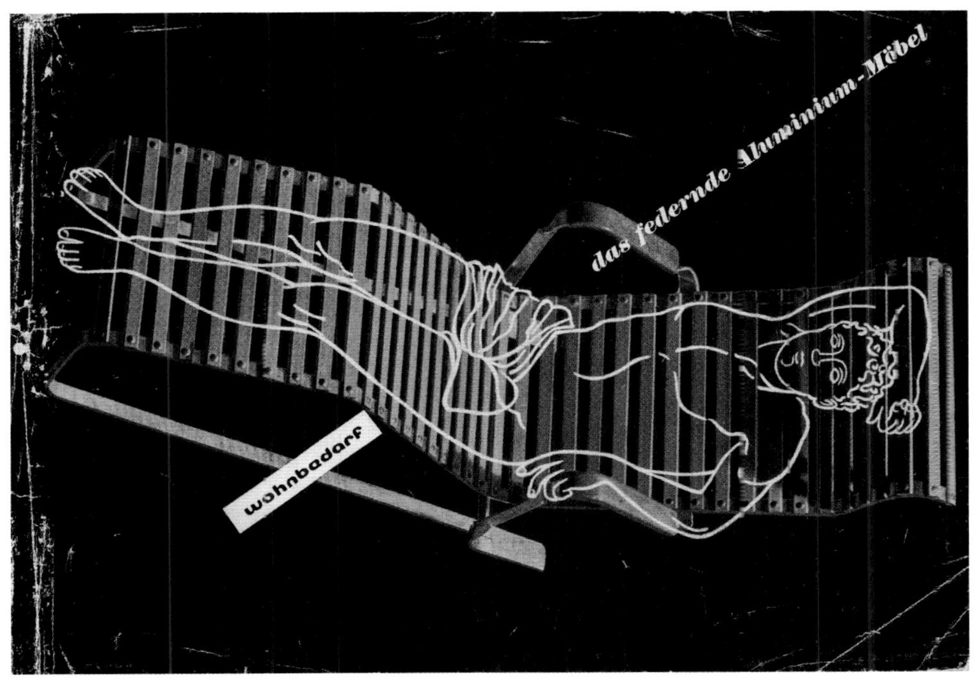

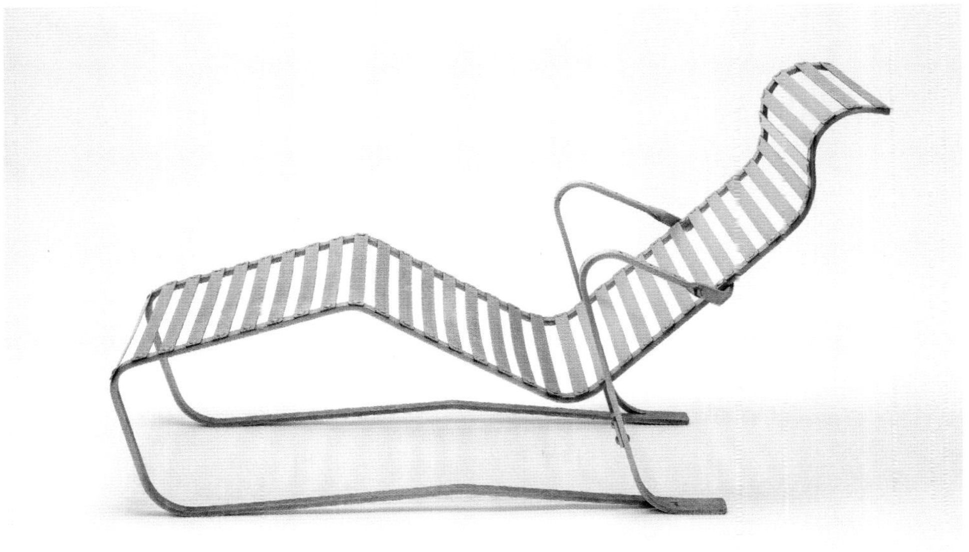

ABOVE: The aluminium Long Chair model 1096 was designed by Marcel Breuer in 1933 for the Swiss company Embru and distributed by Wohnbedarf. Jack Pritchard had imported one from Wohnbedarf for his new penthouse at Lawn Road Flats, and the chair was the direct inspiration fo the plywood Isokon Long Chair.

months refining them and experimenting with prototypes, which were built by
furniture maker Harry Mansell in his workshop in Curtain Road in the East End.

Although it superficially resembled the aluminium recliner, the chair's new
material created new demands. Its seat was formed not from slats, but a single
sheet of bent plywood. Breuer discovered it was impossible, in terms of cost
and practicality, to make the chair's frame out of just two continuous lengths of
plywood. Instead, each side had to be formed from two separate pieces, making
four individual components. The seat had two protruding 'ears', which were
morticed and glued into the supports. The chair was then stabilized with a
crosspiece, which ran at a right angle under the seat and joined the two sides of
the frame. He designed a 'long' and 'short' version of the chair. The seat on the
Short Chair terminated in a downward curve, giving it a slightly more organic
appearance than the long one. In the patent filed on 10 July 1936, which included
drawings for ten possible variations of the chair, Breuer described the distinctive
construction method he had devised.[15]

> *Instead of building up a structure which is complete in itself, so far
> as the load carrying members are concerned and then applying a seat
> to it, I now use the frame members which only become a complete
> structure when parts of them are spanned by the seat.*

The Long Chair's plywood seat was produced and bent at A.M. Luther's factory
in Reval (later renamed Tallinn) and its laminated birch frames, which would be
offered in a choice of veneers, were made in London by Mansell and G. Pfeifer in
a new workshop they set up next to the flats. The ever-inventive (and economical)
Pritchard had discovered they could make the frames by recycling the 1.5mm
thick veneers from the packing cases Luther's used to ship the seats. They began
scouting for the crates all over London.

A prototype Long Chair was delivered in October 1936 and over the next
few months Breuer continued to tinker with the design, adding T-profile fins to
strengthen the laminated arms and putting an extra layer of veneer around the
'ears', which were prone to cracking. The final Long Chair patent (model BC1)
was registered in December 1936. It was 84cm high × 142cm long × 62cm wide
(33 × 56 × 24½in). Pritchard priced the basic birch model with no upholstery at
£3 15s, rising to £8 7s, when veneered in walnut or Zebrano, with a full-length
cushion made of Dunlopillo or Hairlok, which could be upholstered in a range
of fabrics. The Short Chair (model BC2) measured 84 × 91 × 62cm (33 × 36 ×
24½in) and cost £4.[16] Production began in 1937.

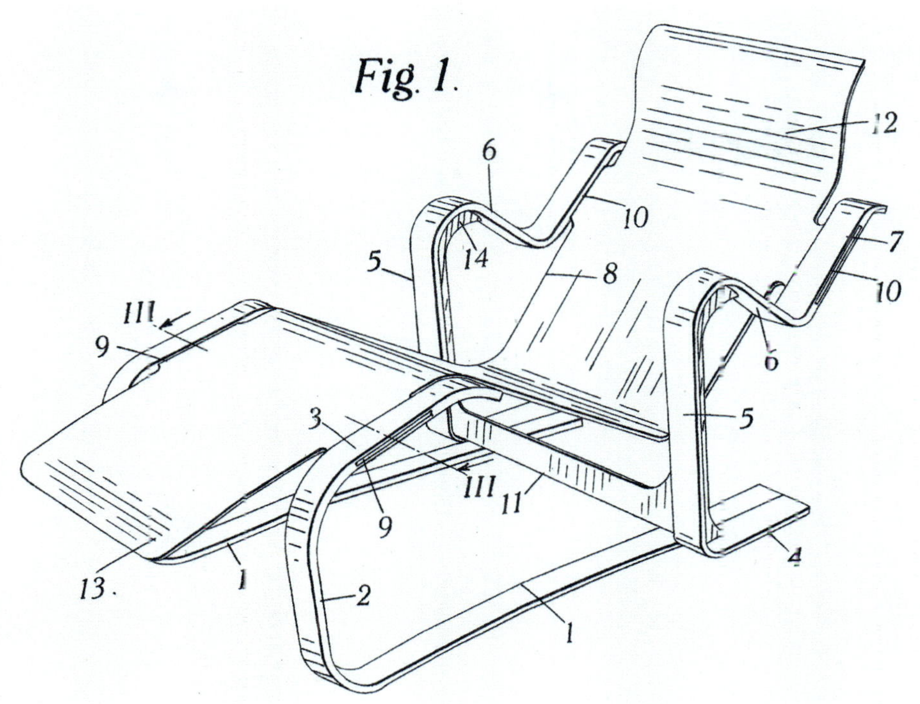

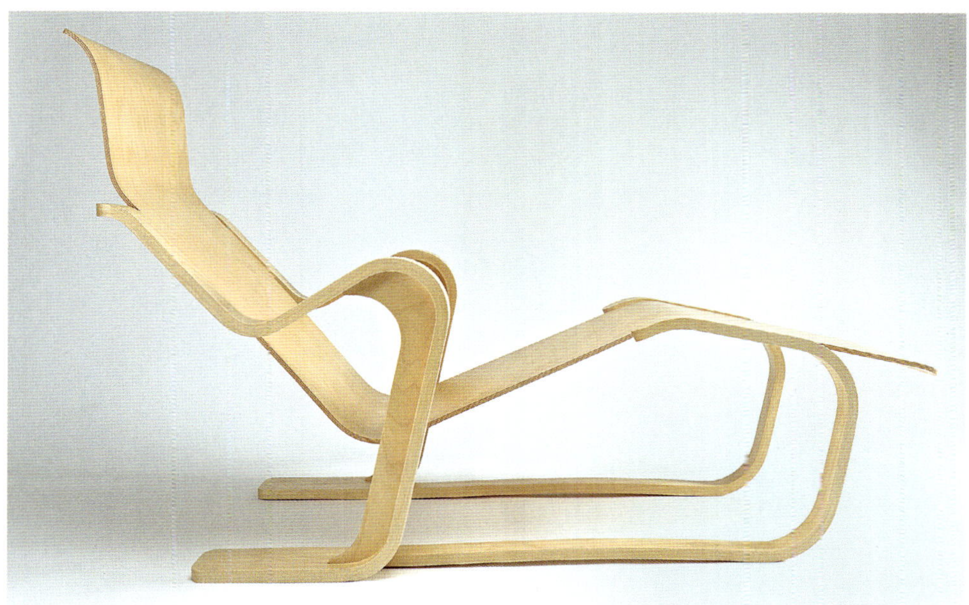

ABOVE, TOP: 1936 patent application drawing for the Marcel Breuer Isokon Long Chair.
ABOVE: The Marcel Breuer Isokon Long Chair, birch plywood.

Throughout this period a legal battle was raging. Shortly after the first Long Chair patent was filed, Pritchard received notice from Finmar that Artek (Aalto's Finnish company, founded in 1935), was taking action against the company for infringing its patent on a laminated wood curve in compression. It demanded that Isokon cease production of the chair. This was an acutely awkward situation for all concerned. Aalto's furniture importer Morton Shand and his wife Sibyl were close friends of the Pritchards and had been involved throughout the Lawn Road Flats project. Breuer angrily denied he could see any similarity between the two designs. 'I do not see any reason for stopping the manufacture of my design,' he retorted. A year of legal wrangling ensued before a compromise was reached. Pritchard had systematically checked through patents in old journals and spotted a plywood chair by Aalto using the wood curve, which predated the patent, thus invalidating it. The Isokon Furniture Company and Artek agreed to 'keep off the designs of the other'.[17]

Jack and Molly had also purchased a set of Breuer's tubular-steel nesting tables from Wohnbedarf. These had been based on simple U-shaped stools he had first designed in 1925–6 for the Bauhaus canteen at Dessau. For Isokon, he designed a set of three nesting tables (model BT2), each cut and bent from a single sheet of 12-mm plywood. The tables, made by Luther's, were incredibly light, yet strong.

Breuer used a similar format for the Isokon dining table (model BT3) of August 1936, but due to its larger scale, the table couldn't be cut from a single plywood sheet. The top of 5mm plywood curved over four tapering plywood legs, which like the Long Chair's frame, were reinforced with a concealed vertical fin. To give the tabletop extra strength, horizontal stretchers were placed under each end. Luther's proposed further refinements to the table to improve stability, which Pritchard and Breuer accepted. Despite measuring 71 × 68 × 138cm (28 × 26¾ × 54¼in), the table weighed a remarkably light 9.5kg (21lb). Breuer also designed a smaller, square version.

When Molly Pritchard went into private practice in 1938, she used the dining table as an elegant desk and chose the nesting tables for her psychiatric consulting room in Upper Harley Street, which was designed by Christopher 'Kit' Nicholson, brother of artist Ben Nicholson.[18]

Breuer's stacking Dining Chair (model BC3) was formed from just two pieces of plywood. Its seat, legs and back support were cut from one sheet. The back itself, with a curved handle for ease of lifting, was cut from another and the design was patented on 4 August 1936.

Pritchard had high hopes for the chair, but it proved unstable and had to be endlessly reworked. The back (which was glued on) was prone to breaking and additional supports had to be added under the seat. The final version of the chair

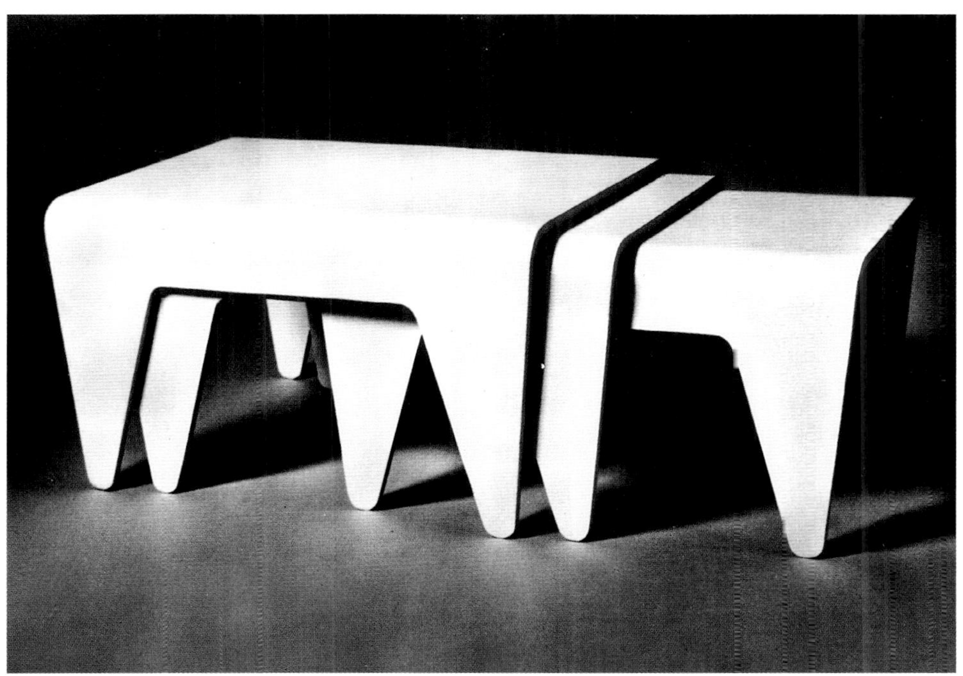

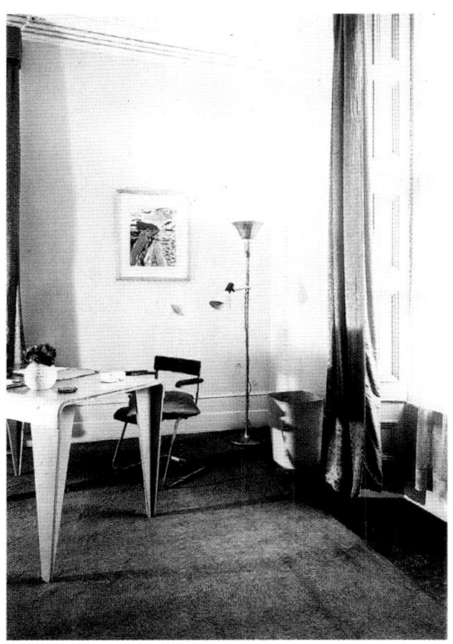

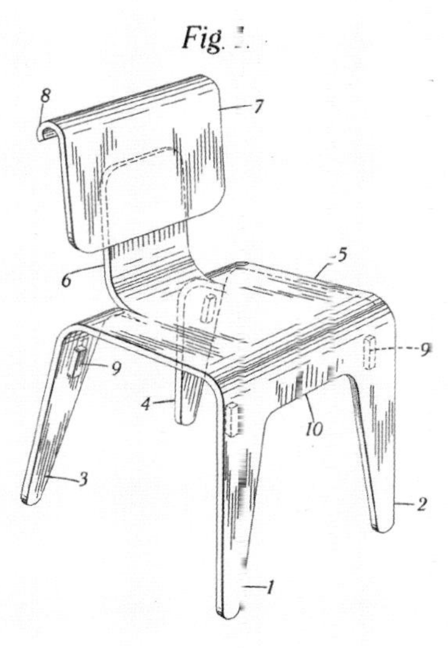

ABOVE, TOP: Marcel Breuer's BT2 Nesting Tables, each cut from a single sheet of plywood. ABOVE, LEFT: Molly Pritchard's Consulting Room in Upper Harley Street, with a Marcel Breuer Isokon table and a floor lamp designed by Sigfried Giedion and Hin Bredendieck. A John Piper collage hangs on the rear wall. ABOVE, RIGHT: Marcel Breuer's problematic BC3 stacking Dining Chair was made from nine pieces of plywood.

was made from nine pieces of plywood rather than two. Produced in birch, it retailed from 1937 for 28s 6d. An upholstered version was also available. Breuer experimented further, producing a model with arms and, in January 1937, wrote to R.C. Swinton of the London Aluminium Co. Ltd enquiring about producing an aluminium stacking chair, but neither went into production.

Walter Gropius also created several furniture designs for the company, but they were not commercially successful. In April 1936, he designed a rectangular 122 × 81cm (48 × 32in) occasional table with a linoleum top and curved legs. In November, he redesigned a smaller, square version of this table (GT1), but the cost of producing the legs proved prohibitive.[19] In July he designed a set of three rectangular nesting trays, but Venesta expressed concerns that they infringed an existing German patent and these were never produced.[20] The following year, he produced another square table with a top shaped like an inverted tray, covered in black Rexine, a synthetic leather. This design was approved and Isokon offered the GT2 table for sale at 30s, but only a handful were produced and sold.

Experimenting with materials was also part of his brief as Controller of Design and Gropius was interested in creating rounded chair legs from plywood. He designed a prototype chair in solid wood, whose arched back and rear legs could be cut from a single sheet of plywood. He also devised a cylindrical plywood tube, from which legs or the rounded edges of furniture could be cut. Pritchard sent both designs off to Estonia to be assessed, but A.M. Luther's reported that neither were viable.

Harry Mansell designed the final item of the Isokon Furniture Company's first range – the MS1 sideboard. This had four doors and was fitted inside with a wine rack for 18 bottles, a shelf for glasses and on the other side, four trays, which could be used for linen, knives and plates. It was available, either entirely in birch for £13 13s, or in walnut with a birch top for £15 15s.

F.C. Pritchard, Wood and Partners produced a series of clear, simple and graphic sales leaflets for the Isokon products, which, although they extolled many of the Bauhaus virtues, lacked dynamism and flair. Gropius suggested Moholy-Nagy should create some new advertising materials. He sent Pritchard an experimental photomontaged showcard, which does not appear to have been used, for the Kienzle bookshelves, and also designed a red transfer paper wrapper for the company's existing advertising card, on which he coined the slogan: 'Invention which makes life more comfortable'.[21]

In March 1937, Moholy-Nagy designed a gatefold sales leaflet for Breuer's Long Chair. The striking cover image shows a white outline drawing of the Long Chair superimposed on a colour-washed background of white, yellow and woodgrain. To underline its versatility, the chair is shown in a range of domestic settings –

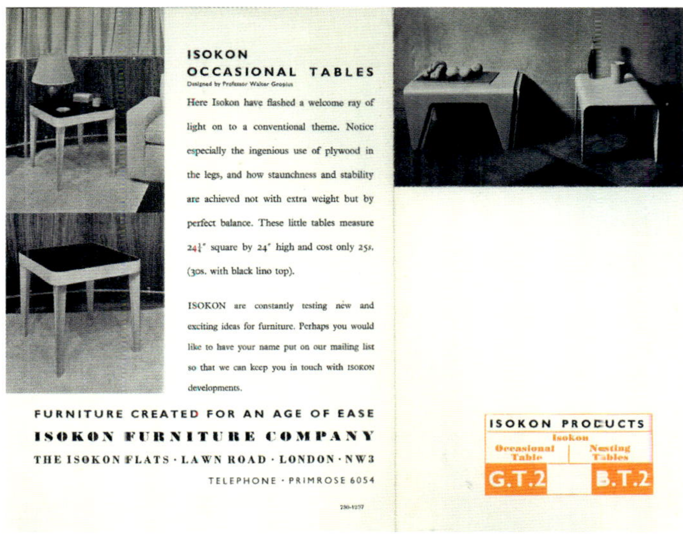

ABOVE: Walter Gropius's GT2 Rexine-topped occasional table. Leaflet design by Fleetwood Pritchard.

on a patio, by a fire, and under a reading lamp. Inside the leaflet, two long chairs are photographed on either side of a Breuer nesting table set for tea. Moholy-Nagy drew a male figure reclining on one chair, with a pipe in one hand and a newspaper in another. Arrows surround the figure indicating the points at which the chair supports his body. The pseudo-scientific text claims:

> *The Isokon Long Chair gives scientific relaxation to every part of the body, immediately creating a feeling of well-being. It is even a better aid to digestion than any medicine under the sun. Admirable for those who take forty winks after dinner. When in an Isokon Long Chair the weight of a person is spread over an area of some 700 square inches, whereas in an ordinary old-fashioned chair it is usually spread over some 250 inches. Thus the pressure of the whole body is concentrated on a narrow area.*

The back of the brochure showed a couple reading in matching Long Chairs. The woman in the photograph was F.R.S. Yorke's wife, Thelma, a professional model. The image was taken by Philip Harben, later manager and chef of the Isobar, who was then working as a fashion photographer. The ads were colourful, modern and differentiated Isokon's products in the marketplace. Pritchard advertised by mail order and in the architectural press, and Breuer's furniture began to appear in features on modern interior design. The revolutionary organic forms made possible by plywood were elegantly described by journalist Clive Entwistle in *Architectural Review*:

> *They have an economy of line and form comparable with that of*
> *a leopard or an orchid.*[22]

Isokon furniture was retailed through forward-thinking stores such as Dunn's of Bromley, Kendal Milne in Manchester and Heal's in London.[23] Pritchard's experience with Venesta helped with marketing and he went on the road to sell the Long Chairs to hotels along the South Coast, offering discounts to those who ordered more than six.[24] Feedback from customers was invaluable in modifying the product.

> *There was great excitement in the early days when we received an*
> *order for a dozen of these chairs from Dolphin Square. This building*
> *had an indoor swimming pool, and the Isokon Long Chairs were placed*
> *around the pool. The floor was tiled and the tiles were warmed, and our*
> *first chair was made using Scotch glue, easy and flexible in use but soluble*
> *when warm and damp. It was not long before our precious chairs became*
> *as John Gloag described them, an 'embarrassing collection of veneer'.*
> *The lesson was learnt fast, and we then used a new ICI product that was*
> *not soluble under Dolphin Square conditions. It was not long before*
> *Bassett Lowke had two or three Long Chairs installed in a municipal*
> *bath-house in similar conditions … and they stood up well.*[25]

Exhibitions continued to be an important but expensive means of raising the Isokon Furniture Company's profile. Pritchard declared the 1936 *Daily Mail* Ideal Home Exhibition at Olympia a 'complete flop', as the show 'did not have a specific point of view'.[26] Even so, he returned to Olympia the following year, showing the Long Chair on a stand designed by Gropius and Breuer, and in 1938 he took another stand at The Woman's Fair and Exhibition at the same venue. He also took out a full-page advertisement, with a drawing by artist and architect Hugh Casson, in the catalogue accompanying the 1938 Modern Architectural Research (MARS) Group exhibition.[27]

In July 1936 Pritchard and Gropius were approached by the John Lewis group. The company was keen to modernize its furniture offering and asked their

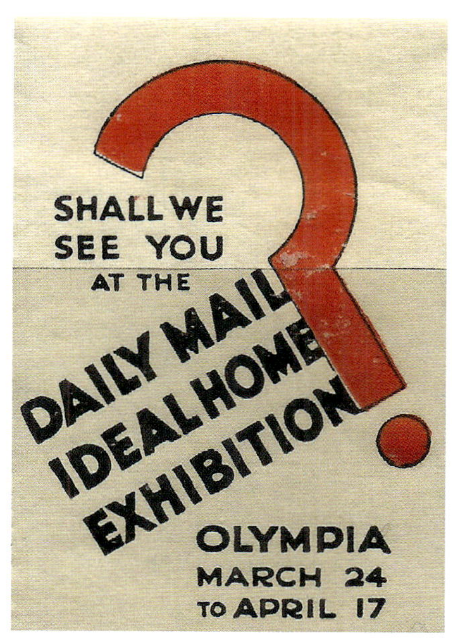

ABOVE: Exhibitions such as the popular *Daily Mail Ideal Home Exhibition* at Olympia were an important way of raising Isokon's profile.

advice on remodelling displays in its flagship Peter Jones branch.[28] Pritchard and Gropius agreed that for a fee of 100–120 guineas, they would propose items for a changing monthly furniture display and put together a selection committee, which included John Gloag, Marcel Breuer and Professor Charles Herbert Reilly (Peter Jones's Consultant Architect). Gropius designed a stand, in a prominent position on the ground floor, which could display fabrics and two or three items of furniture. They reached agreement that for a quarter of the year, this should be used for Isokon products and in summer 1937 the first display of Marcel Breuer's furniture was shown. The concept was rolled out to John Lewis in Oxford Street, where the inaugural display comprised Isokon Long Chairs and trays, the Gropius waste basket, black Finmar chairs, and an Alvar Aalto desk and chair. Pritchard and Gropius further negotiated a permanent 2.4 × 3m (8 × 10ft) of dedicated wall space for Isokon products.[29]

By November 1937 Pritchard was considering a move into retailing. He had found a possible site near Gordon Russell's store, at 128 Wigmore Street, a prestigious West End thoroughfare running parallel to Oxford Street.[30] He asked Breuer and F.R.S. Yorke to survey the building and design the interiors. Although the project fell through, Pritchard continued to explore the idea of a London store for several years to come.

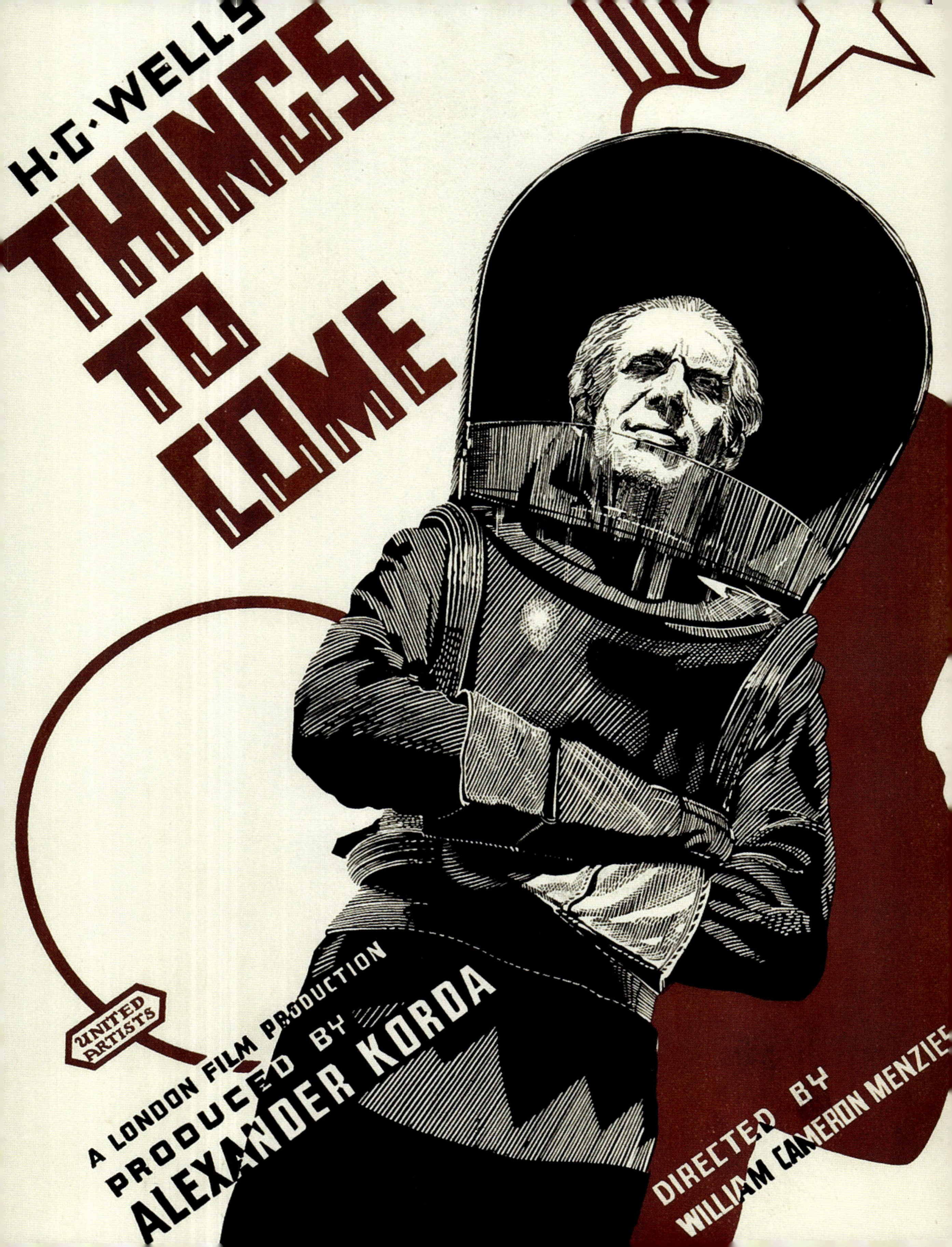

H·G·WELLS
THINGS TO COME
A LONDON FILM PRODUCTION
UNITED ARTISTS
PRODUCED BY
ALEXANDER KORDA
DIRECTED BY
WILLIAM CAMERON MENZIES

THE BAUHAUSLERS' WORK OUTSIDE ISOKON

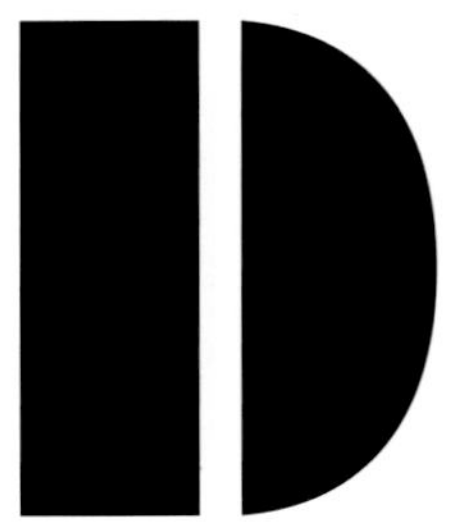URING THE TWO YEARS FOLLOWING THE OPENING OF the Lawn Road Flats, Jack Pritchard attempted to launch three other Isokon housing schemes in Manchester, Birmingham and Windsor, with the aim of employing Walter Gropius and Maxwell Fry as his architects. In February 1935, he began negotiations on a plot of land just north of the Lawn Road Flats and wrote to friends asking if they would be interested in forming a company to build another apartment block. The project, dubbed 'Isokon 1½', included plans for two studios, an office and a restaurant. His ideas about the facilities he wished to offer residents had become more ambitious and he was also looking at extending those at Lawn Road. He approached Hampstead Lawn Tennis Club with a view to building and sharing new tennis courts, a pavilion and swimming pool. This fell through, but Pritchard had other irons in the fire.

'Isokon 2' was the proposed apartment block in Manchester, which he had offered to Gropius, while he was still in Germany. Gropius and Fry travelled to Manchester at the end of October 1934 to survey the riverside site and they presented Pritchard with an estimate of £13,000 to build a block of flats. Pritchard consulted W.H. Robinson, a local estate agent. He advised they could achieve a maximum rent of £75 per annum for a double flat and £50 per annum for a single, but he told Pritchard he doubted there was sufficient demand. Molly, Graham Maw and Robert Swinton met to discuss the finances, but concluded the plan was not viable. The plans for Manchester were shelved.[1]

'Isokon 4' ('Isokon 3' is covered below) was a scheme intended for a site in the Selly Park suburb of Birmingham owned by Philip Sargant Florence. In March 1935 Gropius and Fry went to survey the land and Gropius gave a speech to the local branch of the Design and Industries Association (DIA). He presented Pritchard with a proposal for a block of 24 flats, each 9 × 9m (30 × 30ft) – 10.7 × 10.7m (35 × 35ft)[2] and comprising three rooms, a kitchen and bathroom. He estimated the total building cost would be around £27,500 or £1,150 per flat. When Pritchard informed him that he could only get financing for a project of less than £12,000, Gropius suggested three cheaper options for smaller blocks. However, it transpired that local planning regulations permitted only four houses per acre and the Birmingham plan was also dropped.

WALTER GROPIUS IN LONDON, OCTOBER 1934 TO MARCH 1937

His first spring in London was a difficult time for Gropius, personally and professionally. Although his primary aim in coming to Britain was to establish

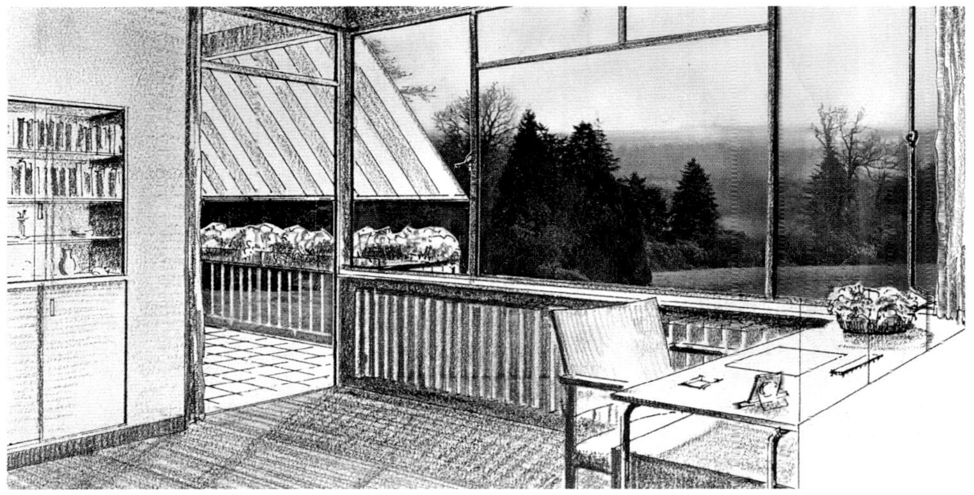

ABOVE: A design for Gropius and Fry's 1935 abandoned Isokon 3 development in Windsor.

an architectural practice, he had briefly considered establishing an 'English Bauhaus' and had discussed the idea with Leonard and Dorothy Elmhirst and the artists Roger Fry, Richard Carline and Henry Moore. With no salary and no architectural commissions, he and Ise were chronically short of funds and in March 1935 he applied for the role of Principal of the Royal College of Art. It would have been the perfect opportunity for him to transform the teaching of art and design in Britain, but he was passed over in favour of the English academic painter Percy Jowett. In April he wrote to Pritchard apologizing for still being unable to pay the rent on his flat. Pritchard generously responded that it was a 'happiness and a privilege' to have the couple staying at Lawn Road and that he only wished their accommodation was better. He wrote: 'It is not you to be ashamed about not being on your own legs, but us, as it was our responsibility that Manchester fell through.'[2]

On 19 April, Gropius's ex-wife Alma Mahler-Werfel sent a telegram informing him that their 19-year-old daughter Manon was dangerously ill. With Pritchard's help, Gropius applied for the necessary paperwork to travel to see her. It came too late. On 21 April he received the devastating news that Manon had died. He and Ise travelled to Germany, but were denied permission to go to Vienna to visit his daughter's grave.

On his return to London, he spent the next months finalizing publication of his book *New Architecture and the Bauhaus* with Faber & Faber. Philip Morton Shand advised on the translation from German and when Moholy-Nagy arrived in London in May, he was asked to design the dust jacket. The book, which contained

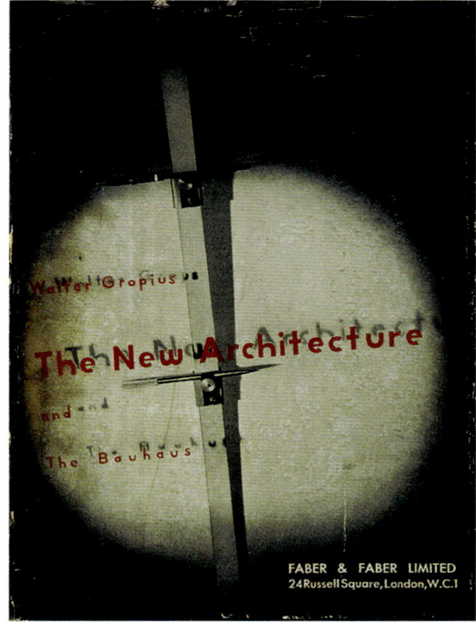

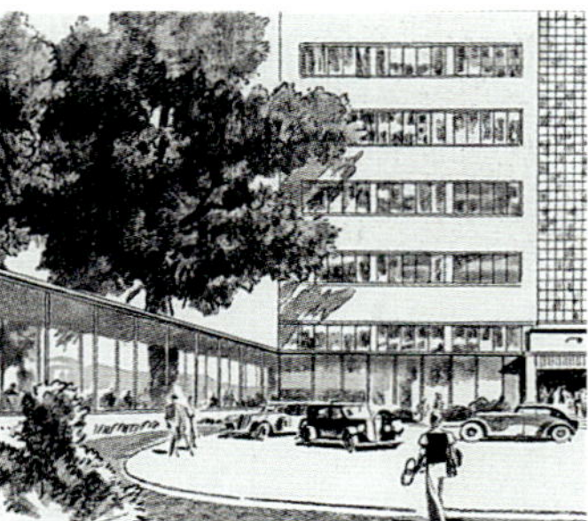

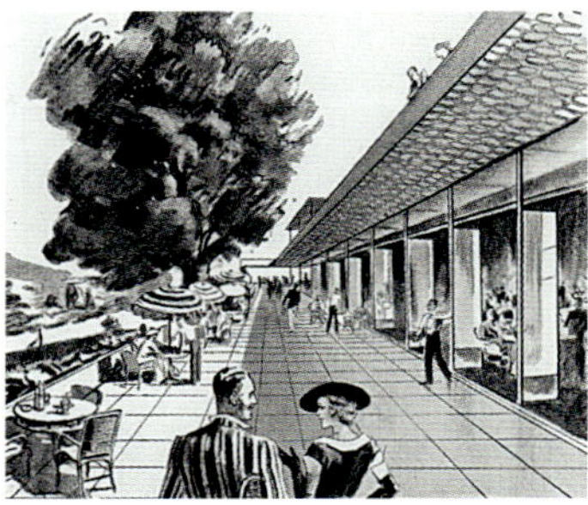

ABOVE, LEFT: Moholy-Nagy designed the cover for Gropius's *The New Architecture and the Bauhaus*. Philip Morton Shand oversaw the translation. ABOVE, RIGHT: Fleetwood Pritchard designed the prospectus for the doomed St Leonard's Hill project in Windsor.

an introduction by the influential Frank Pick (President of the DIA and CEO of the London Underground), was published in June and received favourable reviews from a wide range of publications. In his review for *Scrutiny*, Herbert Read underlined Gropius's influence on modern life:

> *You cannot enter a house anywhere in the world that has any pretence to modernity, which does not bear, in some of its details if not in its whole design, some trace of the Bauhaus influence.*[3]

Architect & Building News, however, queried Bauhaus teaching practices. It asked where the school had found its 'industrial experts', questioned whether they could actually teach and enquired how German industry had responded to the Bauhaus?

In an attempt to foster links between the Bauhauslers and British industry, Pritchard invited Robert Dudley Best, owner of the Birmingham-based lighting company, Best & Lloyd and chairman of the local Birmingham DIA, to dinner at the penthouse to meet Gropius, Moholy-Nagy and their wives. Best had been aware of the Bauhaus since 1926 and had visited Dessau in 1933 with publisher Noel Carrington. He invited Gropius, Sigfried Giedion and Moholy-Nagy to visit his factory in Birmingham and asked what they considered be the most useful activity for promoting good design. Gropius advised: 'Exhibitions. Entrust them to one man at a time. Let him choose his collaborators. Let them be extreme and revolutionary.'

The most ambitious of Jack Pritchard's property plans was 'Isokon 3'. In 1935 he had discovered that a large site at St Leonard's Hill, near Windsor, had come on the market. It consisted of 33 acres of parkland in the grounds of a ruined Elizabethan country house, with far-reaching views over Windsor Castle and Eton College. On 1 July 1935, Pritchard formed a company, Isokon 3, with Fleetwood Pritchard, Graham Maw and Professor Charles Reilly as its directors. He purchased a six-month option on the site and asked Gropius and Fry to design a development of apartments offering 'a country gentleman's life near London'.

Their plan consisted of two parallel blocks containing a total of 110 flats, ranging in size from one to seven rooms. In the larger flats, the separate dining and sitting rooms could be opened up into one generous, double-aspect living space measuring 4.3 × 10.7m (14 × 35ft). As at Lawn Road, it was proposed that a full range of services would be provided and the two blocks were linked by a communal area containing restaurant, bar and ballroom. The grounds would contain a swimming pool, tennis courts and underground car parking. There would be an on-site nursery and playground with 'a fully qualified member of staff' employed to care for children. The proposed rents were £100 – £500 per annum.

Once again, Jack called on the expertise of Fleetwood's marketing agency. They advised pitching the scheme as an environmental one. Rather than destroying the landscape with hundreds of houses, Isokon's St Leonard's Hill development would house 500 people in less than an acre, leaving the surrounding 32 acres of mature parkland untouched. Their plans were outlined in a five-page article in *Architectural Review*, entitled 'Cry Stop to Havoc or Preservation by Development'.[4] A fund-raising launch was held at the Café Royal and an exhibition with models, plans and photographs was held at Hamptons, St James's Square.

The plans advanced. As the project would overlook Windsor castle, approval was sought and granted from the Crown. Jack, however, fell ill at this point (possibly psychosomatically) and was unable to raise enough capital to launch the scheme. Bitter and disappointed, he laid part of the blame at Fleetwood's door.

I should have asked Moholy to design the folder, but instead asked
my brother Fleetwood to do the job. They had a high reputation for

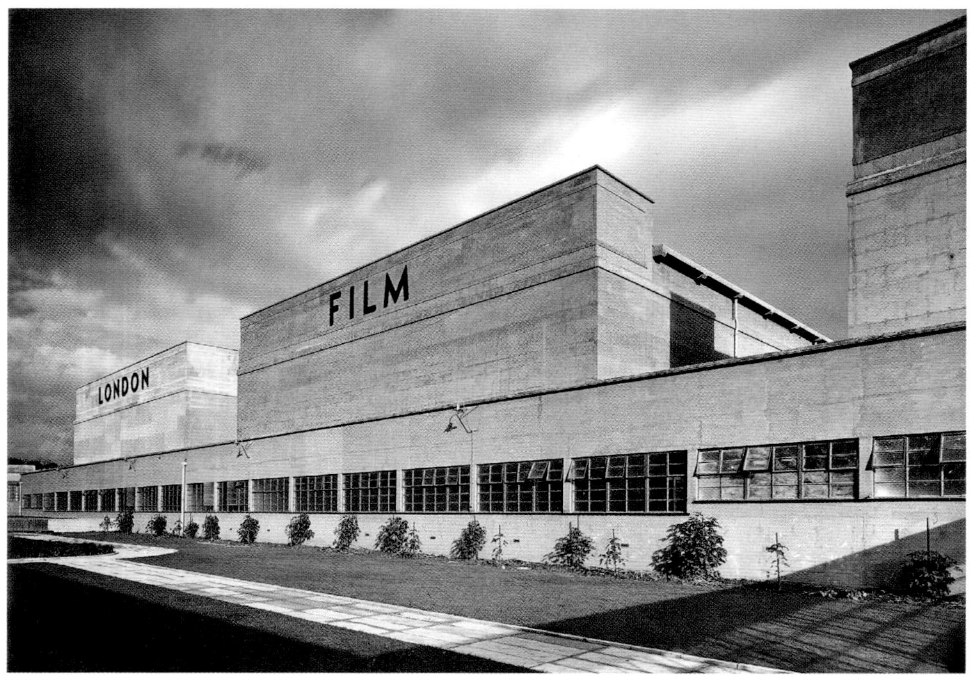

ABOVE: Alexander Korda's London Films studios opened in Denham, Buckinghamshire in 1936. Walter Gropius swore that he would never work for Korda again.

sound marketing and advertising and produced a conventional job but it had no charisma. Had Moholy done the job it would have had a far more powerful influence and might have tipped the balance; as it was, we were not far off from success.[5]

More devastating perhaps, was Jack's sense that he had failed Walter Gropius: 'You will think me a broken reed. First No.2 goes phut – then No.3 … and you will think that we asked you to London for nothing,' he wrote.[6]

On New Year's Day 1936 Ise's sister Hertha died, leaving a 10-year-old daughter, Beate, known as 'Ati', whom Walter and Ise adopted. When she joined them in London, she followed Jonathan and Jeremy Pritchard to Bertrand and Dora Russell's Beacon Hill school, in West Sussex.

Gropius's next commission came via another exile. Hungarian film director Alexander Korda had set up his own production company, London Films, in 1932 and with his brother Vincent working as his artistic director, the pair had established a reputation for the lavishness and scale of their film sets. They were

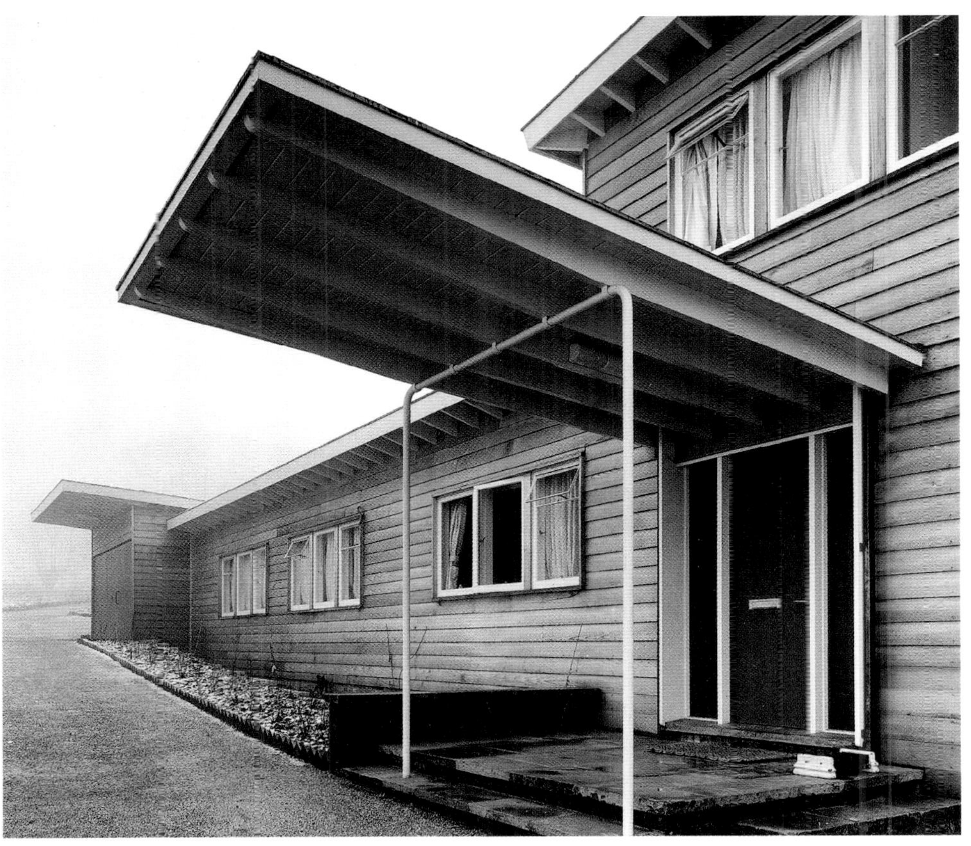

ABOVE: The Wood House by Gropius and Fry, in Shipbourne, Kent.

building Europe's biggest and best-equipped film studio on a 28-acre site at Denham in Buckinghamshire, and Korda asked Gropius and Fry to complete the design of his new film laboratory. Its steel frame had already been erected by the time the architects were instructed, so their creative input in the project was limited.[7] The resulting three-storey building, with its flat roof, steel-framed windows and long, horizontal balconies, bears a passing resemblance to the Lawn Road Flats, but Gropius and Fry were heavily constrained by the existing plans, fire regulations and huge difficulties with the clients themselves. Jack Howe, then a young assisting architect in their practice, recalled that the Kordas:

> *…behaved disgracefully. They gave instructions and counter instructions to the contractors and sub-contractors without any*

Although it had proved an unpleasant commission, it had paid £700 and
Gropius and Fry broke away from the architectural firm of Adams and Thompson
and set up as a two-man practice in offices at 171 Victoria Street. There they were
joined by a steady stream of young architects, some of whom were Fry's students
from the London Polytechnic, where he had lectured since 1932, and others from
Professor Charles Reilly's School of Architecture at Liverpool University (his son
Paul was now Gropius's neighbour in the Lawn Road Flats). Gropius's position
as an elder statesman of the 'new architecture' was reinforced by the publication
that year of Nikolaus Pevsner's *Pioneers of the Modern Movement from William Morris
to Walter Gropius.* The book placed him firmly in a historical trajectory with its
beginnings in England. Gropius now applied for permission to settle permanently
in Britain and his application to the Secretary of State was supported by Ian
MacAlister, Secretary of the Royal Institute of British Architects (RIBA).

Gropius and Fry's first residential commission was a house at 66 Old Church
Street in Chelsea, for playwright Benn Levy and his wife, American film actress
Constance Cummings. Although Gropius had suggested building in brick the
clients insisted on a dazzling white 'Californian style house', which was built
on a site adjoining a newly completed villa by Serge Chermayeff and Erich
Mendelsohn. This was owned by Levy's cousin, the publisher Dennis Cohen,
and the two houses opened onto a large shared garden. Gropius positioned the
Levy house directly against the street, with only its front door, a ribbon of small
windows and garage visible from the road. The building's pristine glamour was
preserved for its private garden view. He and Fry designed an asymmetrical, three-
storey house with a flat roof and curved terrace and loggia to the rear. The living
and dining rooms were linked with full-height sliding screens and the exterior
was punctuated by a series of balconies and terraces. Despite its stark modernity,
Gropius and Fry ensured the roof lines of the house blended in with its historic
Chelsea surroundings and *The Times* noted approvingly:

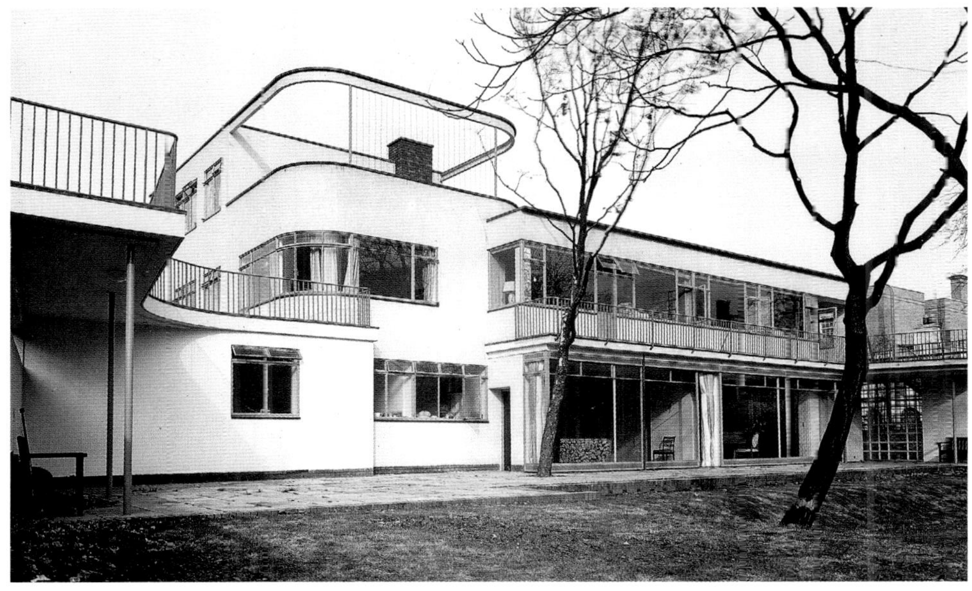

In a sense these are the most advanced buildings in London,
but the odd thing is that they not only tone in with the general
character of the neighbourhood, but seem to have a definite
relationship to some old, possibly eighteenth century houses
in the same street.

The following year, Gropius designed his only English country house for politician Jack Donaldson and his wife Frances, a writer.[9] Their site in Shipbourne, near Sevenoaks, lay on sloping land with long views over meadows and woodland. The Wood House was entirely oak framed, infilled with concrete blocks and clad in cedar planks and the modest, two-storey structure was insulated with wool. Gropius gave it overhanging eaves, a cantilevered porch and a glazed screen of opaque glass at the rear. He created a 'sleeping' porch on the first floor which could be used as an open-air bedroom in the summer.[10] Inside he installed a fireplace made from the local black knapped flints, which he had admired in the local countryside. He had listened carefully to the Donaldsons' requirements and they found the distinguished architect a pleasure to work with.

Although none of Pritchard's Isokon housing schemes had materialized, Gropius's introduction to his greatest friend and mentor Henry Morris, Secretary of Cambridgeshire City Council's Education Committee, did result in one important public commission during his stay in Britain, although it was completed after his departure. In 1925 Morris had written a famous memorandum proposing the establishment of Village Colleges, to stem the tide of rural depopulation, by providing education for entire communities, from 'cradle to grave'.

Two very different visionaries, who nonetheless shared a passion for educational reform, Gropius and Morris had hit it off at their first meeting. Gropius had won over Morris, someone with traditional tastes for 'Mozart, fine hock and Italian architecture' to the cause of Modernism, so that he was now: 'convinced intellectually, technically and aesthetically, not only to the inevitability of the new forms of modern architecture, but eager and enthusiastic to embrace this chance of a new beginning'.[12] He invited Gropius to design a prototype Village College, but knew that persuading the council to employ a foreign architect would be difficult. He enlisted the support of Ian MacAlister of RIBA and the professors of Architecture and Fine Art at the Universities of Cambridge, Liverpool and London. They wrote to Cambridgeshire Council arguing that:

Jack Pritchard mobilized supporters to pay Gropius's fee and managed to raise £1,200 from private sources, some coming from his own pocket. A 12-acre site in

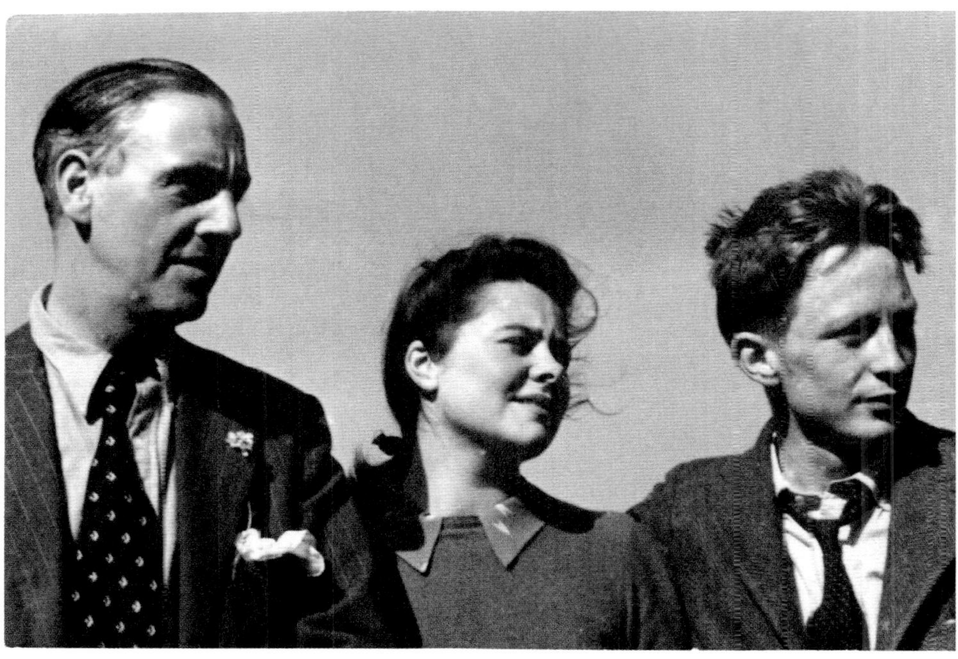

the grounds of Impington Hall, the ancestral home of Samuel Pepys, was donated by the local Chivers family, who topped up the council's contribution of £20,000 with a further gift of £8,000 to fund an adult wing.

Gropius began work on the plans in summer 1936. Building on his experience at the Bauhaus, he allowed the social functions of the college to determine his plan. The school was approached via a welcoming wedge-shaped assembly hall with a broad, overhanging porch. At its heart was a long, broad 'promenade' corridor, which served as the spine and social focus of the college. A single-storey wing, which branched off it, led to bright, airy classrooms with floor-to-ceiling windows opening onto gardens. In the adult wing there was a formal plywood-panelled common room, recreation rooms and a library. Maxwell Fry supervised the construction of Impington after Gropius's departure for America and it was completed in 1939. Due to financial constraints, the library and lecture rooms were reduced in size and the gym and a planned outdoor sculpture by Henry Moore were dropped. Even so, it was an influential design, which provided a template for system-built state schools after World War II. Nikolaus Pevsner described it as 'one of the best buildings of its date in England, if not the best.'

Despite Gropius's rejection by the Royal College of Art, overtures continued to

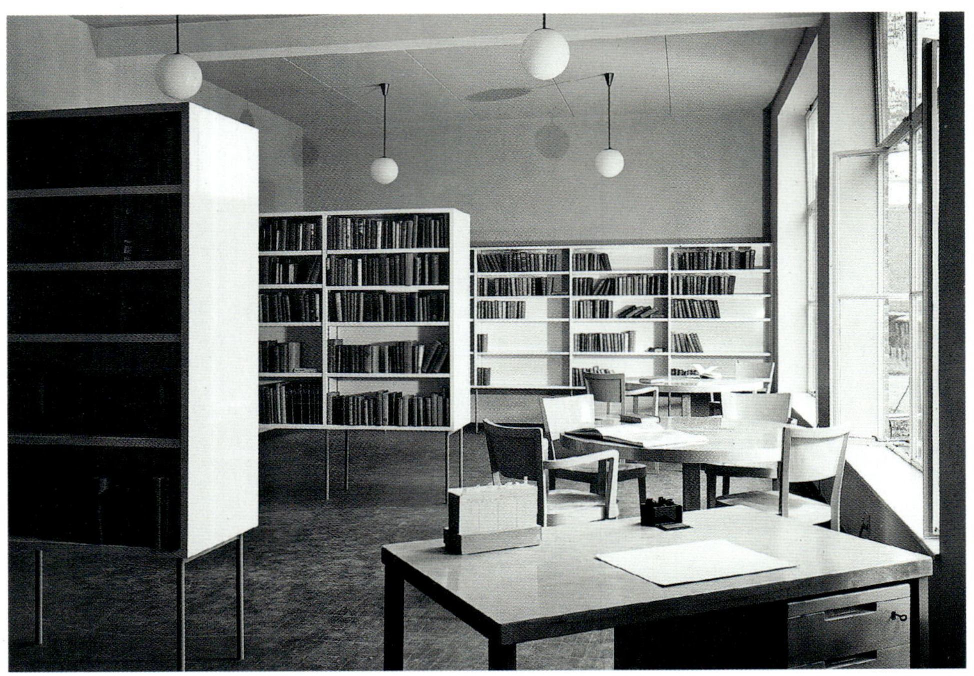

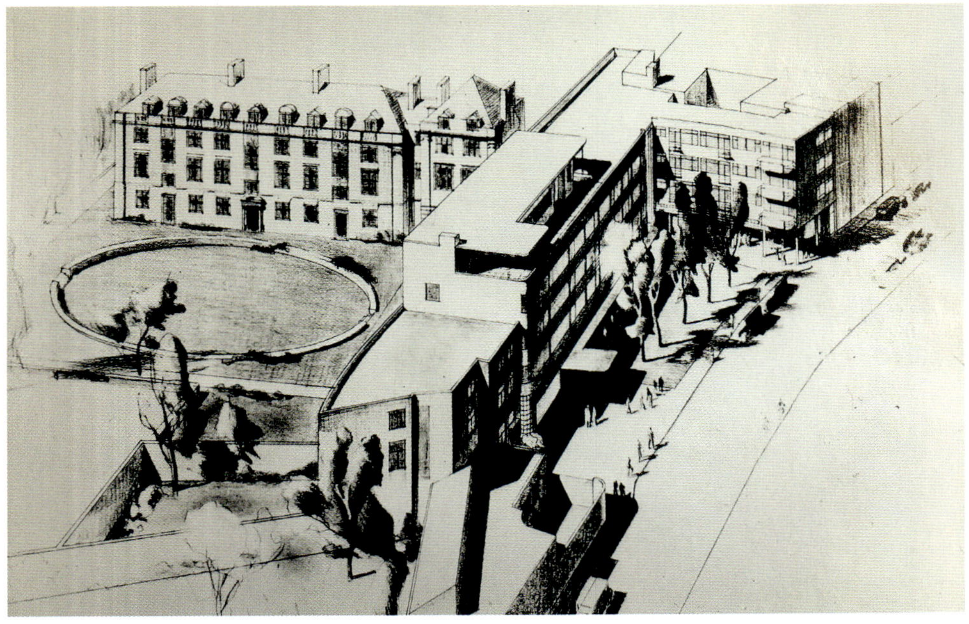

ABOVE, TOP: The light-filled library at Impington Village College, completed after Gropius departed for Harvard. ABOVE: Gropius' radical design for Christ's College Cambridge, which included plans for ten shops on the adjoining Hobson Street.

come from America. In July 1936 Alfred Barr, Director of New York's Museum
of Modern Art visited him in London, in an attempt to lure him to Harvard. In
August, Joseph Hudnut, Dean of Harvard's School of Architecture, met Gropius
in Rotterdam, but still failed to persuade him. Hudnut was persistent, however,
and arranged for James Conant, President of Harvard, to visit Gropius in London
that October. When Conant agreed that Gropius could combine teaching with
a private architectural practice, and would not have to give lectures, a deal was
finally struck. Hudnut delightedly wrote to Gropius confirming that he would be
appointed Nelson Robinson, Jr., Professor of Architecture on 1 February 1937.

> *Your presence at Harvard University will not only be of the*
> *greatest possible value to this institution but, beyond that,*
> *I feel the service you can render to the cause of architecture*
> *in this country is valuable beyond all calculation.*[14]

While these discussions had been taking place, the prospect of a high-profile
commission had emerged from one of Britain's great academic institutions.
Biologist Conrad Hal Waddington invited Gropius to Christ's College, Cambridge,
to discuss a scheme for a new building. The brief was to build a wing on the
north side of the college's Third Court. It should house two 'sets' for fellows of the
college and provide accommodation for as many undergraduates as possible. He
was invited to compete for the £40,000 project against Oswald P. Milne and Percy
Morley Horder.

Gropius proposed constructing a four-storey steel-framed building, clad in local
Ketton stone to harmonize with the rest of the college. The ground floor facing
Third Court would be glazed with glass bricks and, on the three floors above,
each student room would have a balcony overlooking the courtyard, as they had
done at the Dessau Bauhaus. The site ran parallel to Hobson Street and Gropius
suggested building ten shops facing into the road to create a public area in which
pedestrians could meet and shop under mature trees. It was a radical proposal
that would take down the college's historic boundary wall and open it up to the
town.[15] He gave a presentation to the college, reassuring them in confidence
that although he was leaving for the US, the scheme would be continued in his
absence by the capable Maxwell Fry. However, their plans were voted down by
the college by 13 votes to 8, and ultimately with building costs rising the project
was abandoned until after the war.[16] Fry recalled: 'It was a bitter blow for Gropius
and it precipitated the end of our work together, as I sensed growing insistence of
the offers being made to him by Harvard.'

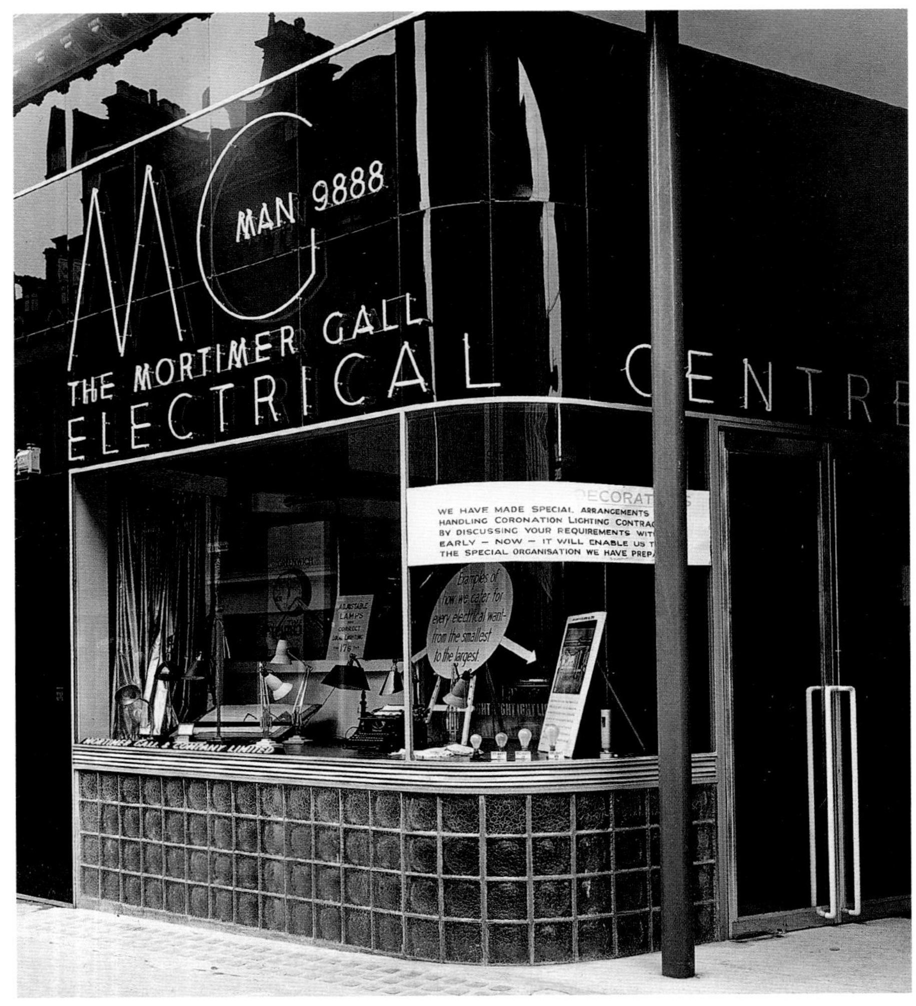

ABOVE: Gropius and Fry's Mortimer Gall Electrical Centre in Cannon Street, 1937.

Gropius had managed to keep his discussions with Conant and Hudnut private, but he informed Jack Pritchard that he had accepted their offer over lunch on 28 November 1936.[17]

In early 1937 Gropius and Fry designed the Mortimer Gall Electrical Centre, a small store in Cannon Street in the City of London. They removed the 19th-century ground-floor shop front and replaced it with a distinctive curved façade faced with black glass and glass bricks. The first storey was supported by a single steel column and its stainless-steel entrance doors were set at a right angle to the street to create a concrete porch.[18]

Gropius's appointment at Harvard was formally announced in *The Times* on 26 January 1937. It was excellent timing, noted Pritchard, for the opening a few days later, of his unlikely swansong – 'The Flat of 1937' at the Kendal Milne department store in Manchester. The suite of rooms contained three Breuer chairs, the Isokon bookshelves and six stools. Showing a surprising sensitivity to Kendal Milne's feminine customer base, Gropius upholstered a Long Chair in quilted chintz. A local journalist observed him making final preparations to the display.

> *The professor regarded the room point by point, from the chromium shades of the indirect lighting on the cedar-panelled walls to the circular turntable fitted dining room table. He frowned. Evidently something was not quite right. Then he bent and moved the large sofa of his own design two-eighths of an inch to the left.*[19]

The store's Coronation Year catalogue contained a centre spread of the Gropius interior-designed flat, which was sent out to 10,000 of its clients.

On 23 February Gropius wrote to Pritchard proposing that Marcel Breuer should succeed him as the Isokon Furniture Company's Controller of Design:

> *He is a most brilliant man, in my opinion even the most gifted original architect of the younger generation, possessing genuine creative power... As a rule I am not in the habit of using superlatives, but I feel Breuer deserves them.*[20]

MOHOLY-NAGY IN LONDON, MAY 1935 TO JUNE 1937

When László Moholy-Nagy and his wife Sibyl arrived in London in May 1935, he had a job waiting at *International Textiles,* the publication he had worked for in Amsterdam. The journal's London office was located on the Strand, between the River Thames, the newspapers of Fleet Street and the flower market and opera house of Covent Garden, giving Moholy-Nagy – a keen social observer – a glimpse into every walk of English life. Initially his unorthodox ideas on type and layout shocked the London printers of *International Textiles,* but soon his work attracted the attention of W.S. Crawford, the journal's publicity agency. Crawford's had an office in Berlin and its London staff were aware of Bauhaus graphic-design ideas. They sent so many commissions Moholy-Nagy's way, that before long he began working 16-hour days.

By the end of 1935, he had created several high-profile advertising campaigns for Trubenizing shirts, Abdullah Cigarettes and Imperial Airways, Britain's only international airline. His brief for Imperial was to convince the public that long-haul air travel could be both affordable and luxurious. To this end, he organized an exhibition on air travel at London's Science Museum and designed 'The Empire's Airway', a mobile exhibition, housed (rather incongruously) in a railroad car, which toured British colonies. While he was still working on this project, London Transport asked him to design a series of posters, promoting the latest technological developments in underground travel. He collaborated on many of these jobs with his artistic partner from Berlin, fellow Hungarian György Kepes, who had joined him in London.

British documentary film-making was coming of age and the pioneering English director John Grierson, owned a copy of Moholy-Nagy's 1930 abstract film *Light-play Black-White-Gray*. Grierson introduced him to John Mathias, a wealthy young producer, who in the summer of 1935 commissioned him to direct *Lobsters*, one of the first aquatic films, for his company, Bury Productions. The film was set on the Sussex Coast and Moholy-Nagy spent several weeks in Littlehampton, getting to know the lobster-fishing community and filming the fleet on its daily outings. The underwater sequences, explaining the life cycle of the lobster, were shot in a specially built tank at Port Erin on the Isle of Man.[21] The 16-minute film contains many of Moholy-Nagy's artistic trademarks – shifting patterns of light, abstract shapes and close-ups of the crustaceans' forms, which reflected his fascination with biological structures. During filming, Mathias invited the Moholy-Nagys to stay at his manor house in Sussex. The artist enjoyed this glimpse into the lifestyle of the English upper-class. Sibyl recalled:

> *Things which irritated me – the feudal relationship between master and servant, the clannishness of the men, the coldness of the women, and the drilled, unnatural politeness of the children – were for him object lessons to which he devoted himself with uncritical attention. He hadn't come to England to judge the English. He had come to demonstrate a new vision, and he was grateful for each clue handed him toward a right psychological approach.[22]*

The film, which was part-funded by Alexander Korda, was completed in June 1936. On a visit to Denham Studios with Gropius, Moholy-Nagy met Vincent Korda, an old friend from Vienna. The Kordas were producing H.G. Wells's dystopian sci-fi fantasy *Things to Come*. Fernand Léger and Le Corbusier had been

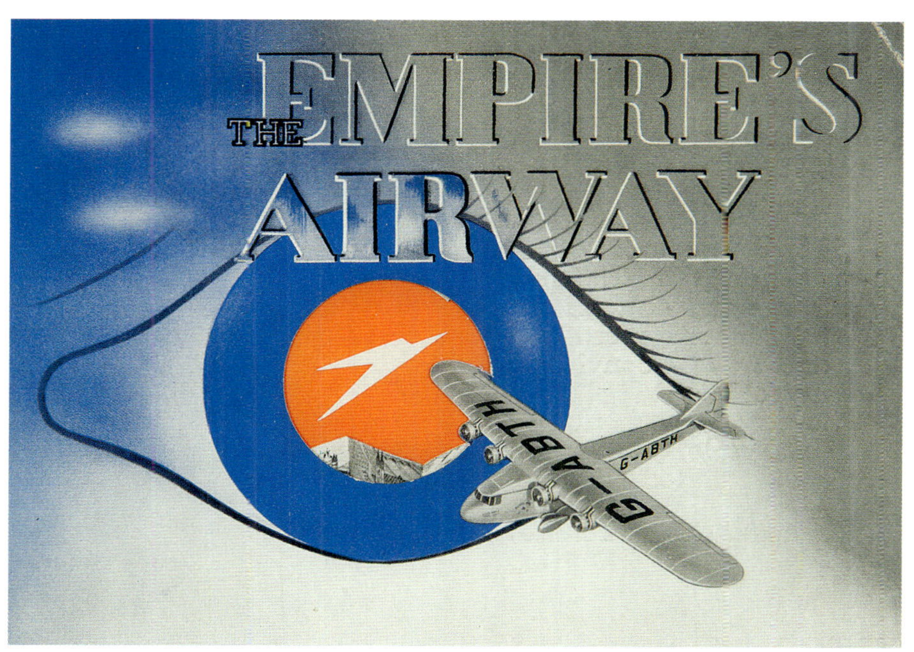

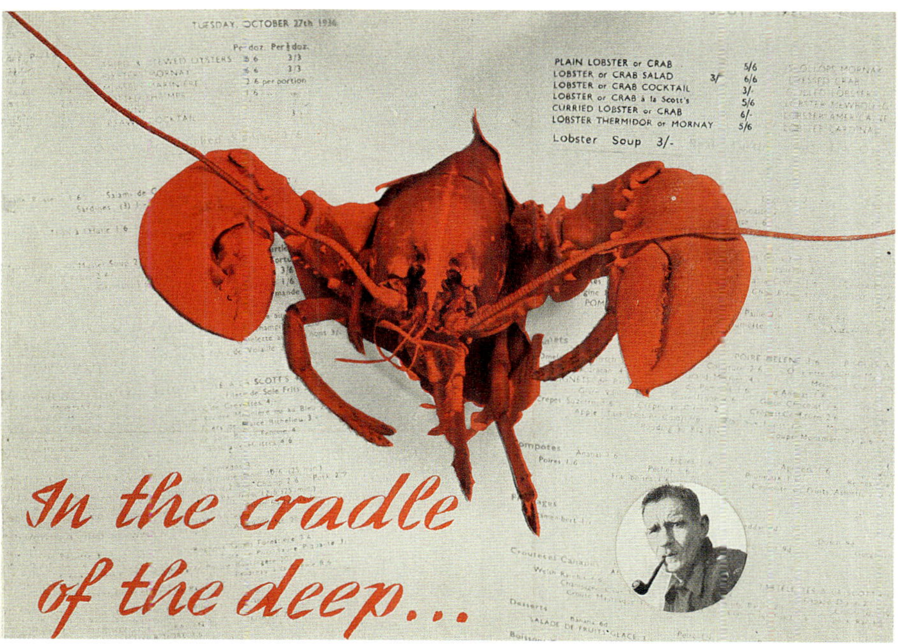

ABOVE, TOP: Moholy-Nagy worked on a range of advertising campaigns for Imperial Airways.
ABOVE: Moholy-Nagy immersed himself in the fishing community of Littlehampton during filming of John Mathias's *Lobsters*.

invited to design the film's sets, but when negotiations with them broke down, Vincent Korda had created them himself, using Le Corbusier's *Vers Un Architecture* as a guide. The Kordas commissioned Moholy-Nagy to create a specific five-and-a-half-minute sequence for the film, depicting the reconstruction of *Everytown* between 1970 and 2054 and Moholy-Nagy worked on the project between November and mid-December 1935.[23] Intrigued by the brightly coloured stocks of Rhodoid, a plastic display material being used on set, he often stayed at the studios late at night to experiment. 'He was fascinated by the idea of constructing scale models which through a skilful use of camera angle and lighting could create the illusion of superhuman dimensions,' Sibyl recalled. At the same time Russian Constructivist, Naum Gabo, who had lectured at the Dessau Bauhaus, and was now living nearby at 11 Lawn Road, was experimenting with the new material, Perspex, which he obtained from a friend working for the chemicals company ICI.

H.G. Wells, who was closely involved in the production of the film, had specified that the sequence should contain a 'fantasia of powerful rotating and swinging forms'. Moholy-Nagy used the score by modernist composer Arthur Bliss to dictate the rhythm of a montage using smoke, glass tubes, mercury, revolving rollers and shafts of light. He was understandably dismayed to find at the film's premiere the following year that all but 90 seconds of his work had been left on the cutting-room floor. (Four short sections of his discarded sequence were rediscovered in 1975.) However, his experiments with Rhodoid proved artistically fruitful. He brought home a sheet of the material to create the first of his *Space Modulator* series, a hybrid of painting and sculpture, exploring light and shadow, and spent the next few months in an enormous surge of creativity. [24]

> *He made numerous pencil and crayon sketches, all marked*
> *'Third Dimension'. He sketched in barber shops and subway*
> *trains, while he had luncheon or waited for an appointment.*
> *Every business letter had a sketch on its back and his shirt*
> *cuffs and handkerchiefs were smeared with crayon, hastily*
> *wiped off his fingers before going into a conference or*
> *shooting a picture.*

In 1935, clothing manufacturer Alexander Simpson was building the largest menswear store in London on a prestigious site in St James's. The six-storey building, designed by Joseph Emberton, was faced in Portland stone and had distinctive concave windows spanning its frontage on Piccadilly and at the rear in Jermyn Street. Simpson wanted to revolutionize men's luxury retailing by

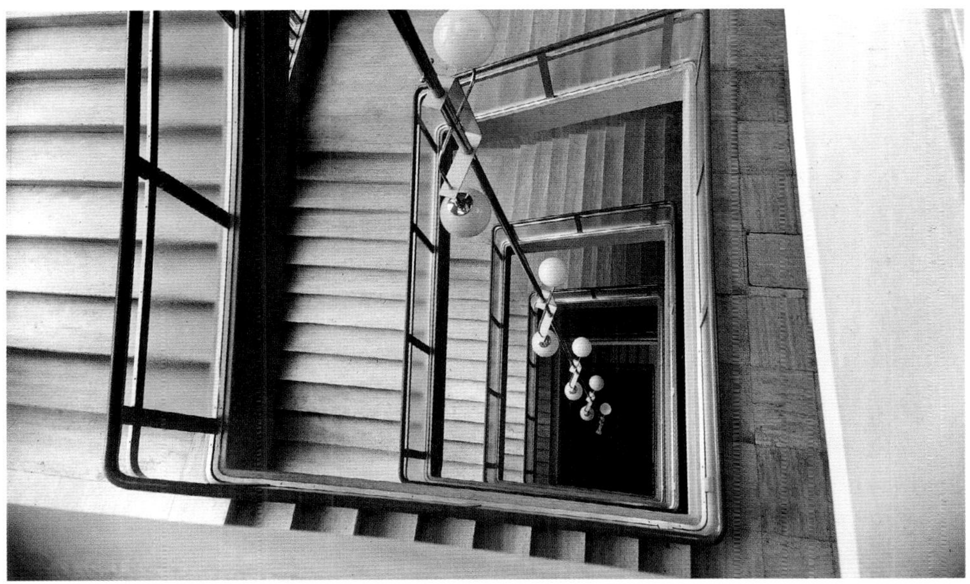

presenting clothes and accessories in a 'modern' manner. Ashley Havinden (head of A.S. Crawford's art department) who designed Simpson's advertising and logos, recommended Moholy-Nagy and Alexander Simpson offered him a permanent position as the store's 'art advisor'.[25] His brief was extensive. It included all signage, visual merchandising, windows and in-store displays. Simpson also employed György Kepes on a similar basis.

Moholy-Nagy's approach was to create visual impact in the store by presenting familiar objects in an unexpected manner, giving what he called 'a mild electric shock to the eye'. He devised heat-formed body shapes of transparent plastic to display clothing and installed Bauhaus light fittings in the store. As the deadline for the opening approached, the work became all-consuming. While the Royal Photographic Society was showing an exhibition of his work in Russell Square, he was organizing an exhibition on aviation on Simpson's fifth floor. He ordered three aircraft, a Gipsy Moth biplane, a Flying Flea and a Supermarine seaplane, which had to be winched up the store's monumental central staircase. When he failed to return home the night before the grand opening on 29 April 1936, a desperately worried Sibyl went to Piccadilly in the early morning. She found him standing on a stepladder in Simpson's window hanging fishing nets, his bare feet bleeding as he chatted to reporters. His colourful and original windows, which resembled 'a still life of men's fashion' were declared a triumph and Moholy-Nagy's aviation exhibition received a great deal of excited press coverage. In July, the planes were replaced by a 'Boat Exhibition', which included speedboats, dinghies and collapsible craft. He also suggested to Alexander Simpson that Breuer should design a 'bachelor's apartment' within the store. Simpson had its own photographic studio and in his spare moments, Moholy-Nagy returned to his experiments with colour film stock. He brought samples of Rhodoid into the studio and shot them using Dufaycolour with different exposures and under different coloured lighting. He also took some early colour portraits, including one of his close friend and colleague, the cartoonist and art critic Harry Blacker.

In 1933 Moholy-Nagy had photographed writer Penelope Chetwode, who was now married to *Architectural Review*'s Assistant Editor John Betjeman. It was to be a useful connection. Betjeman put him in touch with publisher Harry F. Paroissien, who commissioned him to illustrate three books, Mary Benedetta's *The Street Markets of London,* Bernard Fergusson's *Eton Portrait* and Betjeman's *An Oxford University Chest.* Moholy-Nagy approached the subjects with the objectivity of an outsider and like the work of many 1930s émigré photographers, such as Edith Tudor-Hart and Bill Brandt, his images of the street-market traders of Depression London, had a sharp edge of social reportage. By contrast, his impressions of Eton school are cinematic, shot from unexpected angles and framed with his artist's eye. Harry Blacker, who accompanied him on walks, recalled his working methods:

> *Moholy would stop suddenly to frame some object and its surround*
> *with his fingers as he discussed its abstract implications or he*
> *would call at street market stalls to browse through and purchase*
> *Victorian photograph albums which he regarded as highly valuable*
> *social records.*[26]

He used these collected Victorian images in a major commission from J.M. Richards, Editor of *Architectural Review*, who asked him to design and shoot a 28-page feature entitled 'Leisure at the Seaside', which was full of innovative graphic ideas, including a page made from thick yellow card, pierced with circular peep holes through which the reader could view English beach scenes.[27]

Moholy-Nagy was now juggling several careers, working in graphic design, retail display, film and photography and then returning to his studio at night to paint. Sibyl recalled: 'He shuffled his different jobs like a deck of cards, getting innumerable new combinations but finding them all part of the same game.' By summer 1936, his phenomenal workload was taking its toll and he was granted a

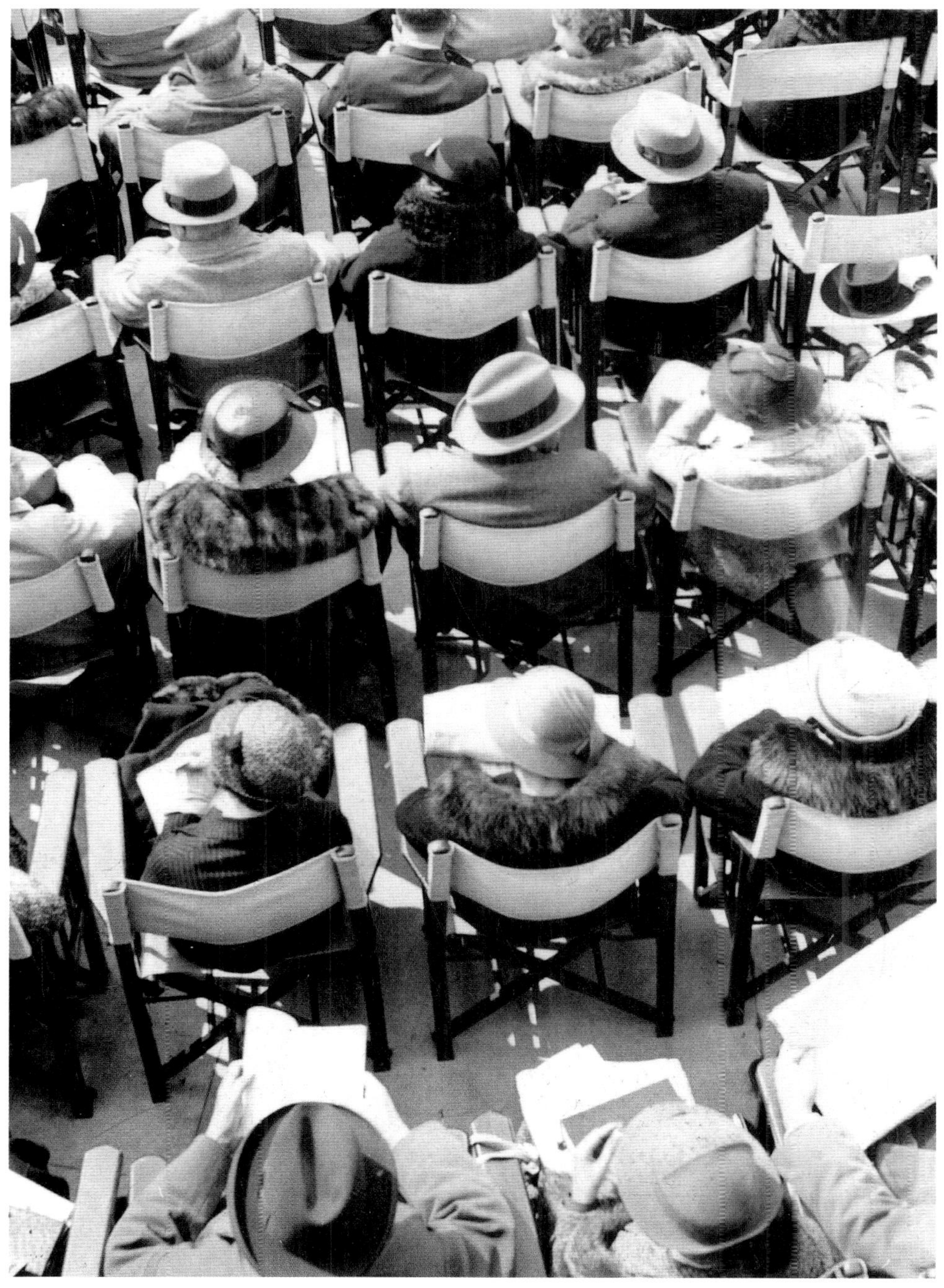

ABOVE: Moholy-Nagy was a keen observer of British social life. In 1936 he designed a 28-page feature entitled 'Leisure at the Seaside' for *Architectural Review*.

two-month leave of absence by Alexander Simpson. Just as he was making plans for a holiday with Sibyl, who had recently given birth to their second daughter Claudia, a photographic agency commissioned him to film and photograph the forthcoming Olympic Games in Berlin. All thoughts of a holiday were forgotten and he headed for Berlin. On the first day of the Games, he bumped into one of his old Bauhaus students, dressed in the uniform of Hitler's SS, who assured the shocked Moholy-Nagy he was simply 'playing the game'. He then discovered that his former Berlin housekeeper had destroyed all of his most recent work. Appalled by what he saw as a sharp decline in Germany's moral climate he abandoned the commission and left after just three days, announcing: 'I'll never go back'.

In London he continued with his commercial work but from autumn 1936, became increasingly preoccupied with painting, finding kindred spirits in the artistic circles of Hampstead, who affectionately nicknamed him 'Holy Mahogany'. He frequented the Old Mall studios, exchanging ideas with sculptors Henry Moore and Barbara Hepworth before returning home to Golders Green to work late into the night. Like Gropius, he explored the possibility of setting up a British Bauhaus with Ben Nicholson, Leslie Martin and Naum Gabo, but any meaningful opportunity to make a mark on art education had disappeared with Gropius's failure to become principal of the RCA.

Through Pritchard, he met Julian Huxley, Secretary of the Zoological Society of London, who had recently instructed Berthold Lubetkin's architectural practice Tecton to design several highly acclaimed animal enclosures. In autumn 1936, the Museum of Modern Art in collaboration with the Architectural Department of Harvard commissioned his third British film project, a documentary on *The New Architecture and the London Zoo*. The silent short featured the revolutionary concrete, wire and glass enclosures, including the penguin pool, gorilla house and giraffe pen. He went to great lengths to capture the images he wanted, including a sequence shot at night, where he had to stand on the roof of the lion's cage, while the animal leapt beneath him, trying to catch his ankles through the bars.

Maxwell Fry asked him to create a photo-mural for his Electricity Showrooms on Regent Street and, at the end of December 1936, the London Gallery in Mayfair held the first one-man exhibition of his paintings in England. It featured his cherished 'Light Prop' of 1930, which had arrived safely from Germany. The opening, at which Gropius gave a speech, was packed and the exhibition received positive reviews. Even so, he was frustrated by how few people he could reach through his work and expressed a desire to Sibyl that he should return to the classroom:

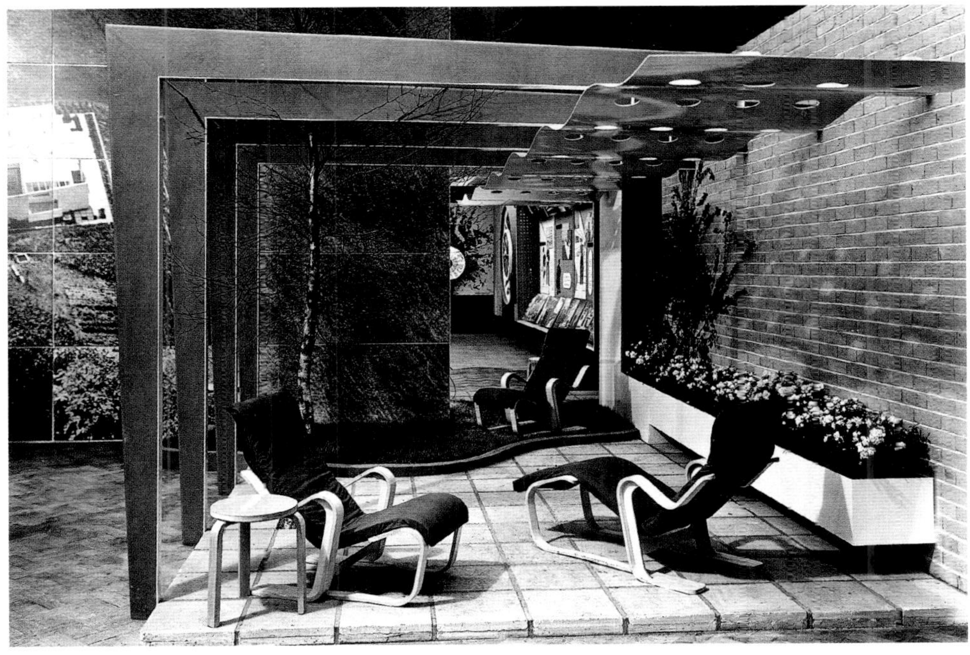

ABOVE: Le Corbusier gave the MARS exhibition of 1938 an enthusiastic write-up. It featured graphic designs by Moholy-Nagy and Isokon Long Chairs.

> *There are very few people who can look at a picture and take*
> *its basic problem home to work on it. No money one makes in*
> *the industry and no satisfaction of shows and public recognition*
> *can equal teaching.*[28]

Moholy-Nagy's role as a committee member of the Modern Architectural Research Group (MARS) resulted in his last work in Britain, the design of its landmark exhibition at the New Burlington Galleries, which opened in January 1938, after his departure for America. The graphic displays, showcasing the whole spectrum of ways in which the New Architecture, town planning, construction and technology could improve peoples' lives, drew together all of his most successful ideas on display, using photography, illustration and innovative materials. It was praised for its 'elegance' and 'the intimate eloquence of its sequence of presentations' by Le Corbusier who visited for the opening and gave it an enthusiastic write-up in *Architectural Review*.[29]

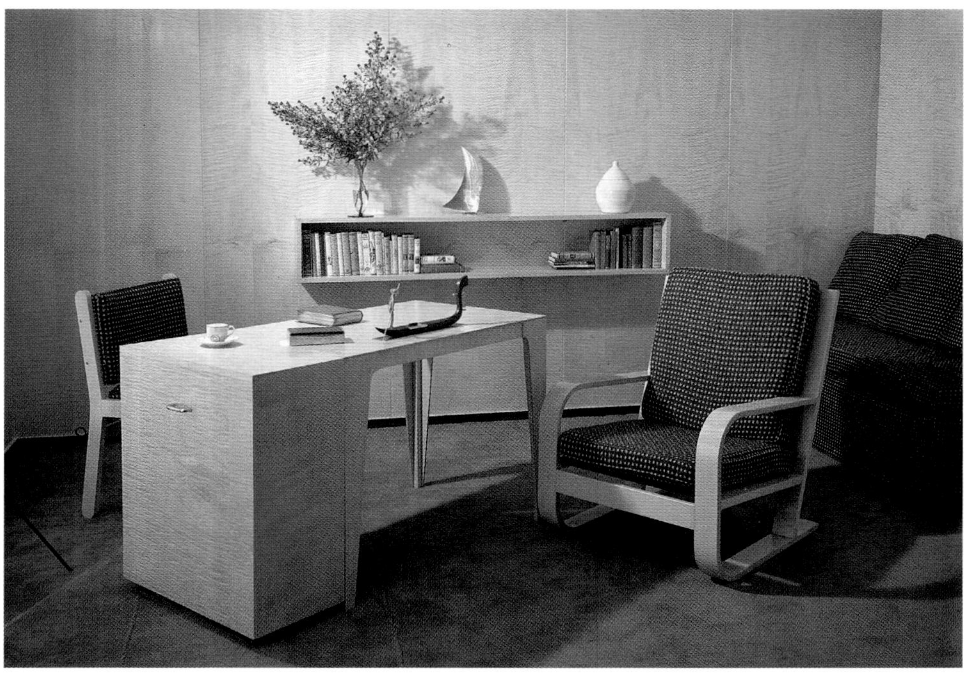

ABOVE: Much of the furniture Marcel Breuer designed in 1935 for Crofton Gane's showcase home in Bristol had to be carved from solid wood to imitate bent plywood.

MARCEL BREUER IN LONDON OCTOBER 1935 TO DECEMBER 1937

By the time Marcel Breuer arrived in London in October 1935, he already had a network of friends and acquaintances in the city, whom he had met travelling, skiing and during Les Congrès Internationaux d'Architecture Moderne (CIAM). His well-connected and famously charming new architectural partner, F.R.S. Yorke, who was Secretary of the MARS group, wrote for the architectural press and made many useful introductions. They agreed to split all revenues and expenses and that their work, including drafts, sketches, publications and exhibitions, would be signed off in both partners' names. Whose name took precedence, depended on who brought in the client.

Breuer's relationship with the Bristol furniture manufacturer and retailer Crofton Gane, whom he met through the DIA, was to be a fruitful one for the partnership. He began work for Gane on his arrival at Lawn Road in autumn 1935. Gane had just purchased a two-storey Edwardian villa in the Bristol suburb of Clifton, which he wished to transform into a showcase for the latest ideas in Modern design. He asked Breuer to remodel the interiors and design new furniture for the rooms that would be produced by his factory in the city's College Green. Breuer travelled to Bristol and began work on the project even before he agreed terms with Jack Pritchard for his role at Isokon.

He reorganized the interior spaces of Gane's house using new materials, which included a wall of white-painted corrugated asbestos sheeting in the dining room, a device he had previously used on the exterior of Sigfried Giedion's Wohnbedarf store in Basel. He also installed Britain's first cantilevered metal, open-tread interior staircase. In the dining room he used some of his own metal furniture imported from Switzerland and designed built-in cabinets of black lacquered wood. For Gane's study, Breuer designed an asymmetric plywood desk and chair, glass-topped occasional tables with plywood corners and organic, Aalto-esque bentwood armchairs. He worked closely on these pieces with P.E. Gane's chief designer J.P. Hully and his team, at the company's workshops. What they produced was a strange marriage between Modernist ideas and 19th-century workmanship. Lacking the necessary equipment to steam-bend wood, they had to carve solid timber to replicate Breuer's designs. Crofton Gane, however, was delighted with the results, which demonstrated that modern furnishings could be successfully incorporated into a real British home. Breuer's designs featured in several editions of *The Architectural Review* and provided rooms sets for Gane's 1936 catalogue *Modern Furniture*.

Another important interiors commission followed. In November 1935, just over a year after the Lawn Road Flats were completed, Highpoint One, the first of the Tecton group's pair of Modernist apartment blocks opened in Highgate. Designed by Berthold Lubetkin, the seven-storey concrete building was commissioned by office-supplies magnate Sigmund Gestetner and like the Pritchards' development, was aimed at middle-class clients. In 1936 Dorothea Ventris, a wealthy collector of modern art, who had moved into the block with her young son Michael, asked Breuer to design and decorate her apartment. Mrs Ventris had seen and admired photographs of Breuer's 1929 Harnischmacher apartment in Wiesbaden and, sacrificing her 'Persian rugs and period furniture' to make a clean break with the past, gave him *carte blanche* to create a total interior in the Modern style. Breuer designed a number of important bespoke furniture pieces for the apartment in sycamore-veneered plywood, which he had manufactured at P.E. Gane's factory.

He covered the living-room walls with tatami-style panels and, dispensing with the traditional focus of a fireplace, arranged the furniture, which included an Isokon Long Chair and Nesting Table, around a centrally placed plywood floor heater. He designed a cut-out plywood sofa and matching armchair with upholstered seats and distinctive plywood loops attached to their arms, which

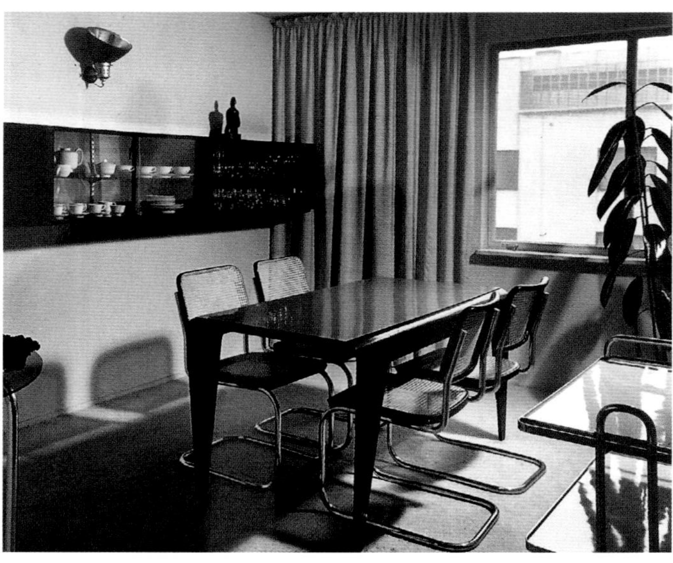

ABOVE: In 1936 Breuer used a combination of his Bauhaus, Isokon and bespoke furniture designs for the Highpoint apartment of art collector Dorothea Ventris. They were arranged together with works by Pablo Picasso, Juan Gris and Henry Moore. The dining room featured black-framed Cesca dining chairs and a black-stained Isokon table.

could be used to store books or drinks. The dining room featured a black laminated Isokon dining table with a blue Bakelite top, a set of his 1928 Cesca chairs, wall-mounted black shelves with sliding glass doors and a tubular-steel serving trolley.[30] For Dorothea Ventris's bedroom, he designed an asymmetrical dressing unit, consisting of a long wall-mounted mirror, two drawer units with red laminated tops and a pair of circular viewing mirrors for applying cosmetics. In addition to Breuer's obvious skills as architect and designer of interiors, Dorothea Ventris believed he had 'the colour-sense of a painter'.[31]

> *The terra-cotta chair-covers reminiscent of a Greek vase; the raw silk curtains; the fragility and discreetness suggested by an almost Japanese use of screens – these cultural associations make the work of Mr Breuer extraordinarily rich and enable a Sung bowl to find its perfect home as easily as a painting by Juan Gris or a piece of sculpture by Henry Moore.*

In October 1935 Maxwell Fry had written to Breuer asking if he would participate in Heal's forthcoming 'Exhibition of Contemporary Furniture by Seven Architects'. Breuer had only a few weeks to submit his design, but the fee for the work was £40 and it promised to be well-advertised. For the exhibition, which opened in March 1936 and ran throughout the summer, Breuer created a Living Room in Sycamore, which featured a full-length cantilevered wall unit, housing a cocktail cabinet, desk and gramophone. 'The housemaid's sweeping is simplified and the room gains in spaciousness' explained Heal's catalogue.[32] He also designed a sycamore-veneered plywood reclining chair with solid sides, which he upholstered in red leather. *The Evening Standard* compared it to the 'most comfortable lounging place in the world – a dentist's chair'.

Yorke and Breuer received a commission in early 1936 from the British Cement Association to create a showpiece for the Ideal Home Exhibition at Olympia demonstrating the possibilities of their new building material. Although Yorke was credited first on the project, their utopian 'Civic Centre of the Future' bears many hallmarks of Breuer's future work and contains a vocabulary of architectural forms that he would use throughout his later career. Their model contained many town-planning ideas that were well ahead of their time. All the proposed buildings were made from reinforced concrete. The centre contained a business quarter of Y-shaped office blocks and a residential sector adjoining open countryside. The housing was a combination of 12-storey apartment blocks raised on piloti and individual houses, all set in large expanses of open space, containing schools and tennis courts. The model included a hospital, theatre, a shopping mall and restaurants. An arterial road and underground railway linked the suburb to a city and aerodrome. It was the most complete vision of a Modernist utopia seen in Britain and received widespread press coverage.

In 1936, another significant commission for Breuer arrived courtesy of Crofton Gane – a trade stand for his company at Bristol's Royal Agricultural Show. Breuer designed a compact, flat-roofed pavilion, with walls of glass and large blocks of exposed local Cotswold stone. The interior spaces flowed in an open-plan arrangement and the floors were paved in a chequerboard pattern of birch plywood squares. Although intended as a showcase for P.E. Gane's furniture, including Isokon's Long Chair, the modern display was wasted on the provincial audience and when a royal courtier arrived to arrange flowers for the official opening by the king, they enquired: 'When will the furnishings arrive?' Rain kept visitors away and not a single order was placed for Gane's furniture. However, in its frank use of materials, local stone, glass and wood, the building was a precursor of Breuer's later houses in the USA. Its importance was underscored by the fact that 20 years later, when asked to name the buildings of which he was most proud, Breuer selected the Gane Pavilion alongside his monumental UNESCO headquarters in Paris.[33] He worked on two other exhibition stands that summer, for Wood Products and The Architectural Press at the Building Exhibition in

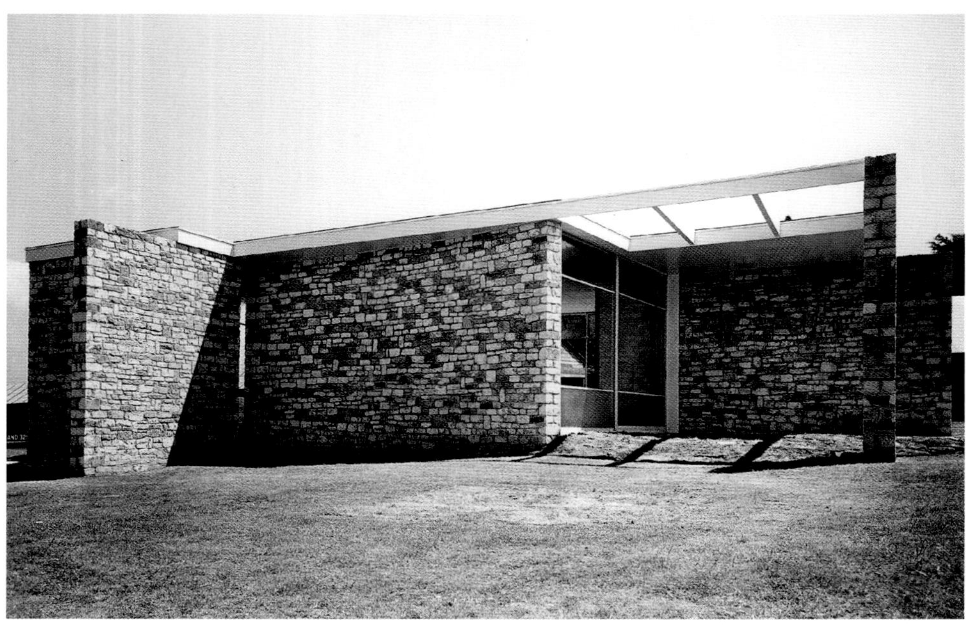

ABOVE: Years later, Marcel Breuer named the Gane Pavilion of 1936, which featured large blocks of exposed Cotswold stone, as one of the two buildings of which he was most proud.

London, both of which were featured in September's *Architectural Review*.

The houses Breuer worked on with F.R.S. Yorke during his time in Britain were also important testing grounds for his architectural ideas.[34] In 1936 they designed Sea Lane House at Angmering-on-Sea in Sussex for bandleader James MacNabb.[35] Constructed from brick and reinforced concrete, the dramatic T-shaped building was raised on oval piloti to afford maximum views over the sea. Painted a monolithic white, the building presented a strong sculptural presence in the flat landscape. Its living and dining rooms opened on to a great curved terrace, which led down an external staircase to the lawn.

In autumn 1936, the partners collaborated on a house at Lee-on-Solent for barrister Hubert Allan Rose, a client for whom Yorke had already built a reinforced-concrete swimming pool at his home in Hampstead.[36] Rose had requested a replica of the 1935 cast-concrete Hertfordshire house, Torilla, that Yorke had built for Christabel Burton of the Harmsworth newspaper dynasty. Shangri La, constructed from steel and reinforced concrete, was based on a series of geometric cubes. Its open-plan interiors were organized around a central monumental chimney breast.

Yorke and Breuer also worked on two identical masters' houses, known as Ainger and Benson at Eton College, which were completed in 1937 after Breuer's

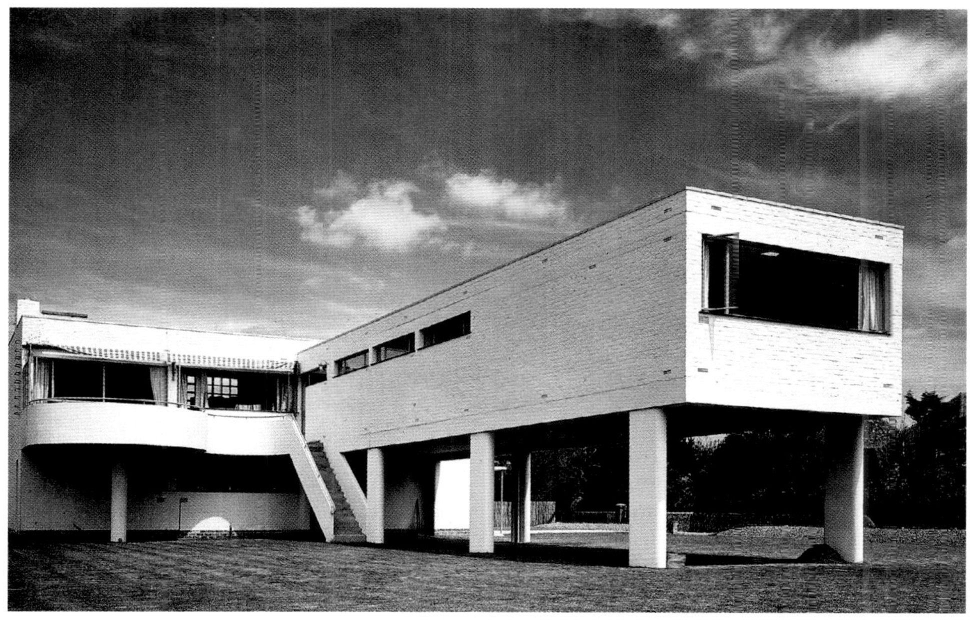

ABOVE: Breuer and Yorke's 1936 Sea Lane House on the Sussex Coast was constructed from brick and concrete and raised on piloti.

departure for the USA. With a tight budget of £2,500 per unit, including built-in furniture and fittings, they created remarkably spacious living quarters in the pair of flat-roofed, two-storey brick houses. Each had seven bedrooms and the luxury, in the 1930s, of two bathrooms. A small canopied porch led to the front door and, at the rear, a terrace was covered with a wood-framed pergola – motifs Breuer employed later in his houses in Massachusetts.

In summer 1936, the acclaimed French theatre director, Michel Saint-Denis and his partners, theatrical manager George Devine and actor Marius Goring, opened a revolutionary new theatre school in London. The London Theatre Studio, whose directors included John Gielgud and Laurence Olivier, offered training not only to actors (early alumni included Michael Redgrave, Peter Ustinov and Alec Guinness), but also provided Britain's first course in stage design. Saint-Denis commissioned Breuer to convert a Methodist chapel at Providence Place in Islington into a two-storey, 200-seater theatre, with office, rehearsal rooms and changing facilities. Inside the chapel Breuer constructed a plywood stage and proscenium with a built-in plywood sound gallery and created an innovative lighting box at the rear of the theatre. He laid a floor of Californian redwood, and transformed the interiors very simply, covering the walls and windows of the chapel with floor-to-ceiling tatami blinds. He had intended using solely Isokon furniture for the commission, but Jack Pritchard was unable to have enough chairs manufactured within the three-month deadline, so in addition to 100 of his own plywood stacking chairs and 92 Isokon stools in natural birch, he filled the auditorium with rows of Alvar Aalto's '611' chairs, purchased from Morton Shand's Finmar.[37]

The course in set and costume design was run by a trio known as 'The Motleys': Elizabeth Montgomery and sisters Sophie and Margaret Harris. In 1937, they branched out into fashion design, and asked Breuer to create the interiors of their new store, Motley Couture in Garrick Street, Covent Garden. The results, run over two pages in December's *Architectural Review*, demonstrate Breuer's skills at creating an elegant, feminine interior. He used a simple palette of white walls and blue-grey carpeting as an understated backdrop for their clothing. The furniture consisted of black, cord-upholstered armchairs and black Isokon nesting tables. He built a small stage halfway down the staircase, for models to show their outfits and installed a full-length rotating photo-mural of a forest landscape, so customers could view themselves in a town or country setting.

Towards the end of 1936, Breuer's supporter Lady 'Peter' Norton, asked him to design The London Gallery, her new space for showcasing modern art on Cork Street. He ordered two Long Chairs, eight Stacking Chairs and two Nesting Tables for the space, hoping it might lead to further orders from browsing collectors.[38] Norton's Gallery showed the work of several Bauhäuslers, with Moholy-Nagy's paintings in July, followed by an exhibition of the work of the Circle group, including Naum Gabo and, in 1937, she showed works by Herbert Bayer.

Breuer spent Christmas 1936 with J.M. Richards and then went skiing over the New Year, a trip that led to one further commission.[39] The following summer his old friend Hans Falkner, a ski-instructor, asked him to design a small winter sports hotel in Obergurgl in the Austrian Tyrol. Using an Alpine farmhouse as his inspiration, Breuer drew up plans for a three-storey building, with ribbon windows and massive rough-stone walls reminiscent of those in the Gane Pavilion. Unfortunately, before the hotel could be built, the Austrian Anschluss took place and Falkner fled to Canada. Another disappointment was a *News Chronicle* competition for an ambitious urban elementary school that he and Yorke entered, but failed to win.

Although he had escaped persecution in Germany, these years in London were personally and professionally unfulfilling for Breuer. Unlike Gropius and Moholy-Nagy, he had neither wife nor family and his stream of small commissions did nothing to satisfy his architectural ambitions, although coverage in publications such as *Architectural Review* and *The Architectural Journal* did maintain his profile. His tubular-steel furniture, manufactured by Thonet continued to be retailed in the

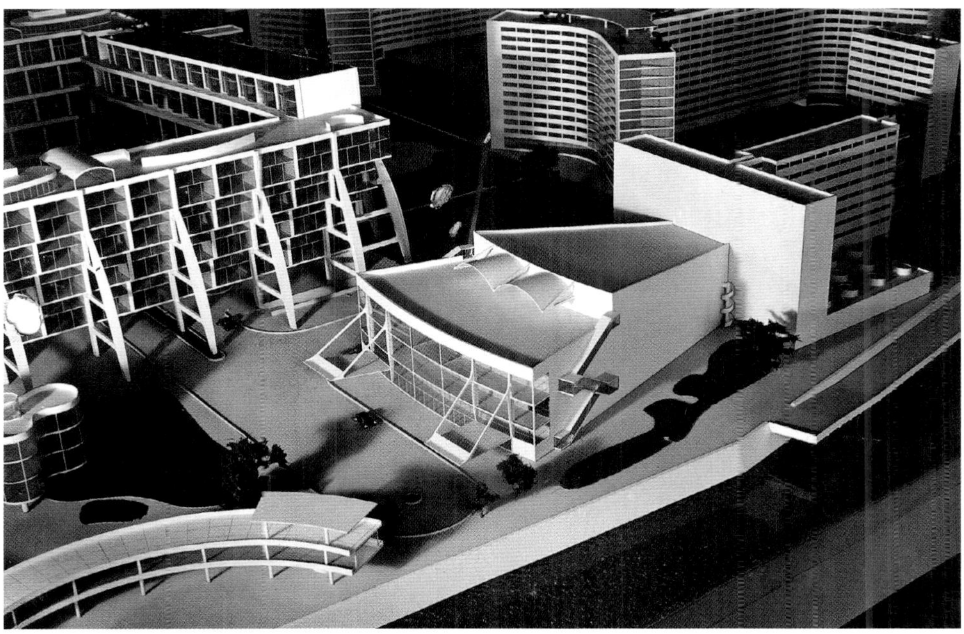

ABOVE: Breuer and Yorke's concrete Civic Center of the Future of 1936 contained a wealth of architectural forms Breuer employed throughout his later career.

US until 1936, when sales were hit by rising exchange rates and import taxes.[40] However, at the end of that year, his designs for the Gane Pavilion were included in a MoMA (Museum of Modern Art in New York) catalogue. Lawrence Kocher of *Architectural Record* wrote asking for more images of his work and proposed having some of Breuer's furniture manufactured under licence in the US to satisfy the growing demand for affordable, mass-produced furnishings.

Breuer was not keen to promote himself as designer of furniture and while living in Britain, turned down several opportunities to talk or write about this aspect of his work, using his poor English as an excuse. He confessed to John Leslie Martin, Editor of *Circle*: 'I do not regard furniture as a separate problem, but merely as part of a building. I do not want to make propaganda for myself as a furniture designer.' However, he did accept invitations to talk about his 'Civic Centre of the Future' at the London Polytechnic School of Architecture in December 1936 and Hull University in May 1937, using Philip Morton Shand's help with translation. In February 1937, Dr Maria Adler, who had taught Art History at the Weimar Bauhaus, invited him to give a talk at New Herrlingen School in Otterden in Kent. As most of the pupils were German refugees, he had the pleasure of addressing them in his native tongue.

THE BAUHAUSLERS DEPART

Jack Pritchard organized a grand farewell dinner for Walter and Ise Gropius, on 9 March 1937, at the Trocadero in London. Moholy-Nagy designed the distinctive 'bill of fare' listing the 135 guests – friends, colleagues, clients and luminaries from the worlds of architecture and science – including H.G. Wells and Julian Huxley, who chaired the event. In his speech Gropius paid tribute to the kindness he had encountered in England, but also expressed sadness at how little he had done to progress the cause of Modernist architecture. On Friday 12 March, he and Ise set sail for America.

The departure of Gropius for a new life in America and all it promised professionally, unsettled his colleagues. Breuer was already disillusioned and Moholy-Nagy was exhausted and melancholy. Within weeks of his departure Gropius sent this euphoric account to Breuer.

> *It's wonderful here. Don't tell the English, but we are both heavenly happy to have escaped from the land of fog and emotional nightmare. Air clear as glass, lots of sun and blue Roman skies. All around an unspoiled, untamed landscape, most of which has not been degraded into parks and in which one doesn't always feel like a trespasser. In addition, fine wooden houses in the Colonial style, painted white, which will delight you as much as they do me. In their simplicity, functionality and uniformity, they are completely in our line. The inviting appearance of these houses mirrors the incredible hospitality of this country, which probably comes from old pioneer times.[41]*

Gropius suggested that Breuer should join him in the Harvard architectural faculty and offered his old Bauhaus protégé the irresistible prospect of setting up together in a joint architectural practice. On 21 May Breuer celebrated his 35th birthday in London. That evening he received a cable from Walter and Ise Gropius that read:

> *Cheers Lajkó. 35 is a good number for a promising new partnership.[42]*

He did not need to be persuaded: on 15 June he replied:

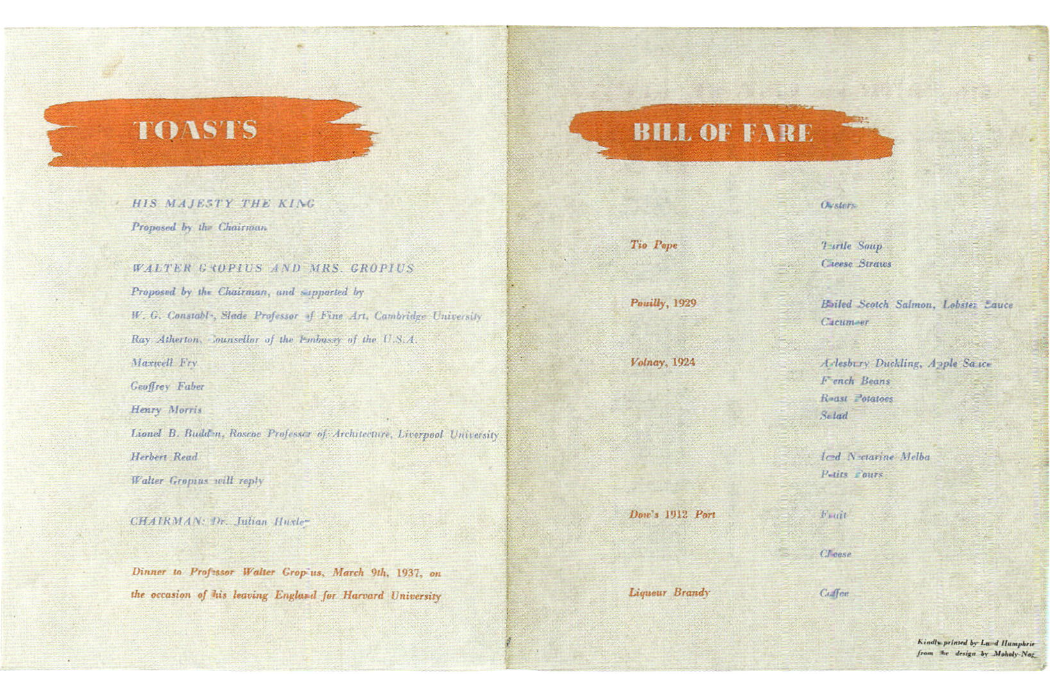

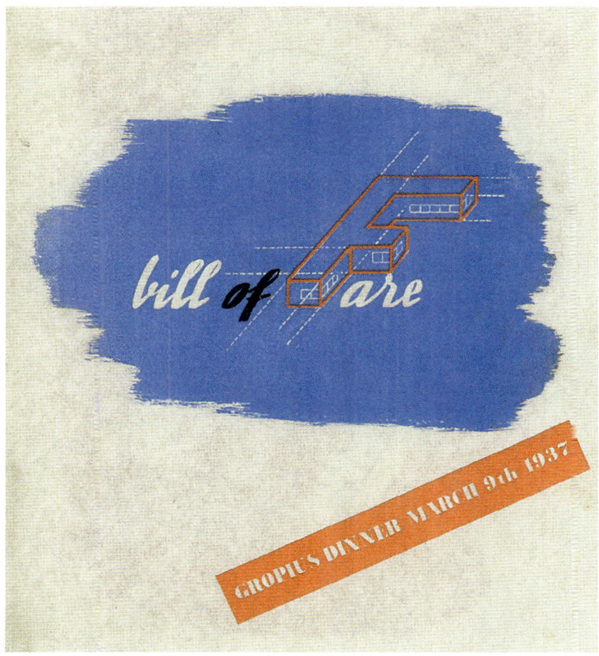

ABOVE: Jack Pritchard organized the Farewell Dinner for Walter and Ise Gropius at the Trocadero at Piccadilly Circus, London.

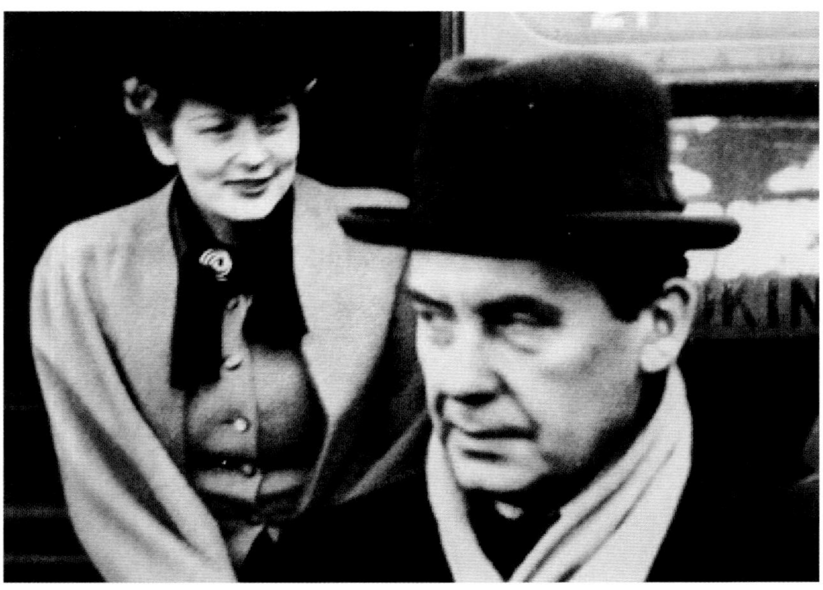

ABOVE: Jack and Molly Pritchard accompanied Ise and Walter Gropius to Waterloo Station, to board a train to Southampton, for their sea crossing to the USA and a new life at Harvard.

What the two of you write looks as favorable for me as I could possibly imagine. I would be quite satisfied with $5,000 a year to start with [at Harvard] and later even more of course with $8,000 in case it goes that far. But the main thing for me would always be our joint private office… So we'll be earning something yet from architecture, I would never have believed it.

On 23 July he set sail for the US, ostensibly to investigate new markets for Isokon products in his new role as Controller of Design. Before he left he struck a deal with Jack Pritchard regarding licensing and royalties. They agreed he would receive a salary of £100 a year: 'Substantially on the same terms as Gropius acted as adviser, an appointment to last for one year certain and thereafter so long as both parties agree.'[43]

He arrived in New York on 2 August and after a few days in the city travelled to Marion on the Massachusetts coast to spend the month with Walter and Ise Gropius. It was an idyllic summer and he fell in love with the country. He returned to London to wind up his affairs and on 23 December, Jack Pritchard held a farewell dinner for him in the newly opened Isobar, the ground-floor dining club and bar Breuer had designed for the Lawn Road Flats earlier that year. Chef Philip Harben cooked a seasonal dinner of brown onion soup, a two-bird special and Christmas pudding for the 26 guests, who included Wells Coates, Ernst Freud, Harry Mansell, Christopher Nicholson, Herbert Read, Dick Russell, architects F.R.S. Yorke and Mischa Black and J.M. Richards.

Gropius had also been working on Moholy-Nagy's behalf and had recommended his old friend for a prominent role he himself had turned down. On 29 May he received a letter from Norma K. Stahle, Executive Director of the Association of Arts and Industries in Chicago. The association was planning to open a school of Industrial Design with workshop practices following the Bauhaus model and had the backing of a number of prominent industrialists. 'I am wondering,' she wrote, 'whether it would interest you to become the head of the school.'

Moholy-Nagy left for New York on the SS *Manhattan* at the beginning of July. On 8 August he presented his proposals for a four-year programme for the New Bauhaus, American School of Design to the Board of the Association of Arts and Industries. He wrote to Sibyl, in London:

> *There's something incomplete about this city and its people that fascinates me; it seems to urge one on to completion. Everything seems still possible. The paralyzing finality of the European disaster is far away. I love the newness of expectation around me. Yes, I want to stay.*

On 13 August, he cabled simply. 'Signed five-year contract for Bauhaus. Opening October eighteenth. Liquidate everything. Details follow.'

And so, the three leading Bauhaus Masters were gone. The London sojourn of Gropius, Breuer and Moholy-Nagy had been a brief one. Between 1934 and 1937 they received no major, large-scale public commissions. The slow development of Modernism in pre-war Britain coupled with challenging economic conditions and a lack of enlightened patrons made opportunities scarce. However, their friendships, partnerships and support for organisations such as the DIA, MARS and the Unit One collective of artists had added momentum to the movement. Their teaching, writing and discussions with fellow artists during this period provided an important legacy, which was not realized, or even calibrated until long after World War II. London, the Lawn Road Flats and Isokon had been their stepping stone to a New World.

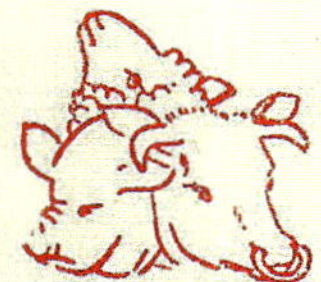

POTAGE DI GARBANZOS   6d   BREAM PIE   1/3

Very Special:
Lobster Americaine   3/-

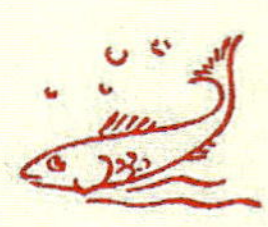

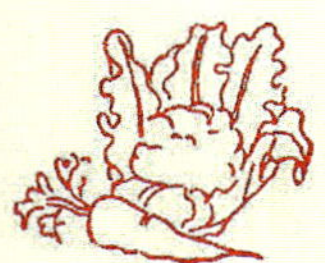

BOILED FRESH BEEF FRENCH STYLE   1/6

Braised Lamb's Tongues and Parsley sauce   1/9

To-day's Spanish dish – profits for
Spanish Medical Aid:

F i d e u s   C a z u e l a   2/6

This is a Spanish way of cooking
spaghetti with chicken so that the
spaghetti absorbs the flavour of
the chicken

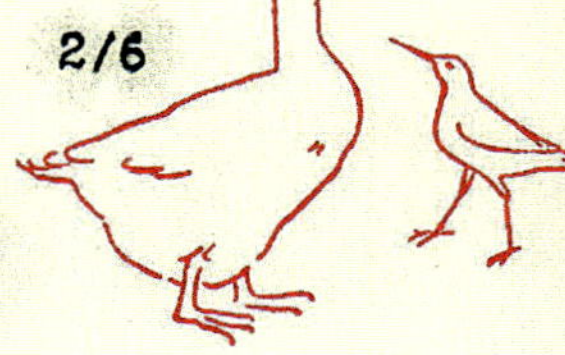

SPRING GREENS
    4d
SPINACH
    4d
CAULIFLOWER   4d
NEW POTATOES   5d

CHEESE (various)
    5d.

Strawberry Fool   6d

Millefeuilles   4d

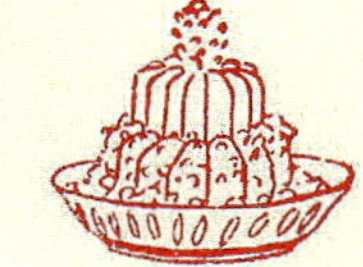

Fontainebleau in a bowl of cream 1/-

S H I L L I N G   S P E C I A L

Sweetbread cutlets and rice

Salads to order, from 10d.   Omelettes plain 1/- others 1/3   Sausages and Mash 1/-

COFFEE MOCHA-JAVA OR VIENNESE, PER PERSON AD LIB.   6d.

Given sufficient notice any dish can be specially prepared or any special menu arranged.
Suggestions for new dishes will always be cordially welcomed.

MEMBERS OF THE ISOBAR TAKING CONTRACT MEALS RECEIVE 23/6 WORTH OF FOOD FOR £1

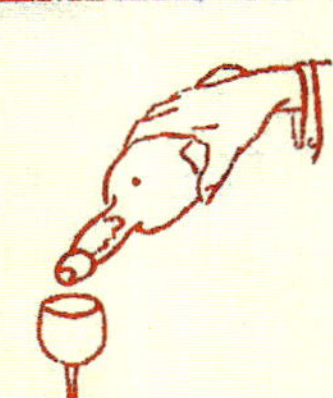

HAVE YOU LOOKED AT THE WINE LIST ?

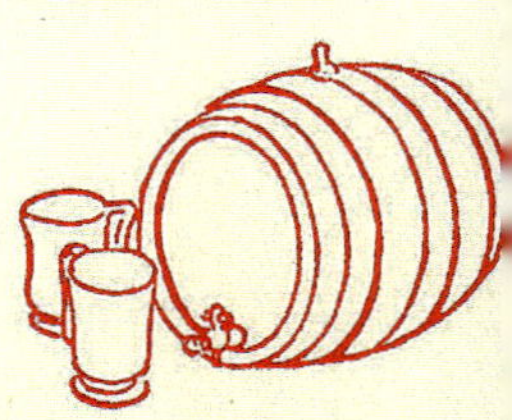

CHAPTER 8

FOOD, BOOKS AND SPIES

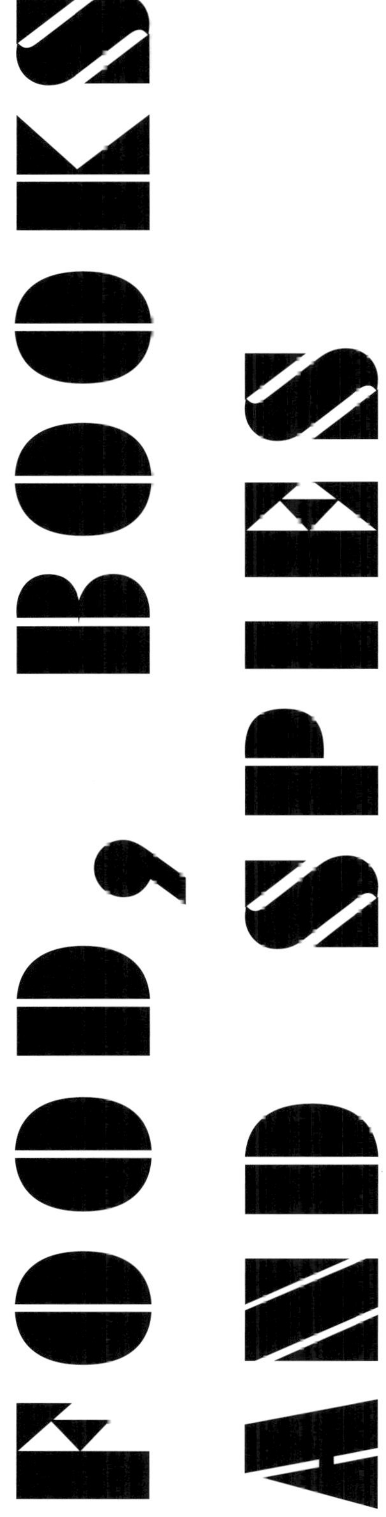

DINING AT LAWN ROAD FLATS

Although the departure of Marcel Breuer as Controller of Design left a creative vacuum at Isokon, the Isobar dining and social club he designed for Jack and Molly Pritchard was a wonderful legacy, not just for the Lawn Road Flats, but also for the cultural life of London.

Jack Pritchard had been an enthusiastic club man all his life and he seized on the opportunity to create his own establishment with relish. What he sought with the Isobar were the material comforts of the traditional gentlemen's club, combined with the lively intellectual atmosphere of his Cambridge days, all in an appropriately modern setting. In addition to being a first-class networker, Pritchard was also a gourmet and he knew that an excellent restaurant would be critical to the Isobar's success. At the end of September 1937 he secured the services of Tommy Layton, a well-known figure in London's restaurant scene. His appointment was a coup.

The Isobar was open to tenants of the flats, their friends and Hampstead residents. In Breuer's sleek new ground-floor clubroom, they could recline in comfortably upholstered Isokon Long Chairs beneath a wall-sized map of Hampstead and drink from a well-stocked bar, which included, at Layton's instigation, a range of 'interesting' and rare beers. The restaurant, which in good weather spilled out onto an *al fresco* deck, overlooking a wooded garden at the rear, was furnished with Breuer's dining tables, wall-mounted seating and Isokon stools. The club's name was a pun on the English obsession with the weather and a Weather Committee, headed by Molly Pritchard, posted daily updates

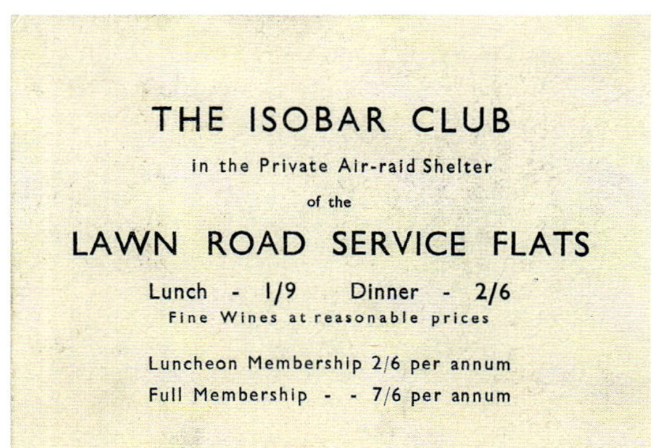

ABOVE: During the war, Jack Pritchard capitalized on the flats' concrete construction. He claimed the building was 'the safest in London'.

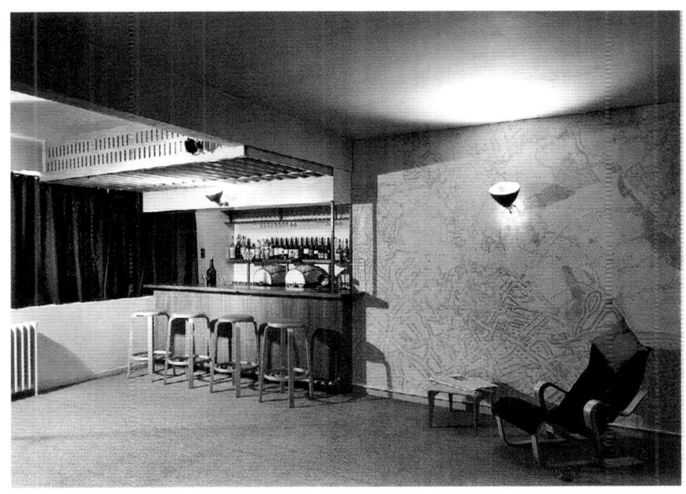

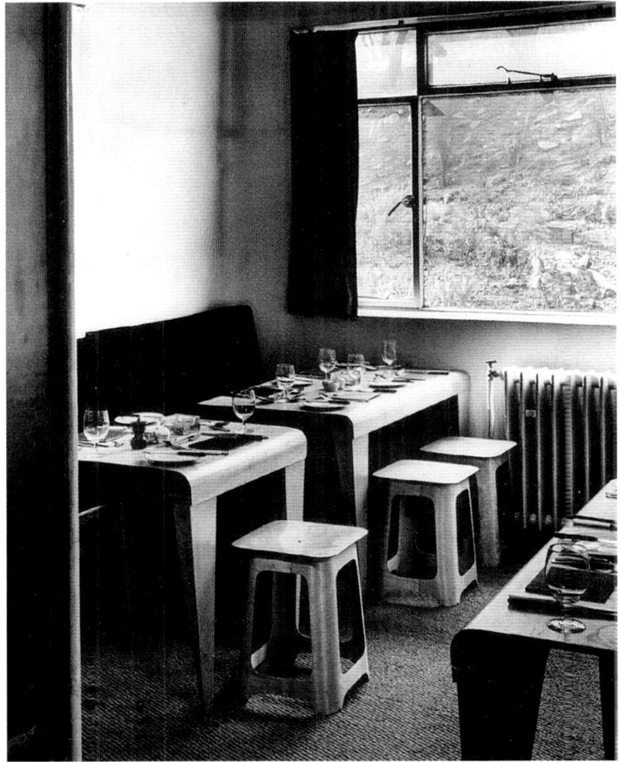

ABOVE, TOP: Marcel Breuer's design for the Isobar, featured a map of Hampstead, Long Chairs and bar stools by Alvar Aalto. A wall-mounted barograph recorded the London air pressure for the flats' Weather Committee.
ABOVE: In the dining room guests could enjoy Philip Harben's adventurous dishes, accompanied by an extensive list of fine wines and Cuban cigars.

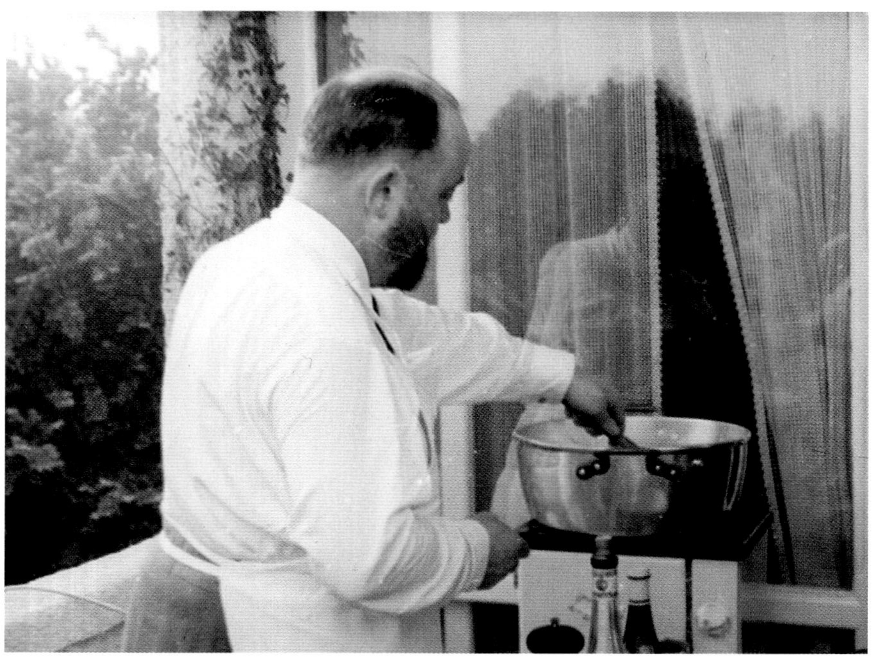

ABOVE: Philip Harben making fondue on the Penthouse terrace. His *joie de vivre* and exotic dinners made the Isobar a mecca for London's intellectual community.

compiled from Air Ministry reports. At one end of the room, Breuer had installed a barograph in a glass case, under a blown-up photograph of clouds. Pritchard joked: 'At the other end of the room was a bar, so that should members find their pressure low they could get it raised at the bar.'[1]

The club provided members with a wide selection of contemporary periodicals and 'all the more important foreign newspapers'. Regular exhibitions were staged by artists including Henry Moore, Kenneth Rowntree and Edmond Kapp (all residents at various periods), Leslie Hurry, John Kenneth Green and Gerald Leet.[2] In July 1938, the Isobar hosted the second series of pictures produced by Contemporary Lithographs Ltd, which included works by John Piper, Vanessa Bell and Edward Ardizzone and, later that year, an exhibition on Czech architecture.[3]

Tommy Layton did not stay long. He hosted Marcel Breuer's leaving party over Christmas 1937 and left to set up his own independent wine merchants. His replacement, Hampstead-born Philip Harben, who took over in January 1938 and would later become Britain's first television chef, was an old friend of Pritchard's and a man of immense charm and energy. His parents Mary Jerrold and Hubert Harben were successful actors and Harben had also dabbled with an acting career

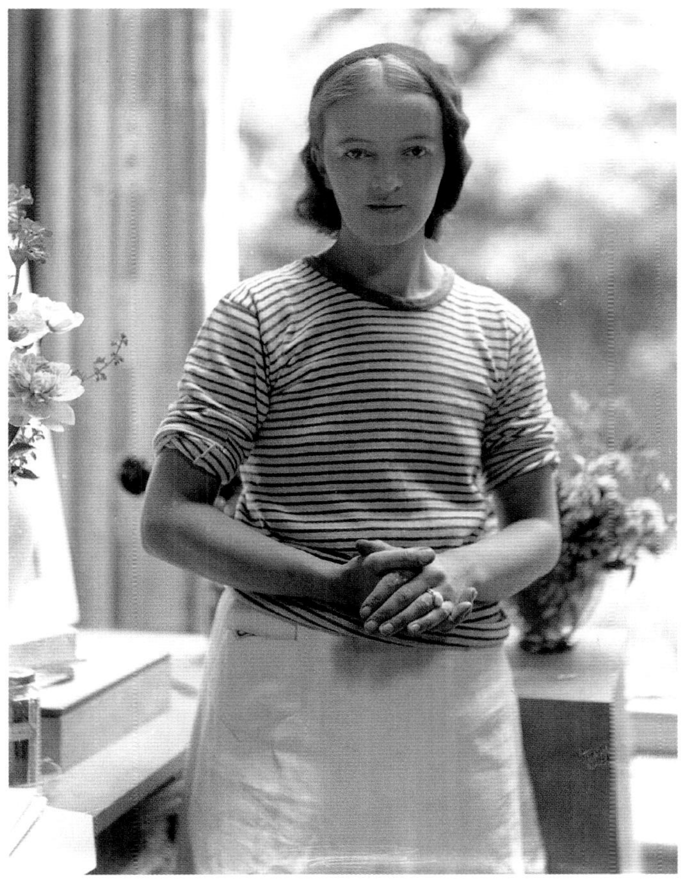

himself, before working as a fashion photographer. However, food had long been his first love and he boasted that he 'could scramble eggs and make mayonnaise long before [he] could read Thucydides or solve a quadratic equation' [4]

Harben and his wife Kathie moved into Flat Seven on the building's first floor. While he ran the Isobar, she managed the building and became the Secretary of the Isokon Furniture Company. Pritchard reported that the club's atmosphere changed at once. Harben's larger-than-life personality and adventurous culinary offerings added greatly to the club's popularity. It quickly established itself as a mecca for local artists (Adrian Stokes, Henry Moore, Barbara Hepworth, Ben Nicholson and Naum Gabo), as well as designers, journalists, critics (Nikolaus Pevsner and Herbert Read), statisticians, philosophers (Cyril Joad) and architects (Erich Mendelssohn, Serge Chermayeff and Wells Coates). In summer 1938

Pritchard invited Sigfried Giedion and Swedish art historian and modern design promoter Gregor Paulsson to stay in the flats and entertained them in the club.[5]

Harben was an adventurous cook, who introduced diners to a wide range of foreign dishes, unusual for Britain in the 1930s. He and Kathie were also committed Socialists, albeit of the champagne variety, and they organized themed fundraising events for left-wing causes, inviting Labour politicians, including Megan Lloyd George, the first female Welsh MP and the well-known union leader Ben Tillett. In November 1938 the Isobar celebrated its first birthday. Harben organized the party, at which he served oysters and a large birthday cake and a darts tournament was played. The club now had a waiting list for membership.

The combination of good food and good conversation was so irresistible that in 1937 the Pritchards, Harben and Raymond Postgate, editor of the left-wing journal *Fact* (later founder of Britain's *Good Food Guide*), founded the Half Hundred dining club, which usually convened in the penthouse apartment. This rather disingenuously styled 'poor man's food and wine society' had 25 members, each of whom could bring along one guest. The rules stated that each member should plan, supervise and, if possible, cook a dinner for their fellow members, the cost of which was not to exceed £1 per head for food, wine and service. Members competed to see who could devise the wittiest and most abstrusely themed menu. Philip Harben directed the first dinner, held in the Pritchards' flat on 19 January 1937. His invitation to fellow diners was issued in verse. The guests included Postgate, Walter and Ise Gropius, Marcel Breuer, Fleetwood Pritchard, child psychologist Theodora Alcock, anaesthetist Eva Hargreaves, and publisher and poet Francis Meynell. As Meynell recalled, members were 'all word-wise as well as food-wise'.[6] They included: Julian Huxley, Director of the British Zoological Society; designers Dick Russell and his wife Marian Peplar; eminent psychotherapist Dr Wilfred Bion; psychiatrist Ronald Hargreaves; model Thelma Yorke; art critic Herbert Read; film director Mary Field; feminist journalist Lella Florence; and documentary producer F.S. Fairfax Jones.

Undoubtedly the most *outré* dinner was that directed by Julian Huxley in November 1938, which was held at London Zoo. The menu included bison tail, antelope fillets and roast bison served with creamed fennel. Members were warned that 'the meal was private and must not be spoken of to strangers, as the spreading of rumours about it would embarrass the Zoo Authorities'.[7]

Food had always been an important symbol of friendship for Pritchard and that Christmas he sent a tin of *foie gras* to Marcel Breuer in Cambridge, Massachusetts. Breuer wrote back thanking him for the gift, which he said: 'brings to me a lot of continental atmosphere'.[8]

REFUGEES FROM EUROPE

From November 1938, following the *Kristallnacht* pogrom of Jews and the *Anschluss* in Austria, the number of refugees arriving in London increased dramatically. They included many who had taught at, or attended, the Bauhaus. Mies van der Rohe and Paul Klee passed through Hampstead, the latter holding his first London exhibition at the Everyman Cinema's Foyer Gallery and from 1938 until 1941, Dutch de Stijl artist Piet Mondrian lived at 60 Parkhill Road in a flat overlooking Barbara Hepworth's Mall studio.

On 13 November, Pritchard wrote to Prime Minister Neville Chamberlain, berating the government's failure to condemn Hitler's anti-Jewish policies.[9] He redoubled his efforts to take in exiles, offering them free accommodation in vacant Lawn Road Flats and making introductions to help them find work. Two months later, he wrote again to the Prime Minister explaining that he was currently housing refugees from Germany and Czechoslovakia and feeding them for £1 a head, but that understandably he 'could not look after them entirely for nothing'. Through the press, he called on other property developers to follow his lead and make their apartments available to refugees.[10]

The Architects' Czech Refugee Relief Fund introduced him to Egon Riss, an Austrian architect of Jewish descent who had moved in Bauhaus circles in the 1920s and was friends with Wassily Kandinsky and Paul Klee. He had gone into private practice in Vienna, from where he fled to London via Prague. Jack Pritchard offered him a flat and he soon became an invaluable member of the Lawn Road community, affectionately nicknamed 'Chips'. At first, he carried out odd jobs around the building including stoking the boilers in exchange for rent and later organized the building of a protective wartime wall of sandbags around the flats, dubbed the 'Isokon Line'.

Pritchard soon offered him employment in the Isokon Furniture Company and he produced several designs for him of 'great wit and charm', including what could have been, had it not been for the outbreak of war, Isokon's most commercially successful product, the Donkey. This was a small plywood bookcase, so named as it had four legs and two 'panniers' to hold books, and a central hollow with space for newspapers and magazines. It was an ingenious product that tied in with Isokon's philosophy for compact modern living. Allen Lane, founder of the newly formed Penguin publishing company, was so impressed with the Donkey that he offered Isokon the opportunity to place 100,000 leaflets in his paperback books, free of charge and the design was renamed the Isokon Penguin Donkey.[11] Manufacturing began and both parties had high hopes, but production had to be cancelled with the outbreak of war. The 50 or so Donkeys that had already been manufactured

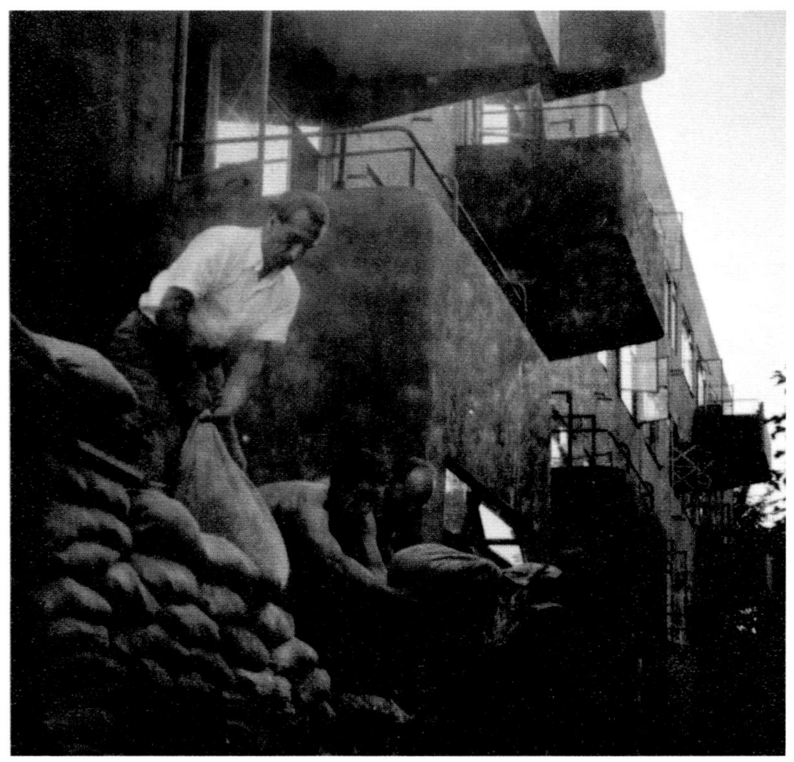

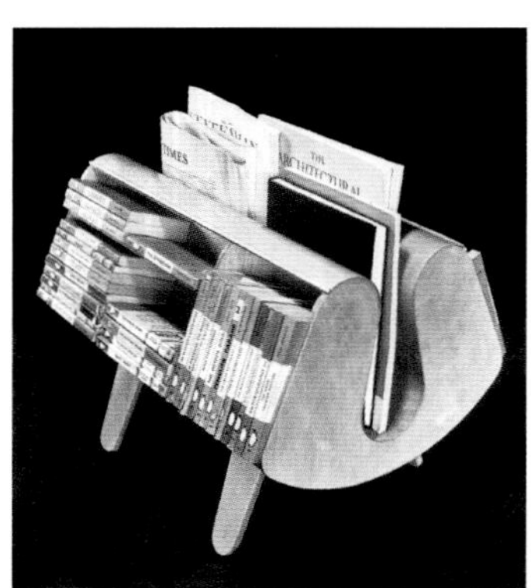

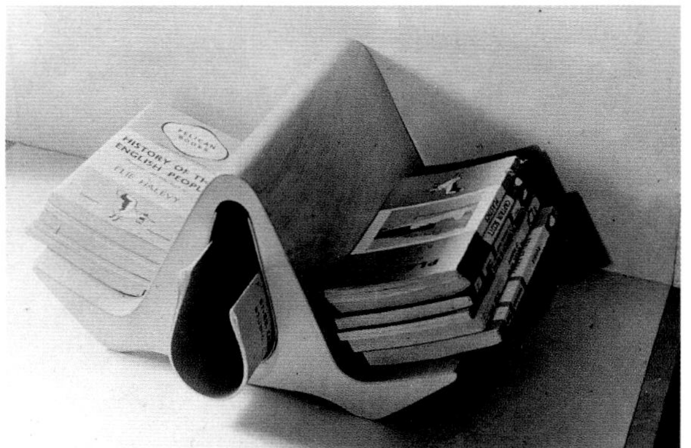

ABOVE, TOP: Austrian architect, Egon Riss, helping to construct the 'Isokon Line' of sandbags outside the windows of the Isobar. ABOVE, LEFT: The Isokon Book Donkey of 1939, was perfect for storing Penguin's new and inexpensive paperback books. ABOVE, RIGHT: Egon Riss's plywood Isokon Gull mini bookshelf could be wall hung.

were snapped up at once and this model, along with some later models is now on the books of Isokon Plus.

In 1939, Riss also designed the Isokon Gull, a miniature inverted version of the Donkey that could be wall hung. His Pocket Bottleship (its name reflecting current political preoccupations), a modified version of the Gull, could be used as a small, portable drinks cabinet, accommodating a bottle and glasses, with a space for newspapers and magazines. Prototypes of the designs were produced for Isokon by Pfeifer in Camden Town. Pritchard considered employing other designers including Christopher Nicholson, R.D. Russell and architect F.R.S. Yorke, but other than a 1937 sketch for a moulded plywood armchair with pierced circles by Nicholson (who designed a range of plywood furniture for the Pioneer Health Centre in Peckham), nothing remains of these potential collaborations.

From early 1939, Pritchard attempted to find a role at Isokon for German architect Arthur Korn. Korn had worked with Erich Mendelsohn and associated with Gropius and *Der Ring* group in Berlin in the 1920s. His prophetic book *Glass in Modern Architecture,* which featured the Dessau Bauhaus building, was published in 1929. Blacklisted from practising architecture by the Nazis, he arrived in London in 1934, and took Flat 24 in the Pritchards' building. Korn was an enthusiastic member of the Modern Architectural Research (MARS) Group and became chairman of its town planning sub-committee. In February 1939 he and Pritchard looked into the possibility of reviving plans to develop the site next to the Lawn Road Flats.[12] In May, they discussed opening a store in Wigmore Street (based on Giedion's Wohnbedarf in Zurich), which would sell modern English furniture. In the uncertain geopolitical climate, Pritchard even considered dropping the 'foreign-sounding' name Isokon. He went as far as proposing that Korn would manage the shop and have a share in its profits. In June, he attempted to involve Korn in the design side of the business. They discussed producing Breuer's stacking chair more cheaply and adding other items to the Isokon range, including a 'Windsor-style' chair, in which Heal's expressed an interest.[13] In July, he asked if Korn would join the firm as its designer and for an investment of £300, take a 40% stake in the parent Isokon Control Company. Harry Mansell, Isokon's furniture manufacturer, had by this date become a director and now owned a 10% stake in the firm. Korn asked to look at the company accounts, but mislaid the books. Relations between the two men grew strained and Korn asked for his money back.[14]

War with Germany was declared on 3 September 1939. By November, Isokon had an overdraft of £528 and Pritchard took out a life-insurance policy to cover his debts.[15] It was now difficult to find residents who were prepared to take out long leases on flats, and as he was no longer able to import supplies of plywood from the Baltics, Pritchard was forced to close the Isokon Furniture Company. He described his dilemma:

> *When the War started it was quite clear that my small Isokon*
> *furniture business would be unable to go on; the essential supplies*
> *of plywood parts for assembly would dry up, and anyway we only*
> *had a couple of men working and it would not be possible to get*
> *any war contracts, however small."*[16]

At the end of November 1939, when news of the outbreak of the first Russo-Finnish war reached Pritchard, he wrote to Alvar Aalto in Helsinki offering him refuge and a flat at Lawn Road.[17]

In autumn 1940, Egon Riss moved into Flat 31 next to the Pritchards' penthouse. Shortly afterwards another Bauhaus Master took up residence in Flat 2. The Ukrainian, Naum Slutzky, had taught in the Metal Workshops at Weimar from 1919 to 1922 and then set up in private practice as a designer and goldsmith in Hamburg. He fled to London in 1933, but lost all his tools and jewellery *en route,* when his ship, the *Guildford Castle,* was lost in a collision on the River Elbe. Although he had letters of recommendation to several art colleges, including the Royal College of Art and Edinburgh College of Art, his poor English prevented him from gaining a teaching position.

In May 1934 he met Walter Gropius, while he was in London giving his landmark speech at the Royal Institute of British Architects (RIBA). On his return to Germany, Gropius sent Slutzky a certificate authenticating his Bauhaus experience to show to potential employers. Following his move to Britain, it is likely that Gropius also introduced Slutzky to Leonard and Dorothy Elmhirst at Dartington Hall. In 1935, they offered him a part-time position, teaching metalwork in their school. While working at Dartington, Slutzky had an affair with the young dancer Birgit Cullberg, a member of the visiting Ballet Jooss, who later founded a famous dance theatre in Sweden. Gropius also introduced Slutzky to Robert Dudley Best of Best & Lloyd. He worked as a freelance designer for the Birmingham-based lighting manufacturer between 1936 and 1937. Slutzky designed a version of the company's Bestlite, with two illuminators, one which reflected light downwards by a shallow spun aluminium bowl, and the other upwards by means of a conical reflector. The desk lamp, priced at 58s 6d was illustrated in *Architects' Journal* in January 1937, but does not appear to have been put into general production. In his memoirs, R.D. Best noted that this form of uplighter was ahead of its time and was not widely adopted until the 1950s.[18]

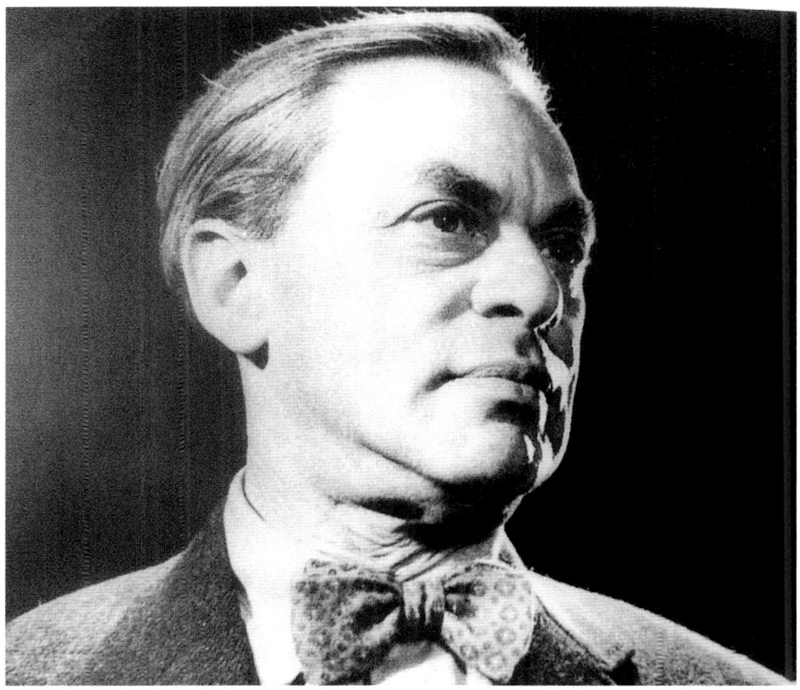

Slutzky frequented the Lawn Road Flats for several years before moving into the building. Pritchard recalled him meeting his old friend, the Russian constructivist artist Naum Gabo (who lived almost opposite the flats at 11 Lawn Road):

> One delightful episode which took place after the Isobar was
> opened was the reunion of Gabo and Slutzky. They met there
> for the first time since leaving Russia. They were both small
> men. They rushed towards each other and embraced with such
> delight that all in the Club were entranced.

Following the outbreak of war Slutzky was interned as a German-speaking immigrant and spent time between June 1940 and February 1942 at a camp in Douglas on the Isle of Man. On his release, he moved back into the Lawn Road Flats and remained there until May 1946. He paid his rent through 'experimental work' for a company known as the Cheriot Trust, and applied for a patent for fixing diamonds into specialist tools. There are also unconfirmed reports that he worked for the Ministry of Defence. After the war he returned to teaching, first at Burgess Hill School in Hampstead, then teaching interior design at Central School of Art. He moved to the Royal College of Art, and between 1950 and '57 was the head of their new Engineering Design department, becoming the only Isokon-connected Bauhausler to have a leading role in a British art school.

He continued to work for Best & Lloyd throughout this period, producing designs for a new anglepoise lamp for the company. In 1957 he was appointed Head of Industrial Design at Birmingham Art College. As at the Bauhaus, he championed the cause of student placements in industry, so that they could obtain practical experience producing designs. For 30 years Slutzky's background as a Modernist goldsmith was virtually unknown in Britain, but in 1961 his pre-war work was included at an important exhibition 'Modern Jewellery 1890–1961' held at Goldsmith's Hall, which was organized by the Victoria and Albert Museum.

Another Bauhausler with a connection to the flats was Croatian weaver Otti Berger, who enrolled at the Dessau Bauhaus in 1927 and took the preliminary *Vorkurs* under Klee and Moholy-Nagy. One of the most talented students who trained in the weaving workshop, she ran the department for a period after the departure of Gunta Stölzl and developed her own curriculum. Berger was the only Bauhaus textile designer who sought patents for her textiles, which included plastics. She set up her own studio in Berlin in 1932, but due to her Jewish background was banned from practising by the Nazis. In 1936, she fled to London and spent several years in Hampstead, living for a time at 66 Belsize Park. Due to a hearing defect and lack of English she had difficulty finding work, but her Bauhaus colleagues in Lawn Road attempted to support her. Gropius and Breuer discussed helping her set up a weaving workshop in London or Bristol and Marcel Breuer took her to meet his patron Crofton Gane in the hope of obtaining a contract for her to produce textiles.[19] In 1938 Moholy-Nagy invited Berger to join him at the New Bauhaus in Chicago. Her fiancé Bauhaus architect Ludwig Hilberseimerand had already fled to the US, but she was unable to obtain a travel visa and returned to look after her mother in Zmajevac, Croatia. Tragically her whole family was deported to Auschwitz, where she was murdered in 1944.

THE BLITZ

The Blitz commenced on 7 September 1940, as the German Luftwaffe began a systematic bombing campaign over London, which lasted for 56 days. On the second day, windows on the top floor of the Lawn Road Flats were blown out by a blast nearby. Londoners sought shelter in their local underground stations, but Wells Coates's steel-framed, reinforced concrete block, surrounded by Egon

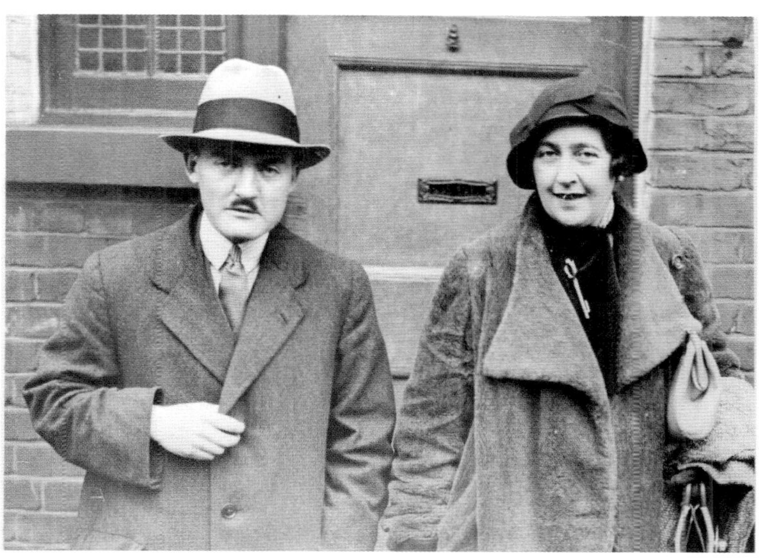

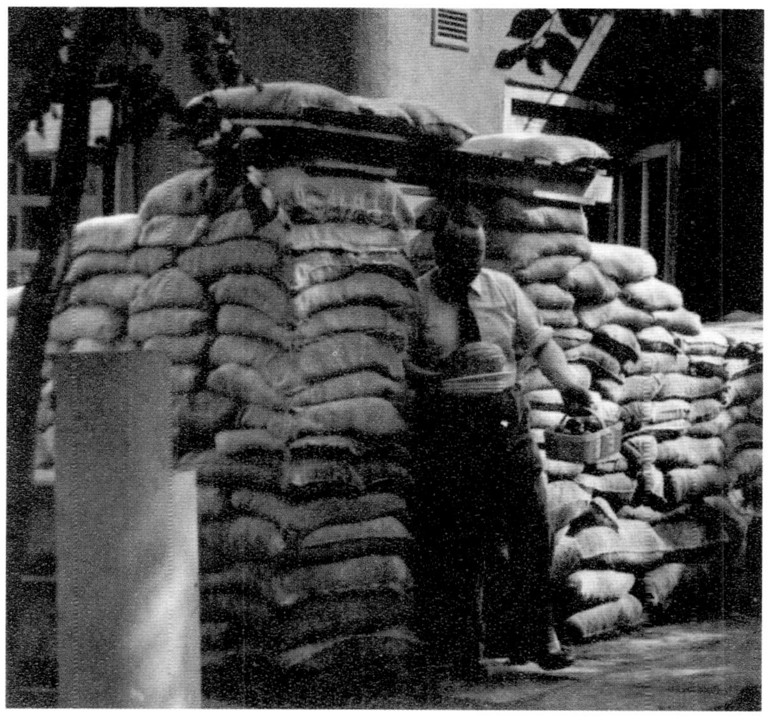

ABOVE, TOP: Max Mallowan and his wife, the author Agatha Christie spent an 'eventful, exciting and often amusing' year together in Flat 22 before he was sent to Cairo. During the Blitz, Christie kept a Sealyham terrier for company and slept with her fur coat over her bed. ABOVE: Harben maintained service as usual in the Isobar during the Blitz, although the kitchen was often challenged by food shortages.

Riss's Isokon Line of sandbags, was deemed one of the structurally safest buildings in the area and when the bombs began to fall, residents gathered in the ground-floor Isobar. In October, the canny Pritchard advertised the flats in *The Times*, highlighting the block's 'club renowned for cuisine in private air raid shelter'.[20] He had a surge in applications for apartments.[21] One of these came from the *grande dame* of crime fiction Agatha Christie and her husband the eminent archaeologist Max Mallowan.

Christie had a large property portfolio, but her London home in Sheffield Terrace, South Kensington was bombed in the first weeks of the Blitz and her large country house, Greenways in South Devon, had been requisitioned by the Admiralty. Possibly on the advice of Professor Stephen Glanville, an old friend of Mallowan, who lived in Flat 2 and was working with him in the Air Ministry, Christie and her husband moved first into Flat 20 and then into Flat 22 in March 1941. Christie later recalled the impact the building made as she approached it along Lawn Road:

> *Coming up the street the flats looked just like a giant liner which ought to have had a couple of funnels, and then you went up the stairs and through the door of one's flat and there were the trees tapping on the window.*

For the next year Mallowan worked for the Directorate of Allied and Foreign Liaison, the intelligence branch of the RAF, while Christie took a job with the Voluntary Aid Detachment in the chemist's dispensary at University College Hospital. This work with pharmaceutical drugs is thought to have provided inspiration for her novels and she amassed a comprehensive medico-legal library in her apartment. Mallowan recalled their first wartime year together in the flats as 'eventful, exciting and often amusing', but in 1942 he was sent to Cairo to establish a branch of the Directorate of Allied and Foreign Liaison. It was the first time since they had married that the couple had lived apart and Pritchard permitted the author to keep a Sealyham terrier in her flat for company. She recalled:

> *Lawn Road Flats was a good place to be since Max had to be away. They were kindly people there. There was also a small restaurant with an informal and happy atmosphere. Outside my bedroom window, which was on the second floor, a bank ran along behind the flats planted with trees and shrubs. Exactly opposite my window was a big, white, double*

cherry tree which came to a great pyramidal point… It was one of the
things in spring that cheered me every morning when I woke.[22]

With Mallowan stationed in the Middle East for long periods, Christie grew close to Glanville, who was an eminent Egyptologist. He advised her on *Death Comes as the End*, a violent whodunit set in ancient Egypt, which she wrote in 1943 and she dedicated *Five Little Pigs,* written the same year, to him. Following its publication, she treated Glanville to a lavish dinner in her apartment. 'What a meal! What hospitality,' he wrote in thanks.[23]

The six years Christie spent at Lawn Road were prolific. *Evil Under the Sun* and the spy novel *N or M?* were published in 1941, followed by *The Body in the Library* in 1942 and *The Moving Finger* and *Towards Zero* in 1943. *Absent in the Spring,* which she wrote in just three days and published in 1944 as one of her Mary Westmacott novels, was a psychological study about a woman alone in the desert. *Death Comes as the End* and *Sparkling Cyanide* were released in 1945, *The Hollow* in 1946 and her short stories from this era included *eight* Hercule Poirot adventures. In addition, she successfully dramatized several of her works for the London stage, including *Appointment with Death* (1945) and *Murder on the Nile* (1946). Christie also penned a short autobiographical memoir entitled *Come, Tell Me How You Live* in 1946 about her travels with her husband to Syria and Iraq.

Mallowan returned from Cairo in May 1945 and they were reunited. Although by December, Greenway was derequisitioned, they kept Lawn Road as their London base until June 1948 and Pritchard allowed them to remove the party wall between Flats 16 and 17 to create more space. The deep affection with which they regarded the building is revealed in a letter Christie wrote to her husband:

How odd, to think that as I pass a funny old building like a liner
I shall always look up at it and say to myself 'I was happy there!'
No beauty to speak of … but oh darling I did have so much
happiness there with you.[24]

A COMMUNITY OF SPIES

N or M?, the spy novel Agatha Christie wrote just before moving into the flats, had brought her to the attention of Britain's intelligence agency, MI5. She had called one of the characters Major Bletchley, a name shared with Britain's secret wartime codebreaking centre, Bletchley Park. Following interrogation, Christie maintained that she had simply chosen the name after being delayed near Milton Keynes

during a train journey. It has also been suggested that the book was inspired by the
network of Soviet spies who, it later emerged, lived in and around the Lawn Road
Flats in the 1930s and early 1940s but the time-frame for this novel, published a
short time after she moved into Lawn Road, and the dates of her own tenure in
the flats do not coincide with most of the individuals involved, ruling out this
theory. The connection between the Lawn Road Flats and the shadowy world
of interwar Soviet espionage falls outside the remit of this book but the Socialist
beliefs, left-wing circle and open marriage of the Pritchards undoubtedly created a
conducive ambience for the community of spies who inhabited their building.

At its centre was Edith Suschitzky. Jack's mistress Beatrix Tudor-Hart met Edith,
a brilliant young Austrian girl who was interested in the educational theories
of Maria Montessori, during her training in Vienna. Edith came from a middle-
class Jewish family, who owned a Socialist bookshop and publishing company in
the city. In 1925, at the age of 15, Edith came to London and met with Beatrix
and her brother Alex, who was a medical student and ardent Communist. She
returned to Vienna and began teaching in the city's slums. At the age of 17, she
met Arnold Deutsch, an older, married Soviet agent. They began an affair and
he cultivated her Communist beliefs. When he left Vienna to live in Russia,
he gave Edith a Rolleiflex camera as a farewell present and she developed a
passion for photography. In 1928 she enrolled at the Dessau Bauhaus, during the
politically-radical era of director Hannes Meyer. She completed the *Vorkurs* and
studied photography under Walter Peterhans. In 1930, she returned to Vienna,
was recruited by Comintern (the internationalist arm of the Soviet state) and
began working as a photojournalist and portrait photographer for the Soviet press
agency TASS.

During another visit to London she began an affair with Alex Tudor-Hart,
who took her to a left-wing rally in Trafalgar Square. The couple were spotted by
Special Branch, who noted they 'appeared to be on friendly terms with many of
the Communist leaders' and that their home was a meeting place for 'well-known'
persons connected with extremist propaganda.[25] When Edith was expelled from
Britain in January 1931, Tudor-Hart followed her to Vienna and the couple were
married. They were recruited as agents by Arnold Deutsch, who gave them the
joint codename 'Strela'.[26] At the same time, Edith's best friend Lintzi Friedmann
married a young Englishman named Kim Philby. The Tudor-Harts returned to
London in August 1933 and Edith set up a photographic studio on Haverstock
Hill, a short walk from Lawn Road. Following an introduction from Beatrix,
Pritchard commissioned her to take a series of photographs of the Lawn Road
Flats under construction and also of the grand opening in June 1934. Unlike other
photographers, such as Ashley Havinden who shot the flats for *Architectural Review*

in 1934, Tudor-Hart's images often explore human interaction with the building.

Pritchard also introduced her to R.S. Lambert, Editor of *The Listener*, who used her work in his magazine, including on several covers. In 1935, she was involved in the production of 'Jubilee' Chimp, published by the National Unemployed Workers' Movement, a protest at the excesses of King George V's Silver Jubilee celebrations. The pamphlet showed images of 'Jubilee', the first chimp born in London Zoo and compared its privileged living conditions to the poor diet and slum housing of Britain's working class.

In May 1934 Arnold Deutsch visited London. His orders from Moscow Central were 'to cultivate young radical high-fliers from leading British universities before they entered the corridors of power' and asked Edith to help him find suitable candidates. She introduced Deutsch to the Pritchards, and in autumn 1935 he moved into Flat 1. He took up an academic position at the University of London as his cover. His wife Josefine (a Soviet secret-police radio operator) joined him in London in April 1936 and the couple moved into Flat 7, where they lived for the next five months. Deutsch became one of the most notorious Soviet agents of the inter-war era, who with Tudor-Hart's help, recruited more than 20 spies in Britain. In June 1936 she set up his fateful meeting on a Regent's Park bench with Kim Philby (later the most successful Soviet double agent of the Cold War period.) Deutsch asked him to compile a list of his Cambridge peers who 'could penetrate into the bourgeois institutions'.[27] Philby recommended Guy Burgess, Anthony Blunt, Donald Maclean and John Cairncross – later known as the notorious 'Cambridge Five' spies. Burgess worked as a producer for BBC radio during the 1930s. A number of the Lawn Road Flats tenants and Isobar members (including pioneering television producer Lance Sieveking) were employed by the corporation. One of the block's first residents was Anthony Gordon Lewis, a member of the Communist party of Great Britain (CPGB), who was employed in the BBC Listener Research Department. Lewis moved into Flat 4 in September 1934 and retained a lease there for the next 19 years. In 1936 he married Brigitte Kuczynski whose German-Jewish family lived in an apartment at 12 Lawn Road, just across from the flats. There were six Kuczynski siblings, five of whom became Communists and three – Jürgen, Brigitte and Ursula – who became involved in Soviet espionage linked to the Lawn Road Flats. Following her marriage, Brigitte worked at the London School of Economics. Her older sister Ursula, codenamed 'Sonya', was one of the most successful and decorated secret agents of GRU, Soviet military intelligence. In 1938 she was ordered to recruit operatives to carry out 'illegal dangerous work inside Germany' to assess the state of the country's armaments industry.[28] Sonya decided to use English agents and on a visit to London, asked Brigitte to vet potential candidates for her. In October

1938, Brigitte invited Alexander Allan Foote, a car mechanic who had fought in the Spanish Civil War, to the Lawn Road Flats for a meeting. He recalled their encounter in Flat 4:

> *I pressed the bell and walked in… You will proceed to Geneva. There you will be contacted and further instructions will be given you. The voice of my vis-à-vis was quiet and matter of fact and the whole atmosphere of the flat was one of complete middle class respectability. Nothing could have been more incongruous than the contrast between this epitome of bourgeois smugness and the work that was transacted in its midst.[29]*

As instructed, Foote met Sonya in Geneva and she told him to move to Munich, where he made contacts within the Messerschmitt aeroplane factory. Sonya also used Brigitte to vet the man who would become her second husband, 25-year-old Len 'Jim' Beurton. Brigitte vetted him over lunch in the Isobar, gave him a £10 note for travelling expenses and instructed him to meet her sister in Switzerland. He carried out several missions, including establishing contacts within I.G. Farben, the pharmaceutical company, which would later supply poison gas to the Nazi concentration camps, and reconnaissance of the factory where the Zeppelin hot-air balloon was being built. In 1939 GRU ordered Sonya to divorce her estranged husband Rolf and marry Foote, so that she could gain an English passport. They married in February 1940 and Sonya arrived in Oxfordshire in December, where she was put under immediate surveillance by MI5. From her small village she continued to control Soviet agents in Britain and set up a radio system to send secret messages to Moscow.

While Sonya acclimatized to life in the shires, her elder brother Jürgen Kuczynski, a journalist and highly regarded economist, had just moved into Flat 6 in the Lawn Road Flats. 'JK', as he was known, had emigrated to Britain from Berlin earlier that year and had spent three months in Seaton detention camp in Devon as an enemy alien, but had obtained an early release after a campaign organized by a number of high-profile English supporters. From his flat in Lawn Road, where he lived for the next 18 months, JK, a man of enormous personal charm, headed the exiled German Communist party and helped form the Free German League of Culture with Fred and Diana Uhlman, whose home on nearby Downshire Hill became a meeting place for refugee artists. Kuczynski sent reports to Moscow on the political and economic situation in Britain and entertained both the Russian ambassador Ivan Maisky and Anatole Gromov, the

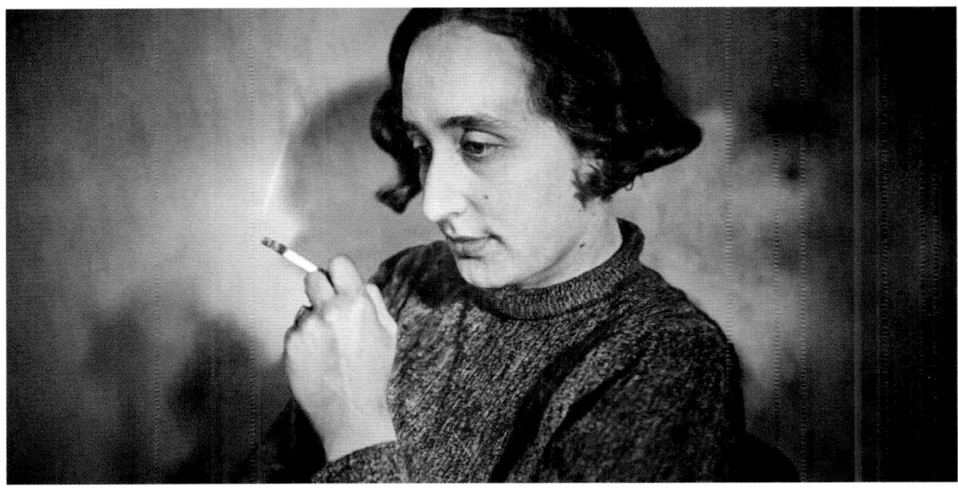

Soviet press attaché, in the Lawn Road Flats and Isobar. He also introduced one of their colleagues Simon Davidovitch Kremer to the apartment block. At the end of 1936 Kremer moved into Flat 1, which Arnold Deutsch had vacated. Kremer hid his espionage career in plain sight. Employed at the Embassy as Secretary to the Military Attaché, he was also a professional spy, an officer of the Red Army's foreign military intelligence directorate. He recruited several key agents for the GRU and had a reputation as one of their best officers in London.

It was through the triangular axis of Simon Kremer, Jürgen and Sonya Kuczynski that one of the most audacious acts of 20th-century espionage was committed – and one that arguably changed the course of world history. Klaus Fuchs was a gifted German physicist and member of the Communist party who arrived in England from Leipzig in 1933. He had escaped from Germany the day after the arson attack on the German parliament building, the Reichstag, which had been blamed on Communists, and claimed that the party had ordered him to continue his studies abroad: 'They said I must finish my studies because after the revolution in Germany people would be required with technical knowledge to take part in the building up of the Communist Germany.'[30]

Fuchs completed his PhD at Bristol and then moved to Edinburgh, where he worked under fellow German émigré Professor Max Born, who is credited with developing quantum mechanics. In 1939 his scientific career was put on hold while he was interned abroad as an enemy alien. However, as with Jürgen Kuczynski, a group of influential friends, including Born, secured his release, on the basis of his scientific ability, and he returned to Britain. In May 1941 he joined

Professor Rudolf Peierls's team at Birmingham University and was asked to sign the Official Secrets Act. Peierls was working on the British atomic bomb project and Fuchs became involved in investigating the potential scale and efficiency of a nuclear blast, in a mission codenamed 'Tube Alloys'.

At the end of 1941 Fuchs received the news that Hitler's army was advancing on Moscow. Horrified at the prospect of Germany obliterating Russia, he decided to share the ground-breaking research he had been working on. He contacted Jürgen Kuczynski at Lawn Road and asked him to open channels with Moscow. JK first put Fuchs in touch with Simon Kremer and then Sonya became his handler, meeting Fuchs in the Oxfordshire countryside for regular updates and arranging a system whereby he left classified documents from the Tube Alloys project in a series of rural drop-off points, including holes in tree roots. At their last meeting in 1943, Fuchs gave Sonya a massive dossier detailing how far the atomic bomb project had developed. He then left for New York with Peierls, where they joined the Manhattan Project, which developed the first nuclear weapons used in World War II. In 1951 Fuchs was interrogated by MI5 and confessed to his actions. He was sentenced to 14 years in prison and stripped of his British citizenship, but he defended his actions:

I never saw myself as a spy. I just couldn't understand why the
West was not prepared to share the atom bomb with Moscow.
I was of the opinion that something with that immense destructive
potential should be made available to the big powers equally.[31]

Welcomed as refugees by the Pritchards, the spies were rendered inconspicuous by the tide of fellow exiles fleeing persecution from Germany and Austria. The physical design of the Lawn Road Flats was also advantageous to anyone wishing to come and go unobserved. Arnold Deutsch, Simon Kremer, Jürgen and Brigitte Kuczynski all rented apartments on the ground floor, with easy access to the street and to Belsize Park Underground Station along a wooded path at the rear. They did not have to cross paths with other tenants on the internal staircase.

MI5 investigated other Lawn Road Flats residents, including heiress Eva Collet-Reckitt, owner of Collet's political bookshop in Charing Cross Road, the poet and publisher Francis Meynell and philosopher Cyril Joad. Author David Burke has estimated that a total of 32 individuals associated with Soviet espionage lived in the flats or around Lawn Road during the 1930s and early 1940s.[32] How many others with hidden agendas and secret foreign paymasters visited the building and Isobar during this time, we will never know.

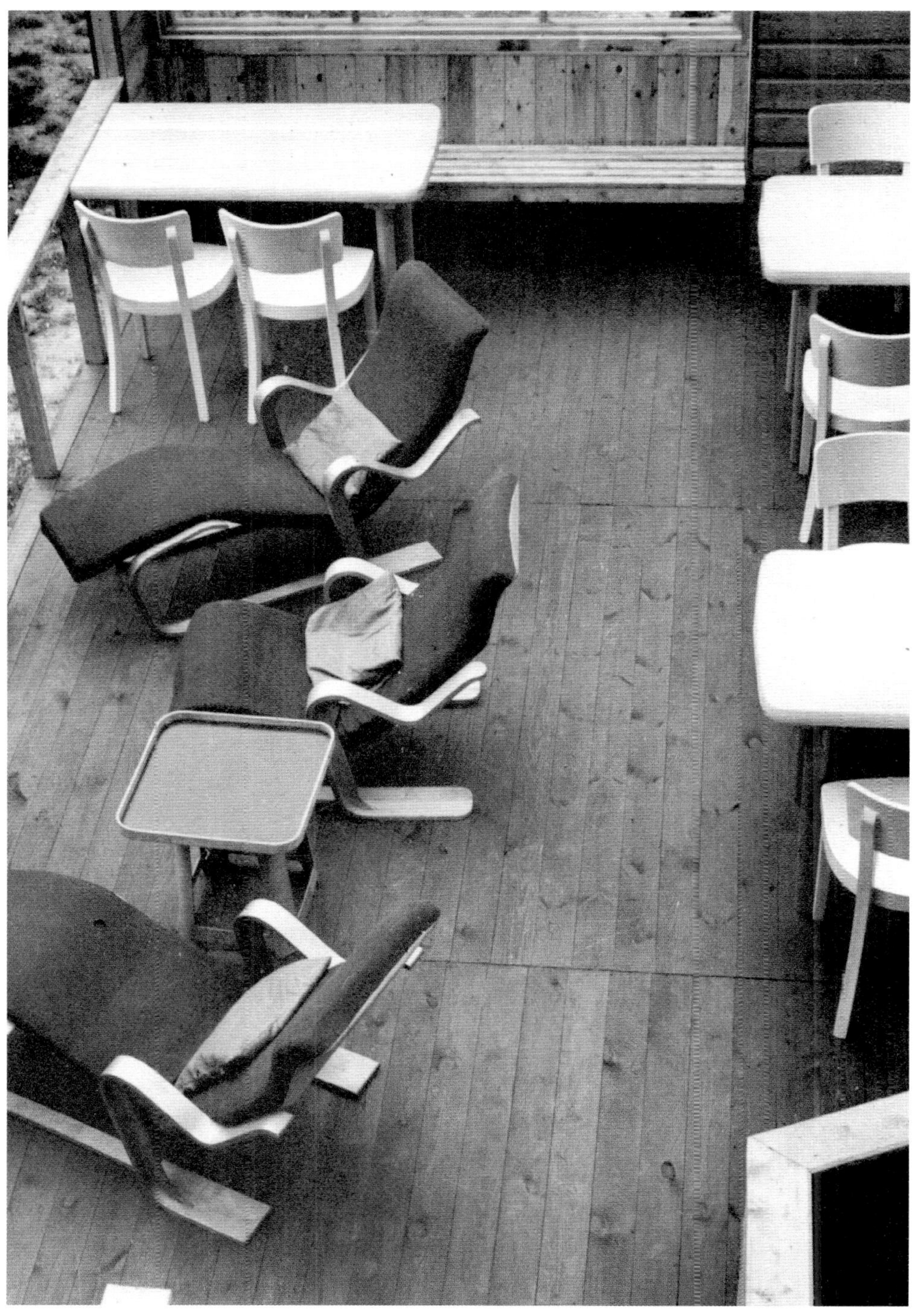

ABOVE: Guests could enjoy al fresco dining overlooking the Isobar garden. Pritchard designed a square tray to convert the Isokon stool into a handy side table.

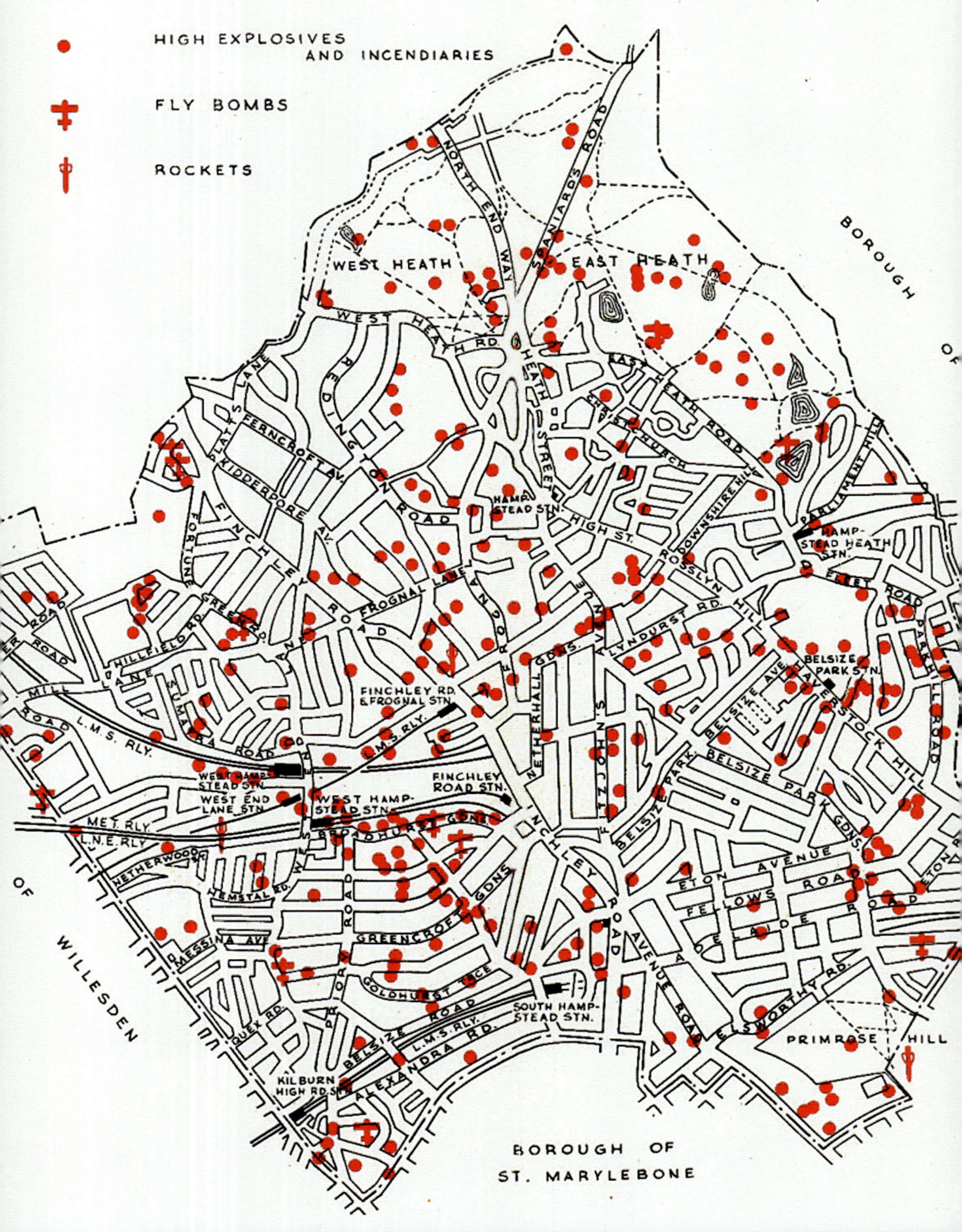

HIGH EXPLOSIVES AND INCENDIARIES
FLY BOMBS
ROCKETS
WEST HEATH
EAST HEATH
SPANIARDS ROAD
NORTH END WAY
BOROUGH OF
WEST HEATH RD.
HEATH STREET
EAST HEATH ROAD
PLATTS LANE
FERNCROFT AV.
REDINGTON ROAD
KIDDERPORE AV.
FINCHLEY ROAD
FORTUNE GREEN RD.
HAMPSTEAD STN.
HAMPSTEAD HIGH ST.
DOWNSHIRE HILL
CHURCH ROW
ROSSLYN HILL
PARLIAMENT HILL
HAMPSTEAD HEATH STN.
HILLFIELD RD.
SUMATRA ROAD
FROGNAL LANE
FROGNAL ROAD
LYNDHURST RD.
FLEET ROAD
HAVERSTOCK HILL
BELSIZE PARK STN.
FINCHLEY RD. & FROGNAL STN.
NETHERHALL GDNS.
FITZJOHN'S AVENUE
BELSIZE AVENUE
BELSIZE PARK GDNS.
MILL ROAD
L.M.S. RLY.
L.M.S. RLY.
WEST HAMPSTEAD STN.
WEST END LANE STN.
WEST HAMPSTEAD STN.
FINCHLEY ROAD STN.
MET. RLY.
L.N.E. RLY.
NETHERWOOD RD.
BROADHURST GDNS.
FINCHLEY ROAD
BELSIZE PARK
ETON AVENUE
FELLOWS ROAD
ADELAIDE ROAD
ETON ROAD
HEMSTAL RD.
MESSINA AV.
GREENCROFT GDNS.
GOLDHURST TERRACE
SOUTH HAMPSTEAD STN.
AVENUE ROAD
ELSWORTHY RD.
PRIMROSE HILL
QUEX RD.
PRIORY ROAD
BELSIZE ROAD
L.M.S. RLY.
ALEXANDRA RD.
KILBURN HIGH RD. STN.
OF WILLESDEN
BOROUGH OF ST. MARYLEBONE

THE WAR AND ITS AFTERMATH

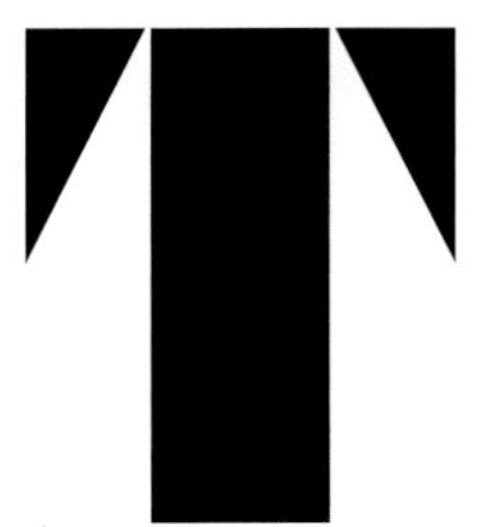

HE FIRST MONTHS OF THE WAR WERE A BLEAK TIME
for Jack Pritchard. In debt, with no hope of government
war contracts for the Isokon Furniture Company with
timber supplies from the Baltic cut off, he took a desk
job at the Ministry of Information. He worked in the
Censorship Division, assessing the suitability of illustrations
for publication, but rapidly grew critical of the Ministry's
work. One evening in the Isobar he confided his frustrations to his friend and
fellow Design and Industries Association (DIA) member Hugh Weeks, who was
living in Flat 1. Weeks was setting up a statistics section at the Ministry of Supply
and invited Pritchard to join his team as a Temporary Statistical Officer. Their task
was to provide the minister with a weekly report on how the production of war
materials was meeting War Office demands. It was confidential and demanding
work for which Pritchard was required to sign the Official Secrets Act. He
frequently invited his colleagues back to Lawn Road during the Blitz: 'It would be
a late session and sometimes a few members of the department would come to the
Isobar and maybe stay the night if the bombing was troublesome.' While he was
working in the Ministry, Pritchard met Leonard Tregoning, whose family owned a
steel mill in South Wales. He suggested that Pritchard could use his plant to restart
Isokon for the government's Utility furniture programme. The proposal got the
green light from Hugh Dalton, President of the Board of Trade, but fell through
when the mill was requisitioned by the Army for other uses.

The war transformed the lives of all those involved in the Lawn Road Flats.
Wells Coates returned to the RAF to work on fighter aircraft development, for
which he was later awarded an OBE and Philip Harben left the Isobar to join the
RAF, where his job, Pritchard rather dismissively claimed, 'was to provide Winston
Churchill with hot coffee and boiled eggs when flying high without a pressurized
cabin.'[1] In 1942, Harben compered a BBC radio cooking programme, which led
after the war to his role as Britain's first television chef, presenting *Cookery*, a show
which ran from 1946–51 and turned him into a household name.

Fleetwood Pritchard, who was now employed as Head of Public Relations
to the Minister of Transport, moved into Flat 8 and brought with him Harben's
replacement Robert Braun, who had worked in his advertising agency. Braun had
big boots to fill, but proved himself up to the task. Building on Harben's legacy,
he initiated a series of themed dinners and provided members with exotic dishes
made from scarce wartime ingredients, which he ingeniously sourced. The Isobar
became the only restaurant in London where 'bananas and cream' were served one
evening, at the height of the Blitz, when US Ambassador James John Winant and
his wife dined in the club with Philip and Lella Sargant Florence.

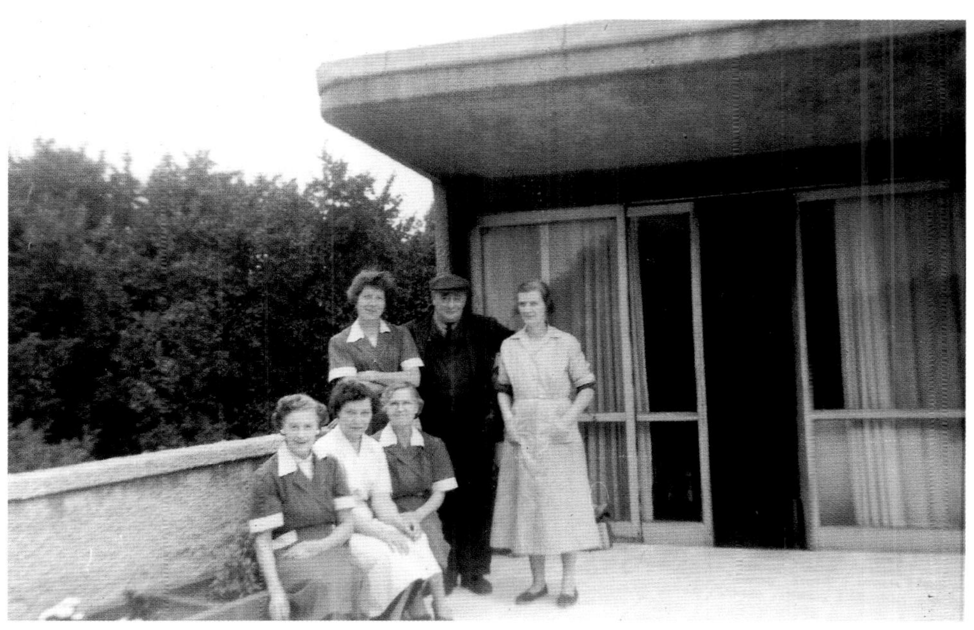

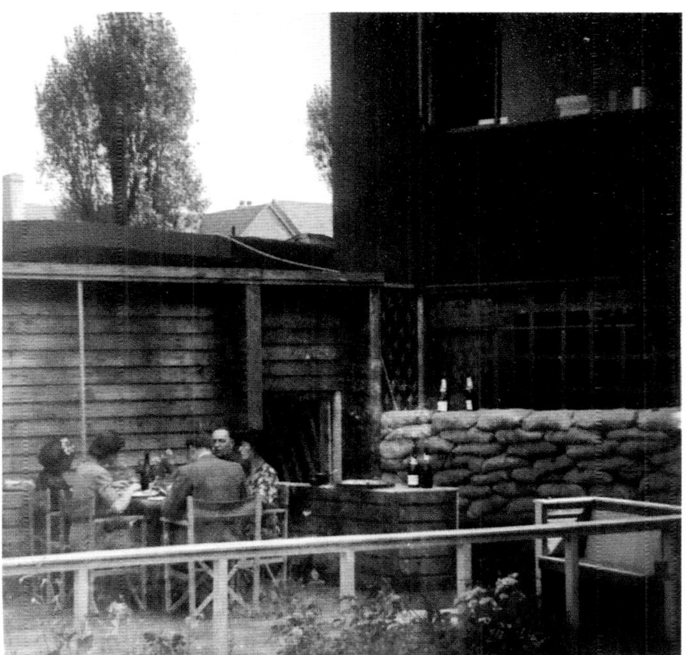

ABOVE: The first staff included Mrs Turner, 'a homely type' who dealt with all the domestic arrangements, Mrs Snooks, the charwoman and 'star turn', and former police officer, Bob Wilson, who amused everyone with his spontaneous wit. ABOVE: Pritchard frequently invited his colleagues from the Ministry of Supply back to the Isobar. Harben's successor Robert Braun proved talented at sourcing scarce ingredients.

During the air raids some tenants brought their bedding down to sleep in the Isobar at night. On occasion there were spats between those who wanted to sleep and those of a hedonistic nature who wanted to dance the night away. Agatha Christie preferred to brave the nightly bombing in her own bed, 'face covered with a pillow as a protection against flying glass, and on a chair by my side my two most precious possessions: my fur coat and my hot water bottle'.[2]

The residents had formed an Executive Committee and the Isobar was well-stocked with a range of emergency equipment and a battery wireless set so members could keep abreast of news developments. The war of wireless propaganda was closely monitored by a group of intellectuals living in the flats. Between 1 December 1939 and 16 March 1940 a weekly bulletin entitled *Comparative Broadcasts* was compiled in Flat 7, edited by economist L.W. Desbrow and his advisors, the MPs Vyvyan Adams (Conservative) and John Parker (Labour), General Secretary of the Fabian Society. They analysed how radio stations in different countries reported the same wartime events. Isobar members were informed:

> *A group of private members of the club propose running a service of great political and sociological interest. Each subscriber to the service will receive through the post a weekly bulletin containing a comparison of the various national broadcasts on the same subjects. The editors will make an objective precis of the broadcast propaganda of each of several nations and will collect together those dealing with a few specified subjects each week and post them to subscribers.*[3]

While the BBC had closed down stations at the outbreak of war, Germany had expanded its broadcasting network. In December 1939 the bulletin reported that Germany was winning the propaganda war because if 'you turned the knob of a wireless on medium or short waves you find that nearly every second station you get is a German one.'[4] Another bulletin observed many British listeners were tuning in to German stations for their good music and that the Nazis were exploiting the situation by 'sandwiching propaganda between large slices of entertainment.' It also covered the development in the Balkans of 'Germany producing very clever imitations of British programmes "twisted" to German purpose'. In an observation relevant to our own era of 'fake news', *Comparative Broadcasts* concluded 'this opens up a marvellous vista of doubts and suspicions.'[5]

On 13 June 1940 Paris fell to the Nazis, and with the threat of a British invasion, the government initiated a mass evacuation scheme to remove children to safety overseas. Molly had continued to see patients in her Harley Street consulting rooms, but now the Pritchards agreed she would take Jonathan and Jeremy out of school and accompany them to Canada. Separately Beatrix Tudor-Hart arranged for Jack's daughter Jennifer to travel to Canada to stay with her grandfather the artist Percyval Tudor-Hart at his riverside mansion in Quebec.

Molly enrolled her sons in Upper Canada College, a private boys' boarding school in Toronto and in October travelled to Lincoln, Massachusetts, where she moved in with Walter and Ise Gropius in their recently completed house at 68 Baker Bridge Road. Shortly after arriving in the US, Gropius had been given a plot of land by local philanthropist and art patron Mrs James Storrow. Gropius had built his house, the first in the US to be constructed on Bauhaus principles, totally from prefabricated industrial components, but in a nod to his new homeland, had included some local details, such as white clapboarding (applied vertically), a brick hearth, fieldstone foundations and a screened porch. Gropius had sent to London for his Isokon furniture and the living room and study both contained Long Chairs. Marcel Breuer and his new wife Constance had built a home on a neighbouring plot, with a monumental wall and fireplace of rough local stone, reminiscent of the Gane Pavilion. The Gropius' home in Lincoln became a refuge for many European exiles during the war. Molly lived on and off with the couple for the next two years, occasionally moving into an apartment in Cambridge when they were short of space. She noted there were tensions in the marriage and wrote to Jack: 'Ise is terribly annoying at times – not to me – but if I were Walter I'd want to kill her! So beautiful, so hard – so un understanding [sic].'[6] Molly and the former German cavalry officer shared a passion for horses and frequently went riding together. 'When Walter is riding he loses all that sad look and looks really happy and serene', she observed.[7]

With his help Molly found a position at the Harvard University Psychological Centre under Dr Harold Stuart. Between 1940 and 1942, she worked on research into the development and structure of the Personality and was able to maintain her therapeutic practice by analyzing several students in the postgraduate School of Psychology. The Lawn Road fixation with propaganda and her knowledge of *Comparative Broadcasts* also proved extremely useful. She joined a team at Harvard run by Dr Harry Murray researching the psychological effects of propaganda and the factors involved in building and maintaining morale. They used nearby Boston as their case study – a city in which 'rumours' between various ethnic groups were causing social tensions. Molly helped set up a 'Rumour Clinic', collecting the rumours that were circulating and having them analysed by a psychologist. Each Sunday, the rumours were published in the city's largest newspaper together with explanations and, where possible, accurate information to refute them. Molly later

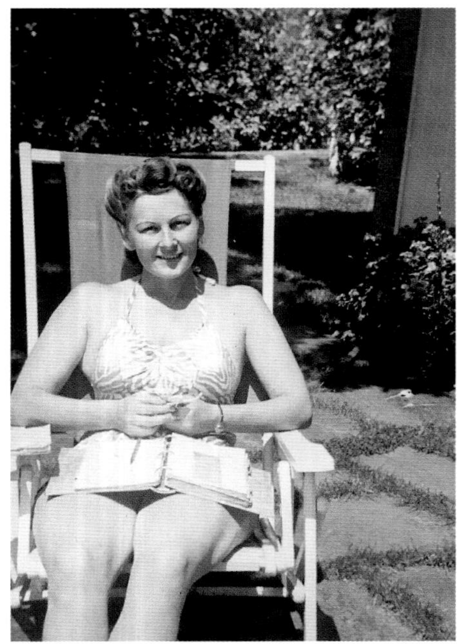 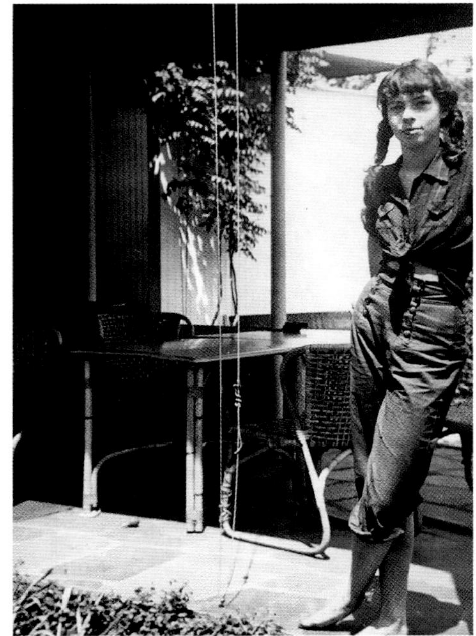

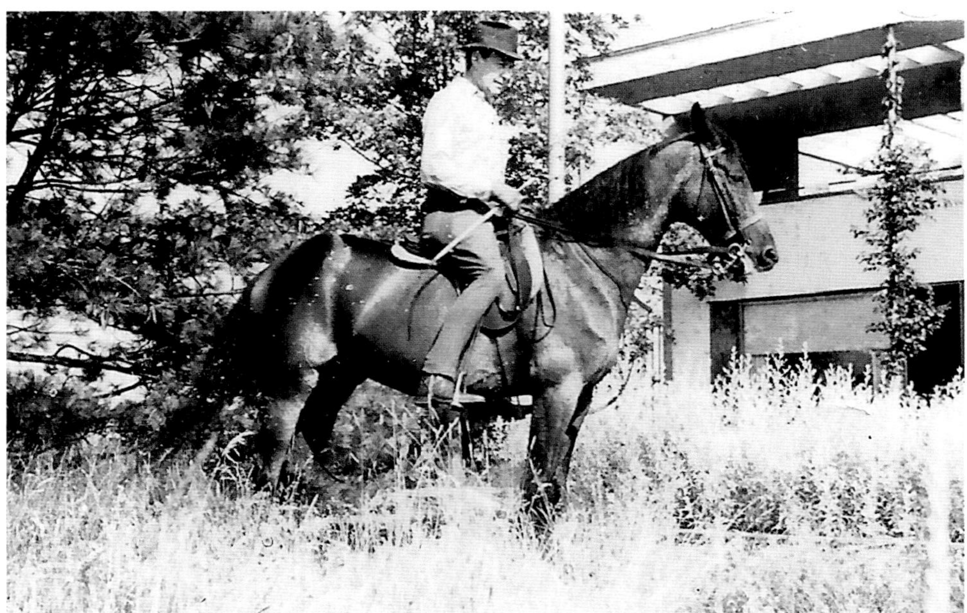

ABOVE, TOP-LEFT: Ise Gropius sunbathing at the Gropius house at 68 Baker Bridge Road, Lincoln, Massachusetts. ABOVE, TOP-RIGHT: Ati Gropius ABOVE: Molly Pritchard observed that Walter Gropius was never happier than on horseback. They often rode together in Lincoln.

published a paper on this research in London and, throughout her stay in the US, she made useful new contacts for Jack and Isokon.

Had it not been for the interruption of the war, Isokon might have successfully launched its furniture range in the hugely lucrative North American market. When he had tendered his resignation as Controller of Design, Breuer had offered to help Jack Pritchard promote the company in the US. Breuer had used Isokon furniture, including the Long Chair, Short Chair, Nesting Table and Dining Chair on his Unit stand at the Golden Gate Exhibition in San Francisco in early 1939. The pieces could be ordered through New Furniture Incorporated in New York's Rockefeller Plaza. The store (which also sold Alvar Aalto's furniture) wished to acquire exclusive rights to retail Isokon in the US until production in Britain was halted by the war.

In September 1940, Molly and Breuer travelled to New York. He took her to see Eliot Noyes, Director of the Museum of Modern Art, who advised her to approach several American manufacturers with a view to producing Isokon models in the US. She met Penguin Books to investigate marketing the Book Donkey, but was told the young US division had no time or resources for such a tie-up. It suggested she meet with rival company, Pocket Books.[8] Molly also went to see Howard Myers, Editor of the *Architectural Record*, who offered to show photographs of Isokon furniture to his retail contacts. In October Breuer met with the Herman Miller Furniture Company in the hope of persuading the firm to manufacture his plywood designs, but was informed it did not wish to add to its existing lines.[9] Breuer became increasingly preoccupied with his new architectural practice and teaching at Harvard, and further momentum was lost. In January 1941, the prestigious New York department store James McCutcheon & Co. contacted Molly at Harvard, to enquire about obtaining furniture it had seen illustrated in *Architectural Forum*.[10] She replied: 'I am trying to arrange for the models to be manufactured in this country. Timber control has put a stop to its manufacture.'

Back in London, Jack had become firm friends with Henry Moore, now an Official War Artist. He frequently dropped in to see Pritchard after sketching in Belsize Park and Hampstead Underground Stations, which were being used as air-raid shelters. He wrote to Molly: 'Sometimes on a Sunday I would take a train and then walk to Perry Green and have lunch with Irina and Henry Moore. I might take a bottle of wine or something to contribute. In the garden there was a small pile of hay; after lunch I would sleep on one side and Henry on the other.'[11]

In 1941 the artistic community in the flats was boosted by the arrival of the Czech architect Jacques Groag, and his wife Jacqueline, a textile designer. Jacques Groag, who had worked in Adolf Loos's office in Vienna, joined Gordon Russell's team designing Utility furniture. Jacqueline had studied under Josef Hofmann in

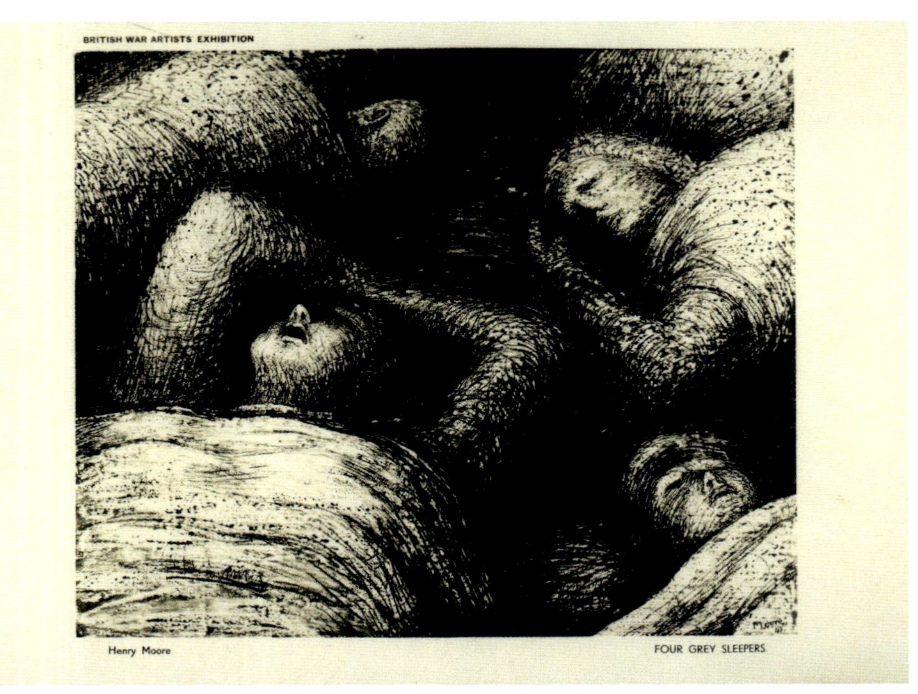

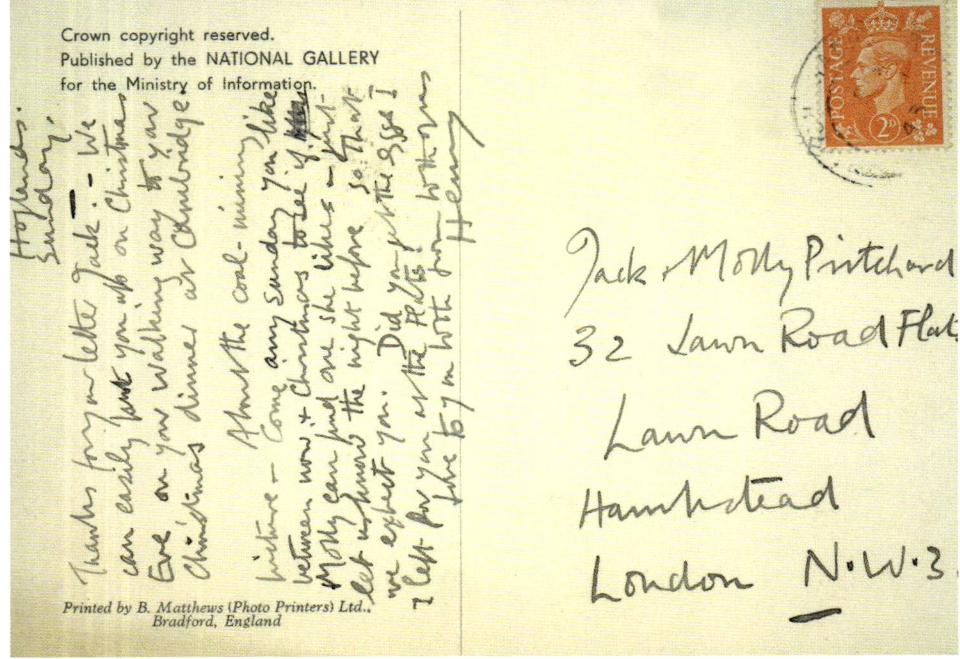

ABOVE: Artist Henry Moore sketched Londoners sheltering in nearby underground stations during the Blitz. Pritchard brought Gropius, Breuer, and Moholy-Nagy large-format books of his works as gifts after they moved to the USA.

Vienna and worked for the Wiener Werkstätte. She received a gold medal at the
Paris World Fair of 1937 and had designed textiles for Chanel, Jeanne Lanvin and
Elsa Schiaparelli. Her designs for Edinburgh Weavers and David Whitehead were
influential during the 1940s and her work featured prominently at the Festival of
Britain. The couple lived in the Lawn Road Flats until 1958.

Molly returned to London towards the end of summer 1942, leaving her sons
at school in Canada. She offered her paper on 'Rumour' to the Army Bureau
of Current Affairs, who, claiming it would 'do a lot of good', published it as
a pamphlet in 1943 and again in 1947.[12] She wrote another paper proposing
methods of undermining Nazi ideology among German prisoners of war.[13]
In 1943 she began work for the Ministry of Supply, touring factories to study
women's working conditions and produced a report suggesting psychological
techniques to improve productivity.[14] Meanwhile the Gropiuses acted as surrogate
parents to the teenage Jonathan and Jeremy Pritchard. Walter Gropius advised
Jonathan on an application to Harvard and, with his help, he won a full scholarship
to study Engineering.[15] Jeremy remained at Upper Canada College until 1944,
when he returned to England and finished his education at Bryanston School
before going up to Cambridge. To thank Walter Gropius for his support, Jack
Pritchard sent him a drawing by Henry Moore. It was delivered by Hugh Weeks,
who had travelled across the Atlantic on official business with Winston Churchill
on board HMS *Duke of York*.

By the end of 1944 Pritchard moved to the Ministry of Fuel and Power.
Anticipating a shortage of fuel after the war, it was looking into ways of improving
the efficiency of domestic heating. Jack proposed a research trip and travelled to
the US in December. As always, he managed to combine business with pleasure
and on his arrival in New York, telephoned Gropius, Breuer and Moholy-Nagy,
for whom he had brought books of Henry Moore's latest work He travelled
to Lincoln in the depths of the New England winter, spent a snowy weekend
with Walter and Ise, went to see Breuer's house and visited Aluminium City
Terrace, Breuer and Gropius's 1941 housing development in New Kensington,
Philadelphia, built by the federal government to house defence workers.

*Two hundred and fifty dwellings were scattered on a steeply sloping
site. They had taken full advantage of the slope to let the sun in, and
the living rooms had long windows on the south side. The value of
winter sun for space heating through large glass windows was
demonstrated on many occasions. Even when there was heavy*

He travelled to Chicago, where Moholy-Nagy took him to a Christmas eggnog
party in the Tavern Club at the top of a skyscraper. Jack recalled:

*I wanted to take the opportunity while in the city to see something of
the new Bauhaus at the Institute of Design. Moholy's enthusiasm for
fun and all technical innovations was infectious. After the Eggnog
party we went to the Institute. To get there we had to go through the
old slaughter houses… We went up in a lift, getting out at the kitchen
of a night club and then through into the Institute… It was exciting
to see the work being done there and to see for the first time Moholy's
Light Modulator. It was an exhausting evening.[17]*

Moholy-Nagy also took Pritchard to the furniture research department of the
mail-order firm Sears Roebuck: 'Moholy insisted that we must see their "fucking
machine". It was of course a simple device for testing the springs in mattresses.'[18]
It was the last time he would see his Hungarian friend. Moholy-Nagy died of
leukaemia on 24 November 1946.

Jack called in to see Ati Gropius at Black Mountain College in North Carolina.
He also met former Bauhaus master, Josef Albers, who, with his wife Anni, was
teaching in the art school, and bought several paintings from him. In addition
to catching up with his Bauhaus friends, Jack and his colleagues managed to
interview 160 people and cross America from Washington to Seattle, looking
at new forms of heating. His report was published in 1946 but its enthusiastic
recommendations for domestic solar power were thought far-fetched.

On his return to England, Pritchard turned his attention back to the flats. The
building had emerged from the war years structurally unscarred, but looked shabby,
having been hastily painted dark brown during the Blitz (to avoid the German
bombers using the building as a navigation aid), and was now in urgent need of
repair. In December 1946, it was voted 'joint-second ugliest building in London' in
a competition run by *Horizon* magazine. Wells Coates was furious, telling Pritchard
he had been 'shocked and surprised' at the building's condition on a recent visit.[19]
Showing the old wounds had still not healed, he wrote of 'the many serious
knocks re LRF' he had endured 'since the day it was opened by a ceremony on
the roof: when Miss Cazalet was instructed to make a speech which gave nearly all

the credit for the ideas behind the building to Molly and I was rather offhandedly referred to as "Mr Russell Coates". I realise, that with the Blitz, the war, the lack of licenses etc. things are difficult to arrange at the moment, but I hope that as soon as you can manage it the building will be restored properly.'

Jack turned to Walter Gropius to defend the flats. The Harvard Professor of Architecture wrote to *Horizon*'s Editor Cyril Connolly acknowledging that the brown paint was a mistake, but stating it could not 'veil the basic soundness of this handsome building of which I thought London could be proud.'[20]

The war behind him, Jack began a succession of largely unfulfilling jobs. Sir Stafford Cripps invited him to join the Furniture Working Party and in October 1945 he was made chairman of the Design Sub-Group, which looked at the use of alternative materials in the furniture industry. The group which included Gordon Russell, travelled to Switzerland, where Pritchard arranged for them to meet Sigfried Giedion in Zurich. They also visited the Kunstgewerbeschule, headed by former Bauhaus Master, Johannes Itten, which Pritchard described as 'an eye-opener', noting his latest syllabus used 'art to expand his students' ideas and technology to keep their feet on the ground'.[21] At the end of the trip, Gordon Russell wrote a report on their findings, which included a proposal from Pritchard for the establishment of a British Standards Institution for testing the performance of furniture.

After a short and unhappy stint at Utility furniture maker Harris Lebus, Pritchard resolved to go it alone. On 2 February 1949, he left for America to pick up contacts he had made during the war in the heating and furniture industries. Although reviving Isokon may have been on his mind, shortly after he arrived in the US, he received an invitation from Britain to become the first Director and Secretary of the Furniture Development Council and was asked if he could keep his eye out for any useful information about testing the performance of furniture on his trip. He travelled from New Orleans to Wisconsin, stopping off to meet many of his old friends including Gropius and Breuer at Harvard. In Chicago he visited Serge Chermayeff, who was now President of the Institute of Design. He also went to see Sibyl Moholy-Nagy and bought three of László Moholy-Nagy's pictures, including a crayon drawing he completed just before he died.

On his way through New York he purchased an extravagant selection of cheeses – whole large Cheddars, Stiltons and Roqueforts unobtainable in ration-hit Britain. He carried these back to Lawn Road, arriving just in time to make a grand entrance at the wine and cheese party Molly had thrown in the penthouse. He went to meet the Furniture Development Council and accepted their job.

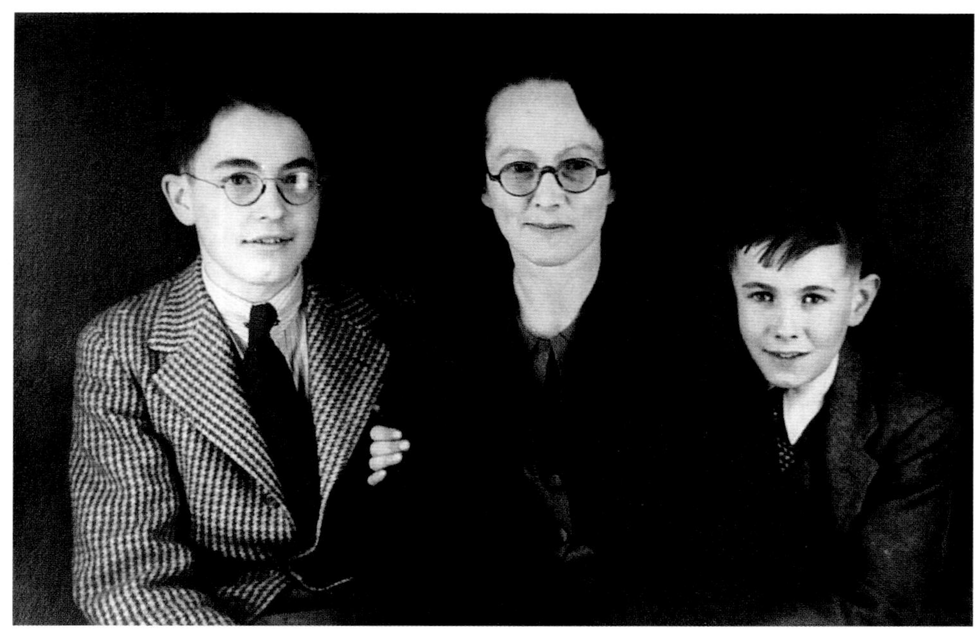

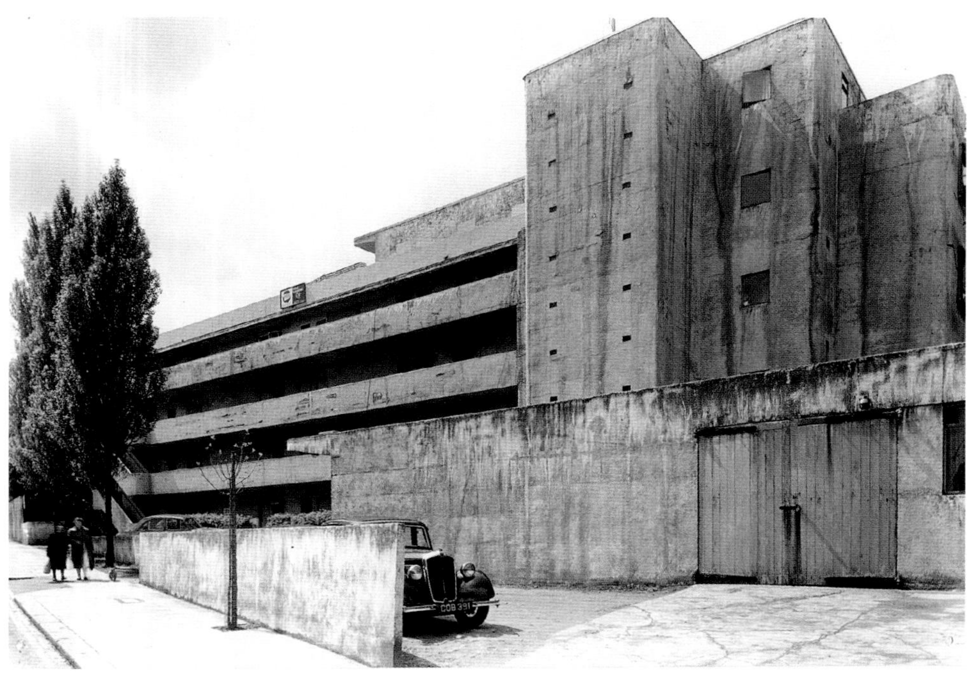

ABOVE, TOP: Molly, Jeremy and Jonathan Pritchard left Liverpool on board RMS *Samaria* on 3 July 1940. The other ship in their evacuee convoy was torpedoed. ABOVE: Lawn Road Flats were painted dark brown during the Blitz to prevent the Luftwaffe from using them as a navigation landmark.

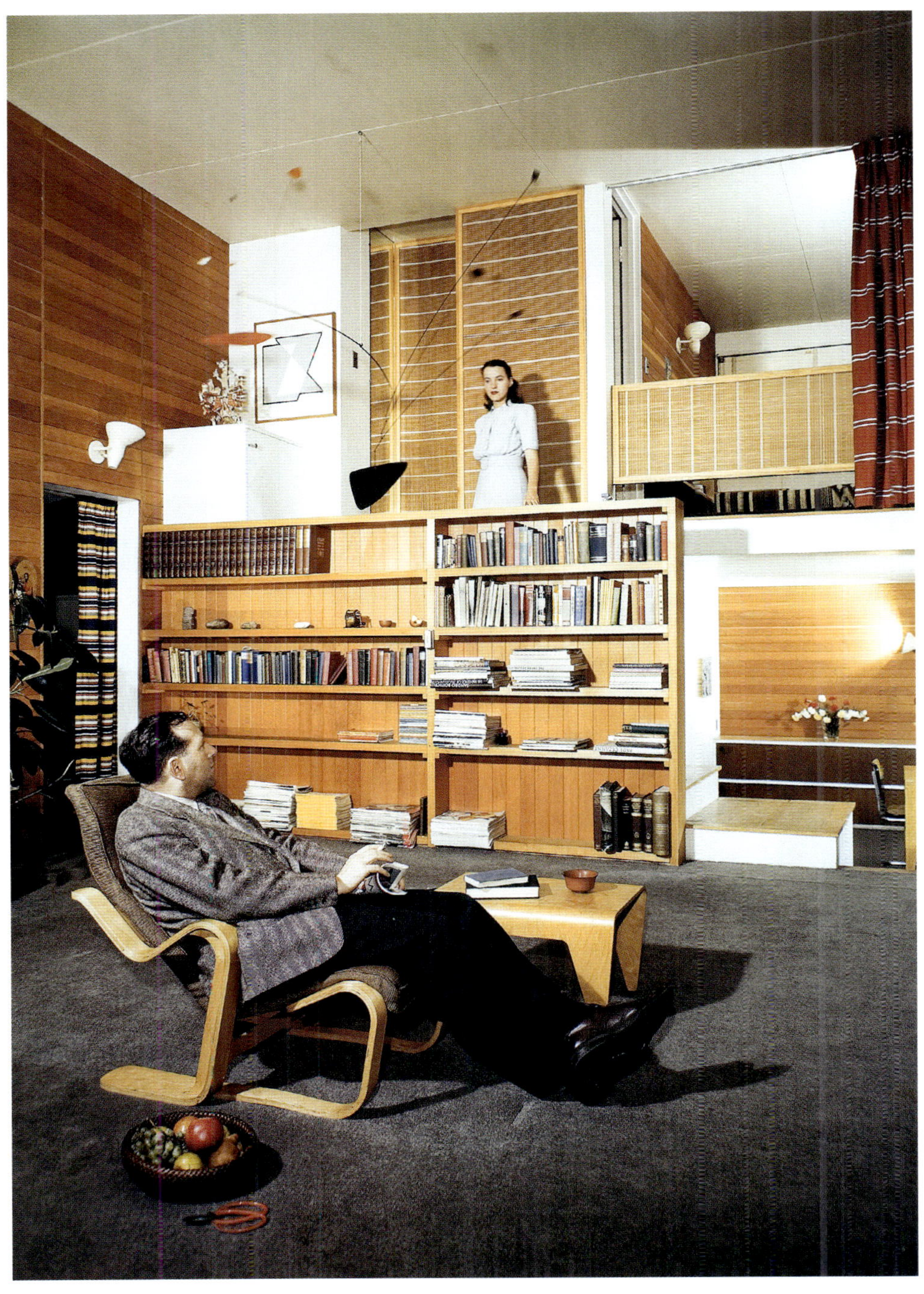

ABOVE: Marcel and Connie Breuer in their 1939 home in Lincoln, Massachusetts, with a giant mobile by Alexander Calder. Breuer shipped his Isokon furniture from London.

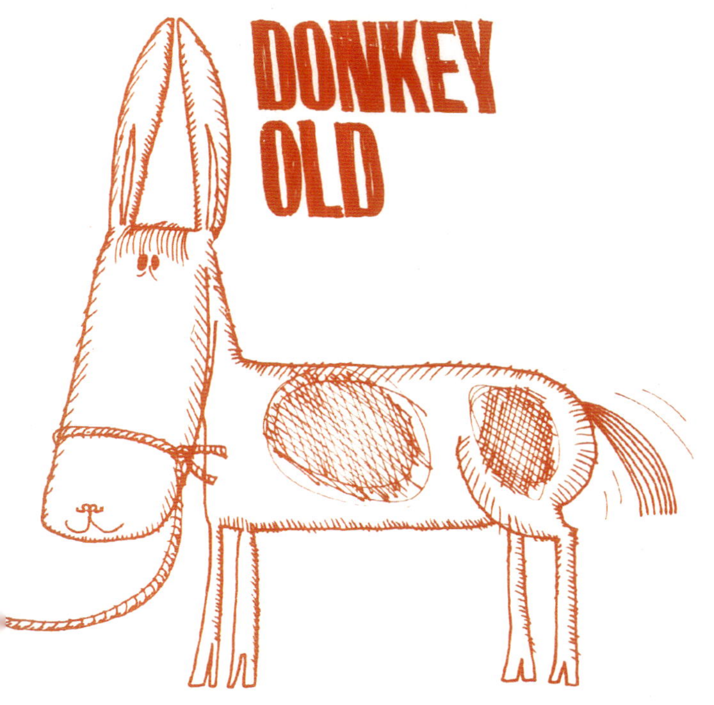

DONKEY
OLD

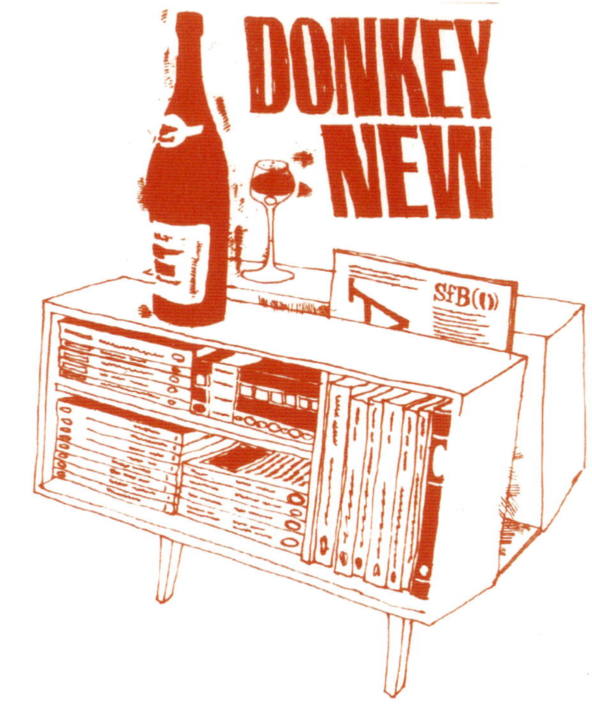

DONKEY
NEW
SfB(0)

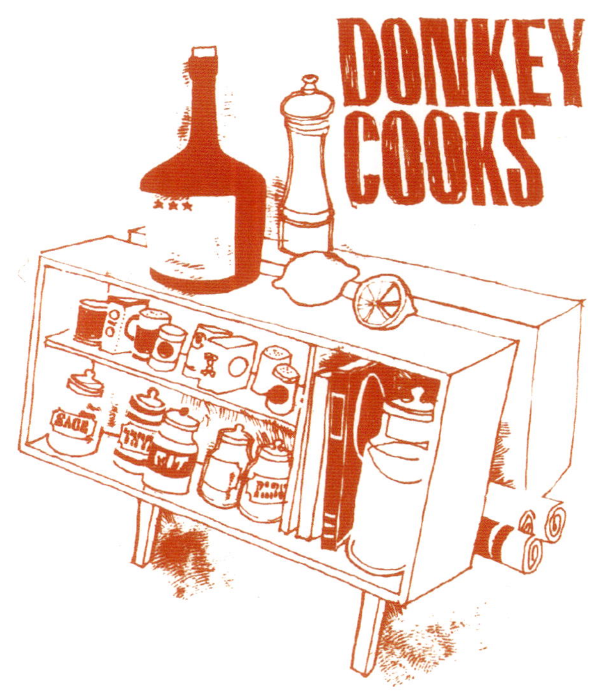

DONKEY
COOKS

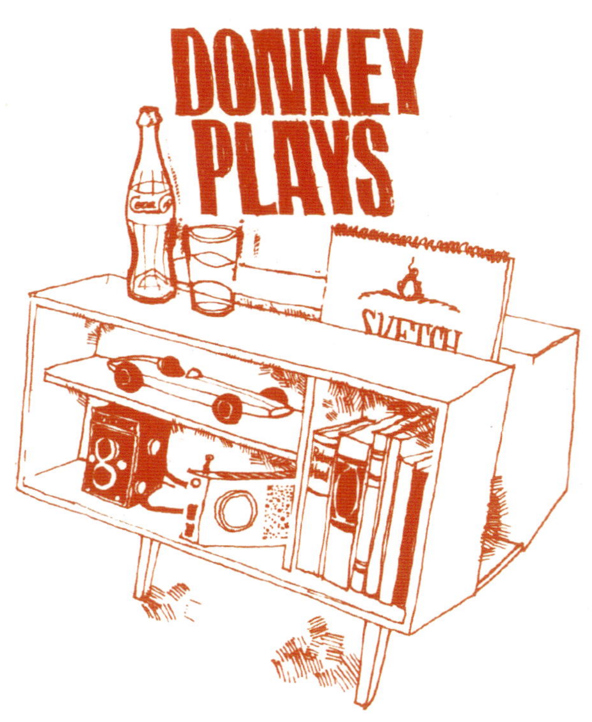

DONKEY
PLAYS

CHAPTER 10

THE 1950S AND 60S – THE REBIRTH OF ISOKON

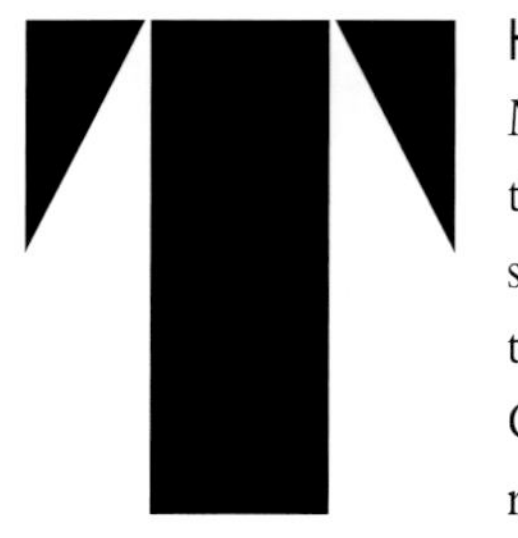

HE FIRST GREAT GATHERING OF THE INTERNATIONAL
Modernist architects after the war took place in 1947 in
the English market town of Bridgwater in Somerset. Over
seven days, more than eighty leading architects, writers and
town planners gathered to discuss the future of urban design.
Gropius, who was advising the US government on the
reconstruction of Germany, arrived in Britain straight from a
classified fact-finding mission on the state of Berlin and the possible establishment
of Frankfurt as the new West German capital. He was shocked by what he had seen:

Berlin is a has been! A disintegrated corpse! Impossible to describe.
The people bent down, bitter, hopeless. In the evening a meeting with
Scharoun, Max Taut, Redslob, Lilly Reich – all so old looking that I
scarcely recognised them.[1]

It was a key moment in Les Congrès Internationaux d'Architecture Moderne's
(CIAM's) history. The war had devastated cities across Europe and rebuilding now
presented exciting opportunities for architects and planners. It seemed Modernism
had at last come of age, as Gropius observed to Philip Morton Shand:

By momentum of ideas the movement has spread on its own without
our knowing it. New groups like the Czech, Argentine and Cuban
are certainly encouraging and it seems to be worth going on pushing
in the same direction as we have done since 1928.[2]

The war had proved a watershed for modern architecture in Britain and the
1951 Festival of Britain, brainchild of John Gloag, was to herald the virtual state
sponsorship of Modernism. Over the next decade it was used for public buildings
ranging from schools and hospitals to public housing. The pioneering MARS
(Modern Architectural Research Group) members had become the movement's
elder statesmen and a new generation of English architects and designers were
emerging in the more receptive cultural climate. Gerald Barry who had reported
on the opening of the Lawn Road Flats for *The News Chronicle* in 1934, was
the Festival of Britain's Director General and Hugh Casson, a former student
of Christopher Nicholson, was the Director of Architecture. Coates designed
the Television and Telecinema pavilions; Fry, the Waterloo Gate Entrance and
Harbour Bar; and Ernest Race (who would later rework several Isokon designs)

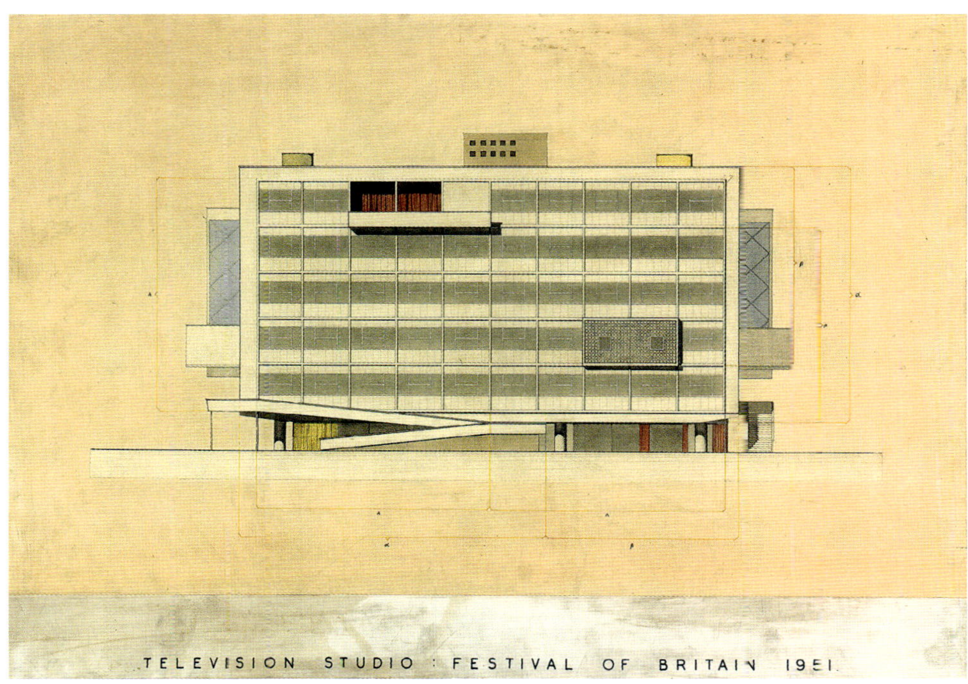

ABOVE: Wells Coates designed the 400-seater Telekinema for the 1951 Festival of Britain. Constructed from light steel, it was the first cinema designed to show both regular and 3D-films and television.

designed the outdoor furniture including the popular Antelope and Springbok chairs. The influence of Jacqueline Groag's textiles was evident everywhere. Jonathan Pritchard, who after Harvard and Cambridge had joined Felix Samuely's engineering practice, worked on the Skylon, the streamlined, futuristic sculpture that became the abiding symbol of the exhibition. A popular joke of the period was that, like the Labour–led British economy of 1951, 'It had no visible means of support'.

The Festival's construction coincided with the Eighth CIAM Congress in Hoddesdon, Hertfordshire. Its proximity to London allowed the delegates, including Gropius, Breuer and Le Corbusier, to attend the Festival site. Gropius, who had last been in the capital in 1937, found post-war London transformed into a 'jewel of a city', but gave a muted response to most of the Festival architecture.[3]

In the spring of 1952 Breuer wrote to Pritchard asking for his help in organising a two-month tour of Europe with his wife Connie. Pritchard put a great deal of effort into ensuring the visit was a success and offered them Flat 15 for the duration of their stay in London. The Breuers landed in Plymouth at the beginning of May. Pritchard arranged for them to purchase a British MG sports

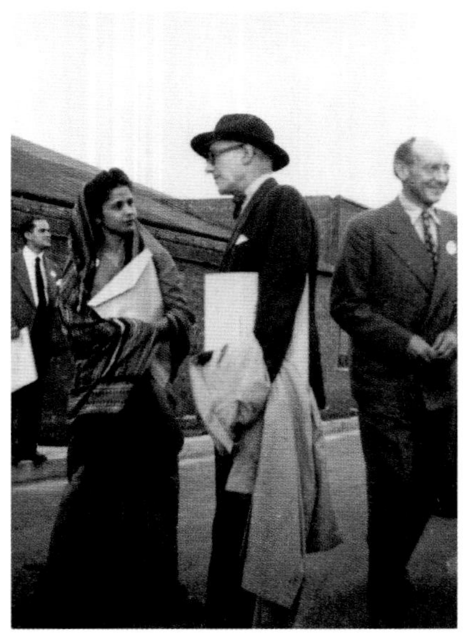

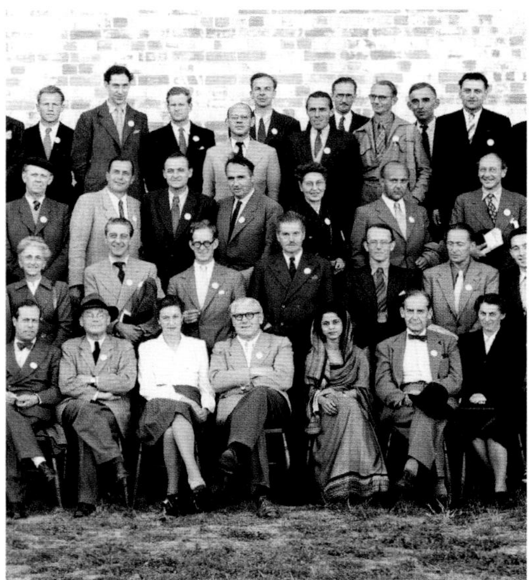

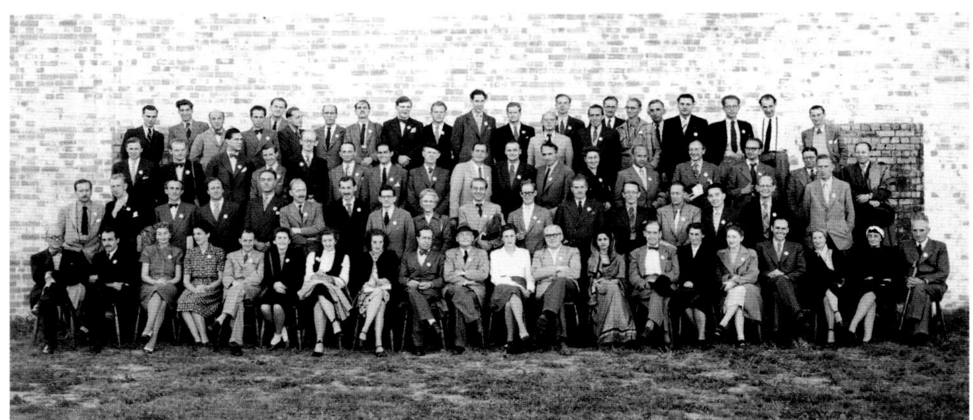

ABOVE, TOP-LEFT: The Indian architect Minette De Silva, Le Corbusier and Jack Pritchard arrive in Bridgwater for the 1947 CIAM Conference. ABOVE, AND ABOVE, TOP-RIGHT: The 1947 CIAM conference had delegates from Algeria, Argentina, Austria, Belgium, Canada, Cuba, Czechoslovakia, England, Finland, France, Greece, Hungary, India, Ireland, Italy, Netherlands, Poland, Switzerland and the USA. Delegates included Walter Gropius, Jack Pritchard, Wells Coates, Maxwell Fry, Siegfried Giedion and J.M. Richards. Jack Pritchard has the widest smile of all the delegates.

car and drew up an itinerary that took in Oxford, the Cotswolds, Stonehenge and a trip to Bristol, to visit Breuer's old patron Crofton Gane.[4] Jack and Molly held a party for the couple and their Isokon friends in the penthouse and Geoffrey Dunn also organised a dinner in their honour.[5] Leaving Britain, they motored on through France and Switzerland to Germany, stopping off to visit Breuer's first house commission at Wiesbaden, which now lay in ruins. On their return to New York at the end of June, Breuer was awarded the most prestigious architectural commission of his career, the UNESCO headquarters in Paris.

In July 1955, Jack and Molly Pritchard celebrated the Lawn Road Flats' 21st birthday. The guests included designers Robin and Lucienne Day and architects Alison and Peter Smithson; critics, Nikolaus Pevsner, J.M. Richards and Reyner Banham; and retailers Anthony Heal and Geoffrey Dunn. Wells Coates, who was now teaching at Harvard, travelled back to attend the event. The building had been repainted after the war and the celebrations took place on the penthouse terrace, just as they had done for the opening 21 years before. Philip Harben provided a suitably lavish feast and Raymond Postgate, now author of *The Good Food Guide*, chose the wines. As a silver-haired Coates stood on the crowded terrace, he at last received the credit he felt he deserved, as Pevsner, in his welcoming speech described the flats as 'a manifesto':

> *Now we are standing in it – with Wells Coates, whose after-life as long as architectural historians will busy themselves with English architecture is at once secured. It was sure enough a milestone – it looks too as if it were built of milestones. Now you must allow me to say that the Lawn Road Flats looked at in 1955 are extremely dated and they are extremely dated because they are giant's work of the 1930s.*[6]

Other accolades were read aloud. From Walter and Ise Gropius:

> *It is hard to think of any other shelter in London that would have made us quite as happy... We cherished the privilege to be among the first to explore the features of this radically new attempt at apartment living. We loved the sociability of the whole lay-out, the honest unpretentiousness of the exterior and the excellently planned flats.*[7]

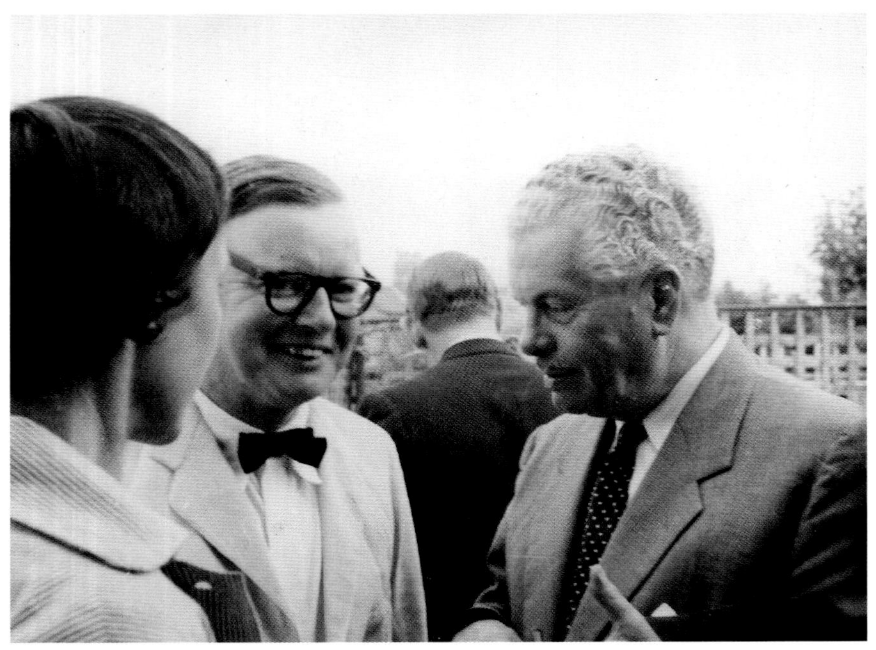

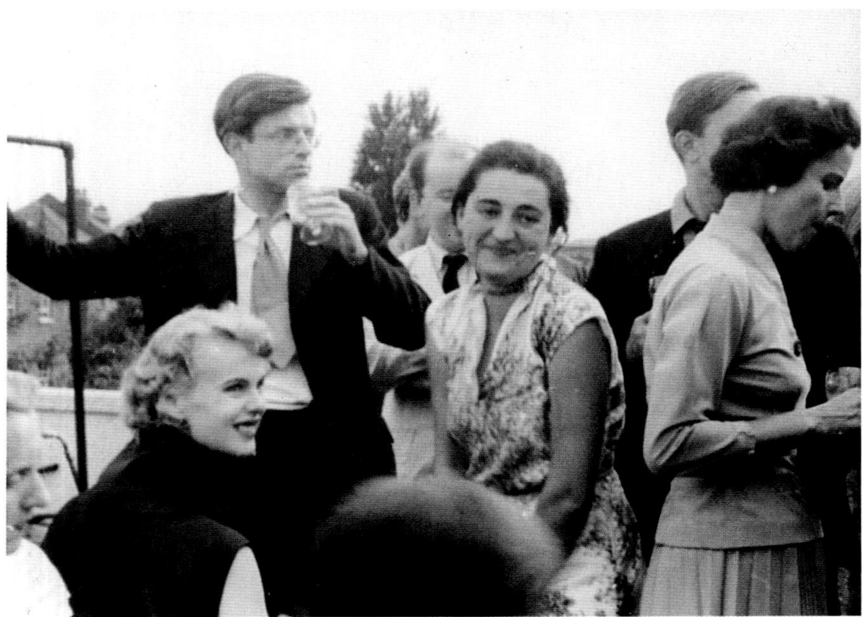

ABOVE, TOP: Wells Coates returned for his building's 21st birthday party on the 9th July 1955, finally receiving his accolades, including a speech delivered by Nikolaus Pevsner, who described the flats as 'giant's work'. ABOVE: The guests that gathered to celebrate included Robin and Lucienne Day, furniture makers Hille, *Architectural Review* editor J.M. Richards and architects Peter and Alison Smithson (centre).

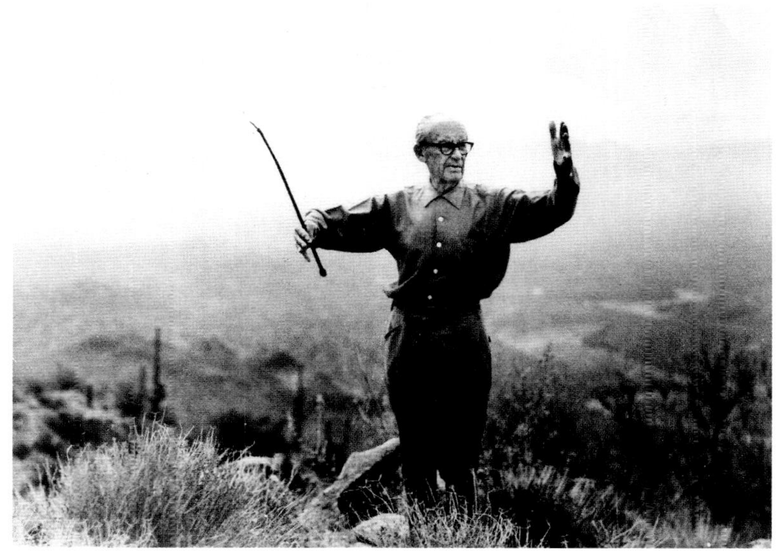

This from Marcel Breuer:

It is good to know that the Lawn Road Flats will have a birthday, just like any other human being. I always liked that girl, and I think she is getting younger from year to year. She is a generous wench, a friendly and hospitable one – not too careful with what she has. I wish all pretty girls were the same … I'm sure you agree![8]

And Agatha Christie

I certainly was a very contented inhabitant of Lawn Road Flats… My chief memories are of the fascination of finding a place where like the wood in Dear Brutus, trees really seemed to have moved close to the windows That, meals in the garden, and one particularly beautiful white blossoming cherry tree are the things I have never forgotten.[9]

It was a busy summer. The Pritchards next travelled to Helsingborg in Sweden for the H55 Exhibition, where Jack had organized a conference for British and Swedish furniture manufacturers. They stayed with Gregor Paulsson, and then Jack proceeded to Finland to meet up with Alvar Aalto.[10] In July, Jonathan Pritchard married the beautiful Czech refugee Maria Pollak, and held their wedding reception on the penthouse terrace. Maria took over the management of the flats and for a time the young couple lived in Flat 25.

Jack's daughter Jennifer Tudor-Hart, who studied at the AA, also managed the flats for a period in the late 1960s, while she was a jobbing architect. She designed a fitment with a hot-plate, refrigerator and sink for use in the three single flats without kitchens, which had originally been designed for short-stay tenants.

In April 1956 Gropius returned to London to be honoured with the Royal Gold Medal by the Royal Institute of British Architects. A dinner was held at the City Company of Ironmongers at which many of those who had attended his farewell party at the Trocadero in 1937 were present, including Pritchard, who gave a speech.

In 1958 Gropius's monumental Pan-Am building opened in New York. One of its investors was the flamboyant Birmingham-born property developer Billy Cotton. In the early 1960s Cotton attempted to involve Gropius in three major commercial developments in Britain. The first was the proposed redevelopment of the Monico site in London's Piccadilly Circus. He invited Gropius to consult on the scheme alongside Richard Llewelyn-Davies and his partner John Weeks. Llewelyn-Davies was Professor of Architecture at the Bartlett School and had based his new curriculum directly on Gropius's Bauhaus model, combining art and science.[11] It was a controversial project, dogged by interminable delays and costly challenges, and by 1964 Gropius dropped out of proceedings. Cotton also invited him to design a shopping, entertainment and hotel development in the centre of Birmingham. In mid-1960, Gropius travelled to the city with his partner in The Architects Collaborative (TAC) Benjamin Thompson and revisited the site of the aborted Isokon 4 in Selly Park. Although the Gropius–Thompson plans were praised, this scheme was also doomed. Cotton's third project for Gropius, 45 Park Lane in London's Mayfair, went ahead, although his architectural input was limited to the building's elevation, as Cotton's in-house architectural firm had already completed the preliminary plans. The ten-storey concrete office block, occupying a prestigious corner site, was from 1965 let to Hugh Hefner's Bunny Club, earning it the soubriquet 'The Hutch on the Park', an association that apparently amused Gropius.

In 1961, he was awarded the prestigious Albert Medal by the Royal Society of Arts in a ceremony at Buckingham Palace. He joined a cast of distinguished former recipients including Winston Churchill and Louis Pasteur. Despite the lack of worthy commissions, it was an acknowledgement of his contribution to architecture, design and art education in Britain.

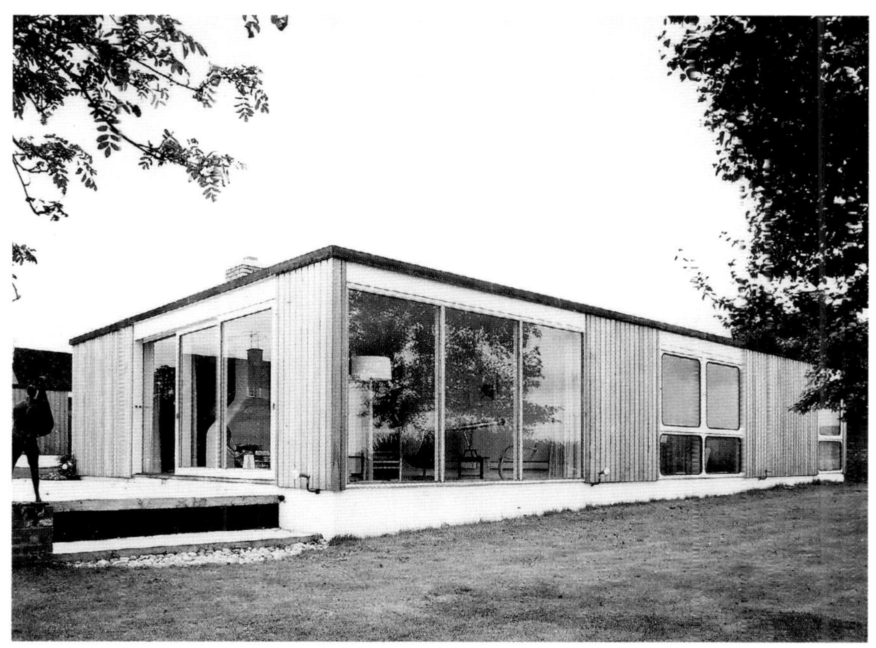

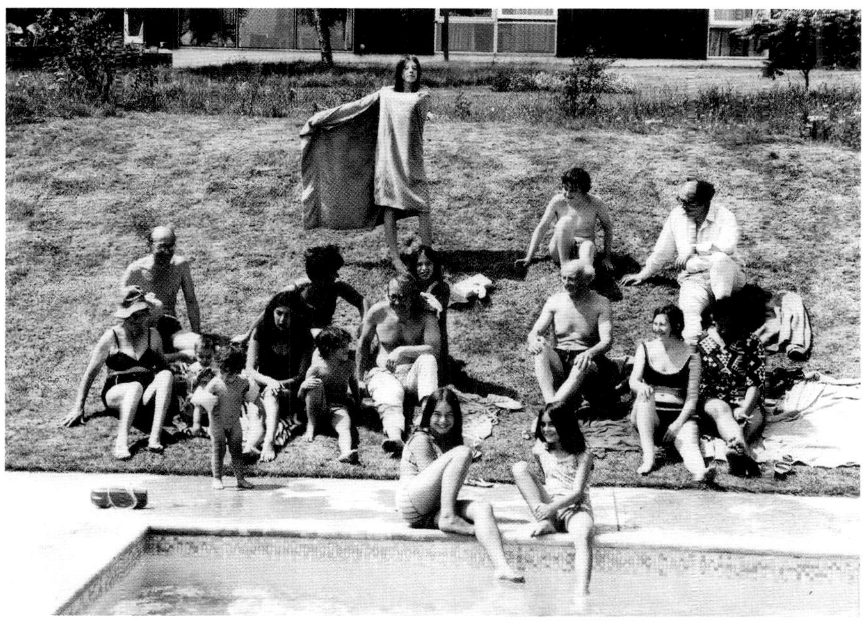

ABOVE, TOP: Jack's daughter Jennifer Jones designed Isokon, the elegantly minimal house in Blythburgh, Suffolk, where the Pritchards retired. ABOVE: Three generations of Pritchards beside the solar-heated pool in Blythburgh. A sauna followed by a swim became a compulsory family tradition on Christmas Day.

Wells Coates died in Canada on 16 June 1958, after suffering a heart attack on a beach in Vancouver. His daughter Laura wrote that he had been bathing and picnicking with friends and taking pictures of a sailing schooner from Japan when he collapsed.[12]

In 1962, Jack and Molly bought a plot of 50 acres in Blythburgh on the Suffolk coast. Surrounded by birch trees with lovely views across water, it had the added attraction of abundant birdlife for Molly, who had become a dedicated birdwatcher. They asked Jack's daughter Jennifer and her husband Colin to design a modern weekend house, which they called ISOKON. The single-storey, flat-roofed house was clad in wooden panels, and had an open-plan living and dining room with glass walls to take in the landscape beyond. The small galley kitchen was meticulously planned to facilitate Jack's interest in food and cooking. He installed an outdoor swimming pool, using the solar-powered technology he had seen at Massachusetts Institute of Technology (MIT) in the 1940s to heat the water. Influenced by his many trips to Finland and Scandinavia, he also built a sauna. The couple increasingly spent time at Blythburgh, sailing, birdwatching and entertaining. Guests were typically encouraged by Jack to take a group sauna followed by a dip in the pool, regardless of the weather conditions.

When they were in London the Pritchards still dined in the Isobar most evenings. The club remained a social hub for the Hampstead intelligentsia and was open to the public for lunch. During the mid-1960s it was managed by actor Roger Worrod, who continued Harben and Braun's tradition of themed events. The most memorable was 'Russian month', during which the Isobar showed an exhibition of prints by Marc Chagall, organised by the Russian Embassy, which also laid on a chef. Worrod remembered: 'His dishes, especially the borscht were exquisite, but on the gala evening, we discovered he had other talents. He had been a member of the Red Army Choir and at the end of the night he came out of the kitchen and sang for us, closing his recital by leading us all in a robust "Kalinka".' The Embassy also provided a selection of vodkas, which were laid out on an open table, guarded by an armed Russian 'heavy'. Given the building's connections with Soviet espionage, it was an interesting collaboration.[13]

Between 1949 and 1963 Jack Pritchard worked as Director of the Furniture Development Council. At the age of sixty-four, when most people's thoughts turn to retirement, he decided to revive the Isokon Furniture Company, choosing to reintroduce the three designs he believed would do best in the post-war market. First was the Long Chair. He wrote to Breuer asking him for clarification on some modifications he had suggested in 1952, but Breuer, who was focused on his architecture was irritated by the queries:

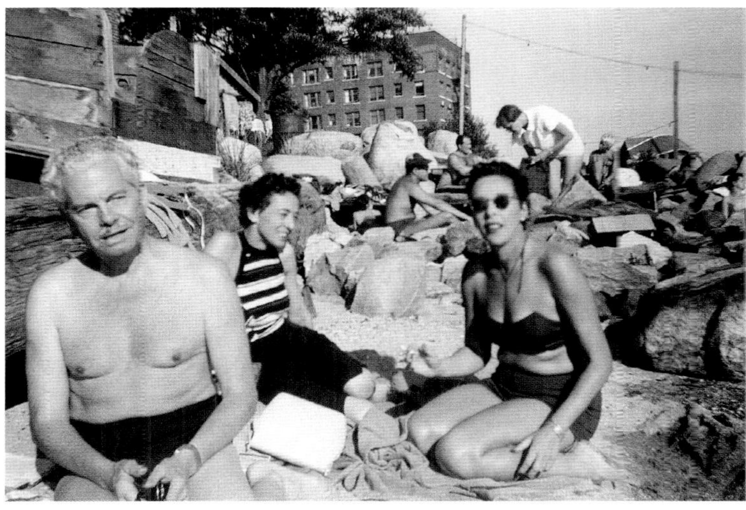

I will not have much personal time to spend with the problems which automatically come up with such a production. I am simply at the limit of my capacities and we have to reject more and more quite a few interesting building projects. However I would like to answer your questions as much as I can as I have a long-standing attachment to Isokon and to my designs which you have produced.[14]

Pritchard followed Breuer's instructions about widening the seat and adding a cross-rail to the back of the Long Chair, and had it manufactured by Alesbury Bros in Kent. The parts were then assembled in London by Remploy, a government-backed scheme employing disabled workers. He also experimented with a new method of applying the upholstery directly to the plywood seat. This new Long Chair, priced at £19.11s.6d, was exhibited at the Design Centre in London's Haymarket and at Dunns of Bromley store in May 1964.

Pritchard also had Breuer's Nesting Table manufactured by Alesbury Bros, and he asked Ernest Race, well-known following his Festival of Britain success, to redesign the Pocket Bottleship and Penguin Donkey. For its 1960s reincarnation, Race sharpened up the Donkey, making it geometric rather than organically curvy. He gave it a practical flat top on which to place 'coffee cups, glasses or a tray of hors d'oeuvres' and coated the plywood with wipe-clean, white acid catalyst lacquer.[15] The Isokon Penguin Donkey Mark II was priced at £7, or £6.10s to Penguin book readers. Nikolaus Pevsner expressed his delight at Isokon's return and wrote a message for the company to use in its advertising leaflets as did Penguin's Allen Lane. To keep his costs down, Pritchard marketed the piece, as he had done in the 1930s with the Embru, as a simple do-it-yourself project. The advertising text announced:

> *And for you, we've saved the pleasure of final assembly. It involves the turning of eight screws (we provide the screwdriver) which gives you five minutes of delicious do-it-yourself satisfaction and years of faithful service.*

Race's transformation of the Bottleship was much more radical. He reinvented it as a wedge-shaped, free-standing drinks cabinet with a hinged lacquered lid. Inside there were neat compartments for up to eight horizontally stowed glasses and storage space for bottles. The exterior had a magazine rack, several shelves for books and cut-out handles to facilitate lifting. Pritchard set up a new Isokon office in the Lawn Road Flats, assisted by his secretary Christine Webber.

The rebirth of Isokon coincided with the launch, in 1964, of Terence Conran's first Habitat store on London's Fulham Road, which revolutionised British furniture retailing. At the same time, a few streets away, another important newcomer arrived on the London design scene. Zeev Aram, a design graduate of Central School of Art, who had worked with architects Ernő Goldfinger and Basil Spence, opened a small, white-washed showroom at 57 King's Road, Chelsea.[16] He was the first retailer in London to offer furniture by Le Corbusier, Achille & Pier Castiglioni and Carlo Scarpa, which was produced under licence by Gavina in Italy. One day, not long after the opening, Jack Pritchard announced himself at Aram's office above the store. 'This is just like coming home!', he declared, as he strode into the room. The two men hit it off at once and Pritchard convinced Aram to stock the Long Chair, Nesting Tables and Penguin Donkey, advising him: 'Young man, live dangerously! Don't be comfortable. Take chances!' Pritchard became a frequent visitor to the store, often coming in 'to relax', sitting on furniture in the window display. Aram suggested to Dino Gavina that the Italian company should produce the Long Chair to complete its range of Breuer's products. Gavina asked for two Long Chairs to be shipped to Milan. He made slight modifications, widening the arms and improving the fit of the upholstery and showed it on the Gavina stand at the 1965 Milan Furniture Fair.

1968 was a landmark year for the Pritchards. Jack and Molly had been living in the Lawn Road Flats for 34 years. Now both approaching 70 years of age,

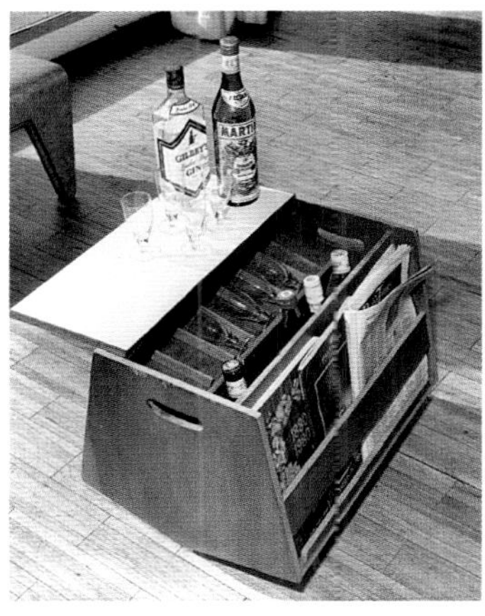

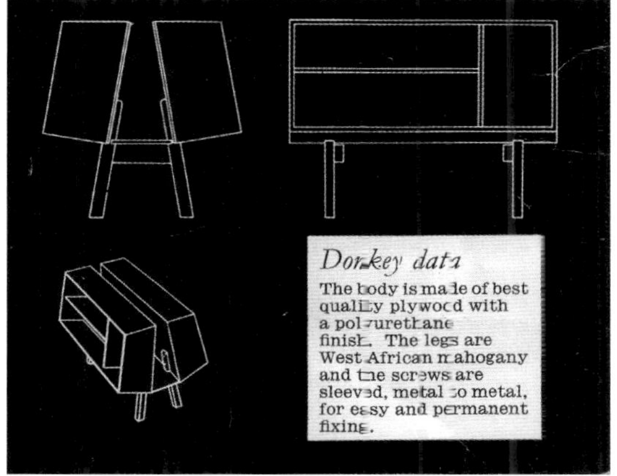

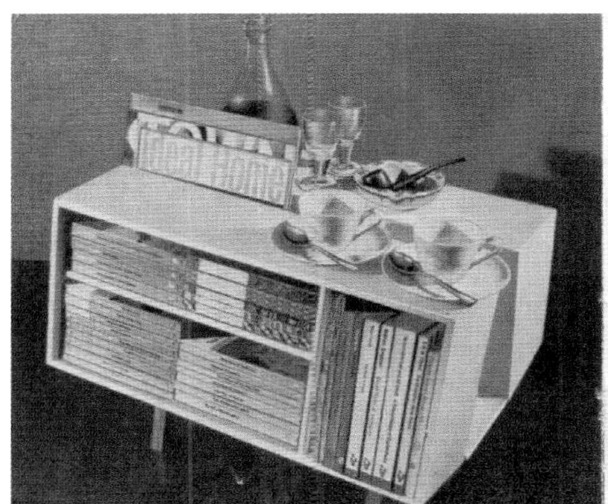

10/- off for Penguin readers

The Isokon Donkey is being made available to Penguin readers at a special introductory price. This offer is available only to those Penguin readers who receive this leaflet and use the reply-paid card.

The normal purchase price is £6.14.6. plus 5/6 postage and packing. The price to you is £6.4.6. plus 5/6 postage and packing, a clear and immediate saving of 10/-.

Moreover, if you fill in the reply card now, we shall be delighted to send you a Penguin Donkey at absolutely no cost to yourself. When you receive it, take it out of its carton, examine it, assemble it, live with it for 7 days. We think you'll like it. But if you don't, pop it back in its carton and return it to us. You won't be charged at all.

But we think you *will* like it. In that case send us a cheque, money order, credit transfer or cash for £6.10.0 and the Donkey is yours.

The reply-paid card is simplicity itself to fill in. Why not do it now?

... *without this?* THE ISOKON PENGUIN DONKEY MARK 2.

Patent application No. 26407/63
Design application No. 911722

This is the Isokon Donkey. Designed by Ernest Race to make living so much more civilised. It sits splendidly in any room. Holds up to 90 of your best liked Penguins. Plus your magazines, Radio Times, T.V. Times, what-have-you. Plus your ash tray, coffee, decanter and glasses. And holds everything neatly. Now you can spend the most relaxed sort of evening and win nothing but approval for your tidyness.

The Donkey boasts an eggshell finish in Oyster white lacquer, a surface which allows splashes and stains to be wiped clean at a touch. The horizontal shelves are horizontal because Penguins should lie flat. They keep better that way and you can read every title from your chair. The depth of the shelves is just right to allow every Penguin to slide out easily. The upright ones? They're to take your maps, hard-backs, Peregrines or whatever you like. Very thoughtful. More, you have the pleasure of putting it together. This involves the turning of 8 screws only and the screwdriver is included. Just 5 minutes' work for you followed by many years of faithful service from your Donkey.

Overall height: 15¾". Overall length: 20¾".
Overall width: 15¼".

ABOVE: Penguin Books founder Sir Allen Lane stood by his pre-war offer to help Isokon promote the Isokon Penguin Donkey. Nikolaus Pevsner wrote a message for use in the advertising leaflets.

they decided to sell the building to relinquish the responsibility and also raise some capital for themselves and their sons. At the end of January, Pritchard asked Richard Llewelyn Davies to help find a buyer for the building. He then received an exciting invitation from The Architects Collaborative, the practice Gropius had formed with seven other architects in 1945 in Cambridge, Massachusetts. They were planning a surprise 85th birthday party for Gropius in May and invited Jack and Molly to attend.[17] Pritchard accepted with pleasure and headed straight to Loeb's wine merchant in Jermyn Street, in search of a suitable gift. It transpired that the proprietor knew of Gropius, and he produced a wine that he promised Pritchard was 'just right'. The Pritchards flew to New York on 13 May and stayed in Sibyl Moholy-Nagy's apartment at 330 East 33rd Street, and Marcel Breuer took them to supper that evening in a Japanese restaurant. The next day, Jack went to see Stendig Inc, a wholesale retailer Breuer had recommended, to investigate prospects for Isokon, but he came away disappointed. They travelled on to Harvard, where a rather nervous Pritchard was asked to make an impromptu speech at Gropius's party in front of 500 guests. Deciding to play it for laughs, he told the story of Gropius's first weekend in England and their trip through 'Courage country' to Stonehenge.

The Pritchards spent the next few days staying at the Gropius house in Lincoln. At Walter's private birthday party, he and Ise asked the assembled guests to: 'Raise your glasses to Jack and Molly for saving our lives'. While they were in Boston, the Pritchards visited an exhibition of Josef Albers's work and watched Oskar Schlemmer's film *Triadic Ballet*. It was a Bauhaus-immersion experience and, feeling inspired, Jack began to draft a talk entitled 'Gropius, the Bauhaus and the Future', which he later delivered around the world. On their return to London, he received a note from Gropius, thanking him for 'the poem of a wine'.[18]

In September 1968, the Royal Academy staged an international Bauhaus retrospective in London. Walter, Ise and Ati Gropius arrived in London on 17 September and a reception was hosted at the Academy for them by the German Ambassador. In his opening speech, 85-year-old Gropius proved he had lost none of his ability to electrify an English audience. *The Times* reported: 'Those who expected to see an elderly gentleman step up to the rostrum for a few faltering words of thanks were taken aback by an address delivered in trombone tones and packed with combative matter.'[19]

The exhibition attracted close to 100,000 visitors, but received mixed reviews from leading critics. Norbert Lynton in *Burlington Magazine* claimed it 'lacked objectivity', while in *The Listener*, Reyner Banham declared the Bauhaus image had 'ossified'. The show coincided with a new wave of scholarship, including Gillian Naylor's 1968 study, *The Bauhaus*. Capitalising on the surging interest in

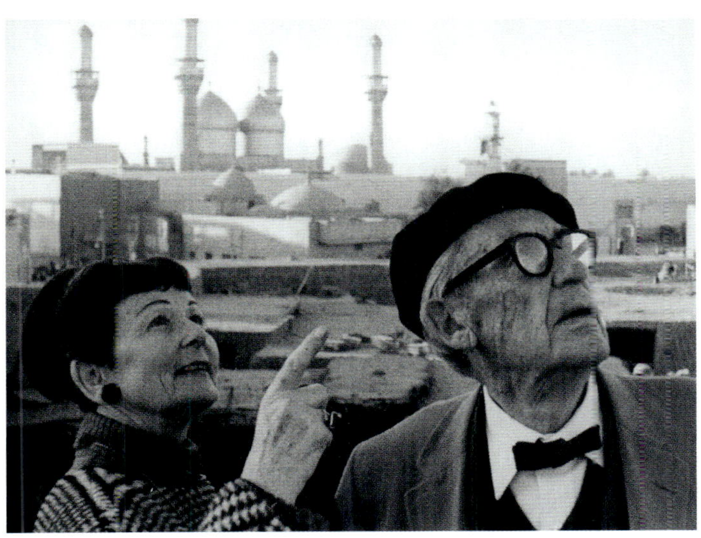

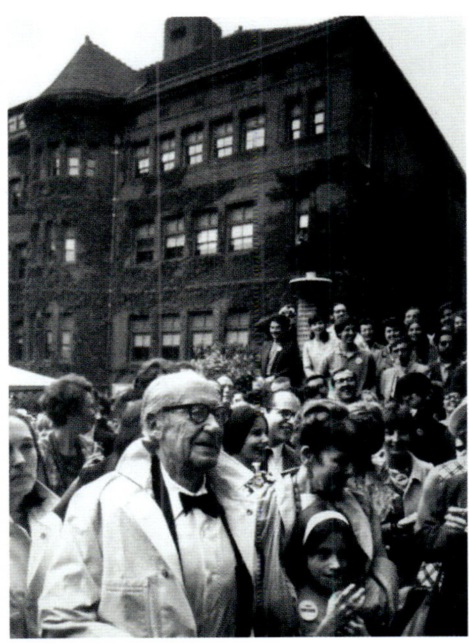

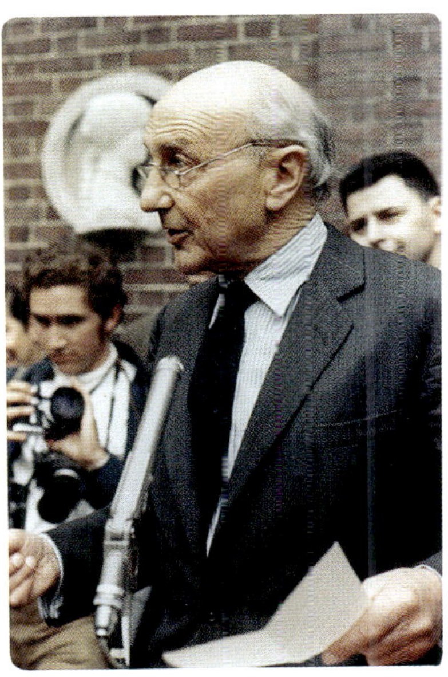

ABOVE, TOP: Towards the end of his life, Walter and Ise Gropius visited Baghdad, where the volatile regime had commissioned a major university campus. Only a handful of buildings were ever completed. ABOVE, LEFT: Five hundred guests attended Walter Gropius's 85th birthday party at Harvard. ABOVE, RIGHT: Pritchard, who had been flown over by TAC had little time to prepare an off-the-cuff speech at the celebrations.

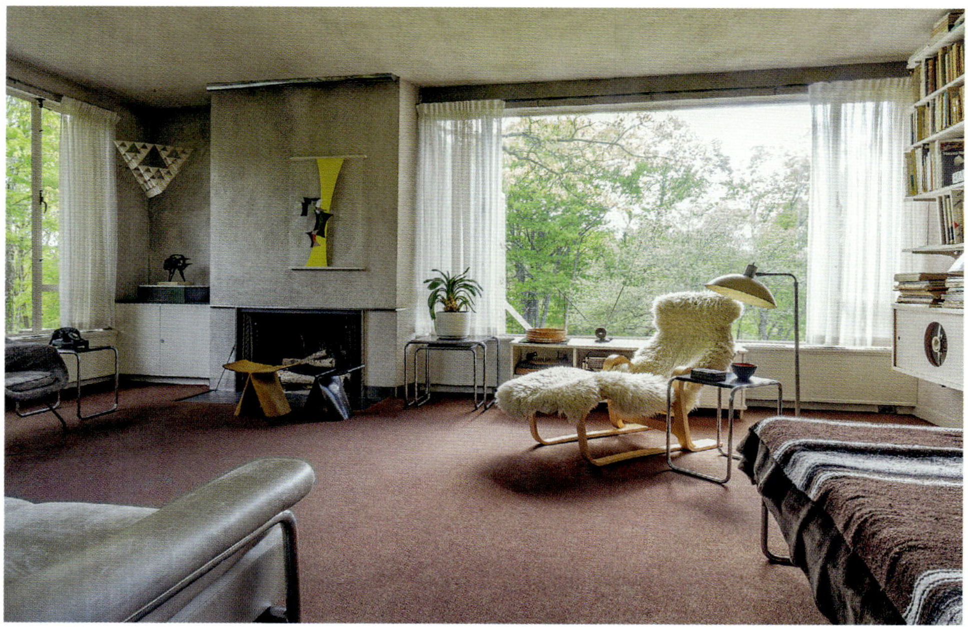

ABOVE: The living room of Walter and Ise Gropius' house in Lincoln, with a sheepskin-covered Isokon Long Chair taking centre stage.

Bauhaus masters, both The Marlborough Gallery and New London Gallery in Cork Street staged selling exhibitions of the work of Lyonel Feininger, Moholy-Nagy and Herbert Bayer.

Pritchard's long association with the Bauhaus and its masters was by now well established. In November he gave his 'Gropius, the Bauhaus and the Future' speech, at the Royal Society of Arts, and enjoyed the lively discussion it sparked. Now that he and Molly were planning to spend more time in Suffolk, Pritchard licensed Christine Webber and her husband John to produce and market the Isokon Long Chair (now priced at £389), the Isokon Penguin Donkey Mark II and the Nesting Tables through their North London based company, John Alan Designs, with its small shop at 98 Parkway in Camden. In the summer of 1968 Gavina was taken over by the American furniture company Knoll (known in Britain as Form International). Although they had dined together in New York just a few months previously, in August Jack received the following message from Marcel Breuer, who had heard the corporate news and was making plans of his own:

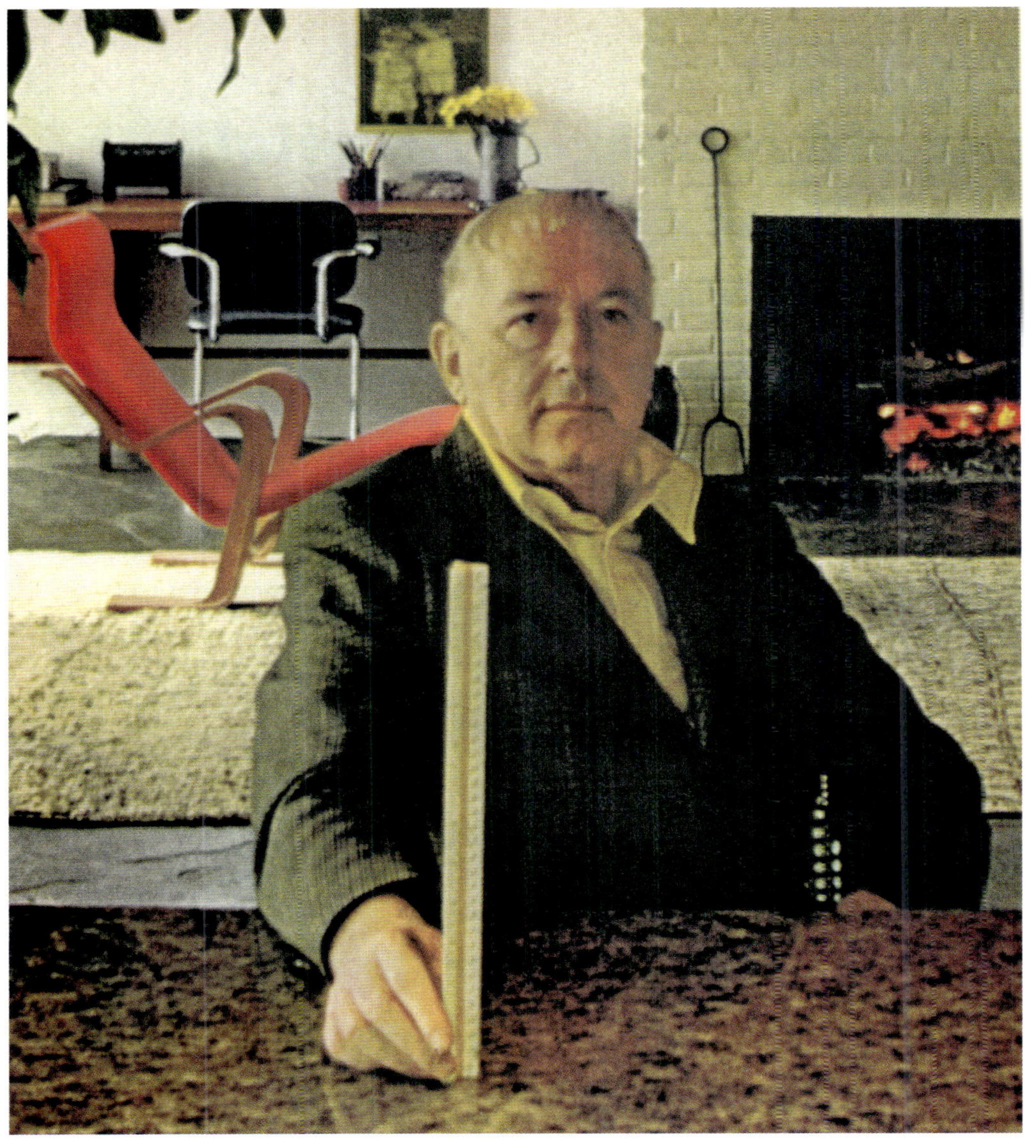

ABOVE: For a period in the 1970s Knoll International had their own production of the Isokon Long Chair, which caused frictions between Pritchard and Breuer, by then an internationally renowned architect, with limited interest in his old furniture designs.

It was a crushing missive from the man whom Pritchard had helped in the
1930s. He took a few months to respond:

In December 1968 the left-wing publication the *New Statesman* purchased the
Lawn Road Flats for £67,500. It appeared to the Pritchards that they had found
the perfect successors, and that the flats and their residents would be in safe hands.
They negotiated a clause to retain the penthouse for themselves for a fixed rent of
£92.7.10 for the following five years. Jack invited board members Kingsley Amis,
Gerald Barry and Jeremy Potter to lunch in the Isobar to seal the deal.[22]
The publication assured tenants that everything would 'continue as before'.
However, the local *Hampstead and Highgate Express*, wrote a cynical report asking
how the '*New Statesman*, protector of the pragmatic left' could justify entering 'the
lush and profitable pastures of the property market'. The publication's secretary,
Jack Morgan, responded with a candour that should have sent alarm bells ringing

SEPT. 12
1976.

DEAR JACK PRITCHARD

YES!

CONGRATULATIONS —

WE HAVE SUCH
HAPPY MEMORIES OF
OUR VISITS — AND LOOK
FORWARD TO ANOTHER
SOON — BEST GREETINGS
NW
♥ RAY EAMES.

ABOVE: Jack continued his legendary networking at Blythburgh, inviting guests including Charles and Ray Eames, Ernő and Ursula Goldfinger and Charlotte Perriand.

in the penthouse: 'It's what you might call a run of the mill investment. We have others. We have simply decided to put some of our reserves into property.'[23]

With the sale apparently resolved, in early January 1969 Jack and Molly Pritchard set off on a world tour. Pritchard had obtained joint sponsorship from the British Council and the Goethe Institute to deliver his Bauhaus speech to a number of institutions in Fiji, India, Australia, Hong Kong, Israel and Italy and he planned the route accordingly, making time to see old friends and colleagues en route.

Their first stop was America, where on 9 January they paid a flying visit to Lincoln to see Gropius, who had just returned from a trip to Mexico. They were shocked by how frail he looked. It was to be the last time they would meet. Walter Gropius died just six months later on 6 July 1969, at the age of eighty-six. In Australia Jack was shown the Sydney Opera House – still under construction – by Harry Seidler. Jack delivered his lecture and showed Oskar Schlemmer's *Triadic Ballet* to architectural audiences in Sydney, Melbourne and by special request to the German Ambassador in Canberra, who had been a young boy in Weimar when the Bauhaus was based there.

In India, the Pritchards stayed in Mumbai, Chandigarh and Ahmedabad with Gautam Sarabhai, the wealthy industrialist who helped start the National Institute of Design and had employed Charles and Ray Eames. They had been introduced by Gita Malhotra, heir to a textile business, who was a tenant in the Lawn Road Flats. Sarabhai entertained them in great style and after dinner Jack showed Schlemmer's film outdoors so that any interested locals could also watch. The Pritchards headed back to London at the end of March. They had been on the road for three months and Jack had given his lecture on Gropius and the Bauhaus on three continents. Within months of their return, it was clear that all was not going smoothly under the *New Statesman*'s ownership. Renée Little, popular manageress of the flats, resigned and the Isobar, which was unprofitable, was converted into three flats. Then in January 1972, after less than three years of ownership, the New Statesman sold the Lawn Road Flats to the Labour-controlled Camden Council for £157,500. It had more than doubled its money on its 'run of the mill investment'.

The Pritchards remained in the penthouse for another year. In 1973 Jack was made a Fellow of the Royal Institute of British Architects. This was recognition, at last, of the important work he had done for architecture and design in Britain. So too was the Bicentenary Medal of the Royal Society of Arts he received in 1976, an award for 'outstanding contributions to the advancement of design in industry and society'. In 1974, after forty years in Lawn Road, Jack and Molly Pritchard left the penthouse and moved permanently to Blythburgh. It was the end of an era.

RIGHT: The Pritchards began working together on a joint memoir, *View from a Long Chair*, which was published in 1984. In the foreground, a bench designed by Robin Day, another of Pritchard's many friends.

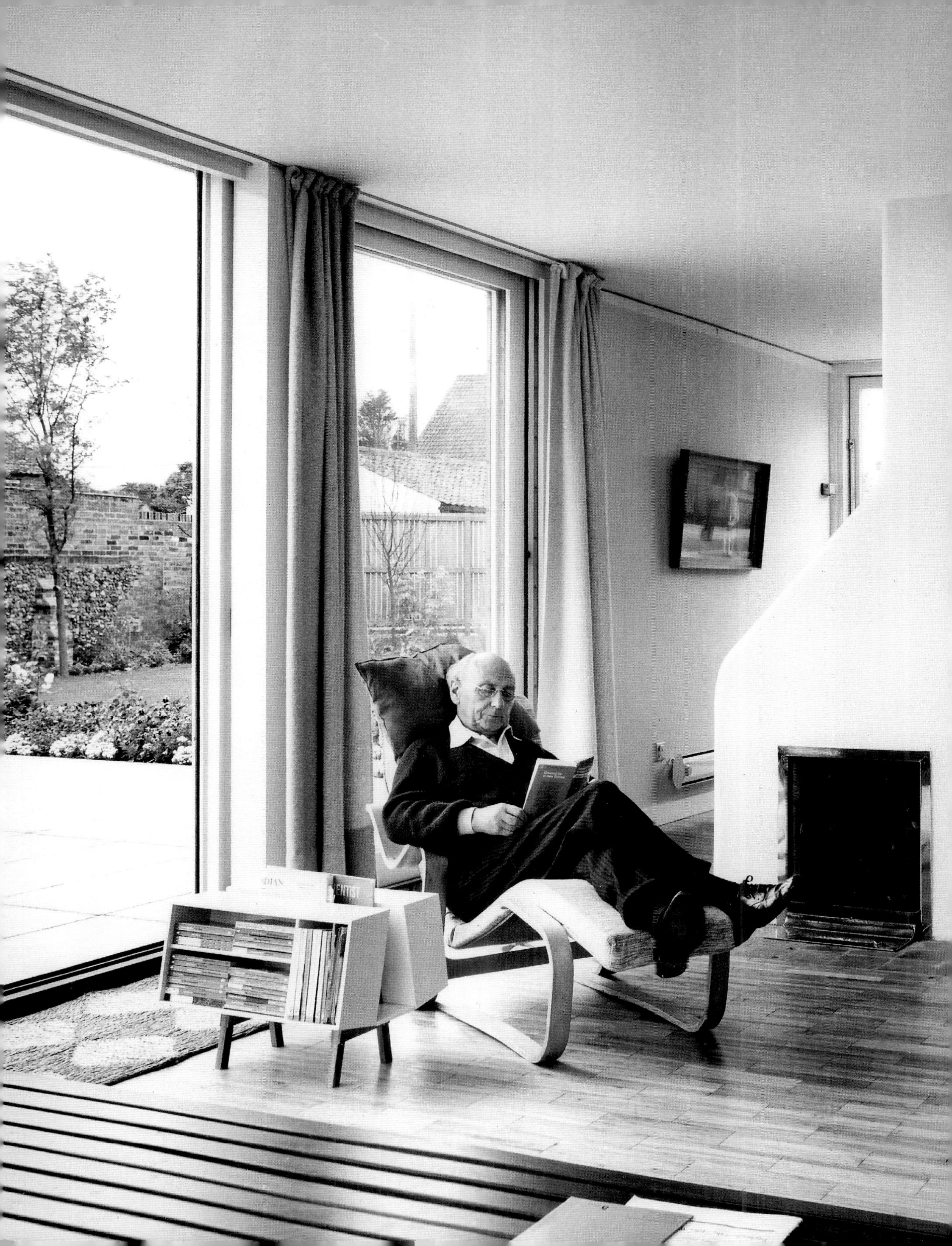

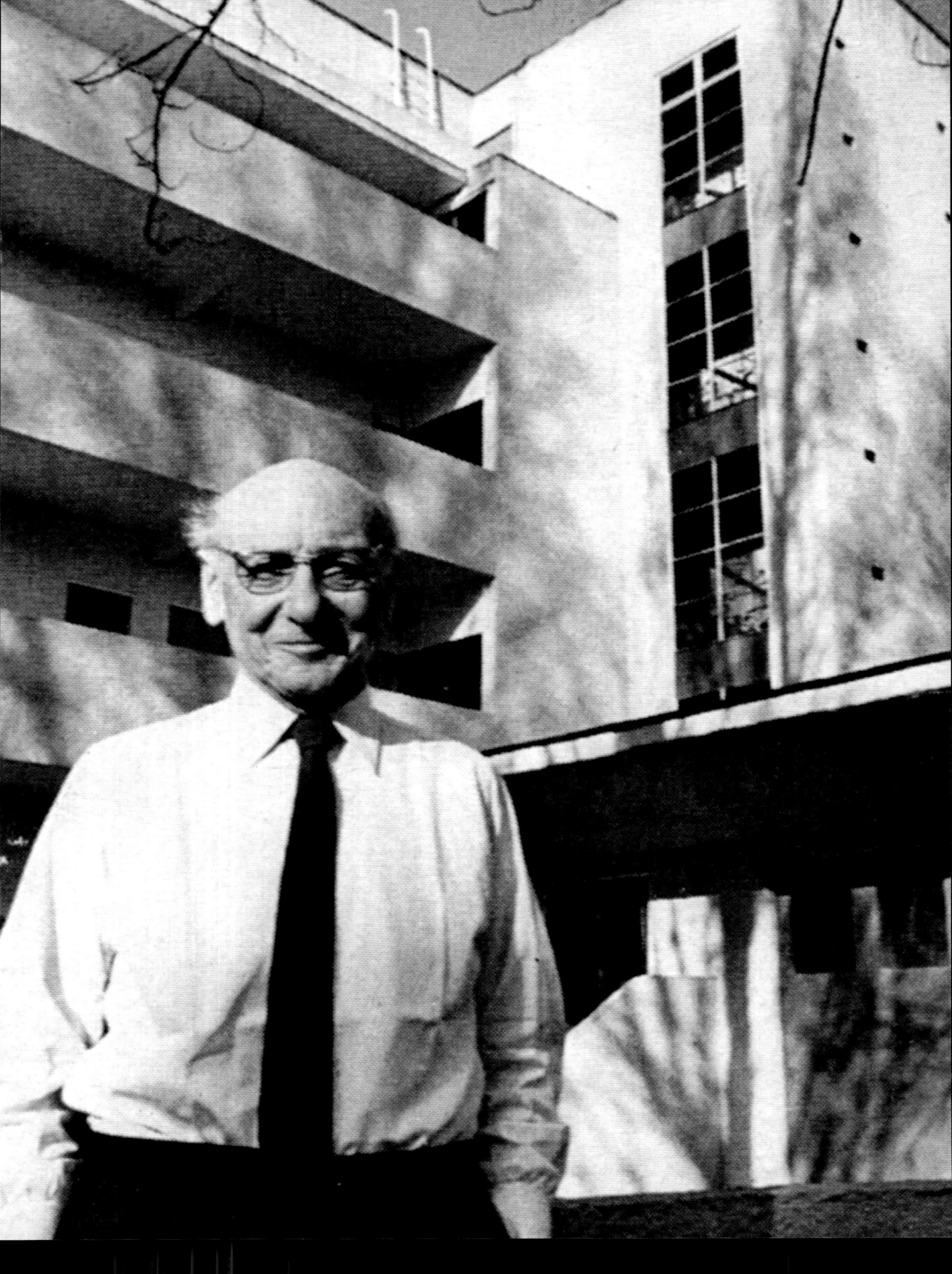

CHAPTER 11

THE DECLINE AND RESCUE OF LAWN ROAD FLATS

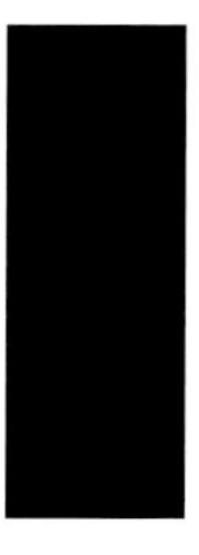

N THE SPRING OF 1994 A COACH PULLED UP OUTSIDE THE
Lawn Road Flats, stopping beside three tall poplar trees. Out clambered
a small group of men and women with cameras swinging from their
shoulders.

*Their initial exclamations as they gazed at the cantilevered balconies
turned to dismay as they took in the broken walls, peeling paint and
empty beer cans surrounding the building. They were, it transpired,
Professors of Architecture from institutions across the USA.*[1]

Watching them was Gerry Harrison, who was campaigning for a Labour seat in
the forthcoming local elections. The building, described as one of the 'architectural
jewels in Camden's crown', was one of the reasons he had chosen to stand for the
South End local ward. Voted in as its Councillor a few months later, he spent the
next eight years fighting to save the building.

Two decades had passed since Camden Council had purchased the Lawn Road
Flats from *New Statesman* and renamed it, simply, Isokon. Initially, Ken Livingstone,
Camden Council's Chairman of Housing (and later Mayor of London) had
wanted to demolish the building and replace it with high-rise flats. English
Heritage responded by giving the flats a Grade II listing, one of the first Modernist
buildings to be protected in such a way.

By the early 1990s Britain was in the grip of another recession and the borough
of Camden had 10,000 homeless people on its books. It began a policy of
rehousing alcoholics, young, single homeless people and mentally ill patients in the
flats, under the government's new Care in the Community programme. Isokon
had begun what one existing resident called 'a remorseless slide into slumdom'.[2]

Wells Coates's daughter Laura Cohn watched the disintegration of her father's
masterpiece with mounting dismay. She, the Lawn Road Flats Tenants' Association,
the Belsize Conservation Areas Advisory Committee, the Thirties Society and
Docomomo UK (the international working party for documentation and
conservation of buildings, sites and neighbourhoods of the Modern Movement),
began lobbying to preserve the building. Its listed status was upgraded to Grade II★
on 3 November 1992.

Now appointed the local Labour Councillor, Gerry Harrison found himself
inundated by desperate Lawn Road Flats tenants at weekly advice surgeries. After
visiting them in the block he realized he was just 'scratching at the surface of the
misery that festers' there. He wrote to Docomomo expressing his horror at the
residents' plight.

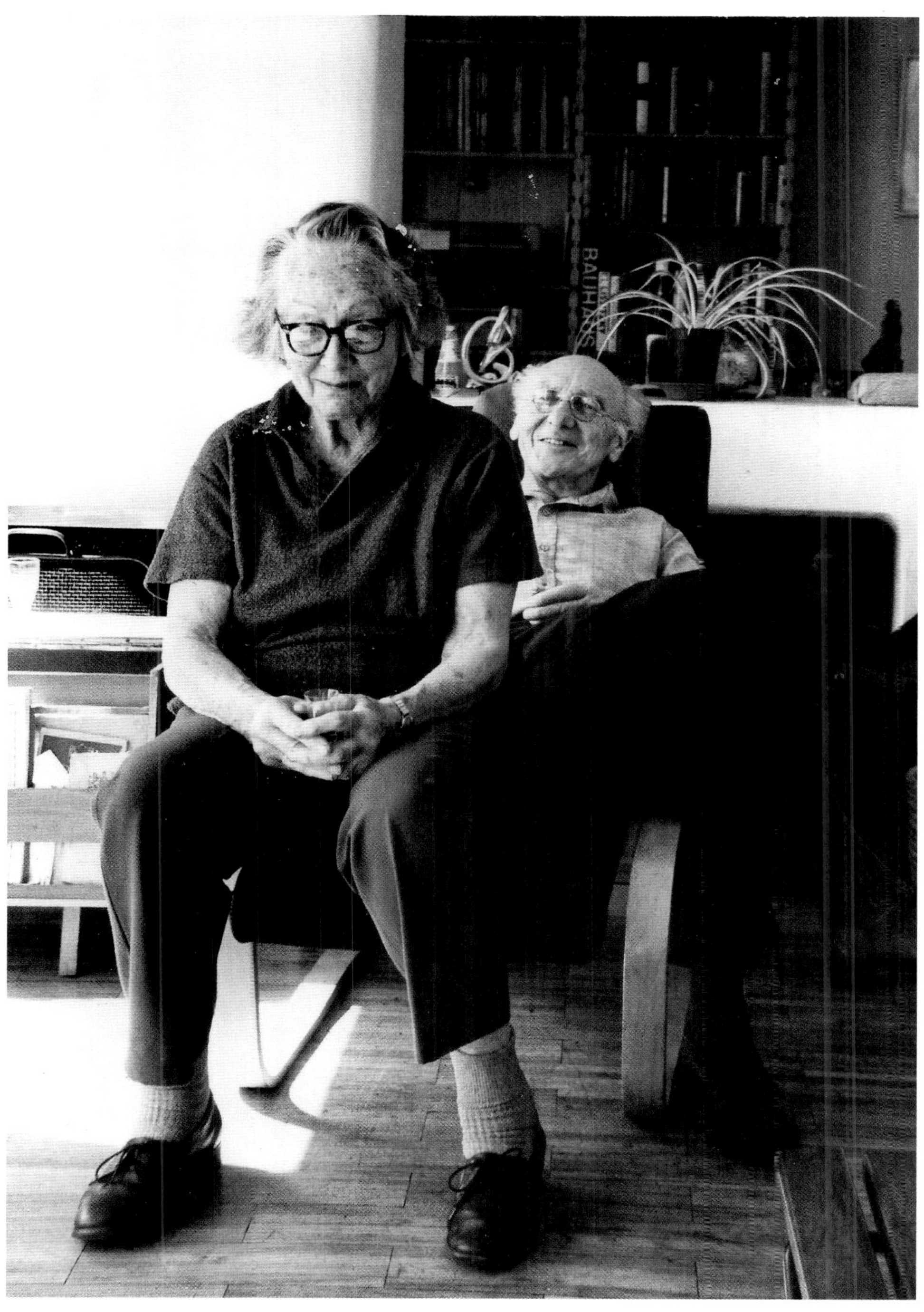

ABOVE: Jack and Molly Pritchard share a Long Chair during their retirement in Blythburgh. Molly died in 1985. She was followed by Jack in 1992.

*The conditions in which they now live is a disgrace. Last weekend sewage
flowed down the balconies … this is not entirely Camden's fault. I realise
now that the architect, Wells Coates (and Pritchard) experimented with a
building whose architecture could not possibly survive sixty years. But it
was then a home for their middle-class artistic and intellectual friends who
always had the opportunity to leave London for their country houses…
Why Camden bought the place from the New Statesman I shall never
know. On Saturday I pushed my finger into one of Coates' world-famous
interior walls. The fabric is damp and crumbling. There is no effective heat
or sound insulation. The plumbing is archaic, illegal and also leaks. The
drainage system which was once designed for people who wanted to share
a liberal communal life, enjoying Philip Harben's meals in the Isobar and
with a separate laundry downstairs, cannot now cope with 34 individual
units. The building is simply a disaster.*[3]

In October 1994, English Heritage put Isokon on its Buildings at Risk register.
In the New Year, Camden Council commissioned architects Troughton McAslan
to produce a survey and recommendations for repairs. It estimated the repairs
(including internalizing heating pipes, illegally installed on the outside of the
building by Camden Council in 1984) would take four years and cost £1,115,500.
There was silence from Camden Council. By the beginning of July 1995, English
Heritage decided to take legal action to force the council to internalize the
disputed heating pipes and to carry out the most urgent repairs. The council at last
greenlighted Troughton McAslan's proposal and issued a press release announcing
its decision on 6 July. The move generated considerable media interest and on
14 September, Isokon was featured in BBC2's popular architectural restoration
programme, *One Foot in the Past.*

Two years later, in June 1997, builders finally arrived and commenced the first basic
renovation work to make Isokon watertight. The council had also decided to restore
Flat 22, to show what might be achieved with proper funding and to raise public
awareness of the block. A total of £300,000 was spent on the improvements.

However, a new freeze on Camden's capital spending meant that the second phase,
due to begin in October, 1997 was put on hold. A final blow arrived in February
1998, with news that squatters had moved into the immaculately restored Flat 22 and
destroyed it.

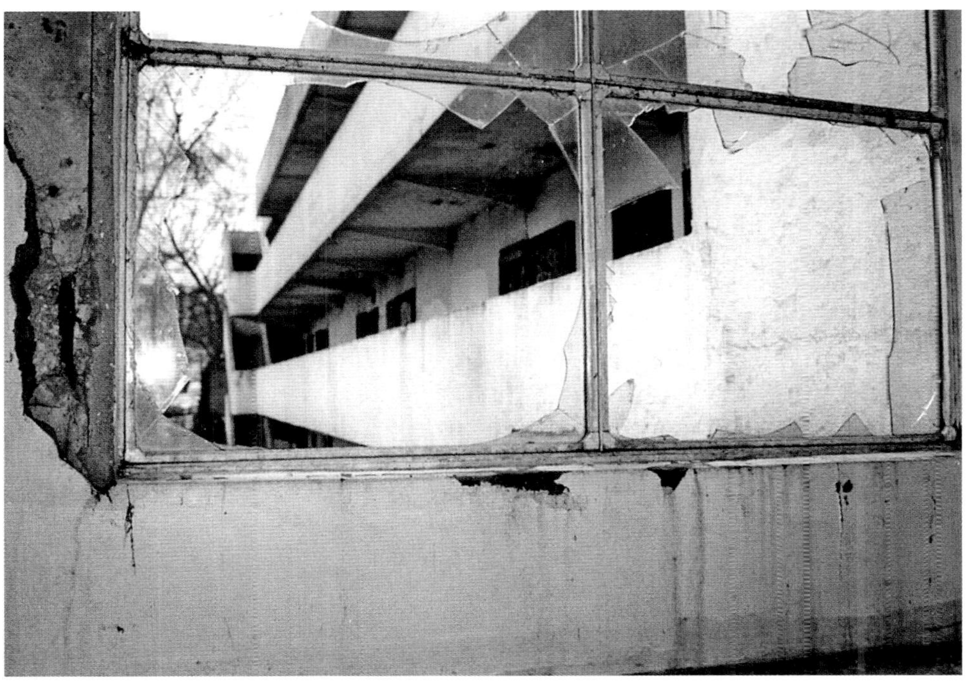

ABOVE: Unloved, vandalized and inhabited by squatters. In 1994, the Isokon was put on English Heritage's Buildings at Risk Register.

By October 1998 there were 14,000 homeless households on the council's waiting list. English Heritage ruled out permitting lateral conversions of the flats to create housing suitable for families, so the council voted to sell Isokon. By this stage two-thirds of the flats were empty and life for the remaining tenants was chaotic and dangerous. One resident, a noted psychiatrist, had died, cutting his wrists in his bath, after finding the anti-social activities of his neighbours unbearable. A murder took place along the same balcony. Cars were often set alight in the carpark opposite the building. In January 1999, English Heritage upgraded Isokon's listing to Grade I, placing further restrictions on its development.

In the spring of 1999, after almost three ignominious decades, Camden Council finally put Jack and Molly Pritchard's Isokon on the market. There were initially over fifty expressions of interest. The council created a shortlist of eleven, which among other criteria, could demonstrate a commitment to and knowledge of the unique nature of the building.

The last remaining tenant finally moved out of the building in November 1999, after her home in Flat 5 was ransacked by thieves. While the council considered the offers on its shortlist, the history of the Lawn Road Flats was celebrated at an exhibition at Hampstead Town Hall. 'Belsize 2000 – A Living Suburb' exhibited artefacts, photographs and furniture about the building's history. It included an original Isokon Long Chair, which Gerry Harrison had found discarded in a nearby skip.

At a meeting on 10 April 2001, Camden Council chose the £1.5 million bid from Isokon Trust and Notting Hill Housing Group, whose architects were the Kentish Town firm of Avanti Architects. It was considerably less than the highest bid, but the group offered to provide starter homes for key-workers in 25 studio units, together with 11 units that were to be sold on the open market. Camden announced they would offer 80 per cent of the key-worker units to teachers and 20 per cent to police. A Shared Ownership Scheme would allow them to buy a 25 to 75 per cent share of their home, while paying a low rent on the remaining sum. When they moved on, the home would be repurchased by NHHG, ready to house another key-worker. It was a proposal that would have appealed to Jack and Molly Pritchard's socialist ideals.

The plans did not, however, include restoration of the Isobar, which the group deemed too expensive, but the Isokon Trust would be involved in managing the garage area as a public-access exhibition space, related to the history of the building. Permission had to be sought from the Secretary of State to accept a price that was so much lower than 'the best consideration'.

In September 2001, the Lawn Road Flats were opened to the public during London's annual Open House weekend. The Pritchards' former penthouse was opened and Chris and Lone McCourt of Isokon Plus lent a selection of Marcel Breuer's furniture, which they arranged in Gropius's Flat 15. 3,000 people visited the building over the course of two days. Later that month the Isokon Trust staged 'Minimal Existence', an exhibition by young London artists. Their work was shown in hallways, staircases and inside the Minimum Flats. Jonathan and Maria Pritchard and Laura Cohn attended the opening, visiting the flats their parents had built. At last, under the stewardship of a knowledgeable and sympathetic team, the Lawn Road Flats were coming back to life.

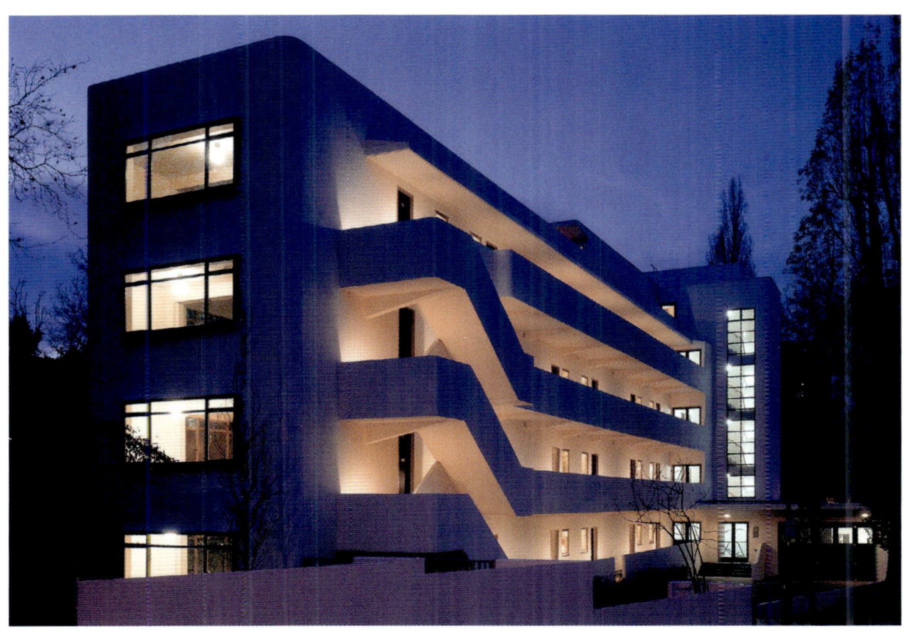

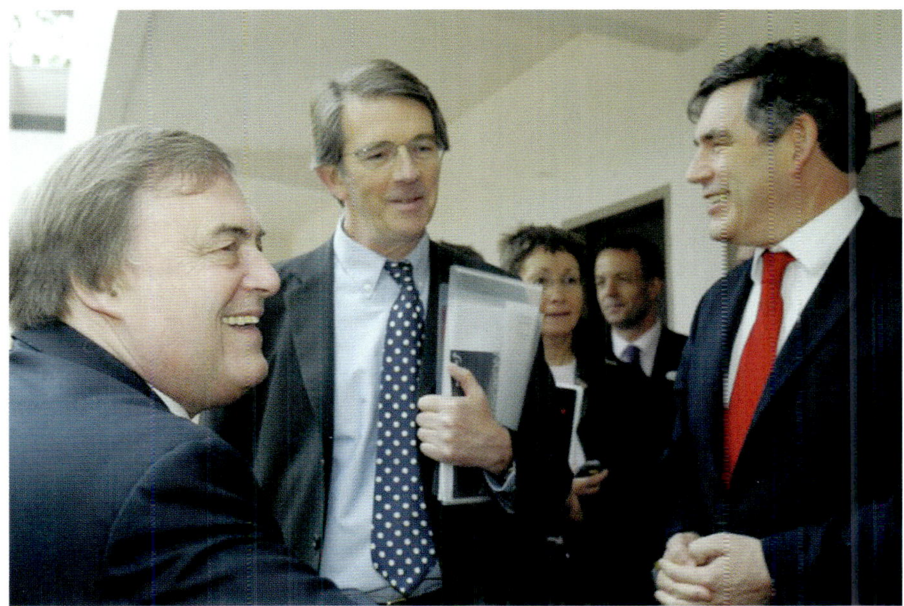

ABOVE, TOP: Rescued, restored and safe under the new ownership of Notting Hill Housing Group after the works by Avanti Architects. ABOVE: Shared ownership was a key policy of Tony Blair's New Labour government, prompting Deputy Prime Minister, John Prescott and Chancellor of the Exchequer, Gordon Brown to tour the newly opened building. John Allan of Avanti greeted the visitors.

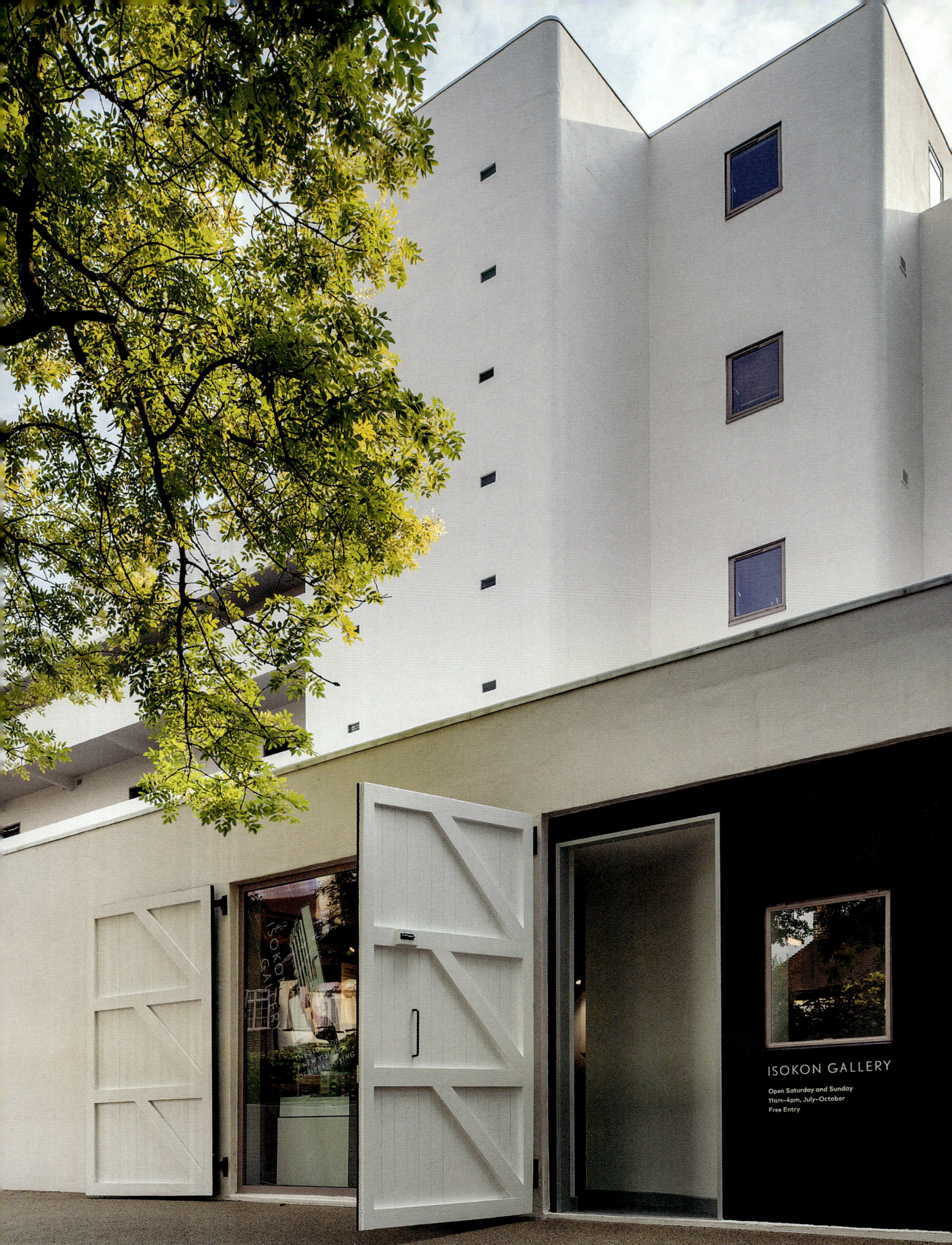
ISOKON GALLERY
Open Saturday and Sunday
11am–4pm, July–October
Free Entry

CHAPTER 12

THE FUTURE
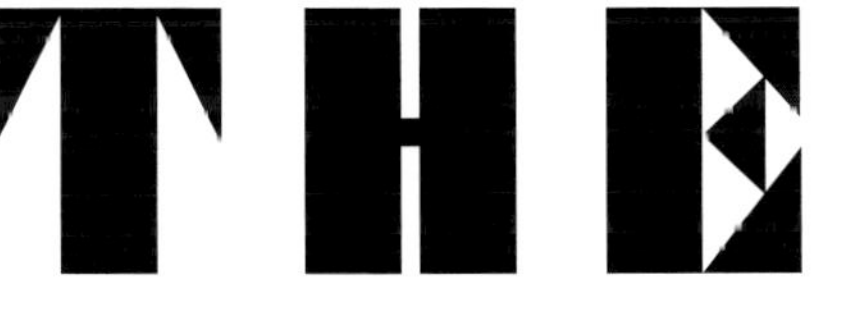

THE ISOKON BUILDING

The task of restoring the Isokon Building fell to John Allan of Avanti Architects, a man with both personal and professional connections to the great Modernists of the 1930s. Allan had first met Jack Pritchard in 1967, while an architecture undergraduate at Sheffield University, writing a thesis on Maxwell Fry. He had called him at Lawn Road to ask for an interview. Pritchard took him to lunch at the Institute for Contemporary Arts (ICA) and a friendship was born.[1]

By 2001, the year Avanti Architects with Notting Hill Housing Trust won the contract to restore the Isokon Building, Allan was a respected figure in the architectural world. He had served as the first Chairman of Docomomo, an international organization dedicated to the documentation and conservation of Modern Movement buildings, and Avanti had already restored several of the great Modernist landmarks, including Berthold Lubetkin's Penguin Pool at London Zoo. Completed in 1934, the same year as Wells Coates's Lawn Road Flats, both structures had pioneered the use of reinforced concrete. In 1992 Allan had also published an encyclopaedic biography of Lubetkin, and his knowledge of the people, techniques and issues of 1930s architecture was extensive. The bravery and ambition of Coates's vision appealed to him, and as he inspected the dilapidated ruin of the Lawn Road Flats, he marvelled at Coates's work – his considerations of the minutiae of domestic living; the efficiency, elegance and self-discipline of his design. There were lessons in 'the social implications of putting together units of that size, for that social group. The organism Coates and the Pritchards created was a real example of how rich an environment can be created out of ordinary things. Rich in the real sense.'[2]

The Avanti team stripped off 11 layers of moisture-trapping coatings, treating or replacing rusted reinforcement to create a sound matrix for the building. They restored the concrete shell and replaced all the party walls to sound-proof and fire-proof the flats. A new roof covering, windows and doors were installed. Modern gas-fired central heating was fitted and the kitchens and bathrooms were reconstructed in keeping with the original layout, but with space for modern appliances. The plywood panelling and fittings in the Pritchards' penthouse were restored by the cabinet maker Nick Goldfinger, grandson of the Hungarian architect Ernő Goldfinger, who had built his own house nearby in Willow Road, Hampstead. Finally, the building's facade was given a coat of the 'pale pink' paint that Coates had originally specified. The work took almost two years.

The Isokon Building was officially reopened on 25 May 2005. In keeping with its left-wing history, Labour's Chancellor of the Exchequer, Gordon Brown and Deputy Prime Minister John Prescott paid a visit.

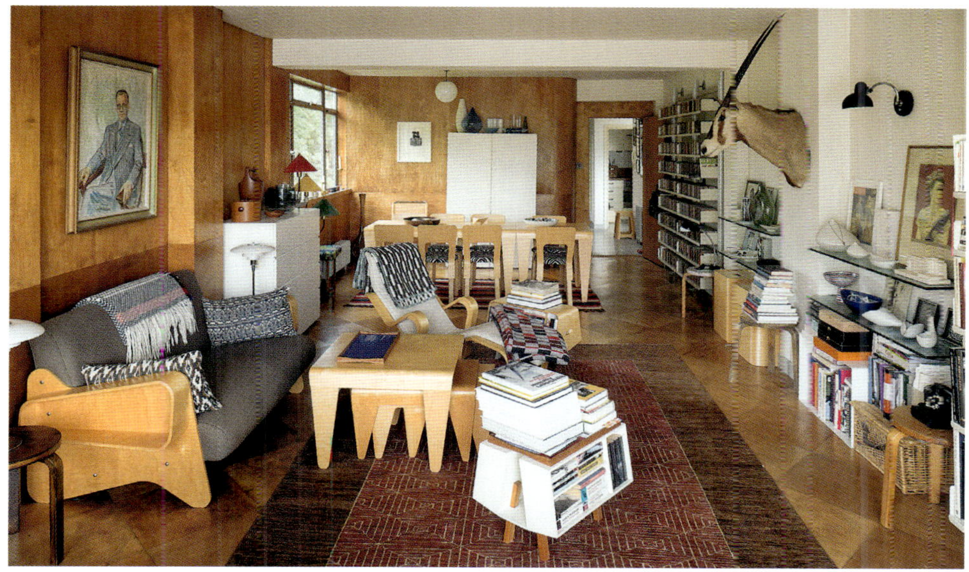

THE ISOKON FURNITURE COMPANY

The year 1980 was a significant one for the Isokon Furniture Company. Its inclusion in three separate exhibitions officially consolidated its position in the annals of British design history. A replica of Wells Coates's Minimum Flat was shown in 'The Thirties' retrospective at the Hayward Gallery on London's Southbank. The University of Newcastle upon Tyne held a dedicated Isokon exhibition and the company featured in 'Homespun to Highspeed: A Century of British Design 1880–1980' at the Mappin Art Gallery in Sheffield.

In 1980 Pritchard ended his association with John Alan Designs and with Claud Bunyard Designs, which was producing the Long Chair for sale in America.[3] In December 1981, he invited the young furniture-maker Chris McCourt, son-in-law of Festival of Britain architect John Morton, to visit him in Blythburgh. McCourt ran Windmill Furniture, a small company making tables in Chiswick, West London. His interview with Pritchard evolved into a visit of several days and included an obligatory session in the sauna, followed by a dip in the freezing swimming pool. Having passed the initiation tests, McCourt was awarded the licence to manufacture the full range of Isokon products.

McCourt made slight refinements to Breuer's post-war Long Chair design, expressing the chair's joints, subtly streamlining it and produced it in birch, as it had been in the 1930s. The Nesting Tables and Isokon Penguin Donkey Mark II came without blueprints, so McCourt had to re-create these from scratch borrowing Pritchard's originals as templates. In 1984, he took out a half-page advertisement in *Design* magazine and initially sold the Long Chair direct to the public, priced at £480.

Marcel Breuer died in New York in July 1981; Molly Pritchard in 1985 and Jack Pritchard in 1992. McCourt's passion for the company and his obsessive focus on quality and craftsmanship ensured their legacy. He continued the sole manufacture of the classic Isokon products until 1996, when he was approached by Edward Barber and Jay Osgerby, two recent architecture graduates from the Royal College of Art. They brought him a scale cardboard model of a coffee table they had designed for an architectural project and asked if he could make it for them in plywood.[4] The table's form was a continuous loop with storage space inside for magazines and menus. McCourt immediately recognised its potential and within weeks had produced a prototype. The minimalist, elegantly sculptural Loop Table marked a turning point for Isokon, and Edward Barber and Jay Osgerby's careers.

McCourt's friend Christopher Wilk, biographer of Marcel Breuer and Curator of the Victoria and Albert Museum's Twentieth-century Furniture Department, saw one of the first Loop Tables in Windmill Furniture's workshop and immediately bought it for the museum. Three months later, Samuel Johnson, Head Furniture Curator of the Metropolitan Museum of Art in New York, purchased one for the Met's permanent collection, along with all the drawings that had been used in the design process. The table was beautifully designed, but it also seemed to capture the zeitgeist. In 1997 Tyler Brûlé, then editor of *Wallpaper*★ magazine asked Barber and Osgerby to design his stand for the trade show, '100% Design' in London. They put the Loop Table centre-stage, flanked by an Eames Lounge Chair and under a classic pendant light by Poul Henningsen. It was quite an audacious statement, but the table caught the eye of Giulio Cappellini, who asked the designers if he could include it in his furniture collection. Barber and Osgerby moved into the Windmill workshop and expanded the Loop concept to produce a floating Shelf and Console and further Isokon products eventually followed: the Flight Stool, 1998; Home Dining Table, 2000; Portsmouth Bench, 2002; Backless Portsmouth Bench, 2005; the competition-winning Bodleian Library Chair, 2014; and stacking Ballot Chair, 2017.

In 1998 McCourt renamed the company Isokon Plus. He began working with a series of international designers, much as Pritchard had done with the Bauhaus masters. In 1999 Michael Sodeau designed the Wing range of finely engineered cabinets. In 2001 McCourt revived Dutch designer Hein Stolle's equilateral

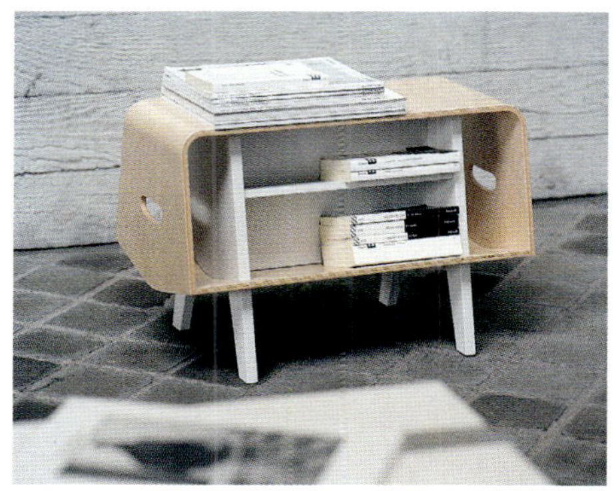

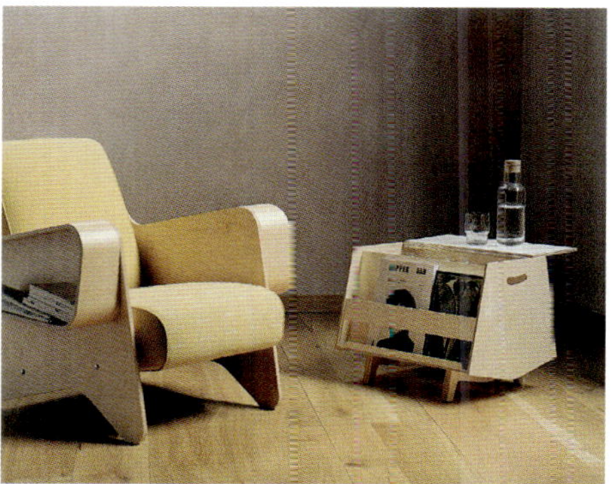

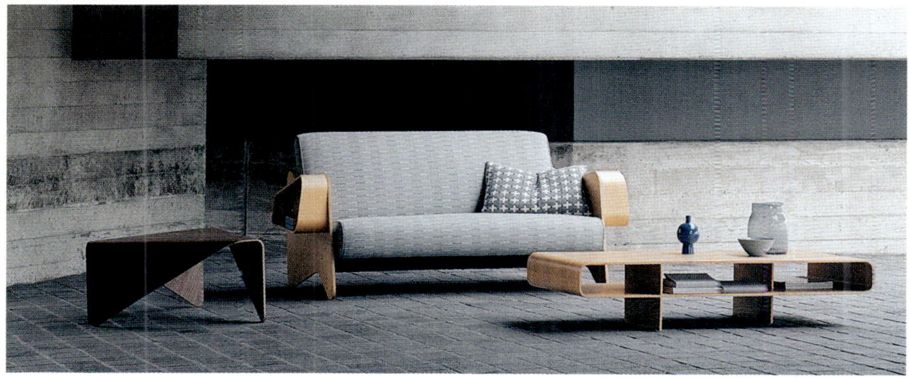

ABOVE, TOP-LEFT: The Isokon Penguin Donkey Mark III, designed by Shin and Tomoko Azumi, 2003. ABOVE, TOP-RIGHT: The Isokon Ventris Armchair, designed by Marcel Breuer, 1935 and Isokon Bottleship Mark II, designed by Egon Riss, 1963. Now in production by Isokon Plus. ABOVE: Isokon T46 table designed by Hein Stolle in 1946; The Isokon Ventris Sofa, designed by Marcel Breuer, 1935; The Loop coffee table designed in 1996 by Edward Barber and Jay Osgerby.

triangle T46 coffee table, made from a single sheet of bent plywood which Stolle had originally designed in 1946. In 2003, Royal College of Art graduates Shin and Tomoko Azumi rationalised both Egon Riss and Ernest Race's Penguin Donkey designs to create the Isokon Penguin Donkey Mark III.

Isokon played a major role in the Victoria and Albert's 'Plywood' retrospective of 2017, curated by Christopher Wilk. Marcel Breuer's Isokon Short Chair, from its permanent collection, was shown together with its moulds and a film demonstrating its construction. The museum also exhibited the original copper Plymax front door from the Pritchards' Penthouse flat, which Jack and Molly had rescued from Camden Council, and through which so many historic characters had passed.

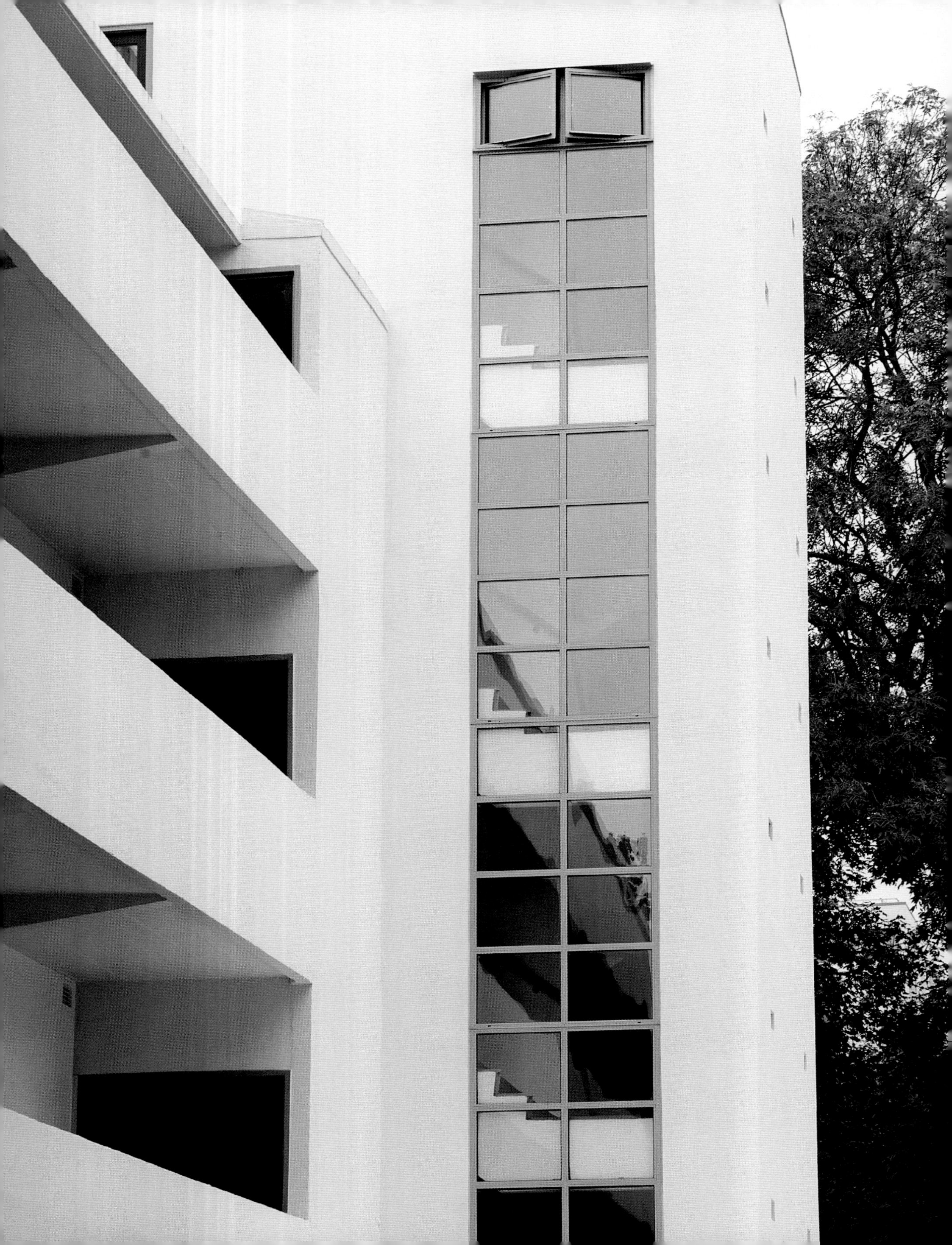

EPILOGUE

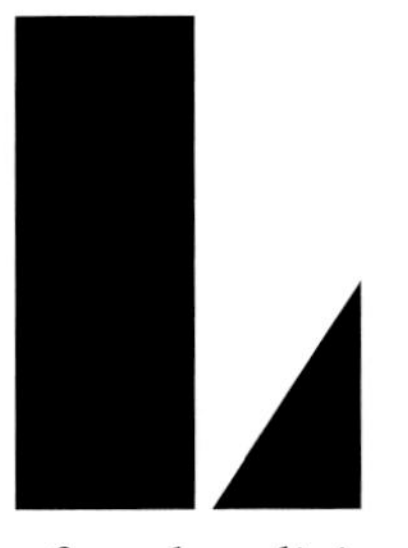EAVING BELSIZE PARK UNDERGROUND STATION AND turning left into Downside Crescent, one can retrace the short walk to the Lawn Road Flats taken by Jack and Molly Pritchard, Walter Gropius, Marcel Breuer, László Moholy-Nagy and all the other long-departed Isokon alumni. Passing the now gentrified Victorian and Edwardian terraces, one comes to a bend in the road and there – suddenly – is Wells Coates's concrete 'manifesto' of modern living. Strangely, time and its rich history have made the building, once voted England's second ugliest, quietly beautiful.

Sculptural, functional and, as Agatha Christie noted, ocean liner-esque, becalmed in its Hampstead backwater for nearly 90 years, its impact has been far reaching: both for what it represents architecturally and as the centre of an extraordinary community.

Although Pritchard's hopes of building a chain of such blocks, prefabricated and furnished with affordable mass-produced furniture were thwarted by the depressed economic climate of the 1930s, Wells Coates's experimental use of materials, radical rethinking of living space and new ideas about architecture as a social mediator became mainstream in post-war Britain. How far the arrival of the three Bauhaus Masters and their brief sojourn in London contributed directly to the development of the Modern movement is impossible to calculate, but it certainly added momentum. Gropius's inspiring speeches to the RIBA and Design Industries Association (DIA) in May 1934 were the first of many exchanges of ideas between the Bauhäuslers and Britain's architectural and artistic community. Lectures, meetings, partnerships, collaborations, congresses, dinner parties and drunken evenings followed. Jack Pritchard's professional network and Molly Pritchard's scientific one widened the sphere of influence and intellectual scope of these conversations, as did the somewhat miscellaneous nature of the Lawn Road Flats' community.

Although Gropius, Breuer and Moholy-Nagy did not found a British Bauhaus, nor take up formal teaching roles, they were natural educators and the models they established at Dessau were later widely adopted by British art schools. The year of their departure, 1937, RIBA set up an Architecture Science Committee and in 1938 Camberwell School of Art began training students in Industrial Design. Naum Slutzky was the only Isokon–Bauhäusler who taught in a major British institution, bringing the Bauhaus ideals of uniting art and industry to his departments at the Royal College of Art and Birmingham Art College.

Through their partnerships with Maxwell Fry and F.R.S. Yorke, Gropius and Breuer left a legacy behind, not solely in the handful of buildings post-war Modernists could learn from, but also through the younger architects who came

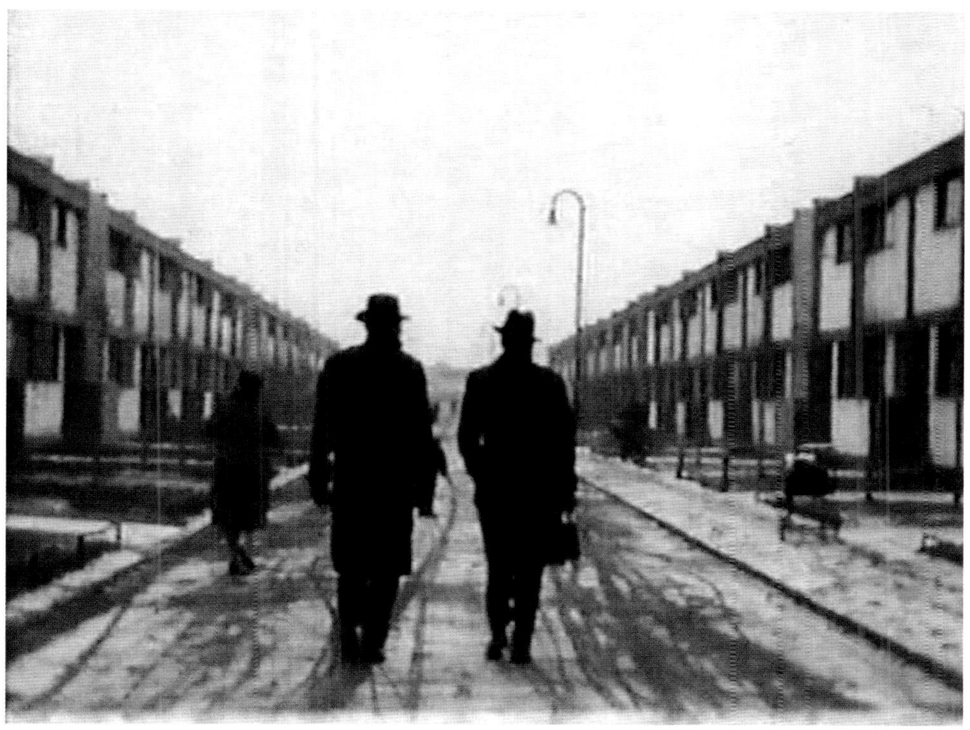

into contact with their practices. Breuer's design work for the Isokon Furniture Company, and Moholy-Nagy's with a range of clients, in fields ranging from graphic design to retail and film, enriched the visual landscape and design vocabulary of 1930s Britain.

In turn, the London years informed the later practices of Gropius Breuer and Moholy-Nagy, both materially and through their artistic contacts. In his architectural *oeuvre* in the US, Breuer continued to work with concrete as he had proposed in his 1936 Civic Centre of the future and with the walls of natural stone he had first employed in the same year. In Chicago, Moholy-Nagy developed further his English series of Space Modulators, hybrid painting-sculptures, using the new material of Plexiglass. Gropius's house in Lincoln echoed motifs from both his Levy and Donaldson commissions. His warm friendship with the Pritchards and their children lasted 35 years.

FOOTNOTES

INTRODUCTION

1 Cine footage of Jack Pritchard's visit to the Dessau Bauhaus, March 1931, Pritchard Family Archive.

2 Jack Pritchard's unpublished memoirs, manuscript, Pritchard family archive.

3 Pritchard, J., *View from a Long Chair*, Routledge & Kegan Paul, London, 1984, p.56.

4 Serge Chermayeff, 'Film Shots in Germany', *Architectural Review*, November 1931, p.131.

5 Chermayeff first met Mendelsohn in London in May 1930 at the Architectural Association. Powers, A., *Serge Chermayeff, Designer, Architect, Teacher*, RIBA, London, 2001, p.65.

6 They may have read F.E. Bennett and K. Winter's 'Berlin, Restaurants, Cafés and Housing', *The Builder*, 4 April 1930, which mentions many of the sites, pp.658–9.

7 Ibid.

8 Chermayeff inexplicably did not mention the Bauhaus visit. Serge Chermayeff, 'Film Shots in Germany', *Architectural Review*, November 1931, p.133.

9 The art school was not illustrated in *Architectural Review* until its special 'Steel and Concrete' issue of November 1932.

10 For a detailed account of these early articles see Alan Powers, 'Britain and the Bauhaus', *Apollo*, May 2006, Vol.531. p.50.

11 Fry, Maxwell, *Autobiographical Sketches*, Elek, London, 1975, p.137.

12 Molly Pritchard, Speech at the Grand Opening of the Lawn Road Flats, 9 July 1934.

13 Wells Coates, Letter to Jack Pritchard, 13 July 1930, Pritchard Papers, University of East Anglia Archive, PP/23/1/26.

14 Grieve, Alastair, *Isokon, For Ease, For Ever*, Isokon Plus, London, 2004.

15 Burke, David, *The Lawn Road Flats, Spies, Writers and Artists*, Boydell Press, Woodbridge, Suffolk, 2014.

CHAPTER 1

1 Pritchard, J., *View from a Long Chair*, Routledge & Kegan Paul, London, 1984, p.37.

2 Lilian Pritchard's travel diary, 1893–1910, Pritchard Papers, University of East Anglia, PP/1/1/4/5.

3 Confidential Report, Pelman Laboratory of Applied Psychology, 17 August 1920, UEA, PP/1/2/11/1.

4 Pritchard, J., *View*, p.38.

5 Ibid., p.32.

6 Ibid., p.33.

7 In an unpublished section of *View from a Long Chair*, Molly describes the May Balls and boat races in detail. Pritchard family archive.

8 Pritchard, J., *View*, p.38.

9 Ibid., p.45.

10 Patent Application No.22690/27, 29 August 1927, UEA, PP/9/5/1.

11 Pritchard, J., *View*, p.69.

12 Interview with Tim Tudor-Hart, Beatrix's grandson, London, February 2016.

13 Ibid.

14 Chaplin's *The Pawn Shop*, a film on the *Lindbergh Transatlantic Flight* and *The Scarlet Woman*, starring Elsa Lanchester, were shown. UEA, PP/7/6/19.

15 Pritchard, J., *View*, p.53.

16 Sigrid Dannius, *Bonnius*, May 1930 (translated) Carey Hugh, op. cit., p.111.

17 Pritchard, J., Unpublished section of *View from a Long Chair*. Pritchard family archive.

18 Venesta Chairman Henry Rutherford 'was wonderfully tolerant, accepting my decision without question,' Pritchard recalled in an unpublished section of his memoirs. Pritchard family archive.

19 Ibid.

20 The plans to build a house for Beatrix on the site are revealed in 1930 correspondence between Jack and Molly, Pritchard family archive.

21 Pritchard, J., *View*, p.79.

22 Read, Herbert, Introduction to *Unit One: The Modern Movement in English Architecture, Painting and Sculpture*, Cassell, London, 1934.

CHAPTER 2

1 Richards, J.M., 'Wells Coates (1895–1958)', *Architectural Review*, November 1958, 357–60.

2 Cantacuzino, Sherban, *Wells Coates*, Gordon Fraser, London, 1978, p.11.

3 Wells Coates, Diary, *Sights and Experiences in Japan*, 27 February 1909.

4 W.C. to Marion Gove, Correspondence, 30 March
1926.
5 W.C. to Marguerite Broad, Correspondence, September
1927–January 1928, WCA Box 35.
6 Wells Coates describes the entire ill-fated trip in
Letter to My Dear Mark, Correspondence, 5 December
1927. The identity of 'Mark' the intended recipient is
unknown.
7 Ibid.
8 Wells Coates to Marguerite Broad, Correspondence,
September 1927–January 1928, WCA Box 35, cited
in Darling, Elizabeth, *Wells Coates*, Twentieth Century
Society, London, 2012, p.5.
9 Patrick Heron, 25 February 1973, quoted in
Cantacuzino, Sherban, *Wells Coates*, Gordon Fraser,
London, 1978, p.43.
10 'Cresta', *Architectural Review*, February 1931, pp.45–6.
11 Jack Pritchard interview, 1981, British Library Archive.
12 W.C. to J.C.P., Correspondence, 17 January 1930,
WCA Box 23.
13 Agenda for the Twentieth Century Group, London, 26
February 1931, WCA Box 12/D.
14 Wells Coates, 'Furniture Today – Furniture
Tomorrow', *Architectural Review Supplement*, Decoration &
Craftsmanship, July 1932, pp.29–38.
15 Goldsmith, V.H., 'The Studio Interiors', *Architectural
Review*, August 1932, pp.52–64.
16 Yorke, F.R.S., 'Details', *Architectural Review*, August
1932.
17 Pritchard, Jack, unpublished draft of *View from a Long
Chair*, UEA, pp.127–8.

CHAPTER 3

1 Isaacs, Reginald, *Gropius, An Illustrated Biography of
the Creator of the Bauhaus*, Little Brown and Company,
Boston, 1991, p.25.
2 Gropius, Walter, 'Monumentale Kunst und Industriebau'
typescript, 29 January 1911, p.13, as translated by Reyner
Banham in *A Concrete Atlantis, US Industrial Building and
European Modern Architecture 1900–1925*, MIT Press,
Cambridge, 1986, p.198.
3 Gropius, Walter, *The New Architecture and the Bauhaus*,
Faber & Faber, London, 1925.
4 Gropius, Walter, *Bauhaus Manifesto*, April 1919.
5 Itten, Johannes, Catalogue for an exhibition of Bauhaus
work, 1919.
6 Paul Citroen, quoted in Whitford, Frank, *Bauhaus*,
Thames & Hudson, 1984, p.127.
7 Moholy-Nagy, László, Constructivism and the
Proletariat', May 1922.
8 Moholy-Nagy, Sibyl, *Moholy-Nagy, Experiment in
Totality*, MIT Press, 1969, p.39.
9 In 1922 Gropius had dismissed three staff members –
Josef Zachmann, Hans Beyer and Carl Schlemmer. They
were the authors of 'The Yellow Brochure'.

CHAPTER 4

1 Pritchard, Jack, *View from a Long Chair*, Routledge &
Kegan Paul, London, 1984, p.79.
2 Ibid.
3 Undated Letter from Molly to Jack in Paris, sent from
Platt's Lane, 1930, Pritchard family archive.
4 Ibid.
5 W.C. Letter to J.C.P., 13 July 1930.
6 The unwinding of the affair with Tudor-Hart is
detailed in Molly's letters to Jack in Paris, February 1930,
Op Cit.
7 Ibid.
8 W.C. Letter to J.C.P., 15 July 1930.
9 HM Inspectorate of Taxes, Wells Coates & Co. Tax
Return, 6 May 1931, UEA, PP/15/1/13.
10 J.C.P. Letter to Lord Pentland, 18 October 1930,
UEA, PP/15/1/11/3/2.
11 J.C.P. Letter to W.C., 4 February 1931.
12 Isokon Ltd was registered in December 1931.
13 W.C. to J.C.P., 12 August 1931, UEA, PP/23/1.
14 'Molly's Brief', 7 September 1932, UEA, PP/16/1.
15 Document entitled 'Multi-Dwellings', UEA,
PP/15/1/26/4.
16 Wells Coates's draft description of the exhibit, UEA,
PP/15/1/17.
17 Erna Meyer's kitchen for J.J.P. Oud, Weissenhof
Siedlung exhibition, Stuttgart, 1927 and Margarete
Schutte-Lihotzky's Frankfurt Kitchen, 1926–7.
18 Pritchard, J., *View*, pp.81–2.
19 Typescript listing the attractions of the flats, c.1932–4,
UEA, PP/16/2/1/44.
20 Dr Rosemary Pritchard's Speech, 9 July 1934, UEA,
PP/16/2/23/3.
21 Gerald Barry, *News Chronicle*, 12 July 1934, UEA,

PP/16/2/23/4/4.

22 Letter from Jack to the Editor of *The New Statesman & Nation*, 17 July 1934.

23 W.C. to J. & M. Pritchard, 23 January 1935.

24 M.P. to W.C., 25 January 1935.

CHAPTER 5

1 Letter to Isokon from R.E. Gathorne-Hardy, 30 October 1934, /16/4.

2 Walter Gropius Letter to Herrn Architekt Lörcher, Pres. Bund Deutscher Architekten, 20 February 1934, UEA, PP/24/1/4.

3 Ibid.

4 Letter to Professor Hönig, President of the Reich Chamber for the Creative Arts, 27 March 1934, UEA, PP/24/1/5.

5 W.G. to A. Lawrence Kocher, Berlin, 9 May 1934, cited in Isaacs, R., p.181.

6 Fry, Maxwell, *Autobiographical Sketches*, Elek, London, 1975, pp.146–7.

7 J.C.P. Letter to W.G., 20 June 1934, UEA, PP/24/3/2.

8 Maxwell Fry Letter to W.G., 22 June 1934, UEA, PP/24/2/4.

9 Maxwell Fry Letter to J.C.P., 28 September 1934, UEA, PP/24/3/17.

10 Pritchard, J., *View from a Long Chair*, Routledge & Kegan Paul, London, 1984, p.103.

11 W.G. Letter to Manon Gropius Burchard, London, 6 November 1934.

12 W.G. Letter to Martin Wagner, London, 26 December 1934, cited in Isaacs, R., p.193.

13 W.G. Letter to the Elmhirsts, 25 December 1934, Isaacs, op. cit.

14 Ibid.

15 E Maxwell Fry, 'F.R.S. Yorke, 1906–1962, A Memoir', *The Architectural Review*, October 1962, pp.279–280.

CHAPTER 6

1 On 14 March 1929, Jack Pritchard wrote to Mansfield Forbes informing him that he had created a chair entirely of plywood. UEA, PP/34/2.

2 Martha Deese, 'Gerald Summers and Makers of Simple Furniture', *Journal of Design History*, Vol.5, No.3, 1992, p.185.

3 Pritchard, J., *View from a Long Chair*, Routledge &

Kegan Paul, London, 1984, p.60.

4 'Furniture, Notes on Costs and Profits', 4 October 1935, UEA, PP/18/1/1/1.

5 Letter to Henry Rutherford, December 1935, UEA, PP/18/1/3/1.

6 UEA, PP/18/4/1/1.

7 Correspondence with Taylor Law & Co. Ltd, 1936, PP/18/8/39.

8 Letter from J.C.P. to W.G., 22 November 1935, Marcel Breuer Digital Archive.

9 Pritchard, J., *View*, p.111.

10 Ibid.

11 Moholy-Nagy moved to 7 Farm Walk in September 1935.

12 *Architectural Review*, February 1936, Plate VI.

13 Pritchard, J., *View*, p.122.

14 Invoice from Moholy-Nagy to J.C.P., 23 January 1936, UEA, PP/18/4/10/15.

15 English Patent, *Improvements in Chairs* (478,138), filed on 10 July 1936.

16 Isokon Furniture Company, Furniture Costing Book, 1938, UEA, PP/18/2/6.

17 Agreement with Alvar Aalto and Finmar Ltd, UEA, PP/18/3/24.

18 J.C.P. Letter to Marcel Breuer, 22 July 1938, UEA, PP/25/1/9.

19 Correspondence with Messrs AM Luther Ltd, Tallinn, 31 December 1936, UEA, PP/18/8/40/15.

20 Correspondence with Venesta over nesting trays, UEA, PP/18/4/40/16/3.

21 Letter and Designs, 17 March 1937, UEA, PP/18/4/4/4.

22 Clive Entwistle, 'An Approach to Interior Design', *Architectural Review*, December 1937, vol. LXXXI, p.226.

23 Dunn's of Bromley showed Isokon furniture at the Design and Industries Exhibition of 1936.

24 Ashley Courtenay, Hotel Advisory Service, Correspondence, March 1938, UEA, PP/18/5/1/7.

25 Pritchard, J., *View*, p.112.

26 Letter from J.C.P. to F.M. Gordon on Women's Fair and Exhibition, 9 November 1938, UEA, PP/18/4/10/42.

27 Letter from Pritchard, Wood and Partners to J.C.P., 4 January 1938, UEA, PP/18/4/8/36.

28 Letter from M. Watkins to J.C.P., 2 October 1936, UEA, PP/18/5/7/19.

29 Letter from J.C.P. to C.G. Holme, 21 June 1937, UEA, PP/18/4/10/28.

30 Memorandum, UEA, PP/25/4/11.

CHAPTER 7

1 Letter from W.H. Robinson & Co. to J.C.P., 16 November 1934, UEA, PP/15/4/2/9.

2 J.C.P. Letter to Walter Gropius, 9 April 1935, UEA, PP/24/4/2.

3 Herbert Read, 'Gropius', *Scrutiny*, December 1935, Vol. IV, No. 3, pp.313–15.

4 'Cry Stop to Havoc or Preservation by Development', *Architectural Review*, April 1935, pp 188–91.

5 Pritchard, J., *View from a Long Chair*, Routledge & Kegan Paul, London, 1984, p.125.

6 J.C.P. Letter to W.G., 31 July 1935, UEA.

7 D. Oliver Letter to W.G., Adams, Thompson and Fry Architects, London, 23 March 1936.

8 Jack Howe Letter to J.C.P., 12 July 1969, UEA, PP/8/29.

9 Donaldson, Frances, *A Twentieth-Century Life*, Bloomsbury Reader, Online Edition.

10 'A Timber House in Kent', *Architectural Review*, January 1938, pp.61–3.

11 Morris, Henry, *The Village College*, 1925.

12 'Architecture, Humanism and the Local Community', Henry Morris Paper RIBA, May 1956.

13 Letter to Cambridgeshire Council, April 1936, signed by W.G. Constable, Charles Holden, S.M. Keynes, C.H. Reilly and J. Craven Pritchard.

14 Joseph Hudnut Letter to W.G., 13 November 1936.

15 Report by Gropius, Christ College Archives, quoted in Alan Powers, 'Conservative Attitudes; Walter Gropius in Cambridge and Maxwell Fry in Oxford', *Twentieth Century Architecture*, Vol.11, Oxford and Cambridge, 2013, p.70.

16 Reply of Messrs Gropius and Fry to Questions concerning Hobson Street Building, Christ's College Archives. Op. cit.

17 Letter from J.C.P. to Walter Gropius, 1 December 1936, UEA, PP/18/7/1.

18 'Working Details', *The Architects' Journal*, 5 August 1937, pp.229–30.

19 'Manchester Sees German Idea, by a Special Correspondent', undated newspaper clipping, UEA, PP/24/2/38.

20 W.G. Letter to J.C.P., 23 February 1937, UEA, PP/18/7/1/8.

21 Senter, Terence, 'Moholy-Nagy's English Photography', *The Burlington Magazine*, 1 November 1981, Vol.123, p.669.

22 Moholy-Nagy, Sibyl, *Experiment in Totality*, Harper & Brothers, MIT Press, 1950, p.125.

23 Hattula Moholy-Nagy recalls staying with the Korda family around this time. Correspondence with Magnus Englund, August 2017.

24 Moholy-Nagy, Sibyl, *Experiments*, Op Cit.

25 Simpson's of Piccadilly is now the flagship Waterstone's bookstore; it still contains a pendant light fitting by Moholy-Nagy.

26 Interviews with Harry Blacker, 1971 and 1981, Senter, Terence.

27 'Leisure at the Seaside, *Architectural Review*, Vol. 80, pp.7–28.

28 Moholy-Nagy, Sibyl, *Experiments*, Op Cit, p.127.

29 Le Corbusier, 'The MARS Group Exhibition, A Pictorial Record', *Architectural Review*, March 1938, pp.109–10.

30 The trolley was illustrated in the *The Architectural Review*, December 1937.

31 Dorothea Ventris, 'London Flat', undated newspaper article, RIBA archive.

32 Heal's 'Seven Architects' Exhibition Catalogue, 1936.

33 Letter from Marcel Breuer to Cranston Jones, 13 January 1961.

34 'Houses 1, 2 and 3 by F. R. S. Yorke and Marcel Breuer', *Architectural Review*, January 1939, Vol.85, pp.29–35.

35 The contract between James MacNabb and builders Peskett & Sons, 8 January 1937, RIBA Collection, YoF/1/1.

36 Contract with Hubert Allan Rose for concrete swimming pool, 8 March 1935, RIBA Archive YoF/1/4.

37 Letters from Marcel Breuer to Jack Pritchard, 10 June 1936, and 7 September 1936, Marcel Breuer Online Archive, Syracuse University.

38 Letter from Peter Norton to Jack Pritchard at Isokon, 26 September 1936, Marcel Breuer Online Archive, Syracuse University.

39 Marcel Breuer Letter to J.M. Richards, 4 January 1937, RIBA Archive, YoF/2/2.

40 Letter from A Lawrence Kocher to F.R.S.Yorke, 1
October 1936, RIBA Archive,YoF/2/2.
41 Letter from Walter Gropius to Marcel Breuer, 17 April
1937, Walter Gropius Papers (Marcel Breuer Letters),
Harvard Library.
42 Cable from Walter and Ise Gropius to Marcel Breuer,
21 May 1937, Marcel Breuer Correspondence, AAA.
43 Marcel Breuer to Jack Pritchard, 20 July 1937, Marcel
Breuer Archive, Syracuse University Library.

CHAPTER 8

1 Pritchard, J., *View from a Long Chair*, Routledge &
Kegan Paul, London, 1984, p.92.
2 Henry Moore's photographs were shown in April 1944.
UEA, PP/8/44.
3 The company was founded by John Piper and Robert
Wellington. UEA, PP/2/2/Z.
4 Caroline Brandenburger, 'TV's First Masterchef', *The
Daily Telegraph*, 24 August 2000.
5 Letter from J C P to Ashley Courtenay, UEA,
PP/18/5/1/34.
6 Meynell, Francis, *My Lives*, The Bodley Head, London,
1971, p.247.
7 Dinner hosted by Huxley at London Zoo, UEA,
PP/39/1/35/30.
8 Letter from Marcel Breuer to J.C.P., 11 January 1939,
UEA, PP/25/1/6.
9 Letter from J.C.P. to Rt Hon. Neville Chamberlain, 15
November 1938, PP/5/1/78.
10 Letter from Harold Outram, News Photo Editor of
The Associated Press, to Philip Harben, 2 January 1939
(misdated 1938), UEA, PP/11/8/10.
11 Ibid.
12 J.C.P. to Arthur Korn, 16 February 1939, UEA,
PP/18/9/2/3.
13 J.C.P. to Arthur Korn, June 1939, UEA,
PP/18/9/2/19.
14 Letter to J.C.P. from Arthur Korn, 20 October 1939,
PP/18/9/2/48.
15 Letter from J.R. Coombe, Manager, National
Provincial Bank, 11 March 1939 to J.C.P., UEA,
PP18/2/4/2.
16 Pritchard, J., *View*, p.129.
17 Letter from J.C.O. to Alvar Aalto, 4 December 1939,
UEA, PP/9/1/2.
18 Child, Kate, *Best & Lloyd Ltd. 1920–1940*,
Dissertation, City of Birmingham Polytechnic, 1989,
p.74.
19 Letter from Marcel Breuer to Walter Gropius, 16 June
1937, Breuer Online Archive, Syracuse University.
20 *The Times*, 1 October 1940, UEA, PP/16/2/32/1.
21 Pritchard, J., *View*, p.129.
22 Christie, Agatha, *Autobiography*, Collins, London, 1977,
pp.486–7.
23 Letter from Stephen Glanville to Agatha Christie, 18
November 1943, op. cit., p.333.
24 Letter from Agatha Christie to Max Mallowan, 26
April 1943, cited in Thompson, Laura, *Agatha Christie*,
Headline, Review, 2007, p.320.
25 Special Branch on Edith Tudor-Hart, 23 February
1934, KV2/1012, TNA.
26 DV2/1613, TNA.
27 Andrew, Christopher and Mitrokhin, Vasili, *The
Mitrokhin Archive*, p.76.
28 Ibid., p.153.
29 Foote, Alexander, *Handbook for Spies*, Museum Press,
London, 1949, pp.9–10.
30 Williams, Robert Chadwell, *Klaus Fuchs, Atom Spy*,
Harvard University Press, 1987, p.15.
31 Green, John, *A Political Family*, Routledge, London,
2017, p.186.
32 Burke, David, *The Lawn Road Flats, Spies, Writers and
Artists*, The Boydell Press, 2014 p.4.

CHAPTER 9

1 Pritchard, J., *View from a Long Chair*, Routledge &
Kegan Paul, London, 1984, p.94.
2 Christie, Agatha, *Autobiography*, Collins, London, 1977,
p.487.
3 UEA, PP/5/1/121.
4 Comparative Broadcasts, Vol.3, 15 December 1939,
UEA, PP/5/1/109.
5 Comparative Broadcasts, Vol.4, 22 December 1939,
UEA, PP/5/1/110.
6 Letter from Molly Pritchard to Jack, Lincoln,
Massachusetts, 7 October 1940, Pritchard Family Archive.
7 Letter from Molly Pritchard to Jack, Lincoln
Massachusetts, 30 September 1940, Pritchard Family
Archive.
8 Molly met Ian Ballantine of Penguin Books in New

York, Sept 1940. Letter from Molly to Jack, 18th Sept 1940, Pritchard Family Archive.

9 Letter from D.J. De Pree of Herman Miller to Breuer, 15 October 1940.

10 John Dowling of John McCutcheon & Co. to Rosemary Pritchard, 22 January 1941.

11 Pritchard, Jack, Unpublished manuscript, Pritchard Family Archive.

12 Pritchard, Molly, 'Rumour', Bureau of Current Affairs, 1943 and 1947.

13 'Application of the Conversion or Decontamination of German Prisoners of War', UEA, PP/31/2/2.

14 Molly Pritchard, Outline of a Policy for a Persuasion Campaign against Lost Time, PP/31/2/2.

15 Letter from Ise Gropius to Molly Pritchard, 6 January 1943, R. Pritchard, Private File.

16 Pritchard, J., *View*, p.138.

17 Unpublished manuscript of *View from a Long Chair*, Pritchard Family Archive.

18 Ibid., p.14.

19 Wells Coates to J.C.P., 21 January 1947, UEA, PP/16/2/27/39.

20 Walter Gropius to Cyril Connolly, Editor of *Horizon*, 19 January 1947, UEA, PP/16/2/27/26.

21 Pritchard, ., *View*, p.153.

CHAPTER 10

1 Letter from Walter Gropius to Ise Gropius, Berlin, 4 August 1947.

2 Letter from Walter Gropius to Philip Morton Shand, 7 November 1947.

3 Pritchard, Jack, *View from a Long Chair*, Routledge & Kegan Paul, London, 1984, p.96.

4 Letter from J.C.P. to Breuer, 28 April 1952.

5 Letter from J.C.P. to Breuer, 5 March 1952.

6 Pevsner, Nikolaus, speech on 9 July 1955, Lawn Road Flats 21st birthday, UEA, pp.16/2/28

7 Ibid.

8 Ibid.

9 Pritchard, Jack, *View from a Long Chair*, Routledge & Kegan Paul, London, 1984, p.97.

10 Letter from J.C.P. to Alvar Aalto, 7 October 1955.

11 Powers, Alan, 'Britain and the Bauhaus', Apollo, May 2006, p.54.

12 Cohn, Laura, *The Door to a Secret Room, A Portrait of Wells Coates,* Scolar Press, 1999, p.236.

13 Interview with Roger Worrod, 23 February 2015.

14 Letter from Breuer to J.C.P., 16 March 1965.

15 Isokon Penguin Donkey Mark II, Advertising Brochure.

16 Interview with Zeev Aram, August 2017.

17 Pritchard, Jack, *Around the World in Four and Eighty Days,* unpublished manuscript, Pritchard Family Archive, p.1.

18 Ibid.

19 *The Times*, London, 20 September 1968.

20 Letter from Breuer to J.C.P., 9 August 1968.

21 Letter from J.C.P. to Breuer, 5 December 1968.

22 Pritchard, Jack, *View from a Long Chair,* Routledge & Kegan Paul, London, 1984, p.99

23 *Hampstead and Highgate Express*, 4 February 1972, UEA, pp.15/2/13

CHAPTER 11

1 Gerry Harrison draft article 'A Tinge of Pink', *The Independent*, September 1995.

2 Peter Abrahams, Chairman of the Isokon Tenants' Association.

3 Letter from Gerry Harrison to Christopher Dean, Co-ordinator, Docomomo UK, 6 September 1994.

CHAPTER 12

1 Interview with John Alan, Avanti Architects, London, 2016.

2 Ibid.

3 Interview with Chris McCourt, Isokon Penthouse, January 2017.

4 Interview with Ed Barber and Jay Osgerby, 20 April 2017.

PICTURE CREDITS AND ACKNOWLEDGEMENTS

We would like to give our heartfelt thanks to the many people who have made this book possible, first and foremost the Pritchard family, who put the authors together and have supplied us with so much unique and previously unpublished material. We would also like to thank Hattula Moholy-Nagy, archivist Bridget Gillies of the Pritchard Papers at the University of East Anglia, John Allan of Avanti Architects, Chris McCourt of Isokon Plus, the late Zeev Aram, the late Stuart Hudson, Edward Barber and Jay Osgerby, Gerry Harrison, the Tudor-Hart family, Gene Adams, Wolf Burchard, the late Wolfgang Suschitzky, the Isokon Gallery Trust, the Bauhaus archives in Berlin and Dessau, the Wells Coates archive in Canada and the Wells Coates family, Jyri Kermik, Valeria Carullo at the RIBA archive, Roger Worrod, Notting Hill Genesis, English Heritage, the Twentieth Century Society, the Association of Estonian Designers, and the past and current residents of the Isokon building. Finally we would like to thank our editor at Batsford; Lucy Smith, and our two patient families; Mark, Astrid, Theodora and Gjøril, who must often have thought that Jack, Molly and Walter were the most important people in our lives over the last few years.

Page 6: Wells Coates and Serge Chermayeff approach the Bauhaus buildings in Dessau, March 1931, filmed by Jack Pritchard. Lost cine footage discovered by the authors in 2017.

Page 12: Pritchard family Christmas card.

Page 28: Wells Coates with a model of his Windsail Catamaran. The 16-feet Catamaran was built and sailed on the Norfolk Broads.

Page 42: Lou Scheper-Berkenkamp photographed in 1927 by László Moholy-Nagy at the students wing of the Bauhaus school in Dessau. These balconies were later seen by Wells Coates and might have helped inspire the balconies at the back of Lawn Road Flats.

Page 54: Pritchard commissioned Edith Tudor-Hart to photograph the construction of the Lawn Road Flats, 1934.

Page 78: Marcel Breuer, Ise and Walter Gropius, July 1935, Lawn Road Flats' First Birthday Party.

Page 94: Laszlo Moholy-Nagy designed a wrapper for the Isokon Long Chair, 1935.

Page 116: *Things To Come* was a film by Alexander Korda after a book by H.G. Wells. Moholy-Nagy created a set of revolving cones and filmed it through multiplying prisms to show the construction of the new Everytown in the film's most futuristic sequence, set in 2036. Most of his work ended up on the cutting-room floor.

Page 152: Philip Harben's daily Isobar menu introduced Londoners to a range of exotic foreign dishes, including Spanish food sold in solidarity with the Republican side of the Spanish Civil War.

Page 174: Belsize Park and Hampstead received numerous direct hits during the Blitz. In 1940, a German bomb fell on the tennis courts adjacent to Lawn Road Flats, destroying most of its windows.

Page 188: The Isokon Penguin Donkey Mk II was marketed as a great improvement on its pre-war older sibling, offering a multitude of new usage possibilities.

Page 210: Selling the Lawn Road Flats to the publication *The New Statesman* in 1969 proved to be a major disappointment, after it demolished the Isobar and sold the building on to Camden Council.

Page 218: The Isokon Gallery was opened on the building's 80th anniversary day in 2014, to tell the remarkable story of this radical experiment in modern living.

Page 224: The window frames of the Lawn Road Flats' stairwell tower have now been restored to their original unique colour, as specified by Wells Coates, after Avanti Architects uncovered traces of the 1934 paint during renovation.

INDEX

These Names Make News

DESIGN FOR LIVING

WORKMEN taking
lunch-hour siesta,
chauffeurs drows-
ing over their
heels in a quiet Hampstead
ad yesterday, were startled by
dden crash of breaking glass,
luge, from above, of beer !
'Wicked waste, I calls it," sa
e.
Bottle - smasher was M.
ELMA CAZALET, there to ope
mally new block of function
ts.

UN beat mercilessly down c
white roof where guests sippe
cktails, sweated, while Mi
zalet—smiling, dumpy, whi
wer pinned on shoulder, re
wer embroidered on dress-
ngratulated architect WELI
ATES on "this beautiful buil
g that we are standing on to
"

Added—almost as tho it we
mething to be proud of !—th
one time she had been
ember of the L.C.C. Housi
mmittee.

LSO spoke: Dr. ROSEMAR
PRITCHARD, originator
heme of building blocks of the
ts in many centres.
Read her speech from typ
ipt, copies of which had bee
culated to us beforehan
itted, alas, the exquisite
oured impromptu : "But I d
t intend to make a speech.
m to have been led on by n
oject. . . ."

LATS are not designed fe
families, but for one or tw
rsons. They are "minimum
ts.
Built-in equipment. . . . Soun
ulated by pumice-stone in con
te walls. . . . Small rents, servi
rown in. . . . Exact amount

with mania for acquiring useless
paraphernalia.
*

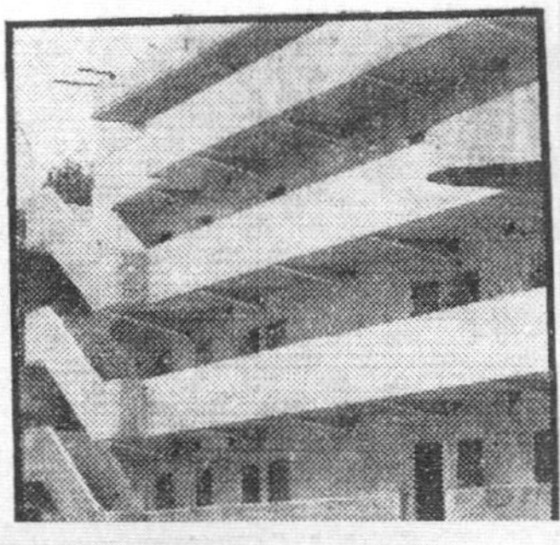

London

Modern Flats:
Problems:
Conserv
The

NDON, WEDNESDAY
T yesterday morn
egarded as the m
in England, a blo
flats in Hampstea
pied, if they are s
er of other provi
a row of houses,
stucco and half o
pe with, rising
hem, a dazzlingly-
block which looks
liner with exter
. The life inside
bear some resem
xistence. There
for communal sun
provided from a
and an economy c
ith an amount of
that is also like th

arrelling Space

the liner life in
no means cheap, although t
supposed to provide accon
ers and are not
ter. It costs a
have a bed-sit
ze with extreme
nd bathroom, or,
term for these

FLATS FOR
MODERNS.

HAMPSTEAD HOUSING
NOVELTY.

———— ♦ ————

HUMAN NEST OF
FLATS.

————

THE MODERN TOUCH.

————

FLATS WITH FURNITURE IN
THE WALL

————

All Tenants Need Is a
Chair or Two

WOMAN'S IDEA

————

All the furniture tenants need provide
r themselves in a block of new flats ir
awn-road, Hampstead, N.W., is chairs !
These flats are the outcome of an idea of Dr
osemary Pritchard, the bacteriologist.
"My husband and I intended building a
bour-saving house for ourselves," Dr. Prit
ard told the *Daily Mirror*. "We had plenty
ideas for making the place as easily worked
possible, and then we decided to share these
eas with other people, by forming a company
d building a block of flats.
"There are thirty flats here, and we are
ing to have the one right on the roof."

ENORMOUS WINDOWS

The position of the block—it faces south-wes
he enormous windows, and the fact that th

More Comfort—Less
Work in These Flats

A new block of flats opened at Lawn-road
Hampstead, N.W., to-day
Cazalet, M.P., will have e
furnished before the tenar
The one-room flats con
living-room, already fitted
mattress, a small dressin
and bathroom.
A sliding dining table o
installed in each living-roo
table fits against the wall
but it can be slid away, pro
four or six people.
The dressing-room is lin
cupboards, and is fitted

FURNITURE AS
OF BUILDIN

Gossip & News

"The Liner Life"—Traffic The Pedestrian Lane— ng Thames Water— Chamberlain Club

Iorning
g in what
t modern
of super-
which are
cessful, in
ial cities.
lf of them
he modern
rprisingly
ite, many
xactly like
r landings
e building
nce to th
an ope
ng, servic
communa
space com
mfort an
of a larg

It has to
of flats ma
adon is b
se flats a
odation
a fashio
least £2
g-room
well-fitt
ecording
"cooki

HE

PAR

HAMPSTEAD HOUSING NOVELTY.

HUMAN "NEST-BUILDING."

Hampstead has been invaded (write a correspondent) by a form of human "nest-building" which the Continen adopted some time ago, and we have bee all too chary of till now. It consists of four-storey structure of a somewhat fo tress type vative-mind partiality i an acquired this phase tages appea

but temptin when to the is added the grace of central s seems as if the modern spirit of volution has things all its own arbiter, however distrustful of n in building, can deny that they a tially healthy, and keep at bay a of epidemics that have haunted and cubicles in the past.

The main conception is that of a dwelling, approachable by lifts, jecting itself beyond the outward means of cantilevered balconies. tion is assured by walls which a tically sandwiches of concrete s imprisoned air. In this way arrested and imprisoned in its o and the man on music bent can say, "the stranger doth not inte with his joy," or vice versa.

In other words, the new type in Lawn-road have each their al of steel or chromium furniture tings, with shelf additions avail

DESIGNED FOR LIVIN

NEW HAMPSTEAD FLATS

No Housewives Needed.

Of a modern villa I heard an e perienced housewife declare t other day that "they call the labour-saving houses, but I thin they are work making." Her vie was that the modern home was b coming so small and compact tha it is getting to the stage where reates work through the nece ties arising out of its own cor actness. I wonder what th ousewife would have thought of ew block of flats I visited in nort ondon yesterday. Here surely he labour-eliminating house. act it seemed to me to make th ousewife herself a superfluit his is due to the service whic ccompanies the flats and to the i enuity of their construction. Th lats are so elaborately fitted tha hey need no furniture exce

Brave New Hampstead

TO-MORROW Miss Thelma Caza M.P., opening a block of flats in Hampstead area which has been design and equipped on a system quite new to t country. They are intended for bu people, on what the architect terms "minimum" basis.

Each flat is fitted not only with all t usual modern comforts, such as central hea ing, ice-cupboards, and so on, but is co plete with built-in furniture, bed, tabl bookcases, and so on, so that the only thin tenants have to supply themselves with a chairs, rugs, and a picture or two.

There is provision for them to do simp cooking in their own flats but there i